Southern African Development Community Land Issues

This book constitutes Volume I of a set of two volumes. Volume I attempts a holistic inter-disciplinary evaluation of the legitimacy of colonial and emergent post-colonial rule property rights in affected States of the Southern African Development Community (SADC) in light of intensifying litigation in national courts, the SADC Tribunal, and more recently the Washington-based International Centre for the Settlement of Investment Disputes (ICSID) regarding counter claims to title to property. Cultural, economic and political drivers at the core of SADC land issues are examined for their significance and potential to contribute to the discovery of a new, sustainable land relations policy that could guarantee social justice in the distribution of all the advantages and disadvantages relating to the allocation and use of land. The book shows that persistent systematic administrative failures by pre-colonial, colonial and post-colonial authorities have made for a very complex challenge that requires Solomonic tools that neither the Courts alone, nor human rights centric morality alone could resolutely attend. Therefore, the book recommends a sophisticated systematic new approach to SADC land issues. That approach is developed in Volume II of this series: *Re-conceiving Property Rights in the New Millennium – Towards a New Sustainable Land Relations Policy*.

Ben Chigara is Professor of International Laws at Brunel University, UK.

Southern African Development Community Land Issues

Towards a New Sustainable Land Relations Policy

Edited by
Ben Chigara

Routledge
Taylor & Francis Group
LONDON AND NEW YORK

First published 2012
by Routledge
4 Park Square, Milton Park, Abingdon, Oxon OX14 4RN
605 Third Avenue, New York, NY 10017

Routledge is an imprint of the Taylor & Francis Group, an informa business

British Library Cataloguing in Publication Data
A catalogue record for this book is available from the British Library

Library of Congress Cataloging-in-Publication Data
Southern African Development Community land issues : towards a new sustainable land relations policy / edited by Ben Chigara.
p. cm.
ISBN 978-0-415-58704-4 (hbk) -- ISBN 978-0-203-80655-5 (ebk)
1. Land reform--Law and legislation--Africa, Southern. 2. Land tenure--Law and legislation--Africa, Southern. 3. Southern African Development Community. I. Chigara, Ben. II. Title.
KQC672.S676 2011
346.6804'32--dc22
2011005403

ISBN: 978-0-415-58704-4 (hbk)
ISBN: 978-0-203-80655-5 (ebk)

Typeset in Baskerville
by Taylor & Francis Books

We shall all become, when our capacities to choose to recognise, promote and protect the inherent dignity of all individuals regardless, shall have become second nature in all our dealings with others.

(Ben Chigara, PhD, Professor of International Laws, Brunel University, UK)

Contents

List of tables

Table of cases

List of abbreviations

AALS	Affirmative Action Loan Scheme (Namibia)
ACHPR	African Charter on Human and Peoples' Rights; African Commission on Human and Peoples' Rights
ADMADE	Administrative Design for Game Management Areas
ANC	African National Congress (Angola)
AU	African Union
AUC	African Union Commission
CAMPFIRE	Communal Areas Management Programme for Indigenous Resources
CBNRM	Community Based Natural Resources Management
CBNRMP	Community Based Natural Resources Management Programme
CEDAW	Convention on the Elimination of all Forms of Discrimination
CFU	Commercial Farmers Union
CIGI	Centre for International Governance Innovation
CITES	Convention on International Trade in Endangered Species
COMPASS	Community Partnerships for Sustainable Resource Management
CPA	Communal Property Association
DRC	Democratic Republic of Congo
DUAT	Direito de uso e aproveitamento da terra
ESAP	Economic Structural Adjustment Programme
FAO	Food and Agriculture Organisation
FIAS	Foreign Investment Advisory Service
FRELIMO	Frente de Libertação de Moçambique
GRAIN	Genetic Resources Action International
GTZ	German Technical Co-operation
ICCPR	International Covenant on Civil and Political Rights
ICERD	International Convention on the Elimination of All Forms of Racial Discrimination
ICESCR	International Covenant on Economic, Social and Cultural Rights
ICJ	International Court of Justice
ICSID	International Centre for the Settlement of Investment Disputes

IDA	International Development Agency
IFAD	International Fund for Agricultural Development
IFPRI	International Food Policy Research Institute
IIED	International Institute of Environment and Development
ILO	International Labour Organisation
Inter-Am Ct HR	Inter-American Court of Human Rights
IPLRAD	Integrated Programme of Land Reform and Agricultural Development
IPP	Indigenous Peoples Plan
IWGIA	International Work Group for Indigenous Affairs
LRP	Land Relations Policy
LRPP	Land Reform Pilot Programme (Republic of South Africa)
LSCF	Large-scale commercial farms (Zimbabwe)
MLRR	Ministry of Rehabilitation and Resettlement (Namibia)
MPLA	Movimento Popular da Libertação de Angola
NAU	National Agricultural Union
NEPAD	New Partnership for Africa's Development
NNTTA	National Native Title Tribunal Awards
OAU	Organisation of African Unity
PECAPDISHD	Pedagogical counter-apartheid-rule psychological distortions of the significance of human dignity
PSA	Production Sharing Agreement
RENAMO	Resistencia Nacional Mocambicana UN
SADC	Southern African Development Community
SADCC	Southern African Development Co-ordination Conference
SAIIA	South African Institute of International Affairs
SAPs	Structural Adjustment Programs
SARPN	Southern African Regional Poverty Network
SIR	Social Indicators Research
SMIF	Sustainable management of indigenous forests
SNL	Swazi National Land
SWAPO	South West Africa People's Organisation (Namibia)
TGLP	Tribal Grazing Livestock Programme
TLGP	Tribal Land Grazing Policy
UNCCD	United Nations Convention to Combat Desertification
UNECA	United Nations Economic Commission for Africa
UPA (FNLA)	Union of Peoples of Angola (Frente Nacional de Libertaço de Angola)
ZANLA	Zimbabwe African National Liberation Army (Zimbabwe)
ZANU	Zimbabwe African National Union (Zimbabwe)
ZAPU	Zimbabwe African Peoples Union (Zimbabwe)
ZIPRA	Zimbabwe People's Revolutionary Army (Zimbabwe)

List of contributors

Martin Adams has over forty years of experience as an international consultant, now specialising in national land policy and related issues. Over the last two decades, he has worked with governments and civil society organisations, mainly in East and southern Africa. He is a member of Mokoro Ltd, a consultancy firm based in Oxford, whose members share a commitment to sustainable international development and poverty reduction.

Samuel Kwesi Amoo holds a BA degree from the University of Ghana, Legon, an LLB from the University of Zambia, and an LLM from the University of Toronto. He is an Advocate of the Supreme Court of Zambia and an Attorney of the High Court of Namibia. He was the Dean of the Faculty of Law, University of Namibia, and is a Senior Lecturer in the same faculty. He has written extensively on the Namibian legal system and has specialised in the property law of Namibia. His latest publication is *An Introduction to Namibian Law* and he is completing his next, *Law of Property in Namibia*.

Ilias Bantekas LLB (Athens), LLM (Liverpool), PhD (Liverpool), Dip. Theology (Cambridge) is Professor of International Law at Brunel University School of Law and Associate Fellow at IALS, University of London. He has held full-time and visiting academic posts at Harvard, Miami, Cleveland State, Trier, SOAS, Westminster and others. He is Head of International Law and Arbitration at Mourgelas & Associates law firm (Athens), where in addition to international law and human rights he specialises in energy and arbitration. He has advised governments, international organisations, NGOs and private clients in most fields of international law. His publications include *International Criminal Law* (4th edn 2010); *International Human Rights Law* (2012); *Trust Funds under International Law: Trustee Obligations of the UN and International Development Banks* (2009).

Hany Besada is Program Head, Governance of Natural Resources and Senior Researcher, Development Cooperation, at the North–South Institute. Previously he was Senior Researcher and Program Leader at the Centre for International Governance Innovation, where he oversaw the Health and Social Governance

Program. He holds a BA and an MA in international relations from Alliant International University, San Diego, where he specialised in peace and security studies. Prior to that, he was the Business in Africa researcher at the South African Institute of International Affairs, Johannesburg, and Research Manager at Africa Business Direct, a trade and investment consulting firm in Johannesburg. He has worked for Amnesty International, United Nations Associations, the Joan Kroc Institute of Peace and Justice and the Office of US Senator Dianne Feinstein. He has published widely in international news media and academic journals. He is the editor of *Zimbabwe: Picking up the Pieces* (2011), *Moving Health Sovereignty: Global Challenge, African Perspective* (2011), *Crafting an African Security Architecture: Addressing Regional Peace and Conflict in the Twenty-first Century* (2010), *From Civil Strife to Peace Building: Examining Private Sector Involvement in West African Reconstruction* (2009), and *Unlocking Africa's Potential: The Role of Corporate South Africa in Strengthening Africa's Private Sector* (2008). His research interests cover an array of themes ranging from Africa's socio-economic and security development, private sector growth, trade and investment facilitation, Middle Eastern politics, fragile/failed states, peace building and post-conflict economic reconstruction

Ben Chigara, PhD, Nottingham University; LLM with Distinction and Josephine Ono Prize, Hull University; BA (Hons), Keele University; CE University of Zimbabwe. Ben joined Brunel University from Warwick in 2003. He is the founding Director of the Centre for International and Public Law that was inaugurated by Lord Bill Brett in 2004. He is founding Director of Brunel University's flagship Master of Law programmes in international economic law, international intellectual property and European and international commercial law. He is founding Deputy Head (Operations) of the Brunel Law School, which was unhinged from the School of Social Sciences and Law in 2005. Ben has also held lectureships at Warwick University, Leeds University and Oxford Brookes University and various teaching positions at Nottingham University and in Denmark, Louisville and Zimbabwe. He is the author of several books, book chapters and journal articles. He is a current and serving consultant to the European Scientific Foundation, the European Commission, the International Labour Organisation and the Organisation for Security and Cooperation in Europe's (OSCE) Office for Democratic Institutions and Human Rights (ODIHR). He is Professor of International Laws at Brunel University, London.

Horman Chitonge holds a PhD in development studies from the University of KwaZulu-Natal, South Africa. He is a senior researcher at the Land Reform and Democracy NRF Chair, University of Cape Town. He has conducted research and published on land-related issues, focusing on a number of countries in southern Africa. He is currently leading a study on land reform and poverty in South Africa. He is also part of the regional team that is conducting research on land use and ownership in Mozambique, Zambia, Malawi, Botswana, South Africa and Tanzania.

Jérémie Gilbert is a Senior Lecturer at Middlesex University, London. He holds a PhD in international human rights law from the Irish Centre for Human Rights. He has published various articles and book chapters on the rights of indigenous peoples, looking in particular at territorial rights. His latest monograph is *Indigenous Peoples' Land Rights under International Law* (2007). He is a member of Minority Rights Group International's Advisory Board on the Legal Cases programme and also regularly works with the Forest Peoples' Programme on their African human rights programme. He is currently involved in research on a comparative legal analysis for the protection of minorities in Africa.

Ariane Goetz is pursuing her PhD in global governance at the Balsillie School of International Affairs and is a Balsillie Doctoral Fellow at the Centre for International Governance Innovation. She has a Master's in public policy (Hertie School of Governance) and a Magister Artium in philosophy and literature science (Free University, Berlin). Her research focuses on peace and security, global environmental governance, international land management and accountability ethics. Previously she worked as a consultant for German Technical Co-operation (GTZ).

Sidney L. Harring holds both PhD and law degrees from the University of Wisconsin, and has taught at the City University of New York's School of Law for many years. He was a Fulbright Professor in Namibia in 1995 and has been working on issues of land rights and indigenous rights there since that time.

Robert Home MA (Cantab.) PhD (London) DipTP (Oxford Brookes) MTRPI is Professor in Land Management at Anglia Ruskin University, UK. His research interests are in the area of planning history and land management, with a strong international focus. His PhD was on the influence of colonial government upon Nigerian urbanization, and he has published books on British colonial town planning, land titling in Africa and the Caribbean, and planning regulations. He has also managed higher education link programmes with South Africa and Zambia, undertaken consultancies in several African countries, and supervised PhDs on African land topics.

David Keane is lecturer in Law at Middlesex University, London. He holds a BCL (Law and French) from University College Cork, Ireland, and an LLM and PhD in international human rights law from the Irish Centre for Human Rights, National University of Ireland, Galway. His most recent book, *Minority Rights in the Pacific Region* (co-authored with Joshua Castellino) was published in 2009. His book *Caste-based Discrimination in International Human Rights Law* (2007) was awarded the Hart Book Prize for early career scholars by the Socio-legal Studies Association. In addition, he has published a number of journal articles on a range of human rights and minority rights issues, including freedom of expression and religion, migrant workers, genetics, environmental refugees and regional systems.

Rachael Knight is an attorney with expertise in the areas of land tenure security, access to justice and legal empowerment of the poor. She is the Director of the International Development Law Organisation's Community Land Titling Initiative, working to document and protect the customary land rights of rural communities in Uganda, Liberia and Mozambique. She worked as a consultant for the Food and Agriculture Organisation of the United Nations from 2004 until 2010 and has completed a book for the FAO entitled *Best Practices For Statutory Recognition of Customary Land Rights*.

Alex Magaisa is a Senior Lecturer in Law at the University of Kent, UK. He studied law at the University of Zimbabwe (LLB) and the University of Warwick (LLM and PhD). He is a registered legal practitioner in Zimbabwe. Previous appointments include the Universities of Warwick and Nottingham.

Oliver C. Ruppel (LLB Hons, LLM, MM, LLD) is a Professor of Law at the Faculty of Law of the University of Stellenbosch, South Africa, and an adjunct professor at the Pupkewitz Graduate Business School at the Polytechnic of Namibia. He served as Director of the Human Rights and Documentation Centre at the Faculty of Law, University of Namibia 2007–10 and is one of the worldwide 14 Founding Chairs in the WTO Chairs Programme of the World Trade Organisation, Geneva. He lectures at various academic institutions worldwide as a (visiting) professor, such as the University of Swaziland, Saransk State University, Russia, and the Institute for Social and Development Studies at the Munich School of Philosophy SJ, Germany. Appointed by the Geneva-based Intergovernmental Panel on Climate Change, he is Coordinating Lead Author for Africa in the IPCC Working Group II at Stanford University, California. He has published widely, especially on public international law and specifically on the law in SACU, SADC and on the SADC Tribunal.

Acknowledgements

Many, many hours of thought, reflection and professionalism of many, many experts in many places, including Australia, the United States, Europe, Canada and Africa, have resulted in this piece of work. These colleagues comprise the invisible majority that needs must remain anonymous in consequence of convention's requirement of non-disclosure of independent expert advisers to projects of this nature. Nonetheless, their visibility is apparent in every chapter of the book as the reader will easily tell. To them all – thank you.

Foreword

The law defines land as 'real property' in nearly all jurisdictions. This distinguishes land from all other forms of property and tells us unequivocally that, in any community, land is the most prized possession. In the *Island of Palmas* case (1928) Judge Huber observed that land was the critical signifier of statehood. No State could exist without ownership over a portion of the globe to the exclusion of all other States (*Netherlands v. US* (1928) 2 R.I.A.A. p. 829).

There is only so much land for any nation, in fact so finite an amount that competition for the best land – whatever the critical purpose in each community – is an inescapable fact of life. Every form of civilisation has been characterised by allocation of land rights. In southern Africa land relations policies of pre-colonial, colonial and even post-colonial administrations have tended to exclude women from the land game. Colonial administrations had extended this disenfranchisement of women to 'natives' in general, and then actively campaigned through a series of legal measures to convert them from landowners and farmers in their own right to farm tenants, wage earners and mine labourers that depended on European enterprises for their existence. Settler Europeans became the new landowners and farmers *par excellence,* from the land thefts of Latin Americans to the 'denationalisation' of Native Americans, then in Australia and New Zealand, and the infamous Land Act of 1912 and 1936 in South Africa.

Colonial-rule land games were guided by constitutional pieces of legislation that completely disregarded indigenous people's own interests in land as farmers in their own right. Consequently, the legacy of foreign rule in southern Africa is typified by unequal land distribution between the native blacks and settler white Europeans. This fact had galvanised the struggle for political independence from foreign rule that had gripped the African sub-region until the collapse of apartheid rule in South Africa in 1994 when the first majority-rule government led by President Mandela took office.

I had the privilege of serving in that government as Minister of Water Affairs and Forestry, from 1994 to 1999, and then as Minister of Education between 1999 and 2004. Immediately after President Mandela's government had taken office, it had categorised land reform in the same basket of acute concerns as national security and development. Water rights, or many would prefer to call it theft, followed the apartheid policy of land expropriation. My task was to prepare and promulgate a Water Act for a post-colonial and a post-apartheid society. This was done in 1998 with the National Water Act, which is now used as a paradigm in other post-colonial countries.

The government wasted little time in legislating to begin to correct the distortions of apartheid rule regarding land rights in South Africa. In the same year of taking office the first non-racial government had passed the Restitution of Land Rights Act of 1994. This was followed by the Land Reform (Labour Tenants) Act of 1996 and the Extension of Security of Tenure Act of 1997. A Land Claims Court empowered to hold hearings in any part of the country was established. The Court was also empowered to conduct its proceedings in an informal way where appropriate.

The challenge to reform land distribution in the Southern African Development Community today requires a cultural paradigmatic shift of near seismic proportions. The passing of legislation for judicial enforcement alone is not sufficient to muster the change required. The people demand and deserve more. It is a reform that touches all with need for land and all with land in excess of their need. It is a challenge that only those with hearts that are strong enough to concede the right of others to be as valid as their own will find manageable. Change with efficiency; reform with a heart and commitment. A recognition that much has still to be done is necessary.

Professor Ben Chigara's two-volume set on this vital matter is a thorough and rigorous effort to date, in my view, to both flag the enormity of the challenge of undoing the distortions in land allocation on racial lines and to end the failed land games of yesteryear in a humane manner.

Its combination of pedagogy of the oppressed, rational choice theory and 'humwefficiency' to arrive at a formulation of a strategy for the realisation of the transformation required to achieve the required culture change among all stakeholders in the Southern African Development Community land issues is commendable.

The contributors have responded so well to the challenge set by him. Professor Chigara's initiative is to be highly commended.

Professor Kader Asmal
Minister of Water Affairs and Forestry 1994–99
Minister of Education 1999–2004
South Africa

Part 1

Problematising Southern African Development Community land issues

1 Introduction

Deconstructing land relations issues of the SADC

*Ben Chigara**

To varying degrees – some more intense than others, several Southern African Development Community (SADC) States are presently engaged in social-reconstruction programs aimed at correcting the salient economic and social legacy of apartheid rule on their territories. To varying degrees, this has triggered a fierce binary opposition between the dispossessed land-hungry black majority and a privileged white-minority farming community that holds and controls lands with the most agricultural potential.

The dispossessed land-hungry black majority question the legitimacy of legal titles to lands that had been expropriated from them without compensation and reserved for white commercial farming under apartheid rule. The white-minority farming community insists on the validity of its land titles at law. It insists also that the Courts should protect its titles from arbitrary alienation.

Nowhere else is this remarkable challenge more apparent than in the former apartheid-ruled States of the SADC that were also the last to achieve political freedom, namely, South Africa, Namibia and Zimbabwe. The challenge is exacerbated by several complex factors.

One is the deliberate intent of SADC governments to substitute equality for inequality as the basic norm for all social-ordering practice in the aftermath of apartheid rule. Protagonists perceive a duty on the part of incumbent SADC governments to pursue this policy without fear or favour because it reflects the foremost reason why so many had fought and died in the struggle against apartheid rule. Consequently, there is a legitimate expectation on the majority's part that the economic and social legacy of apartheid rule will be corrected without much ado.

The other is the duty of current SADC governments to ensure that their countries remain firmly set on a path of sustainable development in order to maximise on their economic potential in an increasingly globalising world economy. Moreover, SADC States have all signed up to the United Nations' (UN) time-bound millennium development goals (MDGs) which require them to ensure certain universally agreed minimum standards of human existence for their populations. The realisation of those goals depends very much on stable and competitive economic circumstances.

SADC States also share in the UN's efforts to prevent desertification and to promote human rights, and to fight discrimination and to promote equality between men and women, particularly with regards the customary right to own, inherit and dispose of property.

Another complicating factor is the duty of SADC governments to ensure the rule of law on their territories, and the protection of individuals against potential excesses of the State itself. The question this raises for SADC governments presently engaged in social-reconstruction programs necessitated by the vagaries of previous white-minority-rule governments on their territories is this: By what paradigm(s) could the correction be successfully implemented to supplant the State's basic norm and general culture of inequality under white-minority rule to equality under black-majority rule without alienating either the beneficiaries or the sufferers/bearers of apartheid rule because of their mutually opposed *legitimate expectations*? By what trick, miracle or method does one liberate both the oppressor and the oppressed from their burdens so that jointly, they arrive at a mutual originary moment of genesis, where they deliberately abandon former positions and choose to reconfigure land allocation/use for instance, in order to ensure equal and not unequal distribution of the advantages and disadvantages of their new reality?

Yet another question is how to go about reversing the economic and social legacy of apartheid rule without upsetting also the apparent economic advantages in comparison to other States. Food security, maintenance of international standards in food production, education, and general service provision all deserve protection if SADC governments are to succeed in making social reconstruction a tool for development rather than self-destruction.

The biggest challenge probably arises from bullish attempts to rationalise and justify the economic and social legacy of apartheid rule. The purpose is to either slow down social-reconstruction-oriented change that is intended by SADC governments' deliberate substitution of equality for inequality under white-minority rule as the basic norm for social ordering under majority rule, or to deny it and kill it off. Often these arguments hang on claims of black unpreparedness to assume the responsibilities inherent in the taking over of large commercial farms for instance. They characterise blacks as lacking in skill, ambition and sense of purpose. But as Brennan J. stated in the seminal *Mabo case No. 2*[1] decision, such bigotry is repugnant to reason.

> If the international law notion that inhabited land may be classified as *terra nullius* no longer commands general support, [then] the doctrines of the common law which depend on the notion that native peoples may be 'so low in the scale of social organization' that it is 'idle to impute to such people some shadow of the rights known to our law' … can hardly be retained. *If it were permissible in past centuries to keep the common law in step with international law, it is imperative in today's world that the common law should neither be nor be seen to be frozen in an age of racial discrimination.*[2]
>
> The fiction by which the rights and interests of indigenous inhabitants in land were treated as non-existent was justified by a policy which has no place in the contemporary law. … The policy appears explicitly in the

> judgment of the Privy Council in *In re Southern Rhodesia* in rejecting the argument that the native people 'were the owners of the unalienated lands long before either the Company or the Crown became concerned with them and from time immemorial ... and that the unalienated lands belonged to them still.[3]

In his *ratio decidendi* Brennan J. summed up the current position as follows:

(i) ... 'a mere change in sovereignty does not extinguish native title to land'.
(ii) The indigenous inhabitants of a settled colony are equal to the inhabitants of a conquered colony ' ... *in respect of their rights and interests in land*'.[4]
(iii) The notion that, when the Crown acquired sovereignty over colonial territory it thereby also acquired the absolute beneficial ownership of the land therein is incongruous with common law.
(iv) Rather, the correct view is that: ' ... the antecedent rights and interests in land possessed by the indigenous inhabitants of the territory *survived the change in sovereignty. Those antecedent rights and interests thus constitute a burden on the radical title of the Crown*'.[5]
(v) Finally, it must be acknowledged that this judgment overrules cases which have held the contrary because '*To maintain the authority of those cases would destroy the equality of all Australian citizens before the law. The common law of this country would perpetuate injustice if it were to continue to embrace the enlarged notion of terra nullius and to persist in characterizing the indigenous inhabitants of the Australian colonies as people too low in the scale of social organization to be acknowledged as possessing rights and interests in land*'.[6]

In short, judicial, academic and any other form of intervention that seeks to characterise as reckless abandon to economic instability, the emergent reconstruction measures aimed at including the previously excluded majority from participating in their own countries' economies point to a deeper, invisible legacy of apartheid rule that is much, much more sinister and profound than the visible one. As this book shows, apartheid rule's invisible legacy heads the threat against SADC governments' social and economic reconstruction agendas. Consequently, SADC governments' appearance of indifference towards it in light of its function as the ultimate guardian and shield of the visible economic and social legacy of apartheid rule in the SADC is most surprising.

The book also shows that apartheid rule was a social experiment whose disastrous consequences now require majority-rule governments to govern only with Solomonic[7] wisdom if they are to succeed. This is because the invisible legacy of apartheid rule, namely, the psychology of distortion which premised the significance of human worth on skin colour had resulted in semi-authentic existence which is contrary to life's purpose of pursuing self-actualisation. It became and still remains the guarantor of the visible legacy of apartheid rule in these predominantly agrarian societies. It is the reason for continuing litigation of land issues in national courts of SADC States, the Windhoek-based SADC Tribunal, and more recently and increasingly, the Washington-based International Centre for the Settlement of Investment Disputes (ICSID).

The hope is that this book will illuminate the issues around social reconstruction in majority-ruled SADC States and assist governments and stakeholders on a path of comprehensive reflection on the challenges that attend that effort locally and internationally. To be efficient, such transitions must not only institute new basic constitutional norms that target the correction of the salient economic and social legacy of foreign rule, namely, unequal land use but also shut out the risk of social fragmentation, seek to promote understanding and healing among agents, and ensure progress towards universal standards of achievement, including the UN millennium development goals, the rule of law and human rights protection.

The pedagogy of the oppressed appears to be an appropriate tool for addressing jointly, the visible and invisible legacies of apartheid rule in the SADC. Its appeal lies in its promise and potential to liberate both the oppressor and his oppressed other from their shared semi-authentic existence to authentic existence. Semi-authentic existence had been entrenched by successive apartheid rule constitutional and administrative requirements, establishing a culture where the significance of human worth depended upon skin colour. The culture that evolved from that social experiment blighted individuals' chances of self-actualising authentic existence. It is not the function of authentic existence to dehumanise people. But apartheid rule constitutional and administrative requirements had quite efficiently served to dehumanise both the oppressed and their oppressors by successfully culturalising them both into accepting the distorted psychology that premised the significance of human worth on skin colour.

Similar irrationalities are evident in efforts to counter majority-rule social reconstruction efforts that are a consequence of their change of basic norm from inequality under white-minority rule to equality under majority rule. Abraham Lincoln thought that some subjects were too serious for casual engagement. I believe that the SADC land issues belong to that category of subjects. They evoke anger, passion, history, pain, misery and bitter/sweet memories especially among vast numbers of people that are now scattered abroad. 'I shall do nothing in malice. What I deal with is too vast for malicious dealing.' – Abraham Lincoln.

Written by the foremost experts on land allocation/use in the SADC, the study has been presented in two volumes. Volume I illuminates SADC land issues from legal, sociological, developmental and practitioners' perspectives. It probes the juridical quality of land issues and the regulatory frameworks that have been instituted to manage the diverse legitimate expectations of stakeholders in time.

Volume II advances the inquiry by analysing the ideological and socio-economic and cultural issues around land in the SADC. It considers opportunities for resolution of land issues in the SADC. In particular, it examines continuing challenges, especially those that are directly linked to SADC States' substitution of equality for inequality under white minority-rule as the basic norm of all social ordering practice.

Notes

* Professor of International Laws at Brunel University, UK.
1 No. 2 [1992] HCA 23 paras 41–42.
2 Para 41 (my emphasis).
3 Para 42.
4 Para 61 (my emphasis).
5 Para 62 (my emphasis).
6 Para 63 (my emphasis).
7 See Holy Bible, 1 Kings 3.

2 The colonial legacy in land rights in southern Africa

*Robert Home**

2.1 Introduction

In the first decade of the twenty-first century southern Africa has seen a new urgency in what is often referred to as the land 'question', 'problem' or 'issue'. This mainly refers to the continued exclusion from land of the African majority population by a white settler minority and foreign investors.[1] In Zimbabwe since 2000 land has emerged as 'the pre-eminent political subject', with repercussions for the whole region.[2] Zimbabwe's Land Acquisition Act 2000 removed the requirement that land redistribution should only take place through the market (the often-quoted principle of 'willing buyer, willing seller'), and empowered the state to seize land for fast-track resettlement, following which a programme of eviction (the so-called third *chimurenga* or revolution) has reduced the number of white farmers from four thousand to a few hundred, transferring a quarter of the land area for the government's accelerated land programme. The underlying paradox is that southern Africa should have enough land to support its fast-growing population, yet in reality lack of access to land for basic shelter and livelihood remains a major cause of poverty. Inequalities created by colonialism (particularly the apartheid system) during the 20th century are seen as the main cause.

Of the European colonial powers in southern Africa (British, Dutch, German and Portuguese) it was the British who contributed the dominant ideologies of colonial rule, such as indirect rule and the dual mandate. It was Britain's larger and older imperial possession, India, that supplied not only immigrant workers (through the indenture labour scheme that brought 150,000 Indians to Natal), but also generated techniques and expertise for colonial management, such as township regulations (based upon those for the Indian military cantonments), labour regulations, worker housing, land surveying and railways.[3]

Of the countries that make up the SADC region, the Republic of South Africa (RSA) is the largest in population and land area, extending its sphere of influence over the whole region. Mineral wealth, initially gold and diamond in the Rand area, but later copper, coal and other minerals in south-central Africa, spurred the dramatic expansion of mining capitalism from the last quarter of the 19th century, drawing in African migrant workers by the million from the whole region (who often suffered high death rates). Rhodes' British South African

Company in 1890 acquired through chicanery the vast lands of Rhodesia (North and South), in hopes of mineral wealth, while similar chartered companies exploited large tracts of Portuguese Mozambique. Three SADC nation states (Botswana, Lesotho and Swaziland), however, escaped rule from South Africa by seeking Queen Victoria's protection, as Bechuanaland, Basutoland and Swaziland respectively.[4] The German colony of South-West Africa (now Namibia) came under South African administration after the First World War, under the League of Nations policy of international trusteeship over 'non-self-governing trust territories', which was intended to be a first step toward the eradication of colonial rule.[5]

The colonial legacy in land rights thus has to be understood in the context of ideologies of indirect rule and the dual mandate, and the derived ideology of *apartheid*. The indirect rule approach (as distinguished from direct colonial rule) was developed in the princely states of India, and sought to incorporate traditional local power structures into the colonial administrative structure, through a system of 'resident commissioners' and district officers. In South Africa it was practiced by British administrators such as Shepstone in Zululand and Lagden in Basutoland.[6] It soon evolved as an ideology of British colonialism between the two world wars into the so-called 'dual mandate', particularly associated with Lord Lugard.[7] As a strategy of separate development, it was notoriously applied in *apartheid* South Africa, whose racially based land laws, starting with the 1913 Natives Land Act, were expanded by the post-1948 Nationalist government.[8] The dual mandate ideology created a dual system of land law and regulation, as this chapter will explore. It distinguished between the plantation estates and townships of the European colonisers, who had one legal system, and the tribal areas where customary land tenure was maintained and codified by social anthropologists (rather than by lawyers). Thus colonialism created and maintained boundaries through dualistic or pluralistic legal structures, boundaries in physical space defined and managed by laws and regulations.

Recent academic study by geographers, lawyers and historians has been exploring how colonial legal and regulatory systems have shaped urban landscapes and the land claims of different social groups, and the place of differentiated territorial jurisdictions in regulating social relationships.[9] Underlying the 'land question' is a continuing tension between private landed property, held in parcels of absolute freehold ownership by individuals or corporate entities, and communal, customary or tribal tenure. When Europeans colonised overseas they imposed their legal systems, took the best land into their ownership, and devised various legal devices and jurisdictional forms, with which to establish, maintain and defend a hierarchy of social and spatial controls, and to dominate the indigenous populations. First, the concept of private property rights requires some interrogation.

2.2 Private property rights

The Dutch colonisers of the Cape after 1653 introduced the Roman-Dutch legal concept of private property, which conferred a virtually absolute right of ownership (*dominium*) with minimal opportunity for legal challenge. Title deeds were maintained through a deeds registry, and conveyancing was co-ordinated with the land survey process to define the land units.[10] The British succeeded the Dutch as colonial power at the Cape after 1796, and brought with them their somewhat different land law, with its feudal origins and the associated doctrine of estates and superior interests, but also asserted the primacy of private property rights through the Lockean philosophy of possessive individualism.[11] Governor Cradock's Proclamation of 1811 confirmed full rights of ownership, including the right to improvements, and did away with the previous informal system of loan tenure.[12]

While there were inevitably local variations, the colonial legal order was essentially imbued with the concept of exclusive private property rights (exclusive, that is, to the colonisers, including corporate entities). Absolute freehold rights provided a philosophical basis for chartered companies to confiscate vast tracts of land through dubious agreements with African chiefs which concealed the true nature of company intentions. Thus could the British South Africa Company in the 1890s lay claim to the whole of Rhodesia (North and South) in absolute ownership, and feel free to subdivide and sell it off to white settlers. Many of the early pioneers brought in by the company were outright adventurers, who, when the promise of mineral wealth was not immediately forthcoming, sought profit through land speculation rather than farming. In Mozambique the Portuguese colonial administration granted long leases to individuals under the *prazo* system (leases usually for three lifetimes, not subdividable), and after 1891 in order to attract external investment granted concessions (conferring a status similar to that of the chartered companies) to foreign entities such as the Zambesia and Nyassa companies.[13] In arid Namibia the colonial regime sold off the better land on advantageous terms to some 7,000 white-owned commercial farms.[14]

In the centuries following the Dutch colonisation of the Cape, many Africans took advantage of the philosophy of private property rights to buy land themselves as individuals, and they often proved to be better farmers than the whites, but after the Union of South Africa in 1910 a stop was put to that by the 1913 Natives Land Act (later the Black Land Act), which has been called the 'first pillar of apartheid'. It excluded Africans from acquiring land outside scheduled 'native' reserves, and a prerequisite to obtaining legal title was proof of 'competence to acquire', a racial test that disqualified them. Formerly independent African land-owners were thereby reduced to becoming labour tenants or wage labourers on white farms, and subsequently Africans' land rights applied to only 13 per cent of the total land area of South Africa.[15] With a population of only some three million estimated in 1913, there was apparently plenty of land, but a century later the South African population had grown to over forty million, with consequent pressures upon productive land. There was the possibility of acquiring possessory title through prescriptive rights after a minimum of thirty years effective occupation, potentially applicable to all property, whether private or public, but the Group Areas Act 1950 stopped a 'disqualified person' (i.e. under racial laws) from benefiting from it.

The prohibition on individual property ownership by Africans, embodied in the Natives Land Act, was also deeply embedded in the dual mandate concept, and the far-away Privy Council in London held in a number of cases in the 1920s that African customary land tenure did not confer individual ownership upon the occupiers of the land.[16] The prohibition on African individual property rights was applied to both urban and rural land, as will be seen, and only ended in South Africa in the 1980s with such initiatives as the home ownership scheme.

At independence the inclusion (at the insistence of the out-going colonial powers) of constitutional guarantees for the protection of private property rights, which had become enshrined as a basic human right after the Second World War, made major land redistribution to the dispossessed majority much more difficult (as indeed was the intention).[17] Transformation of the society through a transformation of property rights was effectively made unachievable.[18] Neo-liberal aid policies included land titling programmes as a precondition of World Bank structural adjustment from the 1980s, but the basic inequalities in ownership and access to land were hardly addressed. While Hernando de Soto through his influential writings has promoted the empowerment of the poor through recognition of property rights, he has shied away from the redistributional implications, and has indeed reiterated white supremacist views about African backwardness (while ostensibly seeking to distance himself from them) in a recent book contribution entitled: 'Are Africans culturally unsuited to property rights?'[19] In 1986 a South African court judgment (by a white judge) could state that 'whites own land by law, whether they are industrious or not, while non-whites must demonstrate their worthiness to own land through their labour'.[20]

2.2.1 'Boundary markers': the land surveyor role[21]

In the words of an early Surveyor-General in New Zealand (someone apparently quite unaware of any concept of indigenous land rights):

> 'The main object of a colonial survey is to enable the settlement of the Crown lands to proceed on a system of survey and record, which, for the settler, will give him possession of a definite piece of land which cannot ever after be overridden by a rival claim.'[22]

It was the colonialists' land surveying profession that had the task of demarcating the precise boundaries of landed property, and from the early days at the Cape, following the Dutch system, title and transfer deeds were officially registered in a public deeds registry.[23] Subsequently British colonial surveyors set out to map the new colonies and protectorates acquired across Africa, importing their so-called 'systematic survey' methods, and the end of the First World War released many trained survey officers from the armed forces into colonial service.[24] The *Empire Survey Review* was their professional publication outlet, and carried articles on such matters as the technical challenges of laying out new townships,[25] creating land titles for large estates,[26] and passionate debates about the relative merits of fixed or general boundary methods of survey.[27]

The concept of a systematic record of land rights, linked to a scientifically surveyed geodetic map base, offered the promise (or illusion) of the 'continuous finality of the register'. An unambiguous map-based demarcation of the land parcel, incorporated in an official certificate of title guaranteed by the state, could be easily amended to accommodate any subsequent changes, through what surveyors called 'mutations' (a term apparently borrowed from Darwinian evolutionary biology). The Torrens system of survey and registration, originating in South Australia, was disseminated across the dominions, colonies and protectorates of the British Empire. The proponents of such modern cadastral systems usually subscribed to an evolutionary theory which justified land registration as part of an inevitable historical process 'towards a greater concentration of rights in the individual and a corresponding loss of control by the community as a whole'[28] – an idea which remains a sensitive issue in recent debates about African land tenure.[29]

Precolonial African perceptions of land were very different, and did not see land as a fixed asset. As a chief of the Ndebele put it in 1887: 'In olden times … we never talked about boundary lines … It is only now they [the British] talk about boundaries.'[30] This failure to recognise the role and power of geographic boundary-setting undermined African counter-claims to land, and only recently has so-called 'cadastral politics' emerged through practices of 'counter-mapping', which seek to record uses of land by groups that have not been recognised by state institutions.[31]

2.3 'Native reserves' and customary land tenure

The idea that colonial subjects deserved to be treated humanely, and that colonies represented somehow a sacred trust placed upon the imperial powers, can be traced to Burke's writings on India in the late 18th century, and to the Aboriginal Rights Society in the 19th, and found a way through the anthropological studies of Maine into Lugardian theories of indirect rule, which aimed to keep traditional tribal societies insulated from the disruptive effects of Western civilisation.[32] In the words of Lugard on Nigeria:

> The British role here is to bring to the country the gains of civilisation by applied science (whether in the development of material resources, or the eradication of disease, etc.), with as little interference as possible with Native customs and modes of thought.[33]

The trusteeship principle under the inter-war League of Nations thus placed a fiduciary duty upon colonial administrations towards the indigenous peoples they governed, because of those peoples' perceived peculiar vulnerability, and customary land rights were to be protected in special trust land areas – the so-called native reserves.

In South Africa the 1913 Natives Land Act legislated for not only the prohibition of Africans from buying land, but also the beginning of a systematic reserves policy. Earlier reserves can be dated from the mid-19th century Cape Colony, and spread not only across southern Africa but widely across the British Empire. They represented a boundary or frontier between black and white, but started out as more of a concept than any physically defined territory; the initial allocations reflected the expedients of conquest and the surviving centres of chiefly political power, rather than the theoretical concerns of such ideologues as Lugard, or the retrospective tidying exercises of later historians. Reserve boundaries were effectively defined by the boundaries of the white settler estates, which themselves were often under-occupied and not clearly fenced. Formal recognition of reserves through a process of official gazetting followed from the 1920s, for example under the Rhodesia Land Apportionment Act 1930, but '[l]and settlement patterns in southern and eastern Africa remained a seemingly anarchic tapestry of white farms, forest areas, unassigned land, and reserves.'[34] The land areas allocated to reserves also fluctuated both up and down. The 1915 Land Commission in Rhodesia recommended reducing the size of reserve areas, and claimed that this would accelerate the end of tribalism (as well as improving the supply of labour to the mines), while subsequently the reserves were enlarged under a new policy to accommodate progressive African farmers. In the protectorates customary land tenure survived, and in Botswana and Zambia still extend to three-quarters or more of the total land area. In South Africa it became the basis of the Bantustans created by the Bantu Authorities Act 1950 and the Promotion of Bantu Self-government Act 1959.

While land surveyors were demarcating boundaries, white social anthropologists were at work describing tribal land tenure systems, often commissioned on behalf of the colonial administration in a form of intelligence-gathering.[35] Customary land tenure was often misinterpreted and undermined by the colonial judiciary, manipulated by administrators, and overlooked in legislation, and was held subject to a 'repugnancy clause' interpretation (if it could be considered contrary to common law principles of fairness, justice or equity). Tribal or customary law was initially primarily concerned with relations between persons, but became increasingly involved with competing claims to land, and by the 1940s Lord Hailey in his African Survey was recording individualistic tendencies in customary land tenure, borrowing lessons from settler ownership.[36]

Customary land has come in recent years to be recognised as an important common property resource, indeed a defence against the forces of globalisation, fulfilling a welfare function, and providing a reservoir of cheap unserviced land in peri-urban areas.[37] Indigenous groups have increasingly pursued legal challenges and human rights arguments to reassert their claims to ancestral lands, notably in the South African *Richtersveld* case.[38] Tests derived from the Australian *Mabo* case required proof of occupation to be mediated by three considerations: the nature of the claimants' economic system (agriculture leaves a permanent record, while pastoralism and hunting/gathering have been interpreted as showing only an ephemeral attachment to land), the exclusion of other groups, and length and continuity of occupation (combined with evidence of a continuous separate identity for the claimant group).[39]

2.4 Public lands and the role of the state

As well as the two above categories of private property and customary tenure, the colonial state asserted its own land rights over what was variously called public, crown or state land (usually subsuming 'native' land). It justified its claim as building up and protecting the 'public interest', on the basis that surplus land was either unoccupied (the concept of *terra nullius*, now discredited since the *Mabo* case in Australia) or not in obviously beneficial use. Once claimed, the state could then transfer that land through grant, sale or lease to new settlers or public bodies, which might be central government itself, regional or local authorities, or parastatal bodies (such as railways). After independence, in a reaction against socialist-driven attempts at land reform, neo-liberal policies have supported large-scale transfers of state land into the hands of private individuals and legal entities.

Along with these separate and exclusionary categories of land went restrictions upon the movement of people, especially of the non-white colonial subjects (such as freed slaves, indentured and migrant workers), applied through requirements to carry travel and work documents. Plantation owners and mining companies wanted to stop their workers from absconding, while the state assumed the role of managing the migration of workers between and within colonies; the transition from private to state control over the mobility of workers has been interpreted as part of a historical dialectical transition from feudalism to capitalism. The most infamous example of controlled population movement was the South African pass laws, which denied access to white or other segregated areas for Africans without the correct pass.[40] Africans occupying land without approval, for example in areas redesignated under the Group Areas Act, could be designated as squatters, and forcibly cleared from such 'black spots' and removed to the black 'homelands' or townships.[41] Such a destruction of complex socio-economic networks of kinship and neighbourhood, as was involved in the racial reordering of Cape Town, for instance (particularly the notorious clearance of District Six), has been likened to 'a man with a stick breaking spiderwebs in a forest'.[42]

2.5 Land in urban areas: the Stallard doctrine and the Durban system

Lugardian Indirect Rule policy supported the establishment of new towns as largely exclusive European residential areas, segregated from the local population, and run under municipal-style by-law regulations, which derived from those applied in the military cantonments of British India. Town planning measures of racial residential segregation and building-free zones were advocated by medical specialists concerned about prevention of plague, malaria and other diseases, notable among them Dr. W. J. R. Simpson. The so-called Stallard doctrine in South Africa regarded towns as European cultural creations, and restricted access by

Africans to those whose labour was needed, while forcing Africans to live in 'locations' or 'townships' (inappropriately named, as these racially segregated housing areas usually lay outside the city limits). As a Durban Police Superintendent stated in 1904: 'I would put my Natives in barracks and let them march into the town as they do with soldiers'.[43]

South Africa was a testing ground for the wider region in the techniques of managing a large migrant labour force, which was needed to serve the sugar estates, mines, ports and railways being developed by colonial capital. The so-called Durban system originated with the *togt* or day-labour system, which was introduced in 1874 by Shepstone in Natal, and under which labourers paid a registration fee which paid for their own policing and accommodation. The Durban system developed into a model for urban control in British central and south Africa, and came to be largely funded by the proceeds of a municipal monopoly of beer-halls, paid into a 'Native Revenue' account which was kept separate from other municipal finances.[44]

The prevention of Africans from legally owning land applied not only on white land after 1913, and in the native reserves, but also in the towns. The Natives (Urban Areas) Act 1923 in South Africa empowered local authorities, in the absence of African property ownership, to build African housing in locations outside the urban area (justified as a measure to prevent non-white, particularly Indian, landlordism).[45] This was a similar model to the contemporary expansion in Britain of council housing, supported by central government grant.[46]

A distinctive urban morphology resulted in what became called the *apartheid* city, which was conceptually mapped in the closing decade of *apartheid* by South African academics, and was applied more widely in the southern African region.[47] British design concepts of the garden city – low-density, self-contained residential neighbourhoods outside the city, with most houses on their own plots with gardens were consciously applied to the planning of African peri-urban townships.[48]

2.5.1 Mining townships

Not only were towns racially segregated, but mining communities were maintained under separate regulatory regimes, following the American model of company town, ie:

> '[A] community which has been built wholly to support the operations of a single company, in which all homes, buildings, and other real-estate property are owned by that company having been acquired or erected specifically for the benefit of its employees, and in which the company provides most public services.'[49]

African mines labour was kept separate from the wider community, fragmenting any union solidarity, and facilitating control. The closed mining complex at Kimberley served as a model for the gold and diamond mining industry, designed to deter diamond theft but also serving a widecontrol function.[50]

A distinctive application of the company town was in the Copperbelt towns of Northern Rhodesia (later Zambia), where the phenomenon of what has been called 'twin townships' evolved through negotiation between the colonial administration and mining corporation.[51] When it became apparent in around 1928–29 that the Copperbelt was set for dramatic growth, the newly-established protectorate administration of Northern Rhodesia was concerned about the management of urban development, and passed both Town Planning and Townships Ordinances in 1929. Three-cornered negotiations ensued between the mining companies, protectorate officials and the Colonial Office in London. The American-controlled mining corporation was anxious to build as quickly as possible to get its workers working, and to reach full production, and so where money could be substituted for time it was spent. Government, on the other hand, was wary, conscious of its status as a protectorate, having responsibilities to the public (especially those providing ancillary services to the mining population), yet itself constrained by meagre financial resources. Ordinances passed by the protectorate eventually provided for two kinds of township – mining and public. Both had township boards, with wide-ranging by-law powers, but crucial differences were that the mining corporations controlled the mining townships, with separate regulations and policing; also they paid no property rates in them, being adamant that, having incurred considerable outlay on social infrastructure, they should not have to pay rates to a local authority as well.

The Copperbelt town of Nkana-Kitwe has been well researched by Emmanuel Mutale as an example of this approach, and its very name reflects its origins as a 'twin township'.[52] Negotiations over the respective roles of the public and mine townships were particularly protracted and difficult. The Rhokana Corporation had surveyed a township site on the Kitwe Farm, east of the railway line, as early as 1928, and invested in basic services. The Colonial Office, however, regarded the transfer of governmental functions to a profit-making private company as 'a grave departure in tropical Africa': ' … it is not our business to increase the profits of a largely American absentee landlord by facilitating their control over *our own people*' (my italics).[53]

The Colonial Office reluctantly agreed that Rhokana could develop a public township, with plots (or stands) allocated by the government with 99-year leases on land donated by Rhokana without compensation, and would undertake engineering works and services at cost price. There was a limit on the number of traders allowed within the public township, and a commitment not to allow the development of another within a 10-mile radius of Nkana's smelter stack earned it the title of a 'closed township'. The mine township at Nkana was declared under the Mine Townships Ordinance in 1935, while commercial trading transferred to the new public township (Kitwe) in 1936, and ceased in the mine township the following year.

2.5.2 African urban housing

The changing physical form of colonial urban housing for Africans is becoming better researched, including the role of official policy.[54] The barrack hostel was the main form of worker housing throughout the British colonies, and spread from the ports into the interior of southern Africa. Natal in the 1870s was significant, with various commissions of inquiry leading to greater regulation, setting minimum space standards and allowing more women immigrants to provide more stable domestic conditions; in Durban at this time one finds the Indian labour barracks (the coolie barrack) physically adjacent to African single-sex hostels. In the early days of mining exploration African workers were housed in barracks on the mine compound, supervised by a compound manager appointed under the Mine Townships Ordinance. The Forster Commission (1937) on riots in Trinidad condemned such barracks as 'indescribable in their lack of elementary needs of decency', and recommended the term be discontinued in future ordinances and by-laws, while the inquiry into the 1935 Copperbelt strike in Northern Rhodesia made similar criticisms, leading British colonial policy to abandon the idea of the barrack, as part of a Colonial Office conversion to a progressive model of colonial development and welfare, which it hoped would secure labour loyalty in a testing time of approaching world war.[55] Officialdom dropped the term 'barrack' (as it had earlier dropped the derogatory term 'coolie') and replaced it with the more neutral 'hostel', which in South Africa first appears in the African (Urban Areas) Act 1923.[56]

To return to the well-researched Nkana-Kitwe case, even before the strikes showed the seriousness of labour unrest, the protectorate administration in Northern Rhodesia had been pressing the mining companies to build bachelor or married huts on individual plots, rather than barracks. The Rhokana corporation in 1935 proposed a native location which would have provided predominantly barrack housing, but colonial officials disapproved of 'the grim barracks which appear to be contemplated … nothing less than the creation of native slums'. Rhokana responded grudgingly by increasing the proportion of married huts, agreeing that all should be 'of the individual type' (i.e. detached on their own plot), although it remained reluctant to build married quarters, reflecting its opposition to stabilisation as well as simple stinginess. The 1935 strike gave the mining companies a severe fright, and in the following years (1939–44) Rhokana built 2,797 dwellings for Africans in Nkana-Kitwe, representing 83.5 per cent of total new dwellings (the rest being built by central or local government, or the railways).

From an organisation of domestic urban space around single men there was thus a shift in favour of family housing under the label 'stabilisation' of African labour. This new concept of family housing for black workers emerged from a discourse on the merits of encouraging a permanent mining population based upon family households, or whether the African miners should regard the village as their base and spend only short periods in the mines. The mining companies generally preferred the latter, with a turnover of cheap African labour, and wanted to avoid detribalisation, unionisation and the establishment of family life in the mining towns. Grudging official recognition that African and Indian workers and families had become a permanent feature of colonial society resulted in a conscious redesign of their housing, informed and prompted by developments in British town planning practice and garden city design.[57] The new forms of housing were contested and negotiated with the employers, both plantation estates and mining companies. By the 1950s family housing was being built in southern and central Africa by both employers and local authorities, although most of South Africa's 700,000 migrant workers were still housed in single-sex barrack or hostel accommodation, and the cultural practices and housing preferences of the occupiers went largely ignored.

2.6 Post-independence developments

The countries of southern Africa have experienced recent massive population growth, with the combined population of the ten SADC countries reaching in 2010 some 130 million. The combined populations of RSA, Zimbabwe and Zambia are now 75 million, compared with less than 8 million – a tenth of that – 80 years ago. Even allowing for census undercounting, these represent astonishing growth rates, and would put pressure on land whatever legal structures were in place. A historically new situation has arisen where labour is abundant but land and work are scarce, what Iliffe has called 'the great transition which has dominated the history of the poor in every continent' – transition from rule by enslavement to rule by enclosure.[58] Controls over the internal movement of people have largely disappeared, but inequitable land ownership remains, and rapid urban growth now poses new governance challenges.[59]

House-building by government and mining corporations was greatly reduced from the 1970s, and largely replaced by the cheaper 'sites-and-services' schemes promoted by the World Bank and aid agencies, which had colonial precedents in 'aided self-help'.[60] Just outside the official urban areas, peri-urban informal settlements arose, within easy commuting distance of the town centre and concentrated along transport corridors.[61] In *apartheid* South Africa successive legislation (eg the Group Areas and Influx Control Acts) struggled with the growing pressures of African population growth and rural-urban migration. As rural impoverishment grew, those tribal or communal lands which lay near urban areas became places where Africans could settle in unregulated, unserviced settlements and gain access to urban employment opportunities. When *apartheid* state power was no longer able to manage these areas, the 'squatter camps' were relabelled as 'informal settlements', designated for upgrading rather than clearance – definitely 'here to stay'.[62]

Since independence several southern African countries have attempted ambitious and complex land tenure reforms, extending the scope of ownership to a wider range of tenures, and giving easier access to title for occupiers in certain circumstances.[63] From the 1980s the World Bank has demanded tenure reform as a precondition for Structural Adjustment Programmes.[64] New land tenure laws in Namibia, Malawi and Zambia facilitated land registration under indigenous tenure, one preferred option being group or community ownership of land. South Africa embarked upon a significant land redistribution and restitution programme. Land redistribution was intended to help those prejudiced under the old regime (the urban and rural poor, farm workers, labour tenants and emergent farmers) to acquire land from willing sellers with state assistance. The 2004 Communal Land Tenure Act allowed community ownership (community being defined as a single juristic person, often a tribal authority) – a move intended to address the chaotic land administration in the former homelands.[65] New land registration procedures in South Africa also allowed the upgrading of rights from the concept of 'initial ownership' under the 1995 Development Facilitation Act.[66]

In spite of an impressive array of new laws and policies, progress in the region has been limited, especially in reducing racial inequalities in land ownership. The South African government, for example, adopted a target in 1994 of transferring 30 per cent of commercial farming land to 600,000 smallholders, but after a decade only 3 per cent of land had been transferred, reflecting institutional weaknesses and the reluctance of owners to offer property for sale. In Zambia land law reforms in 1995 only worsened economic inequality by concentrating land titles in a few hands (Zambian elites and foreigners), with the existing occupiers classed as squatters and then evicted. 'Ironically, a law ostensibly designed to create more secure forms of land tenure is leading to unprecedented forms of dispossession.'[67] In Namibia the Government bought out white-owned ranches (by 2004 120 of them, totalling 700,000 ha), converting freeholds into 99-year leases, but was handicapped by the gap between a high open market price and low government grant that was available.[68]

2.7 Conclusions

The 'land problem' is nothing new in southern Africa, although in the colonial period it referred to rather different issues than it does now. For most of the 20th century land in southern Africa was transferred into the hands of white settlers and capitalist corporations, and a dual legal system was maintained that mostly denied Africans rights to individual property. Recent reforms have focused on new ways of obtaining legal rights as a primary basis of reform, but only since the 1990s, with the lead taken by the post-1994 Government in South Africa, have programmes of land restitution and redistribution gained momentum, while Zimbabwe has moved to over-rule the constitutional guarantee of private property rights. Attempts to unscramble complex and discriminatory laws have, however, often meant replacing them with yet more complex ones, while resource and capacity constraints have held back effective implementation.

Notes

* Professor in Land Management, Law School, Anglia Ruskin University, Chelmsford, UK.

1 Among recent books on the subject are: C. Alden and W. Anseeuw (2009); J. Alexander (2006); J. Hunter (2004); M. C. Lee and K. Colvard (2003); Samuel Moyo (2008); Lungisile Ntsebeza and R. Hall (2007).

2 David Hughes (2006), p xiv.

3 Eric Stokes (1959); T. Holdich (1890).

4 Basutoland, for example, was formally 'disannexed' from the Cape Colony following the so-called 'Gun War' of 1880–82, and in 1884 became 'a Dependency, a Native Territory under the direct control of the Imperial Government', with the Cape Colony paying an annual contribution.
5 'Mandates: League of Nations and United Nations', in K. Shillington (2005), p 933. See also Kenneth Robinson (1965).
6 Theophilus Shepstone (1817–93) was secretary for native affairs in Natal for thirty years, and 'one of the chief architects of segregationist policies used to govern Africans in colonies stretching from the Cape to Kenya' (*Dictionary of National Biography*). Sir Godfrey Lagden (1851–1934) worked in Basutoland 1884–1901 (Resident Commissioner from 1893), and as Commissioner of Native Affairs in Transvaal 1901–07, and was Chairman of the South African Native Affairs Commission 1902–04 (*Who Was Who*).
7 Lord Lugard (1858–1945) was British representative on the League of Nations' Permanent Mandates Commission (1922–36). See his 1922 book *The Dual Mandate in British Tropical Africa*.
8 Saul Dubow (1989).
9 Nicholas Blomley and others (2001); Robert Home (1997); Sandy Kedar (2002); Brenda Yeoh (2000), p 146.
10 R. Zimmermann and D. Visser (1996); D. Carey Miller (2000).
11 Christopher Macpherson (1962); J. Waldron (1988).
12 John Milton, 'Ownership', in R. Zimmermann and D. Visser (1996).
13 Michael Newitt (1973), p 87.
14 Kevin Cahill (2006), p 358; D. Pankhurst (1996).
15 T. W. Bennett (1996); A. Jeeves and J. Crush (1998); S. Banda (2006).
16 T. Allen (2000), p 147.
17 Thomas Allen (1993).
18 L. Ntsebeza (2007).
19 H. De Soto (2008).
20 Quoted in T. W. Bennett (1996).
21 Gabrielle Byrnes (2001).
22 J. McKerrow (1889).
23 The Deeds Registries Act 1937 unified existing practice.
24 G. McGrath (1976); T. H. Holdich (1901).
25 D. L. Reid and D. R. Meldrum (1934).
26 J. E. S. Bradford (1936). The land under survey was in Northern Rhodesia (now Zambia), title granted to the British South Africa Company.
27 C. O. Gilbert (1932); W. M. Edwards (1932). Boundaries, which are often disputed, can be defined either as general boundaries (physical features determined on the ground) or 'fixed' geodetic co-ordinates.
28 J. R. Simpson (1976), p 163.
29 Jean-Pierre Platteau (1996).
30 Quoted in David Hughes (2006), p 7.
31 Ibid.
32 R. Rainger (1980); K. Mantena (2004), p 159.
33 F. D. Lugard (1919), p 9.
34 A. Cheater (1990); 'Land and "Reserves", Colonial', in K. Shillington (2005).
35 Colonial Office (1950); W. D. Hammond-Tooke (1997).
36 Lord Hailey (1956); Martin Chanock (1991).
37 Clarissa Fourie (1994).
38 T. M. Chan (2004); M. Barry (2004).
39 T. W. Bennett (1996).
40 Doug Hindson (1987).
41 L. Platzky and C. Walker (1985); C. Murray and C. O'Regan (1990); D. Van Tonder (1993); J. Western (1984); John Rex (1974).

42 O. Wollheim, quoted in Iliffe (1987), p 263.
43 T. R. H. Davenport (1970).
44 M. W. Swanson (1976); K. E. Atkins (1993).
45 Martin Chanock (2001), p 490.
46 A. D. Roberts (1986).
47 Books on the topic include A. Lemon (1990); Jennifer Robinson (1996); D. M. Smith (1992); M. R. Swilling and others (1991). An extensive journal literature includes A. Mabin (1991); B. Maharaj (1996); B. Maharaj (1997); S. Parnell (1988); H. Southworth (1990).
48 John Collins (1980).
49 J. B. Allen (1966).
50 E. G. Wilson (1972).
51 J. Gardiner (1971).
52 E. Mutale (2004). Nkana is the mine and Kitwe the town. Twin townships are not to be confused with dual cities, another recognised feature of colonialism, which combine traditional and modern urban forms side by side.
53 National Archives (UK) file CO/759/50/36295.
54 R. K. Home (2000); F. Demissie (1998); R. K. Home (1998); J. B. Robinson (1990); J. Wasserfall (1990).
55 Russell Commission (1935).
56 A distinction was made between barracks (provided rent-free by employers) and hostels (municipally owned for 'native' workers of all types). Barracks, hostels and African family housing were all grouped together in a 'sub-economic letting' category. *Durban Housing Survey* (1952).
57 'Stabilisation' (1944), file SEC1/1320, Zambian National Archives, Lusaka.
58 J. Iliffe (1987), pp 4–6.
59 Carol Rakodi (1997); A. Durand-Lasserve and L. Royston (2002).
60 R. Harris (1998).
61 For example, see A. G. Tipple (1981); M. Mulwanda and E. Mutale (1994).
62 D. Hindson and J. McCarthy (1994); R. K. Home and H. Lim (2004).
63 M. Bratton (1990); S. Evers and others (2005); M. Munyuki-Hungwe (2004); A. J. Van Der Walt (2009).
64 A. Manji (2001).
65 R. P. Werbner (1980, 1982).
66 B. de Villiers (2003). Annexure II lists restitution claims settled as at 2002 end: some 85,000 households, 437,000 beneficiaries, 513,000 ha restored. Most claims were urban, and were settled by cash compensation. R. Hall (2007) and C. Walker (2007) in L. Ntsebeza and R. Hall (2007).
67 'Land Reform', in K. Shillington (2005), p 205.
68 Kevin Cahill (2006), p 358.

Bibliography

Alden, C. and Anseeuw, W. (2009) *Land, Liberation and Compromise in Southern Africa* (Basingstoke: Palgrave).

Alexander, J. (2006) *The Unsettled Land: the Politics of Land and State-making in Zimbabwe 1893–2003* (Oxford: James Currey).

Allen, J. B. (1966) *The Company Town in the American West* (Norman, OK: University of Oklahoma Press).

Allen, T. (2000) *The Right to Property in Commonwealth Jurisdictions* (Cambridge: Cambridge University Press), p. 147.

Allen, Thomas (1993) 'Commonwealth Constitutions and the Right not to be Deprived of Property', *International and Comparative Law Quarterly*, 42: 523.

Atkins, K. E. (1993) *'The moon is dead! Give us our money!' The cultural origins of an African Work Ethic, Natal, South Africa, 1843–1900* (Portsmouth, NH: Heinemann).

Banda, S. (2006) 'Land Law Reform: A Comparative Analysis of South Africa's Labour Tenancy Contract and Malawi's Tenant Worker's Contract', *Oxford Commonwealth Law Journal*, 6(2): 201–26.

Barry, M. (2004) 'Now Another Thing Must Happen: Richtersveld and the Dilemmas of Land Reform in post-Apartheid South Africa', *SAJHR*, 20: 355.

Bennett, T. W. (1996a) 'Historic Land Claims in South Africa', in G. E. Van Maanen and A. J. van der Walt (eds) *Property Law on the Threshold of the 21st Century* (Apeldoorn: Maklu).

Bennett, T. W. (1996b) 'African Land: A History of Dispossession', in G. E. van Maanen and A. J. van der Walt (eds) *Property Law on the Threshold of the 21st Century* (Apeldoorn: Maklu).

Bennett, T. W. (1996c) 'Historic Land Claims in South Africa', in G. E. Van Maanen and A. J. van der Walt (eds) *Property Law on the Threshold of the 21st Century* (Apeldoorn: Maklu).

Blomley, Nicholas and others (eds) (2001) *The Legal Geographies Reader* (Oxford: Blackwell).

Bradford, J. E. S. (1936) 'A Three-million-acre Title Survey', *Empire Survey Review* 3: 469–76.

Bratton, M. (1990) 'Ten Years After: Land Redistribution in Zimbabwe, 1980–90', in R. L. Prosterman and T. M. Hanstad (eds) *Agrarian Reform and Grassroots Development: Ten Case Studies* (Boulder, CO: Lynne Rienner).

Byrnes, Gabrielle (2001) *Boundary Markers: Land Surveying and the Colonisation of New Zealand* (Wellington, NZ: Bridget Williams).

Cahill, Kevin (2006) *Who Owns the World: The Hidden Facts Behind Land Ownership* (Edinburgh: Mainstream).

Carey Miller, D. (2000) *Land Title in South Africa* (Cape Town: Juta).

Chan, T. M. (2004) 'The Richtersveld Challenge: South Africa Finally Adopts Aboriginal Title', in R. Hitchcock and D. Vinding (eds) *Indigenous People's Rights in Southern Africa* (Copenhagen: International Work Group for Indigenous Affairs).

Chanock, Martin (1991) 'Paradigms, Policies, and Property: A Review of the Customary Law of Land Tenure', in K. Mann and R. Roberts (eds) *Law in Colonial Africa*, (Portsmouth, NH, Heinemann).

Chanock, Martin (2001) *The Making of South African Legal Culture, 1902–36: Fear, Favour and Prejudice* (Cambridge: Cambridge University Press), p 490.

Cheater, A. (1990) 'The Ideology of "Communal" Land Tenure in Zimbabwe: Mythogenesis Enacted?' *Africa*, 60: 188–206.

Collins, John (1980) 'Lusaka: Urban Planning in a British Colony, 1931–64', in G. Cherry (ed) *Shaping an Urban World* (London: Mansell).

Colonial Office (1950) *Bibliography of Published Sources relating to African Land Tenure* (London: HMSO).

Davenport, T. R. H. (1970) 'The Triumph of Colonel Stallard: The Transformation of the Natives (Urban Areas) Act between 1923 and 1937', *South African Historical Journal*, 2: 77–96.

Demissie, F. (1998) 'In the Shadow of the Gold Mines: Migrancy and Mine Housing in South Africa', *Housing Studies*, 13: 445–69.

De Soto, H. (2008) 'Are Africans Culturally Unsuited to Property Rights and the Rule of Law?' in D. Banik (ed) *Rights and Legal Empowerment in Eradicating Poverty* (Aldershot: Ashgate).

De Villiers, B. (2003) *Land Reform: Issues and Challenges* (Johannesburg: KAS).

Dubow, Saul (1989) *Racial Segregation and the Origins of Apartheid in South Africa 1919–36* (Oxford: Macmillan).

Dugard, J. and Roux, T. (2006) 'The Record of the South African Constitutional Court in Providing an Institutional Voice for the Poor, 1995–2004', in G. Gargarella,

P. Domingo and T. Roux (eds) *Courts and Social Transformation in the new Democracies* (Aldershot: Ashgate).

Durand-Lasserve, A. and Royston, L. (eds) (2002) *Holding their ground: Secure land tenure for the urban poor in India, Brazil and South Africa* (London: Earthscan).

Durban Housing Survey (1952) *A Study of Housing in a Multi-racial Community* (Pietermaritzburg: University of Natal Press).

Edwards, W. M. (1932) 'Relations of Beacon and Deed-Plan in South Africa', *Empire Survey Review*, 2: 203–06.

Evers, S. and others (eds) (2005) *Competing Jurisdictions: Settling Land Claims in Africa* (Leiden: Brill).

Fourie, Clarissa (1994) 'A New Approach to the Zulu Land Tenure System: An Historical Anthropological Explanation of the Development of an Informal Settlement' (PhD thesis, Grahamstown: Rhodes University).

Franklin, A. S. (1995) *Land Law in Lesotho: the Politics of the 1979 Act* (Aldershot: Ashgate).

Gardiner, J. (1971) *Some Aspects of the Establishment of Towns in Zambia during the Nineteen-twenties and Thirties*' (*Zambian Urban Studies* 3, Lusaka: Institute of African Studies, University of Zambia).

Gilbert, C. O. (1956) 'Beacon versus Deed-Plan', (1932) *Empire Survey Review*, 1: 98.

Hailey, Lord (1956) *African Survey* (London: HMSO).

Hall, R. (2007) 'Transforming rural South Africa? Taking Stock of Land Reform', in L. Ntsebeza and R. Hall (eds) *The Land Question in South Africa: The Challenge of Transformation and Redistrbution* (Cape Town: HSRC Press).

Hammond-Tooke, W. D. (1997) *Imperfect Interpreters: South Africa's anthropologists 1920–1990* (Johannesburg: Witwatersrand University Press).

Harris, R. (1998) 'The Silence of the Experts: "Aided Self-help Housing," 1939–54', *Habitat International* 22:165–89.

Hindson, Doug (1987) *Pass Controls and the Urban African Proletariat in South Africa* (Johannesburg: Ravan).

Hindson, D. and McCarthy J. (eds) (1994) *Here to Stay: Informal Settlements in KwaZulu-Natal* (Daldrige: Indicator Press).

Holdich, T. (1890) *African Boundaries, and the Application of Indian Systems of Geographical Survey to Africa* (London).

Holdich, T. H. (1901) 'How are we to get Maps of Africa?' *Geographical Journal*, 18: 590–601.

Home, Robert (1997) *Of Planting and Planning* (London: Spon).

Home, R. K. (1998) 'Barracks and Hostels: A Heritage Conservation Case for Worker Housing', *Natalia*, 28: 45–52.

Home, R. K. (2000) 'From Barrack Compounds to the Single-family House: Planning Worker Housing in Colonial Natal and Northern Rhodesia', *Planning Perspectives*, 15: 327–47.

Home, R. K. and Lim, H. (eds) (2004) *Demystifying the Mystery of Capital: Land Titling and Peri-urban Development in Africa and the Caribbean* (London: Glasshouse Press).

Hughes, David (2006) *From Enslavement to Environmentalism: Politics on a Southern African Frontier* (Seattle, WA and London: University of Washington Press).

Hunter, J. (ed) (2004) *Who Should Own the Land? Analysis and Views on Land Reform and the Land Question in Namibia and Southern Africa* (Windhoek: KAS).

Hyam, R. (1999) 'Bureaucracy and "Trusteeship" in the Colonial Empire', in *Oxford History of the British Empire* (Oxford: Oxford University Press).

Iliffe, J. (1987) *The African Poor: A History* (Cambridge: Cambridge University Press).

Jeeves, A. and Crush, J. (eds) (1998) *White Farms, Black Labour: the State and Agrarian Change in Southern Africa, 1910–50* (Oxford: James Currey).

Kasongo, B. A. and Tipple, A. G. (1990) 'An Analysis of Policy towards Squatters in Kitwe, Zambia', *Third World Planning Review*, 12: 147–65.

Kedar, Sandy (2002) 'On the Legal Geography of Ethnocratic Settler States', *Current Legal Issues*, 5: 401.

Kgabo Commission (1994) *Report of Presidential Commission of Inquiry into Problems in Mogoditshane and other Peri-urban villages* (Gaborone: Government Printer).

Lee, M. C. and Colvard, K. (2003) *Unfinished Business: The Land Crisis in Southern Africa* (Pretoria: Africa Institute of South Africa).

Lemon, A. (ed) (1990) *Homes Apart: South Africa's Divided Cities* (London: Paul Chapman).

Lugard, F. D. (1919) *Revision of Instructions to Political Officers on Subjects Chiefly Political and Administrative, 1913–18* (London: Waterlow).

Lugard, Lord (1922) *The Dual Mandate in British Tropical Africa* (repr. 1965, London: Frank Cass).

Mabin, A. (1991) 'Origins of segregatory urban planning in South Africa, *c.* 1900–40', *Planning History* 13: 8–16.

Maharaj, B. (1996) 'The Group Areas Act in Durban: Central–Local Relations' (PhD thesis, Westville: University of Durban).

Maharaj, B. (1997) 'Apartheid, Urban Segregation and the local State: Durban and the Group Areas Act in South Africa', *Urban Geography*, 18: 135–54.

Manji, A. (2001) 'Land Reform in the Shadow of the State: the Implementation of new Land Laws in Sub-Saharan Africa', *Third World Quarterly*, 21: 327.

McGrath, G. (1976) 'From Hills to Hotine: The Quest for a Central Surveys and Mapping Organization for the British Colonial Territories in Africa', *Cartographic Journal*, 13: 7–21.

McKerrow, J. (1889) 'New Zealand system of survey', *New Zealand Surveyor*, 1: 9.

Macpherson, Christopher (1962) *The Theory of Possessive Individualism: from Hobbes to Locke* (Oxford: Clarendon Press).

Mantena, K. (2004) 'Law and "Tradition": Henry Maine and the Theoretical Origins of Indirect Rule', in M. Lobban and A. Lewis (eds) *Law and History* (Oxford: Oxford University Press), p 159.

Moyo, Samuel (2008) *African Land Questions, Agrarian Transitions and the State: Contradictions of Neo-liberal Land Reforms* (Dakar: Council for Development of Social Science Research in Africa).

Mulwanda, M. and Mutale, E. (1994) 'Never mind the people, the shanties must go: The Politics of Urban Land in Zambia', *Cities*, 11: 303–11.

Munyuki-Hungwe, M. (ed) (2004) *Land Reform and Tenure in Southern Africa: Current Practices, Alternatives and Prospects* (Harare: Documentation Unit).

Murray, C. and O'Regan, C. (eds) (1990) *No Place to Rest: Forced Removals and the Law in Southern Africa* (Cape Town: Oxford University Press).

Mutale, E. (2004) *The Management of Urban Development in Zambia* (Aldershot: Ashgate).

Newitt, Michael (1973) *Portuguese Settlement on the Zambesi: Exploration, Land Tenure and Colonial Rule in East Africa* (London: Longman), p 87.

Ntsebeza, L. (2007) 'Land Redistribution in South Africa: the Property Clause Revisited', in L. Ntsebeza and R. Hall (eds) *The Land Question in South Africa: The Challenge of Transformation and Redistrbution* (Cape Town: HSRC Press).

Pankhurst, D. (1996) *A Resolvable Conflict? The Politics of Land in Namibia* (Bradford: Department of Peace Studies, University of Bradford).

Parnell, S. (1988) 'Racial Segregation in Johannesburg: The Slums Act 1924–39', *South African Geographical Journal*, 70: 112–26.

Platteau, Jean-Pierre (1996) 'The Evolutionary Theory of Land Rights as applied to Sub-Saharan Africa', *Development and Change*, 27: 29–85.

Platzky, L. and Walker, C. (eds) (1985) *The Surplus People: Forced Removal in South Africa* (Johannesburg: Ravan Press).
Rainger, R. (1980) 'Philanthropy and science in the 1830s: The British and Foreign Aborigines Protection Society', *Man*, 15: 702–17.
Rakodi, Carol (ed) (1997) *The Urban Challenge in Africa: Growth and Management of its Large Cities* (Geneva: United Nations University Press).
Reid, D. L. and Meldrum, D. R. (1934) 'Survey and Setting out of Townships and Town Planning layouts, with particular reference to Lusaka', *Empire Survey Review*, 2: 395–400.
Rex, John (1974) 'The Compound, the Reserve and the Urban Location', *South African Labour Bulletin*, 1: 4–17.
Roberts, A. D. (1986) 'The Imperial Mind', in A. D. Roberts (ed) *Cambridge History of Africa*, vol 7, *1905–40* (Cambridge: Cambridge University Press).
Robinson, J. B. (1990) 'A Perfect System of Control? State Power and Native Locations in South Africa', *Society and Space*, 8: 135–62.
Robinson, Jennifer (1996) *The Power of Apartheid: State, Power and Space in South African Cities* (London: Butterworth Heinemann).
Robinson, Kenneth (1965) *The Dilemmas of Trusteeship* (London: Oxford University Press).
Rukuni, M. (1994) *Report of the Commission of Inquiry into Appropriate Agricultural Land Tenure Systems* (Harare: Government Printer).
Russell (1935) *Report of Commission appointed to enquire into the disturbances in the Copperbelt* (Lusaka: Government Printer).
Shillington, K. (ed) (2005) *Encyclopedia of African History* (New York and London: Fitzroy Dearborn).
Simpson, J. R. (1976) *Land Law and Registration* (Cambridge: Cambridge University Press), p 163.
Smith, D. M. (ed) (1992) *The Apartheid City and Beyond: Urbanization and Social Change in South Africa* (London: Routledge; Johannesburg: Witwatersrand University Press).
Southworth, H. (1990) 'Strangling South African Cities: Resistance to Group Areas in Durban during the 1950s', *International Journal of African Historical Studies*, 24: 1–34.
Stokes, Eric (1959) *The English Utilitarians and India* (Oxford: Clarendon Press).
Swanson, M. W. (1976) 'The Durban System: Roots of Urban Apartheid in Colonial Natal', *African Studies*, 2: 159–76.
Swilling, M. R. and others (eds) (1991) *Apartheid City in Transition* (Cape Town: Oxford University Press).
Tipple, A. G. (1981) 'Colonial Housing Policy and the "African Towns" of the Copperbelt: The Beginnings of Self-help', *African Urban Studies*, 11: 65–85.
Van Der Walt, A. J. (2009) *Property in the Margins* (Oxford: Hart).
Van Tonder, D. (1993) 'Boycotts, Unrest, and the Western Areas Removal Scheme, 1949–52', *Journal of Urban History*, 20: 19–53.
Waldron, J. (1988) *The Right to Private Property* (Oxford: Clarendon Press).
Walker, C. (1977) 'Redistributive Land Reform: for What and for Whom?', in L. Ntsebeza and R. Hall (eds) *The Land Question in South Africa: The Challenge of Transformation and Redistrbution* (Cape Town: HSRC Press).
Wasserfall, J. (1990) 'Early Mine and Railway Housing in South Africa' (PhD thesis, University of Cambridge).
Werbner, R. P. (1980) 'The Quasi-judicial and the Experience of the Absurd: Remaking Land Law in North-eastern Botswana', *Journal of African Law*, 24: 131.
Werbner R. P. (ed) (1982) *Land Reform in the Making: Tradition, Public Policy and Ideology in Botswana* (London: Rex Collings).
Western, J. (1984) *Outcast Cape Town* (Cape Town: Oxford University Press).

Wilson, E. G. (1972) *Migrant Labour in South Africa* (Johannesburg: South African Council of Churches).

Yeoh, Brenda (2000) 'Historical Geographies of the Colonised World', in B. Graham and C. Nash (eds) *Modern Historical Geographies* (Harlow: Longman), p 146.

Zimmermann, R. and Visser, D. (eds) (1996) *Southern Cross: Civil Law and Common Law in South Africa* (Oxford: Clarendon Press).

3 Land policy developments and setbacks in southern Africa

Martin Adams and Rachael Knight

3.1 Introduction

In 1998, the late Professor Okoth-Ogendo, a distinguished authority on land policy and land law in Africa, presented a paper at an international conference on land reform at the University of Cape Town (Okoth-Ogendo 1998).[1] He described the unprecedented attention given to land policy in eastern and southern Africa in the 1980s and 1990s. With few exceptions, national governments had been involved one way or another in the evaluation or re-evaluation of their land policies. In his address, he described the drivers of land policy processes and the nature of engagement with land issues. However, he reserved judgment on outcomes because results of land policy development processes had yet to emerge.

In the years since Okoth-Ogendo's speech, land tenure policy and related legislative reform have progressed in several countries, particularly in those nations where efforts have been made to integrate customary and statutory land administration into a national legal system, as well as in nations that have moved to decentralise authority over land administration as a way of strengthening the tenure security of poor rural communities. However, despite promulgating good laws, governments have in many circumstances subsequently amended or implemented them in such a way as to undermine their worthy aims. In the poorer countries in the region, tension between democratic and traditional forces continues to frustrate the development of policies and laws which would improve the administration of customary land, which is most urgently required in rapidly expanding peri-urban areas.

This chapter takes up where Okoth-Ogendo left off, assessing progress in SADC countries by reference to policy drivers and processes, analysing the long-term outcomes and impacts, and highlighting challenges to be overcome.

3.2 Land policy drivers

Land reform efforts entail the redistribution of land, remodelling of land rights and improvement of land administration in a manner that meets the requirements of the political system promoting the reform. Because of the overwhelming impact of the colonial period on African society, especially on agrarian systems and leadership structures, it is inevitable that land reform has remained a major political concern in southern Africa. To this day, a common land policy driver is the repossession of land alienated by Europeans; a second is land tenure reform and the harmonisation of received and customary law; and a third is the transformation of the colonial systems of land administration geared to private and government land, better to serve the majority of the population using customary land.

3.2.1 Colonial policy: land alienation and categorisation

Whether for agriculture, mining or trade, the expropriation of land and property rights was central to the purpose of colonial governments. The impact of colonialism and apartheid on land relations is indicated by Table 3.1, which ranks countries in the sub-region according to the extent of customary land alienated from Africans by 1957.

An intrinsic component of colonial land policy was the categorisation of land for allocation to specific groups, according to state determination. How a colonial government categorised and allocated land has had direct impact, both on national land reform programmes and current land-holding patterns. Table 3.2 is an attempt to group the generic land tenure categories in SADC countries. The first column shows land held in private ownership or under a lease, including a state lease. The second groups land which is administered according to the norms of a sub-state polity (e.g. by Village Councils in Tanzania, Land Boards in Botswana and Namibia, and Traditional Authorities in Malawi, Zambia and Swaziland) for the well being of the community and future generations, as well as the individuals and households who currently use it. In the third column is land held by government for public and domestic purposes.

According to its specific land history, each nation has evolved its own particular land reform strategy. For example, Swaziland achieved repatriation of much of the land previously held by foreigners (see Table 3.1) by repurchase, pre- and post-independence, and by placing it under the control of the Swazi chiefs and

Table 3.1 Land alienated to non-Africans in southern Africa by 1957

Country	*% of total area of the territory*	*Year attaining majority rule and/or self government*
South Africa (Union of South Africa)	89.0	1994
Namibia (South West Africa)	44.0	1990
Zimbabwe (Southern Rhodesia)	49.0	1980
Swaziland	49.0	1968
Botswana (Bechuanaland)	6.0	1966
Malawi (Nyasaland)	5.0	1964
Zambia (Northern Rhodesia)	3.0	1964
Tanzania mainland (Tanganyika)	0.9	1964
Lesotho (Basutoland)	Less than 0.5	1966

Source: Based on Hailey (1958).

Table 3.2 Generic land tenure categories, approximate percentage of national territory, 1999

Country	*Ownership/freehold/ leasehold*	*Customary, communal, tribal*	*State land/public land and protected areas*
South Africa	72	14	14
Namibia	44	43	13
Zimbabwe	34	41	25[a]
Swaziland[b]	27	73	Included in Customary land
Botswana	4	70	26[c]
Malawi	13	69	18
Zambia	n.a.	n.a.	6
Tanzania (mainland)	5	80	15
Lesotho	2	90	8
Mozambique	n.a.[d]	n.a.[d]	n.a.[d]
Angola	n.a.[e]	n.a.[e]	n.a.[e]
Congo-Kinshasa	n.a.[e]	n.a.[e]	n.a.[e]

Notes

a Includes 9% land resettlement with state permit.

b For Swaziland and Lesotho the extent of land dispossession was more severe than is apparent from Table 3.1. The Swazi kingdom lost much of its land to the Transvaal and to Mozambique in the latter part of the nineteenth century. In the case of Lesotho, the border imposed by the Orange Free State in the 1860s took most of the best farming land claimed by the kingdom.

c Includes FPSGs in urban areas.

d No attempt has been made to categorize land tenure in Mozambique in the format of Table 3.2, because of the unique land tenure system introduced under the Land Law 1997 and the lack of related data.

e For Angola and Congo-Kinshasa, areal data for the two principal land tenure categories (customary and state concessions) are not available.

the aristocracy (Levin 1997). Some 73 per cent of Swazi territory is now held by the King in trust for the nation as Swazi Nation Land (SNL) including land held under customary tenure controlled by chiefs and SNL leased to private companies.

In contrast to the situation in the majority of SADC states, post-independence Botswana has found it appropriate to increase the proportion of the country categorised as customary land. At independence in 1966, 49 per cent of the national land area was Tribal Land, less than 4 per cent was held in private ownership and the balance was State Land (White 1999). Today, Tribal Land comprises some 70 per cent of the land area; private 4 per cent and State Land the remainder. Tribal Land may be granted as a common law lease, which reverts to Tribal Land on expiry. A small proportion of the 26 per cent of Botswana's State Land in Table 3.2 is located in the larger towns and held as Fixed Period State Grants (FPSG) – a form of lease – for residential and business purposes.

3.2.2 Legal pluralism and traditional leaders

In his Cape Town conference address, Okoth-Ogendo (1998) expressed surprise that social and cultural impacts had not been more prominent in land policy development. Given the prevalence of chieftaincy-dominated societies in the region, he rightly anticipated that social drivers would assert themselves more strongly.

African lawmakers continue to confront a complex situation, in which the injustices of colonialism and the difficulties of remodelling state land tenure systems have meant that customary land laws and land management practices have continued alongside the formal ones. In some nations, over 90 per cent of land transactions are still governed by customary legal paradigms, and the decisions and rules established under customary systems are recognised as legally valid and binding by their users. The result has been a wide gap between nations' formal legal systems and the rules that govern the lived realities of the majority of those nations' citizens. While the different systems do not operate in complete isolation from one another, a fissure exists between the constructs and laws of the modern nation state and the legal paradigms and rules that dictate the myriad interactions of the rural poor. The end result is that two or more legal systems function side by side, blending and mixing, and occasionally clashing. In some nations, most of the rural populations govern themselves and their land according to a legal system, unregulated by the state.

The issue of chiefly estates of administration (Gluckman 1943) has played out differently in the sub-region, according to each nation's governance options. In Botswana, Seretse Khama, the founding President, moved quickly with the Tribal Land Act 1968 to quash the powers of chiefs and placed the administration of customary land in the hands of Tribal Land Boards, from which chiefs were eventually excluded. A crucial amendment in 1993, vehemently opposed by some chiefs (Mathuba 2001), replaced 'tribesman' with 'citizen' so as to allow land allocation to women and do away with the requirement for ministerial consent for non-tribesmen to hold land within another tribal jurisdiction. In Tanzania, chiefs were swept away by the 1972 'decentralisation' and the Ujamaa Villages Act 1975. The Village Land Act 1999 builds upon Tanzania's system of local government under which Village Councils are, in principle, responsible for the administration and management of village land.

Elsewhere, however, Swaziland's Draft Land Policy of 2000, which was intended to lead to a more democratic system of land administration, has been stalled for over a decade for 'constitutional reasons'. The Swazi aristocracy has been unwilling to surrender the material basis of its wealth and power and its control over the people. The adoption of the new Swaziland Constitution in 2005 was expected to clear the way for a review of the Draft Land Policy, but by mid-2010 this had yet to be completed. Again, in Malawi, there is strong resistance from traditional leaders to the implementation of the National Land Policy, approved by Cabinet in 2002, and its proposal to privatise customary land and register it in the name of individuals, rather than being vested in the President of the Republic and administered by the Traditional Authorities, in terms of the Land Act 1965. The responsibility for the administration of customary land is strongly contested, especially in the peri-urban area of Lilongwe where land for residential, business and commercial purposes is in great demand. In Zambia, as custodians of customary land, chiefs have long been fighting a rearguard action against the

Lands Act 1995, under which large tracts of land are being alienated by government for transfer as state leaseholds for private investors (Adams and Palmer 2007). Over the past decade, the Lesotho government has been engaged in drafting legislation to abolish customary land tenure on the advice of the Prime Minister's Land Policy Review Commission (Kingdom of Lesotho 1999), in the face of opposition by the chiefs who hold sway over land allocation in much of the country.

In South Africa, the opposition of traditional leaders to the reform of communal land tenure has also been strong. With the end of apartheid in 1994, the so-called 'independent' and 'semi-independent' states were integrated into the political structure of South Africa and the underlying title to the land was transferred from premiers to the State President who assigned it to the national Minister for Land Affairs. 'Permits to occupy' (PTOs) land in the former 'homelands' were to give way to enforceable rights within a unitary non-racial system (Department of Land Affairs 1997). Ownership of communal land was to be transferred from the state to its occupants. Traditional leaders on the other hand, had long contended that land rights should vest in themselves, or alternatively 'the tribe', or even the tribal authorities created under apartheid. They argued that, under customary law, they were the custodians of land rights and must now be legally recognised as such. Prior to the general election in April 1999, which followed the first five-year term of an ANC government, a near complete communal land bill, prepared by the Department of Land Affairs, aimed to provide secure tenure rights to occupiers of communal land within a framework of democratic decision-making and dedicated support structures. However, the incoming land minister set aside the proposed bill in accordance with a pre-election pact between the president elect, Thabo Mbeki, and the Congress of Traditional Leaders of South Africa (Contralesa). This pact was to secure the vote of traditional leaders and their subjects for the ANC in the densely-populated, former homelands (Adams 2002). In 2010, a Constitutional Court Judgment declared the Communal Land Rights Act 2004 as unconstitutional in its entirety (Constitutional Court 2010). At issue was the process that the government had used to push the bill through in the build up to the 2004 general election.

3.2.3 International forces

International finance institutions, multilateral and bilateral development agencies are committed to the limitation of direct state intervention in the land market and the ending of state ownership of land. While recognising the role of customary tenure, they tend to promote individual land titling. They claim to support decentralised land administration, although aid and technical assistance tends to flow to central land bureaucracies (McAuslan 2006).

Land policy development in the sub region has been shaped by the wish of governments to secure international funding for land reform and related programmes. Donor support was spurred by the need to foster peace and reconciliation, poverty reduction and economic development, first in Zimbabwe and then in Namibia and South Africa. In South Africa, despite the demands of the 1955 Freedom Charter and the insistence that the redistribution of the land would proceed even if it involved some economic cost, the ANC softened its proposals for land reform in its 1994 election manifesto. Based on experience in Brazil, Colombia and Guatemala, the World Bank was keen to promote decentralised 'market assisted' or 'negotiated' land reform in South Africa (World Bank 1993; Williams 1996). In the event, this proved to be a very difficult approach to scale up. For one thing, unlike in Latin America, the rural poor were not well organised and local NGOs were under resourced and lacking in experience of land reform implementation, as compared with land reform advocacy.

Too great a dependence on donor funding for land policy reform has negatively affected the implementation of Malawi's programme. In the period 1995–2002, there was strong bilateral support for land policy reform, but this fell away about the time of the growing land crisis in Zimbabwe. By 2004, it was clear that donor support for the land sector in southern Africa was decreasing in favour of less politically sensitive social development which had clearer links to poverty reduction, the capacity for higher absorption of development assistance and lower transaction costs for aid agencies.

Arguably, land policies have also been shaped by the failure to obtain international funding. By the mid 1990s, the case for land redistribution in Zimbabwe had been accepted by the UK government as the result of independent evaluations. Yet, despite the several missions mounted in the period 1996–99 to develop proposals for re-financing the government's Phase 1 Land Resettlement Programme, no additional British funds were made available to the Zimbabwe government for land reform in the 1990s. Indecision within DFID (UK Government's Department for International Development) over its Zimbabwe Country Strategy indicated strongly divergent views within the organisation. While technocrats favoured support, the political leadership had firmly made up its mind.[2] In January 2000, DFID finally announced that it would allocate only a paltry £5 million for resettlement projects 'through a Civil Society Challenge Fund'.[3]

3.3 Land reform policy processes

In his paper, Okoth-Ogendo (1998) characterised four different mechanisms for land policy formulation:

- Actions designed to pre-empt land conflicts before they reached a crisis level, when there is no doubt as to what the course of action might be, and the publication of government papers, without waiting for systematic investigation: In this category he placed the development of Mozambique's Land Policy (Republic of Mozambique 1995) and South Africa's Green Paper and the White Paper (Department of Land Affairs 1996 and 1997).
- *Ad hoc*, incremental actions directed at resolving specific land-related problems and not intended to cover the full range of land issues in the country: Here he placed Zimbabwe's Commission of Inquiry (Republic of Zimbabwe 1994) and Namibia's National Land Policy (Republic of Namibia 1997). He would probably have included here the revisions of land policy in South Africa following the 1999 and the 2009 general elections.[4]

- Comprehensive inquiries of a systematic nature: Under this heading he included the type of long-drawn-out enquiries previously used by British Colonial Governments, e.g. Botswana (Republic of Botswana 1983 and 1985), Tanzania (Republic of Tanzania 1994) and Malawi (Republic of Malawi 1999) which was followed by the National Land Policy (Republic of Malawi 2002).
- Finally, he described mechanisms which adopted an incremental 'panel-beating'[5] approach, which proceed on the assumption that the overall legal and institutional framework governing land matters is essentially sound, but which require some *ad hoc* adjustment. In this context he mentioned two East African countries (Uganda and Kenya) and Zambia within southern Africa. Not included in his characterisation were the donor-driven land policy development processes of Lesotho and Swaziland, neither of which has yet been finalised. He would probably have placed these in the same category as Zambia, which has also been slow in finalising its national land policy.

Because of their sensitivity and complexity, land reform policy processes are time-consuming and often iterative in nature. The necessary institutional development can take decades. Progress is dependent on political commitment, appropriate constitutional and legal frameworks and requires thorough public consultation and careful preparation. Table 3.3 provides a snapshot of land policy development activity in the SADC countries since the mid 1980s. Country dates often span a series of consultative processes and publications. The first six countries have made reasonable progress in implementing their land policies. The remainder have yet to announce their policies and/or promulgate the land-related laws and regulations.

The timing of a nation's land policy reform process has proved to greatly influence its resulting land policy, legal framework, and implementation efforts.

Table 3.3 Land policy development processes in southern Africa according to Okoth-Ogendo's (1998) criteria

Country	*Pre-emptive*	*Ad-hoc*	*Comprehensive inquiry*	*Panel beating*	*Policy and laws approved by Cabinet and/or Parliament*
Mozambique	1995–97				Yes
South Africa	1995–97	1999–2003			Yes
Botswana		1989–93	1983–2005		Yes
Zimbabwe		1993–2004			In part
Tanzania			1991–2009		Yes
Namibia		1991–2002			Yes
Angola		2004–06			In part
Malawi			1990–2010		Awaited
Zambia				1993–2010	Awaited
Lesotho				1999–2010	Yes
Swaziland				1996–2010	Awaited
DR Congo					Awaited

Countries that enacted land policy reform directly after the end of the colonial era – in the first years of independence – chose different strategies from those who have restructured their land policies in the post-Cold War era. Examples of these different strategies are described below.

3.3.1 Immediately post-colonial land reform

3.3.1.1 Maintenance of colonial laws

Some newly-independent African nation states simply continued to enact colonial policies after Independence. For example, in Malawi, after independence in 1964, the new government expanded existing colonial laws governing the alienation of customary land.[6] By 1994, when President Banda lost the first democratic presidential election, the area of alienated land under private estates, in terms of ministerial powers granted by the Land Act of 1965, had increased from 6 per cent to 12 per cent of the country, driven by the expansion of tobacco production (Republic of Malawi 1997).

Zambia, like Malawi, continued the colonial policy of alienating customary land and converting it to State Land for leasing; the Land (Conversion of Titles) Act 1975 did not repeal the laws governing the granting of Reserve and Trust Land to investors. To address this, Zambia's more recent Lands Act 1995 requires that the President shall not alienate any customary land without taking into consideration the local customary law on land tenure or without consulting the appropriate chief and local authority. However, fifteen years later no regulations for this purpose have yet been drafted under the Act to implement this provision, and those regulations still in effect are to be found in Circular No. 1, 1985, 'Procedure on Land Alienation'.[7]

3.3.1.2 Nationalisation

Post-independence, some nations sought to nationalise their land as a means of effecting land reform. Tanzania nationalised private land in 1961, Zambia in 1975 and Congo-Kinshasa in 1980. Within one year of their independence from Portugal in 1975, Angola and Mozambique were reborn as socialist states, nationalising land and strategic assets. These programmes of land nationalisation sought to overturn the tenure dualism that African countries had inherited from the colonial era. The outcome was often rather different. Indigenous and settler elites continued to enjoy strong individual property rights both in towns and in the countryside. The rural poor, and some of their urban counterparts, continued to adhere to customary norms, far beyond the reach of the new states' policies and institutions. Few of these early reforms, aimed at strengthening state control over customary land, proved effective or durable. By the end of the 'cold war' most of these statist land policies had been abandoned (Adams and Turner 2005). Botswana has also been involved in nationalising land, but in a cautious way, allowing for leases that have, in time, provided the basis for a flourishing land market.

3.3.2 Examples of more recent and inclusive national land policy processes

Some SADC nations undertaking land policy reform have gone through extended and highly inclusive processes of drafting and vetting their proposed land policies and legislative reforms. The outcomes are most frequently constructive, although lengthy consultation is not a guarantee of success. Some examples follow:

Botswana is alone in the sub-region in having a twenty-year history of cautious land policy development beginning with the Presidential Commission on Land Tenure (1983). Following the implementation of the Tribal Land Act in 1970, the first major review of the country's land policy was the White Paper of 1985. The next milestone was a further review of the Act, land policies and related issues (Mathuba 1989). A Presidential Commission (Republic of Botswana 1991) and White Paper (1992) followed shortly in order to consider land problems in peri-urban areas relating to the transaction, occupation and use of tribal land. Transactions included the unauthorised subdivision and/or sale of arable land for residential and other purposes and the transaction of land allocated for residential purposes before it had been developed for that purpose. The government's response, contained in the 1992 White Paper, examined the status of customary land tenure and explained the pending changes to the law which materialised in the Tribal Land (Amendment) Act 1993. Botswana's iterative policymaking in the different sectors, including land, has followed a process extending up to three years: (i) a commission of inquiry (or an expert review); calls for written submissions; public meetings involving a wide range of stakeholders; (ii) the preparation of a draft report, oral presentations and discussions at a national workshop covered by the media; (iii) a draft paper which is debated in Parliament; (iv) the publication of a government white paper setting out the policy change adopted; the recommendations which have been accepted, amended and deferred (or rejected) with a justification by government; (v) finally, where relevant, the drafting of laws or amending of existing laws (Adams *et al* 2003).

Tanzania provides an example of a remarkably tenacious land policy and legislative reform process extending over 15 years. The sequence of events, based on Alden-Wily (2003), was as follows:

- In 1990, the Minister for Lands decided there should be a national and consultative process to develop a new national land policy.
- A Presidential Commission of Inquiry into Land Matters was launched in 1991 and in 1992 the Commission travelled to all but two districts, held meetings, heard and read complaints, met officials and travelled internationally (Republic of Tanzania 1994). January 1993 the Commission submitted a final report, which was published in 1994, when a provisional response was produced by the Ministry and approved by the Cabinet.
- A National Workshop on Land Policy was held in January 1995 and the policy finalised and approved by Parliament in August 1995.

- In March 1996, the drafting of a new land law began, to be distributed in November.
- In 1998 the draft was revised and divided into two draft bills which were passed by Parliament in May 1999 as The Land Act 1999 and The Village Land Act 1999.
- Regulations under The Land Act 1999 and under the Village Land Act 1999 were published in May 2001 when the two laws came into force as the land law of mainland Tanzania.
- The Ministry of Land's 'Strategic Plan for the Implementation of the Land Laws' (SPILL) was finished in April 2005.

Similarly, on coming to power in 1990, the SWAPO government in Namibia announced its intention of transferring land to the landless majority, but agreed to a constitution in which the property of citizens could not be taken without just compensation. In June 1991, with the support of the parliamentary opposition, it conducted a national consultation on the land question culminating in a six-day national conference of some 700 people in Windhoek, opened by the President and chaired by the Prime Minister. Communities from all over Namibia were in attendance. The aim was to achieve the greatest possible consensus on land issues. Tenure reform in the communal areas (rather than redistribution of white-owned farms) tended to dominate the debate at the conference.[8] Half of the recommendations of the conference related to land issues in communal areas: the need to guarantee land to local people; to abolish land allocation fees demanded by chiefs; to grant land to women in their own right; to establish a system of land administration; to control 'illegal fencing' of grazing areas; and to move the herds of wealthy farmers to commercial farms.

The resulting National Land Policy White Paper (1997) of the Ministry of Lands, Resettlement and Rehabilitation (MLRR) stated that 'government policy will at all times seek to secure and promote the interests of the poor'. These were defined as 'the landless or those with little or insufficient access to land who are not in formal employment or engaged in non-agricultural business activities'. This provided the MLRR with its mandate to resettle the poor on farms acquired and retained by government in terms of the Agricultural (Commercial) Land Reform Act, 1995. The National Land Policy and the draft legislation for the Communal Areas underwent a long process of public consultation. It touched on issues that are sensitive among a large and powerful rural constituency, including traditional leaders who have their roots in the relatively densely populated Communal Areas in the north and provide the bulk of SWAPO support. The Communal Land Reform Act was finally passed in 2002.

In Mozambique, the government established an inter-ministerial land commission to develop a new land policy in 1992. The resulting process may arguably be one of the most participatory law-making processes for a law in the SADC region. The Mozambican land commission included representatives from ten government ministries, two national non-governmental organisations, academics from the Land Tenure Centre at Eduardo Mondlane University, technical advisors for the

United Nation's Food and Agricultural Organisation (FAO), and respected national lawyers and academics. The Commission sponsored a series of consultations across the nation to insure that a wide range of civil society was involved in the drafting process and in accordance with the major tenets of the law. Members of the UN, international donor agencies, FRELIMO and RENAMO, religious groups, the private sector, academic institutions, traditional authorities, and a range of Mozambican NGO's were all invited to comment on and suggest adjustments in the draft law. Once draft versions of the new land law were complete, the Land Commission sponsored a series of provincial and local level consultations to insure that individuals and organisations throughout the nation were involved in the drafting of the new land law. It then held a national land conference in June 1996 that included the above-listed members. For three days, over 200 of these representatives debated the central tenets of the new land law and worked to shape its parameters to balance the need for smallholder tenure security against the need to attract investors who could fuel national economic growth. After the final draft was completed, the land law bill went to the National Assembly. At this time, a massive effort was made to involve the public in debate over the final draft: a full copy of the land law bill was printed in the national daily newspaper, and the text of the bill was read on national radio. Full copies of the bill were made publicly available at the Assembly, and during breaks in legislative debate, members of civil society mingled with representatives to discuss the various points of the law. When the bill finally passed into law, it maintained in full form a majority of the tenets that civil society had lobbied for (Tanner 2002; Negrão 1999).

In 1996, following Malawi's first multiparty elections, the government established a Presidential Commission of Inquiry on Land Policy Reform, which paid close attention to issues relating to customary land, covering some 70 per cent of the country. It reviewed the Lilongwe Land Development Programme, which in the 1970s had pursued a policy of privatising customary land under the Customary Land (Development) Act 1967, to promote agricultural development. The Act provided for the recording of joint ownership or the recording of the family head as owner of family land. The Commission found that none of the predicted benefits, such as greater security of ownership, negotiability of title, and a robust land market, had materialised as a result of the tenureal changes. Further, the programme had tended to erode customary social values and institutions, especially in matrilineal societies. Noting that, before independence in 1964 and under the Land Act 1965, large areas of customary land had been converted into private or public land, the Commission observed that most freehold land in rural and urban areas was still owned or controlled by foreigners. The Commission recommended that all customary land converted to state leaseholds should be restored to Traditional Authorities as the leases expired or were surrendered so as to increase the available stock of customary land (Republic of Malawi 1999). In 2000 the World Bank funded a team to review the Presidential Commission's reports and findings, with the purpose of developing a comprehensive land policy for Malawi. A draft, which departed from the recommendations of the Presidential Commission, was eventually circulated and discussed with all groups including traditional leaders and civil society representatives as well as specialists in land tenure issues. It was followed by three regional consultative workshops. In 2001 a final national workshop on land policy was held in Lilongwe. The Malawi National Land Policy (Republic of Malawi 2002) was then approved by the Cabinet. Under the new policy, customary landholders (entire communities, families or individuals) would register their holdings as private 'customary estates' in ways that would preserve the advantages of customary ownership while providing security of tenure. The property rights contained in a customary estate would be private usufructuary rights in perpetuity. However, eight years later, parliamentary approval of the legislation necessary for implementation had still to be obtained and the role of traditional authorities and local land governance structures for the administration of customary land continue to be strongly debated.

By contrast, the Zimbabwe government's flirtation with public consultation on land policy was relatively brief. Beginning in 1993, a Presidential Commission of Inquiry conducted a thorough review of Zimbabwe's land policy (Government of Zimbabwe 1995). The Commission held numerous public hearings and was assisted by a panel of international land tenure specialists. Implementation of its recommendations could have done much to remove doubt and uncertainty and improve tenure security, both in the communal and the resettlement areas. Sadly, the Cabinet's response to the Commission's findings was tardy and incomplete. Recommendations that were perceived to threaten the powers of the central state over land allocation and natural resources were rejected. Like the Privy Council, the highest colonial court, some eighty years before, the Cabinet ruled that ownership of Communal Land should be retained by the state. Those communities who had used and occupied the land since time immemorial should hold only usufruct rights.

The processes leading to the formulation of Zambia's Draft Land Policy in 1993 and the Lands Act in 1995 were neither thorough nor participatory. There was very limited public consultation in the formulation of the law. In 2002, the Ministry of Lands commenced a review of the land policy and land-related laws. As part of this process, civil society organisations partnered the Ministry of Lands and carried out consultations countrywide in 2004 and 2005. But government delayed releasing the draft land policy for public comment on the grounds that presidential, parliamentary and local government elections were due in 2006. In 2007, the Ministry released a revised draft land policy (Republic of Zambia 2007) and scheduled a national conference to discuss it. Thereafter, it was hoped to finalise the draft and start the process of reviewing land-related laws in line with the new policy, but after a three-year delay the government argued in May 2010 that the process must await a constitutional review.

3.4 Different kinds of land reform initiatives

Land reform can be divided into actions involving direct land redistribution for productive use; land policy reforms that strengthen tenure security; and actions that improve land administration.

3.4.1 Land redistribution

The political circumstances surrounding redistributive land reform have been different, but the main objective has been a more efficient and equitable distribution of land and political power emanating from it. There is strong evidence that too much reliance has been placed on market mechanisms to transfer land to the poor. Demand-led, market-based land redistribution is proving an extremely difficult process to carry through. Outcomes have rarely lived up to expectations. The following examples are illustrative.

Zimbabwe's initial efforts at land redistribution (1980–1994) arguably depict a best-case scenario. In the 14 years following Zimbabwe's 1980 independence, the country's land under large-scale commercial farming decreased by some 3.3 million ha, from 40 per cent to 30 per cent of the total land area, and was subdivided for resettlement by small farmers. Several central government agencies were directly involved in the process: the selection of the participants, the acquisition of the land, the planning of farm layouts, the construction of farm and social infrastructure and the provision of post-settlement support for farm production. According to an evaluation of the programme, it had made impressive strides towards achieving its principal objectives (Cusworth and Walker 1988). The orderly settlement of so many families in such a relatively short time was reported to be an impressive achievement which contributed to post-war reconstruction and stability. The majority of resettled families had benefited from increased opportunities for income generation and from the availability of health and educational facilities. The programme generated an economic return of approximately 21 per cent, which, as *The Economist* commented, 'would make it one of the most successful aid schemes in Africa'.[9] However, the programme presented problems of an institutional nature, particularly over-centralisation and a rigid technocratic and bureaucratic approach. The ambitious programme also weighed heavily on the government budget.

South Africa's land redistribution target in the African National Congress manifesto (ANC 1994) also proved to be overly ambitious and has continued to haunt successive governments. Thirty per cent of South Africa's agricultural land was to be transferred to land reform beneficiaries in five years, equivalent to some 25–30 million ha.[10] The target was set before there was a clear strategy or action plan for the process. In 1995, with the help of an alliance of NGOs engaged in land reform advocacy, a two-year government land reform pilot programme (LRPP) got under way, to test replicable means of helping poor farmers to purchase farms in the land market. Despite grave staffing and institutional problems and lack of post-settlement support, the pilot programme was expanded to a national one in 1997. South Africa developed a household grant mechanism under the powers granted by the Provision of Land and Assistance Act 1993, which aimed to support a demand-led, self-help process.[11] Because land was both relatively costly and unavailable in small grant-sized parcels, poor people wishing to acquire land with government grants had to form groups to acquire a farm. The process resulted in scattered projects, often without regard to farmers' needs for essential physical and social infrastructure. The modest household subsidy encouraged the formation of dysfunctional groups to meet the cost of farm purchase. Inadequate capacity on the part of the Department of Land Affairs was a major factor constraining implementation. There was an acute shortage of well-trained field staff to provide legal advice and facilitate the many complex tasks involved in land transfer. Between 1994 and early 2000, only about 0.8 million ha of land, a mere 0.8 per cent of the country's agricultural land, were transferred to about 56,000 black households. The programme's institutional problems were exacerbated by the fact that, in terms of the South African constitution, land matters are a competence of National Government. Before redistributive reform could proceed at scale, the newly formed national Department of Land Affairs, had to establish itself at the provincial level, in places faced with indifference by unreconstructed provincial officials. Without technical support, farm inputs and markets, the poor were unable to enter the white-dominated commercial agriculture sector, which had evolved with strong government support over some 70 years. Following the general election in 1999, the incoming Minister for Agriculture and Land Affairs announced a number of policy changes relating to land redistribution, the aim of which was to develop a black commercial farming class in South Africa. Grants of up to 80 per cent were to be provided to prospective farmers to purchase small and medium-sized farms. By the end of 2005, land redistribution had increased to 3 per cent of the total area of agricultural land.

In Namibia, in the late 19th century white settlers moved into the sparsely populated semi-arid parts of the country, which hitherto were used seasonally by indigenous pastoralists. A century later, Namibian land redistribution efforts have therefore been primarily concerned with the challenging task of redistributing semi-arid grazing land. A view that received prominent attention at the National Conference on Land Reform in 1991 was that large freehold ranches should be made available on favourable terms to black farmers. The pressure came from whites keen to recruit rich and politically influential blacks into their ranks; from black businessmen and officials who aspired to own farms themselves and from small farmers in the communal areas who resented the pressure on communal grazing exerted by the large herd owners. Thus, one of the first measures to be announced in 1992 was the Affirmative Action Loan Scheme (AALS), administered by AgriBank, to provide for farm purchase by aspiring black entrepreneurs. Evidence collected in recent field investigations of *Livelihoods after Land Reform* by Werner and Odendaal (2010) shows that the AALS enterprises are economically and financially viable only where livestock farmers have access to sufficient finance to service their loans and survive droughts and the predations of wildlife and livestock diseases.

Shortly before Namibia's first general election in 1994, the Agricultural (Commercial) Land Reform Act 1995 was hurried through. It provided for the purchase by the state of large commercial livestock farms at market prices for redistribution to the poor – resettled farm workers and ex-combatants and displaced San people. Statistics for 2006 indicate that since independence in 1990 the government had managed to acquire 201 commercial farms, comprising 1.3

million ha, on which it had resettled a total of 1,561 families (Shivute 2006).[12] Although seen as a political imperative for the incoming SWAPO government, the programme has not provided sustainable livelihoods. Evidence from neighbouring Botswana had demonstrated that the costs of providing social and economic infrastructure and settling poor people in remote, marginal areas were likely to be unsustainable (Adams and Devitt 1992; Purcell 1994). Both local custom and studies of optimal use of the range had pointed to one simple, low-cost solution that was to remove fences and extend communal grazing, an option which has once again been raised by Werner and Odendaal (2010).[13]

In 2004, Malawi's Ministry of Lands commenced a pilot project with a World Bank credit and close supervision and technical support by WB advisors, with previous experience in the planning and mentoring of land redistribution programmes within SADC and elsewhere. This concerned the purchase of former private state leases ('estates') for subdivision and redistribution to poor rural households, drawn from four overcrowded districts in the south of the country. By adopting what is described as a voluntary, community-based, market-assisted approach, the project assists with the provision of grants for land acquisition, the subdivision of the former estates into individual family farms, and the provision of farm inputs (Machira 2009). By September 2009, some 28,000 ha had been redistributed to 12,500 households, each receiving 2 ha of agricultural land for the production of food and cash crops. It is hoped that the pilot phase of careful planning, provision of adequate infrastructure and support services will lead to a successful wider programme, which has evaded even better-endowed SADC countries.

3.4.2 Legislative change to strengthen land tenure security and formalise customary land rights

Over the past two decades, lawmakers across the SADC region have been charged with updating existing legal frameworks to adapt to the evolving realities of the post-colonial political economy. Throughout the 1990s, a variety of nations either enacted new land laws or amended existing laws to improve tenure security. The aims have been to reduce land-related conflicts and to increase national development and prosperity by attracting international investment and strengthening the land claims of the poor. However, faced with the various complex geo-political, historical, cultural, legal and economic situations described above, SADC nations have pursued divergent land policy and legislation drafting processes and have arrived at a wide variety of different legal and administrative mechanisms through which land tenure security – particularly the security of small scale rural farmers – is to be established. Some national examples are explored below.

In 1997 (through the participatory lawmaking process described above) Mozambique elevated all existing land claims into formal, secure tenure. The law allows both Mozambicans and foreigners to acquire a 'right of use and benefit' (*Direito de Uso e Aproveitamento da Terra* or DUAT). Under the Land Law 1997, registration of such existing land claims is not necessary – land holders have enforceable, secure land rights even without paper documentation of any kind. In particular, under the Land Law, 'local communities who occupy land according to customary practices' automatically 'acquire the right of land use and benefit' (Regulations, Article 9 section 1). For these rural communities, the Land Law establishes processes for delimitation and registration of local community lands as a whole, after which the community becomes a legal entity, capable of transacting with outsiders (Article 10 section 1, 2). Such rights of land use and benefit are secure, inheritable, and can be transferred to third parties, either internally within the community or to investors through a formal consultation process (Article 14 section 2). Investors may apply to the government for 50-year leasehold rights, after consultation and approval by the community within which the land requested is located (Article 12(c)). Importantly, the land right is legally the same, regardless of whether it is acquired under customary terms, good faith occupancy, or government concession.

Botswana's and Tanzania's laws, passed in 1968 and 1999, respectively, also automatically legitimised existing land claims, but their legislation does not make this expressly clear. Rather, the right must be inferred from a very close reading of the law. Under Botswana's Tribal Land Act 1968, although never articulated in the text of the legislation, land allocated according to custom before the Act was passed did not need to be formally registered for claims and rights to be legitimate and enforceable: all existing customary land claims were formalised the moment the Act passed into law. The law eliminated the need for residents of the Tribal Areas to immediately undergo lengthy and complex registration procedures – registration of customary land rights was allowed to happen slowly, over time, according to land holders' own volition. Holders of customary land rights in the Tribal Areas have tenure security over their individually-held land, as well as the ability to transfer, sell, bequeath, or assign their land rights. Should an individual or family choose to register and document their land claims in the Tribal Areas, there are three different types of rights to apply for: customary rights, common law rights, and freehold title. Decades later, a majority of rural families have in fact registered their claims with Botswana's Land Board system, as the consequences of not having a formal grant of customary land right have come to light. However, from 1968 until 2008, the Land Boards had not granted one freehold title in the Tribal Areas; only Customary and Common Law leasehold rights were issued (Nkwae 2008).

Tanzania's Land Acts – the Land Act 1999 and the Village Land Act 1999 – focus on protecting the rights of the poor while also striving to regulate what was already, by the late 1990s, a flourishing land market in Tanzania. As in Mozambique, all land in Tanzania is held by the state, and land rights are therefore not rights of private ownership but rather rights of occupancy. Under the Land Acts, land is divided into three categories: Reserved Land (national parks, conservation areas, etc.), Village Land and General Land (Land Act Article 4 section 4). Village Land is the land falling under the jurisdiction and management of a registered village. General Land denotes all land that is neither reserved land nor village land; all urban areas fall under this category. The Acts establish pre-existing customary tenure rights as the basic means of holding property rights in all areas zoned as Village Land. Although not expressly stated, under the law, customarily-held land rights are equal in weight and validity to formally-granted land rights, and there is no need for registration and documentation of one's customary land rights. Should an individual, family or group seek formal documentation of their land claims, they may apply for either a Customary Right of Occupancy or a Granted Right of Occupancy. Both rights are like ownership in that they include the full bundle of rights of freehold title: citizens may freely sell, gift, bequeath, rent and mortgage their Right of Occupancy (Article 30 sections 1, 2). Processes for titling, granting and registration of family and communal land may happen within the village, in new village-level land registries. However, unlike in Botswana, due to various implementation obstacles and the complexity of the text of the legislation, more than ten years after the Land Acts were enacted, very few smallholder Tanzanians have used the legal processes described in the law to document their land rights.

Other nations' laws have given smallholders an established deadline by which they must register their land holdings for these claims to be preserved and respected. Namibia and Angola are two such nations. Although the Namibian Constitution provides that every Namibian has the right to live, work and settle in any part of the country that he or she desires (Article 16 section 1), a large percentage of the nation's pastoral lands continue to be held by Namibia's white settler population as commercial farms established during the colonial era. To ameliorate the legacy of its racially-based and inequitable land tenure laws, Namibia passed the Communal Land Act in 2002. The law provides for the recognition and registration of all customary land rights that existed before the Act, but it required that every individual or family seeking recognition of their land claim must submit an application to the new system of Communal Land Boards within three years of the date specified in the National Gazette. However, the date has been extended from the initial deadline several times.

Similarly, in Angola, the Land Act 2004 provides for a rural family's statutory right of use and enjoyment of lands. It reads: 'The occupation, tenure and the rights of use and enjoyment of rural community lands, occupied and *used in a useful and effective manner* according to custom, by families that form part of rural communities, are recognized' (Article 70 s 3, emphasis added). While this appears to be a guarantee of land rights, it is not clear what will happen to lands that are not used in a useful or effective manner, as defined not by the people claiming the land, but by the state. The Law also grants legal personality to rural communities (Article 70(3)), but makes community land rights subject to official registration of community lands in the national cadastre and the issuance of a title (Article 37). It includes a time limit for all land titling and registration processes, mandating that all citizens, families and communities had three years after the law's enactment to complete the official process of legalising their land rights. However, it seems that the time limits have come and gone. Only with a major public awareness campaign and the allocation of resources to support land adjudication, survey and registration will it be achievable.

3.4.2.1 The land tenure security of vulnerable groups

SADC countries have also grappled with the issue of how best to safeguard the tenure security of vulnerable groups like women, widows, orphans, pastoralists, hunter-gatherers and refugees, and whether such protections should be explicitly or implicitly set out in the law.

Tanzania and Mozambique, among other nations, establish women's rights explicitly. Tanzania's Land Acts have identical provisions protecting 'The right of every woman to acquire, hold, use and deal with land, to the same extent and subject to the same restrictions … as the right of any man' (Land Act Article 3 section 2, Village Land Act Article 3 section 2). The law underscores this by often using the phrase 'he or she' whenever referring to an individual applicant for a right of occupancy. Furthermore, the Village Land Act includes various mechanisms to protect vulnerable groups against bad faith market transactions, including the provision that every assignment of land rights must be reviewed by the Village Council and will be nullified if found to undermine a woman's right to land. Furthermore, pastoralists' land uses and land claims are protected alongside the claims of small scale farmers, including allowance for dual and joint use and management of certain lands by different communities.

Similarly, women's equal entitlement to rights of land use and benefit is a central tenet of Mozambique's 1997 Land Law. Under the law, women have equal rights to hold, to access and to derive benefits from land independent of any male relatives, and the law is clear that this principle overrides any contrary customary rules. The law repeatedly and expressly includes the phrase 'men and women' to make explicit this right: Article 10 makes clear that 'National individual and corporate persons, men and women, as well as local communities may be holders of the right of land use and benefit' (Article 10 section 1). Second, in regard to individual titles, Article 13 section 5 asserts that: 'Individual men and women who are members of a local community may request individual titles … ' Article 16 section 1 decrees that 'The right of land use and benefit may be transferred by inheritance, without distinction by gender'. However, under Mozambique's law, there are no state oversight mechanisms to protect citizens against intra-community injustices, no village-level supports to help women enforce their land rights, and no penalties for intra-community discriminatory practices. Such lack of appropriate state oversight, combined with rural communities' lack of genuine access to state justice forums, has meant that women's land rights have largely not been adequately protected and enforced (Calengo *et al* 2007: 33). The law also validates and legitimises the customary land rights and land administration systems of all ethnic and tribal groups within Mozambique, simply and elegantly equalising all groups and manners of livelihood practiced.

Botswana's Tribal Land Act (1968) does not include any explicit provisions setting out women's right to own land or to protect the land claims of women or minority ethnic groups. The Act's longevity is no excuse; it was amended in 1993. The 1993 amendments, referring to who may hold land, changed the word 'tribesmen' to the more gender-neutral language 'citizens of Botswana', but research has shown that such gender-neutral language has not been a sufficient guarantee of women's land rights (Kalabamu 2006; Adams *et al* 2003). Furthermore, because Botswana's Tribal Land Act was designed around anthropological research on the dominant majority Tswana tribe, it has essentially functioned to entrench Tswana traditions and rules as the customary law of the land. It therefore, by omission, implicitly discriminates against those ethnic and tribal groups that have different residential, land use, and livelihood practices from the Tswana. The customary land rights of non-Tswana tribes have to date not yet been recognised in any statute or law, and their territorial rights to areas for hunting, gathering, and the right to exclude others from their customary lands remain unprotected (Ng'ong'ola 1999).

3.4.3 Reform of land administration systems

Professor Okoth-Ogendo (2002) addressing a World Bank meeting in Uganda, identified land administration as the most neglected dimension in the land reform movement in sub-Saharan Africa.[14] Poorly equipped to manage contemporary land reform programmes, most government land agencies are understaffed and underfunded. They face numerous problems, including: weak legal and institutional frameworks; over-centralised, inaccessible and out-of-date land registries; lack of land information; inadequate arrangements for land dispute resolution; the demise of customary systems of common property resource management; and unsustainable systems of land use. Few countries in the sub-region spend more than one per cent of their annual government budget on land administration, significantly less than the potential income governments could collect in the form of land-related revenues.

Officials often have vested interests in perpetuating the *status quo* and impede the adoption of more simple, accessible, efficient and transparent systems for land transfer, land survey and the registration and collection of land information, which would facilitate the development of land markets and the levying of land-related taxes which could cover the cost of the required reforms. They are 'virtually incapable of managing systems and processes which require transparency and accountability' (African Union Commission 2009: 52).

In very few instances has the planning for the reform of land agencies – including human resource requirements, arrangements for change management and budgetary implications – been matched by the efforts that have gone into the tenureal aspects of land policy. Sadly, in the case of Malawi, one of the few where funds were set aside to upgrade the land administration system for the direction and co-ordination of a new land policy, other factors brought down the programme. These included the unexpected withdrawal of support by bilateral donors expected to fund other key elements of the policy, and the long-delayed adoption of the enabling legislation by the state Parliament.

Land administration functions have often remained highly centralised and have impeded the adoption of more simple, accessible and efficient systems of land transfer, survey and registration for both private and customary land. In those countries that have created new decentralised land administration systems, various approaches have been tried: some have adopted systems that are not customary in structure, but have taken over the management of customary rights (e.g. Botswana, Tanzania and Namibia) while others have made customary institutions the community-level managers of a decentralised state land administration (Mozambique and South Africa). However, no single approach to decentralisation has been found to be without problems and, in most cases, central and provincial governments retain significant control over local land governance, especially in matters relating to the revocation of customary rights and land allocation to outside investors.

3.5 Lessons for land policy

3.5.1 Land redistribution

The challenges encountered by land redistribution programmes in Zimbabwe, Namibia and South Africa (described above) have varied according to the differing impact of colonialism and apartheid on land dispossession and indigenous African farming. Following the relatively successful programme of land redistribution in Zimbabwe in the period 1981–2000, under which some 3.6 million ha of Zimbabwe's large-scale commercial farming (LSCF) area were acquired and subdivided for small farmers, the bulk of the remaining LSCF area (some 8.7 million ha) underwent 'fast-track' land redistribution during 2001–09, which is proving to be less of a disaster than often assumed. A three-year study in Masvingo Province, on small and medium-sized farms with contrasting agricultural potential, found that yields and output on the redistributed farms had increased steadily. Former beef ranches and wildlife farms are now supporting much higher rural populations than they did before redistribution.[15]

Meanwhile, South Africa and Namibia continue to wrestle with poorly performing, market-related land redistribution programmes. With each successive government they have undergone modification, but show little progress in terms of generating sustainable livelihoods or changing the dualistic and racially divided agrarian structure. The lack of advancement is a source of grave concern as the racial disparities in land holding are more severe than they were in Zimbabwe in 2000. Architects of South Africa's demand-led, market-based land reform in the period 1994–2009 seriously overestimated its viability as a vehicle for regenerating African agriculture, which was once as efficient as large-scale white-settler farming based on hired labour (Mbongwa 1991).[16]

These examples serve to illustrate that if land redistribution measures are to contribute to the improvement of the rural livelihoods, they must be part of a broad political, social and economic change, rather than a narrow intervention simply to repossess land alienated by European settlers. The pace of successful land redistribution cannot reasonably run ahead of advances in other related government functions, especially of those for providing infrastructure (potable as well as irrigation water, power and communications) and other services to well-located small farmers – credit, input supply, marketing, extension advice and adaptive research. Nor can it run ahead of government capacity to plan, to co-ordinate land rights delivery and provide support services for small farmers (Adams 2000).

3.5.2 Land tenure reform

New global trends are combining to undermine the tenure security promised in even the strongest of various SADC nations' land laws. Increasing land scarcity across the SADC nations has been caused by population growth, environmental degradation and changing climatic conditions, and by the recent trend of wealthy nations and private investors seeking to acquire large tracts of land in SADC nations for agro-industrial enterprises and forestry and mineral exploitation. SADC countries, among them Tanzania, Zimbabwe and Mozambique, are granting hundreds of thousands of hectares to private investors and other sovereign nations. These land concessions are hemming in rural communities and depriving them of access to resources vital to their livelihoods, food security and economic survival. Overcrowding and over-use of family and communal holdings has led to a breakdown in the rules that govern sustainable community use of common resources. Because land in most African nations is owned by the state, communities often have little power to contest such grants. In many cases, they may not even be aware that their land has been granted to an investor until after the fact. As a result, today, a decade or more after these land laws were adopted, the actual tenure security of their people – particularly the poorest, rural, small-scale farmers – may actually be much weaker than in the past.

While this is due in part to the construction and content of the laws themselves, most of the blame may be placed on lack of appropriate and/or effective implementation. These laws are not being implemented in a manner that protects the land rights of the poor because of two inter-related factors: the lack of resources and political will. Whether or not to allocate sufficient resources to support the state implementation of a law is often a policy choice; many SADC states have simply not directed an appropriate amount of funding to carry out the law's mandates properly. For example, village registration (Tanzania), community delimitation exercises (Mozambique), or the creation of community conservancies (Namibia) have not been found to be particularly expensive, and the legal processes for these efforts are not complicated and can be accomplished in a relatively short amount of time with minimal state resources. However, to date, very few communities have had their land claims formally documented according to the laws' precepts. Some SADC states have gone so far as to issue ministerial orders or decrees that serve to undermine the land tenure security promised in national land legislation.

The Mozambique 1997 Land Law is still far from being properly implemented, despite enormous sensitisation efforts by civil society organisations. To date, the FRELIMO government has not allocated adequate funding, training, or personnel to local, district and provincial land administration bodies to help process community and individual land claims, and has instead focused primarily on promoting investment. In particular, it has not allocated sufficient finances to the process of community land delimitation.[17] As a result, very little land held by communities has been formally delimited and registered in the national cadastre. Meanwhile, the government has taken legislative action to weaken the strength of community land rights. Even though the law provides for communities' customary land rights regardless of formal registration processes, the 2007 changes to Article 35 of the Land Law Regulations have been construed by state officials as signifying that the recognition of community rights is subject to state authorisation. More alarmingly, the Mozambican government has been granting very large land concessions to foreign investors with minimal 'consultation' (Cotula *et al* 2009). Despite various constitutional assurances, there are currently no accessible legal mechanisms by which communities can protest government officials' decisions to cede their land to foreign investors, for, ultimately, the land is owned by the state, and communities hold only 'rights of use and benefit'. This lack of tenure security has been underlined by the government's 2007 declaration that it has the power to declare that 'unused' community land is 'free' and to then claim jurisdiction over such lands. The government has publicly assured communities, which have already delimited and registered large areas of land in the cadastre, that they will not lose this land, 'so long as they keep these areas under use'.[18] There are no definitions of what 'under use' can be interpreted to mean. In the final analysis, it is not clear that even a successful delimitation application could stand in the way of a central government decision to grant land to an investor for large-scale investment.

Similarly, Tanzania's Village Land Act (1999) promises a high degree of tenure security in theory. It sets out myriad protections for every possible vulnerable group and establishes village-level titling and registration systems. However, more than a decade after the law was passed, the state has not yet established the village-level institutions necessary for the full and proper implementation of the law (Republic of Tanzania 2005: 21; Kassim 2009). Of greatest concern, however, is that Tanzania's Village Land Act ultimately fails to provide true land tenure security to villages; the Village Land Act's multiple protections for the land rights of communities are secure and good only until the state decides otherwise. This is best exemplified by the varying definitions of General Land in the two Acts: the Land Act's definition of General Land as 'all public land which is not reserved land or village land and includes unoccupied or unused village land' (Land Act 1999, Article 2) means that the state has the right at any moment to rezone what it feels to be 'unused' Village Land (even lands zoned as communal areas and areas zoned for future village expansion) as General Land, and therefore remove it from village jurisdiction entirely. Also, under Article 4 section 1, 2 the state may compulsorily acquire even clearly used village land for 'investments of national interest' and rezone it as General Lands. There are no clear mechanisms in the Village Land Act through which communities can appeal or block such reclassifications of their lands. This has allowed the government to grant large-scale land concessions that include areas of village land to international investors – and has meant that the villages whose lands are being seized have very weak legal grounds upon which to contest these grants.

In Botswana, although urban and peri-urban communities and individuals (65 per cent of the national population) may have a very high degree of tenure security (particularly as Botswana's courts and policy makers have increasingly interpreted customary land grants within Tribal areas to be akin to ownership rights), the same may not be said of rural pastoralists and non-Tswana tribes. This can be largely attributed to various policy decisions of the central government, in particular the 1975 Tribal Land Grazing Policy (TLGP), which was intended to remedy the perceived overgrazing and degradation of communal areas and to foster private investment and economic growth. Under the TLGP, large areas of the communal grazing areas, re-zoned by the government as commercial land, were allocated to wealthy cattle ranchers under 50-year leases. Despite Article 17 section 4's suggestion that the Land Boards make zoning decisions in consultation with various local authorities, the results of the TLGP indicate that such consultations have been a vastly inadequate check against infringement upon the customary land rights of pastoralists and hunter-gatherers with customary claims to lands suddenly zoned as 'Commercial' (Taylor 2007; Adams *et al* 2003). This has meant that vast territories that poor pastoralists and tribes like the Basarwa (San) have historically depended on for their livelihood and survival have been granted to private ranchers, who have fenced these areas and impeded access. Such policies have drastically reduced the grazing land available to small-scale and subsistence herders within Tribal Areas and led to the growth of a landless rural underclass (Adams *et al* 2003). Although these land claims are protected under the Tribal Land Act, it has never been invoked to protect them. Furthermore, White reports that while in theory all citizens of Botswana have equal access to land in line with the customary edict that all individuals are entitled to land according to their needs, in practice the Land Boards have instead been allocating land according to perceived ability to use it. Wealthy individuals who can demonstrate that they have the capital and resources to make full productive use of land are allocated large areas of land, while the poor (including the Basarwa, widows, disabled individuals, and the landless, among others) who lack the tools, resources and assets to use the land fully are 'effectively denied land' (White 2000: 12).

These are questions of governance and political will; funding/capacity constraints and state emphasis on national economic growth are insufficient explanations for such implementation challenges. McAuslan has warned that the creation, passage and implementation of a new land law is a 'major exercise in institutional reform, and such exercises generate a whole host of problems, challenges and opposition that need to be addressed if reform is to have any chance of being successful' (McAuslan 2003: 21). Similarly, Ouédraogo explains, 'Nor should we overlook the lack of political will shown by the administrative authorities in implementing legislation favourable to local land rights. Either no practical steps are taken to implement the law or, worse still, the administrative – and even judicial – authorities … are sometimes persuaded to take decisions which fly in the face of the law' (Ouédraogo 2002: 84). For these laws to be successful, the full participation and commitment of state officials at all levels of government are necessary.

3.5.3 Land administration

Institutional issues should receive more attention in the drafting of land policies. The *Framework and Guidelines on Land Policy in Africa* provides a candid assessment of the inability of government land agencies to manage change (AUC 2009). Their reluctance to accept change extends to their retention of out-dated technology, for example for land measurement and registration, even when more appropriate alternatives are available. Land agencies must throw off their image as inaccessible, inflexible, highly-centralised bureaucracies and be prepared to engage with the public and civil society organisations advocating change and to deliver a range of affordable services to the majority of the land-using public.

Land reform agencies in Namibia, South Africa and Mozambique, which were created almost from scratch in the 1990s, have been faced with problems of a different nature. From the outset, they suffered from lack of infrastructure and trained land professionals (e.g. land surveyors, cartographers, physical planners, valuers, property lawyers and land economists). With a few notable exceptions, universities and technical colleges in SADC were slow to respond to the demand for relevant post-graduate courses in land administration, both for new graduates and for the retraining of existing staff.

One country, namely Botswana, has stood out as one with a long tradition of strong, decentralised land administration. As a result, it has hosted numerous visits from groups of land administrators from countries in southern as well as East Africa, seeking advice and information on the implementation of land tenure reforms and the administration of state land.

Joint training courses involving land administrators from SADC countries have the potential for spreading knowledge and skills beyond national boundaries, but so far these have received little support within SADC.[19] Until now, member states have not found sufficient reason to collaborate closely in matters relating to land administration and governance.

3.6 Concluding comment

Since Professor Okoth-Ogendo's 1998 Cape Town address, SADC countries have continued to adopt varying approaches to the development of national land policies. The holding of comprehensive, country-wide, consultative processes, has remained fashionable since the 1990s and is recently endorsed by the African Union in its *Framework and Guidelines on Land Policy in Africa* (2009), but such processes carry no guarantee of success. Given strong political leadership and inclusive, consultative processes, some countries have been remarkably successful in initiating fundamental reform of their land tenure arrangements. Other states, however, having engaged in such processes, continue to have difficulty in implementing even modest changes to outdated policies and laws. They continue to wrestle with the increasing complexity of dual land tenure systems and the transformation of unresponsive agencies responsible for land administration. Successful set piece land policy development processes, like those conducted in Tanzania and Mozambique in the 1990s, may not be a politically feasible strategy for some countries, which will have to tackle their many and complex land issues by adopting a more incremental approach.

Whatever the process, some common pitfalls await policy makers. For example:

- not fully considering how aspects of the policy are to be implemented;
- adopting a piece-meal approach without adequate attention to knock-on effects and unintended consequences within the sector as a whole;
- failing to consult with land users affected by land policy changes, during both the development of the policy and the related legislation;
- not taking account of the financial implications: i.e. the resources needed for recruitment and training, for physical infrastructure and for compiling land information and baseline data;
- failing to take account of the need to overcome the conservative orientation of government land agencies and their lack of capacity to manage change;
- underestimating the length of time needed to bring about change and, in the meantime, losing momentum and political support for land reform.

This last point is a reminder that political priorities can change and so can the support of politicians and officials for the implementation of key legislation for redistribution and/or land tenure reform. An initially strong political commitment to pro-poor land reform is often followed by a switch of emphasis to so-called economic goals. This may again be followed by a reaffirmation of the needs of the landless. The policy cycle relates to changes in the balance of influence of the landless lobby on the one hand and that of landowners and commercial interests. Debates about land reform everywhere have seen a confrontation between those who believe that land reform must be centred on pro-poor redistribution and control over productive agricultural land and those who wish reform to focus on measures to raise agricultural productivity.

Notes

1 Professor H. W. O. Okoth-Ogendo died suddenly in Addis Ababa, 24 April 2009, where he was chairing the African Task Force on Land and finalising their Framework and Guidelines on Land Policy.

2 In May 2000, the then Minister with responsibility for Africa, Peter Hain, told the House of Commons Foreign Affairs Committee that this was because that government was running 'a corrupt, inefficient land reform programme. We cannot put British taxpayers' money into that.'

3 Briefing, Land Resettlement in Zimbabwe, DFID, January 2000. Also see AAPPG (2009).

4 Although the Restitution of Land Rights Act was the first law passed by the Mandela government in April 1994, the land policy development process extended over three years. A Land Policy Framework Document was distributed by the Ministry of Land

Affairs in May 1995 to which 50 organisations responded. This was followed by a National Land Policy Conference in August 1995, which was attended by over 1,000 delegates and for which a consultative Statement of Land Policy and Principles was prepared. In turn, this was followed by a Green Paper in May 1996, which was discussed in 30 workshops all over the country. The White Paper on South African Land Policy which explicitly took account of the workshops was published in April 1997 (source: White Paper, Introduction, p 1).

5 'Panel beating' is the process of fixing dents in automotive vehicles.

6 During both the colonial and post-colonial periods, the Malawi state regarded customary users as a residual group, to be mobilised for labour or limited to only the production of staple food crops.

7 The Ministry of Lands has a backlog of many years of applications for all types of leases. Consents continue to accumulate, without the updating of the land register (Adams 2003). Thus the 93.6 per cent of Zambia held under customary tenure quoted by Roth and Smith (1995) must now be considered long out of date.

8 However, following the conference, tenure reform in the communal areas received little attention. One of the first measures to be announced was an Affirmative Action Loan Scheme, which was introduced in 1992 as a result of a Cabinet decision. The five-year scheme aimed to provide black farmers with access to subsidised loans, repayable over 25 years. No more generous than a similar scheme provided for mostly white farmers up to independence, it represented a huge subsidy to a small group monopolised by businessmen and officials.

9 'Land-hungry', *The Economist*, 28 October 1989, p. 90.

10 An objective deferred in 2010 to 2025.

11 The Zimbabwe land settlement model was rejected by the ANC because of its association with the type of social engineering associated with the so-called 'betterment schemes', which forced blacks off their farms and on to 'native reserves' under the apartheid regime.

12 This excluded direct farm acquisition by black farmers through the Affirmative Action Loan Scheme.

13 The absorption of freehold land into tribal land in Botswana has been achieved at relatively low cost and without the administrative complexities contemplated by the workshop. Likewise, the purchase of freehold land for grazing commonages has been relatively successful in broadening the ownership of land in RSA.

14 For example, most government land agencies in anglophone countries in southern Africa were established in the colonial period, under a Commissioner for Lands assisted by a Chief Surveyor, Registrar, Physical Planner, etc., for the administration of private and Crown/government land, in terms of received laws. In some countries these institutions have barely changed since.

15 See <http://www.lalr.org.za> and Scoones *et al* (2010).

16 The Native Land Act 1913 put an end to competitive African farming by segregating the races and designating only 7 per cent of the country for Africans, who were otherwise forbidden to own, rent or share crop land in white areas. They could work only as labourers.

17 In 2001 the Mozambican government allocated only enough funding to complete 10 community delimitation exercises. In 2003 it allocated only enough to fund three to four (Tanner and Baleira 2006; Norfolk and Tanner 2007: 11–13). The government has largely relied on private donors and NGOs to provide the funds and technical support necessary for successful delimitation exercises.

18 Website 'Portal do Governo de Moçambique', <http://www.portaldogoverno.gov.mz/news_folder_politica/outubro2007>.

19 At the height of the land-related crisis in Zimbabwe and a related 2001 SADC Summit a decision was made to develop a regional strategy for land reform. A Land Reform Support Facility was eventually established in 2006 under the SADC Food, Agriculture

and Natural Resources Directorate, but it has since remained more or less dormant due to lack of funding.

Bibliography

Adams, Martin (2000) *Breaking Ground: Development Aid for Land Reform* (London: Overseas Development Institute).

Adams, Martin (2002) 'Unscrambling the Apartheid Map', <http://www.oxfam.org.uk/resources/learning/landrights/south.html#southafr> (accessed 1 December 2010).

Adams, Martin (2003) *Land Tenure Policy and Practice in Zambia: Issues relating to the Development of the Agricultural Sector* (Mokoro: Oxford), <http://www.oxfam.org.uk/resources/learning/landrights/downloads/zambia_land_tenure_policy_and_practice_adams.pdf> (accessed 1 December 2010).

Adams, Martin and Devitt, Paul (1992) 'Grappling with Land Reform in Pastoral Namibia', Pastoral Development Network 32 (London: Overseas Development Institute), <http://www.odi.org.uk/work/projects/pdn/papers/paper32a.html> (accessed 1 December 2010).

Adams, Martin, Kalabamu, Faustin and White, Richard (2003) 'Land Tenure Policy and Practice in Botswana; Governance Lessons for Southern Africa', *JEP*, 19: 55, 66, <http://www.oxfam.org.uk/resources/learning/landrights/south.html#botswana> (accessed 1 December 2010).

Adams, Martin and Turner, Stephen (2005) 'Legal Dualism and Land Policy in Eastern and Southern Africa', *Land and Property Rights for African Development* (Nairobi: UNDP-DDC, <http://www.google.ie/search?sourceid=navclient&ie=UTF-8&rlz=1T4RNWN_enIE324GB325&q=%27Legal+Dualism+and+Land+Policy+in+Eastern+and+Southern+Africa%e2%80%99> (accessed 1 December 2010).

Adams, Martin and Palmer, Robin (2007) *Independent Review of Land Issues, Eastern and Southern Africa*, vol III, *2006–07* (SARPN), <http://www.oxfam.org.uk/resources/learning/landrights/horn.html> (accessed 1 December 2010).

Africa All Party Parliamentary Group (2009) 'Land in Zimbabwe: Past Mistakes, Future Prospects', <http://www.royalafricansociety.org/images/stories/pdf_files/aappg_report_land_in_zimbabwe.pdf> (accessed 1 December 2010).

African National Congress (1994) *Reconstruction and Development Programme: A Policy Framework* (Johannesburg: ANC).

African Union Commission, United Nations Economic Commission for Africa and African Development Bank (2009) *Framework and Guidelines on Land Policy in Africa* (revised version), <http://www.pambazuka.org/aumonitor/images/uploads/Framework.pdf> (accessed 1 December 2010).

Alden-Wily, Liz (2003) 'Community-based Land Tenure Management: Questions and Answers about Tanzania's new Village Land Act, 1999', Issue Paper 120, Drylands Programme (London: IIED), <http://pubs.iied.org/9295IIED.html?s=DIP (accessed 1 December 2010).

Calengo, André Jaime, Monteiro, José Oscar and Tanner, Christopher (2007) *Mozambique Land and Natural Resources Policy Assessment* (Maputo: Centre for Juridical and Judicial Training).

Constitutional Court (2010) *Tongoane and Others v Minister for Agriculture and Land Affairs and Others*, Case CCT 100/09 [2010] ZACC 10, South Africa, 11 May, <http://www.constitutionalcourt.org.za/site/Tongoane.htm> (accessed 1 December 2010).

Cotula, Lorenzo, Toulmin, Camilla and Hesse, Ced (2004) *Land Tenure and Administration in Africa: Lessons of Experience and Emerging Issues* (London: IIED), <http://pubs.iied.org/9305IIED.html?k=Cotula (accessed 1 December 2010).

Cotula, Lorenzo and others (2009) *Land Grab or Development Opportunity? Agricultural Investment and International Land Deals in Africa* (London: IIED), <http://pubs.iied.org/12561IIED.html?k=Cotula (accessed 1 December 2010).

Cusworth, John and Walker, Judy (1988) *Land Resettlement in Zimbabwe: A Preliminary Evaluation*, Evaluation Report EV 434 (London: Evaluation Department, Overseas Development Administration).

Department of Land Affairs (1996) *Green Paper on South African Land Policy* (Pretoria: DLA).

Department of Land Affairs (1997) *White Paper on South African Land Policy* (Pretoria: DLA).

Government of Lesotho (2000) *Land Policy Review Commission* (Maseru).

Gluckman, Max (1953) *Essays on Lozi Land and Royal Property* (Rhodes-Livingstone Papers 10 (repr. 1968, Manchester: Manchester University Press).

Hailey, Lord (1958) *An African Survey: A Study of Problems arising in Africa South of the Sahara* (revd edn, Oxford: Oxford University Press).

Kalabamu, Faustin (2006) 'Patriarchy and Women's Land Rights in Botswana', *Land Use Policy*, 23: 237.

Kassim, S. (2009) 'Decentralization of Land Administration and Women's Rights in Tanzania: the Case of Mvomero District', Analytical Workshop on Decentralisation Women's Land Rights and Citizenship, Kampala.

Knight, Rachael (2010) *Statutory Recognition of Customary Land Rights: A Preliminary Investigation into Best Practices for Lawmaking and Implementation* (Rome: Development Law Service, FAO).

Levin, Richard (1997) *When the Sleeping Grass Awakens: Land and Power in Swaziland* (Johannesburg: Witwatersrand University Press).

Machira, Stephen (2009) 'Pilot-testing a Land Redistribution Program in Malawi', in H. Binswanger-Mkhize, C. Bourguigon and R. van der Brink (eds) *Agricultural Land Redistribution: Towards Greater Consensus* (Washington, DC: World Bank).

Mathuba, Botshelo (1989) *Report on the Review of the Tribal Land Act, Land Policies and Related Issues* (Gaborone: Government Printer).

Mathuba, Botshelo (2001) 'Reflecting on Customary Tenure Issues in Botswana', National Land Tenure Conference: Finding Solutions, Securing Rights, Durban.

Mbongwa, Masiphula (1991) 'Nationalisation of the Land', in S. Matlhape and A. Münz (eds) *Towards a New Agrarian Democratic Order* (Amsterdam: South Africa Economic Research and Training Project).

McAuslan, Patrick (2003) 'A Narrative on Land Law Reform in Uganda', Lincoln Institute of Land Policy Conference, <http://www.lincolninst.edu/pubs/809_A-Narrative-on-Land-Law-Reform-in-Uganda> (accessed 1 December 2010).

McAuslan, Patrick (2006) 'Improving Tenure Security for the Poor in Africa', FAO Regional Technical Workshop for sub-Saharan Africa on Legal Empowerment of the Poor, Kenya, <ftp://ftp.fao.org/sd/SDA/SDAR/sard/Africaframework.pdf> (accessed 1 December 2010).

Moyo, Sam and Nyoni, Joshua (1991) 'Land Reform Experience in Zimbabwe', National Conference on Land Reform and the Land Question (Windhoek: National Economic Policy Research Unit).

Negrão, José (1999) *The Land Campaign in Mozambique*, <www.oxfam.org.uk/resources/learning/landrights/downloads/mozcamp.rtf> (accessed 1 December 2010).

Ng'ong'ola, Clement (1999) 'National Land Boards: The Experience of Botswana', National Stakeholder Workshop on National Land Policy, Zimbabwe.

Nkwae, Boipuso (2008) 'Botswana's Experience on Recognizing Traditional Land Rights on a Large Scale', World Bank Conference on Challenges for Land Policy and

Administration, Washington, DC, <http://siteresources.worldbank.org/INTIE/Resources/475495-1202322503179/NKwae_Paper2008WB.doc_2_.pdf> (accessed 1 December 2010).

Norfolk, Simon and Tanner, Christopher (2007) 'Improving Tenure Security for the Rural Poor: Mozambique Country Case Study', Legal Empowerment of the Poor (Nakuru: FAO), <ftp://ftp.fao.org/SD/SDA/SDAR/sard/Mozambiquecase.pdf> (accessed 1 December 2010).

Okoth-Ogendo, H. W. (1998) 'Land Policy Development in Sub-Saharan Africa: Mechanisms, Processes and Outcomes', International Conference on Land Tenure in the Developing World with focus on Southern Africa, Cape Town, <http://www2.gtz.de/dokumente/bib/00-0591.pdf> (accessed 1 December 2010).

Okoth-Ogendo, H. W. (2002) 'Land Administration: The Neglected Factor in Land Reform in Africa', World Bank Regional Workshop on Land Issues in Africa and Middle East, Entebbe.

Ouédraogo, Hubert (2002) 'Legal Conditions for the Recognition of Local Land Rights and Local Land Tenure Practices' in P. Lavigne-Delville, H. Ouédraogo and C. Toulmin (eds) *Making Land Rights More Secure: International Workshop for Researchers and Policymakers* (London: IIED), <http://www.iied.org/pubs/display.php?o=9446IIED&n=3&l=17&k=Ouedraogo (accessed 1 December 2010).

Purcell, Ray (1994) 'Economic Analysis of Land Reform Options in Namibia', Working Paper 41 (Windhoek: Namibian Economic Policy Research Unit).

Republic of Botswana (1983) *Report of the Presidential Commission on Land Tenure* (Gaborone: Government Printer).

Republic of Botswana (1985) *National Policy on Land Tenure* (Gaborone: Government Printer).

Republic of Botswana (1991) *Report of the Presidential Commission of Inquiry into Land Problems in Mogoditshane and other Peri-urban Villages* (Gaborone: Government Printer).

Republic of Botswana (1992) *Land Problems in Mogoditshane and other Peri-urban Villages* (Gaborone: Government Printer).

Republic of Botswana (2003) *Botswana National Land Policy: Issues Report* (Gaborone: Department of Lands, Ministry of Lands, Housing and Environment).

Republic of Malawi (1997) *Estate Land Utilisation Study: Land Use on the Tobacco Estates of Malawi* (Lilongwe: Ministry of Lands and Valuation).

Republic of Malawi (1999) *Final Report of the Presidential Commission of Inquiry on Land Policy Reform* (Lilongwe: Government of Malawi).

Republic of Malawi (2002) *Malawi National Land Policy* (Lilongwe: Ministry of Lands, Physical Planning and Surveys).

Republic of Mozambique (1995) *A política nacional de terras e estrategia para a sua implementação* (Maputo: Council of Ministers).

Republic of Namibia (1991) *National Conference on Land Reform and the Land Question* (Windhoek: Office of the Prime Minister).

Republic of Namibia (1998) *National Land Policy* (Windhoek: Ministry of Lands, Resettlement and Rehabilitation).

Republic of Tanzania (1994) *Report of the Presidential Commission of Inquiry into Land Matters* (Dar es Salaam: Ministry of Lands, Housing and Urban Development).

Republic of Tanzania (2005) *Strategic Plan for the Implementation of the Land Laws* (*SPILL*) (Dar es Salaam: Ministry of Lands and Human Settlements).

Republic of Zambia (2006) *Draft Land Administration and Management Policy* (Lusaka: Ministry of Lands), <http://www.oxfam.org.uk/resources/learning/landrights/downloads/zambia_draft_land_policy_oct_2006.pdf> (accessed 1 December 2010).

Republic of Zimbabwe (1995) *Report of the Commission of Inquiry into Appropriate Agricultural Land Tenure Systems* (Harare: Government Printer).

Roth, M. J. and Smith, S. G. (1995) *Land Tenure, Land Markets and Institutional Transformation in Zambia*, LTC Research Paper 124 (Madison, WI: Land Tenure Center, University of Wisconsin), <http://minds.wisconsin.edu/handle/1793/21877> (accessed 1 December 2010).

Scoones, Ian and others (2010) *Zimbabwe's Land Reform: Myths and Realities* (Oxford: James Currey).

Shivute, Nashilongo (2006) *Consultative Workshop, Perceptions on Land Reform: Proceedings* (Windhoek: Legal Assistance Centre), <www.lac.org.na/projects/lead/Pdf/landworkshop.pdf> (accessed 1 December 2010).

Tanner, Christopher (2002) *Law Making in an African Context: the 1997 Mozambican Land Law* (Legal Papers Online 26, Rome: FAO), <http://www.fao.org/legal/prs-ol/lpo26.pdf> (accessed 1 December 2010).

Tanner, Christopher (2005) 'Land Rights and Enclosures: Implementing the Mozambican Land Law in Practice', *International Conference on the Changing Politics of Land in Africa* (Pretoria: University of Pretoria QUAE Press), <http://www.oxfam.org.uk/resources/learning/landrights/south.html (accessed 1 December 2010).

Tanner, Christopher and Baleira, S. (2006) 'Mozambique's Legal Framework for Access to Natural Resources: The Impact of new Legal Rights and Community Consultations on Local Livelihoods', FAO Livelihoods Support Programme (Working Paper 28, Rome: FAO), <http://www.fao.org/es/esw/lsp/workingpapers.html> (accessed 1 December 2010).

Taylor, Michael (2007) *Rangeland Tenure and Pastoral Development in Botswana: Is there a Future for Community-based Management?* (Cape Town: CASS/PLAAS), <http://www.landcoalition.org/pdf/07_PLAAS_common_ rangelands_southern_africa.pdf> (accessed 1 December 2010).

Werner, Wolfgang and Odendaal, Willem (2010) *Livelihoods after Land Reform: Namibia Country Report* (Windhoek: Legal Assistance Centre), <http://www.lac.org.na/projects/lead/Pdf/livelihoods_report_a.pdf> (accessed 1 December 2010).

White, Richard (1999) 'Livestock and Land Tenure in Botswana', Africa Studies Centre, Conference on New Directions in Land Tenure (The Hague: University of Leiden).

White, Richard (2000) 'Land Issues Paper', Conference on Networking as a Means of Managing the Environment (Gaborone: Kalahari Conservation Society).

Williams, Gavin (1996) 'Setting the Agenda: A Critique of the World Bank's Rural Restructuring Programme for South Africa', *Journal of Southern African Studies*, 22(1): 139–66.

World Bank (1993) 'Options for Land Reform and Rural Restructuring', Land Redistribution Options Conference (Johannesburg: Land and Agriculture Policy Centre).

4 Land resources ownership and use in 'Africa of the Labour Reserves' (the Southern African Development Community)

*Horman Chitonge**

4.1 Introduction

The Southern African Development Community (SADC) is one of the many Regional Economic Communities[1] (RECs) in Africa. SADC is composed of 14 countries, covering a total surface area of about 9.9 million km^2 with a total population of about 256 million in 2007, accounting for over 32 per cent of the total population in Sub-Saharan Africa (SSA) (see Table 4.1). Although the countries in SADC are varied in many aspects, most of them share a common economic, political, cultural and geo-typological background. In terms of land resources, though not all the countries in the region face the same challenges, all the countries have unresolved issues around land. Unresolved land issues in the region range from the problem of distribution or ownership patterns of land, to the lack of capacity, commitment and appropriate institutions for land administration, management and effective use.[2] This chapter focuses on land use and the closely related theme of ownership, both of which have a bearing on food security and poverty reduction in the region.

Diverging from the dominant literature on this topic, which has largely focused on land tenure reforms,[3] the chapter looks at the size and main characteristics of the land resources in SADC, how these resources are distributed between the different types of users and how the resources are utilised. While acknowledging that tenure, institutional and legal reforms are important in the region, the chapter highlights landownership and use, linking these two themes to issues of food insecurity. It is argued here that, even after discounting the precarious climatic conditions in the region, SADC has sufficient land and human resources, which if used effectively should eliminate the perennial problem of chronic and transitory food insecurity among its population. Land resources play a central role in addressing the challenges of food security and environmental sustainability.[4] Current patterns of land ownership, management, and especially land use, represent serious constraints to addressing the challenges of food security and sustainable development in the region. As population increases and as arable land becomes a limited factor, the spotlight should be on how the available land resources are being used, in view of the region's vision of using land as an instrument for poverty reduction.[5]

Table 4.1 SADC: land and human resources, 1997 and 2007

Country	*Land area* (km^2)	*Agricultural area (000 ha)*		*Agricultural area % land*[a]		*Population*[c] *(million)*	*Density per* km^2
		1997	*2007*	*1997*	*2007*	*2007*	*2007*
Angola	1,246,700	57,500	57,590	46.12	46.19	17.0	14
Botswana	581,730	25,901	25,852	44.52	44.44	1.9	3
DR Congo	2,344,860	22,880	22,650	09.76	09.66	62.0	28
Lesotho	30,350	2,329	2,304	76.74	75.91	2.0	65
Madagascar	587,040	37,490	40,843	63.86	69.57	20.0	34
Malawi	118,480	4,430	4,970	37.39	41.95	14.0	148
Mauritius	2,040	112	101	54.90	49.51	1.3	662
Mozambique	799,380	48,135	48,800	60.22	61.05	21.0	27
Namibia	824,290	38,820	38,805	47.10	47.08	2.0	3
South Africa	1,219,090	99,650	99,378	81.74	81.52	48.0	39
Swaziland	17,360	1,341	1,342	77.25	77.30	1.3	67
Tanzania	947,300	34,003	34,200	35.89	36.10	40.0	46
Zambia	752,610	24,419	25,589	32.45	34.00	12.0	16
Zimbabwe	390,760	14,200	15,450	36.34	39.54	13.0	35
SADC	**9,861,990**	**411,210**	**417,874**	**50.3**	**51.0**	**255.5**	**84.8**
SSA				42.1[b]	43.9[b]	800	34

Sources: based on data from FAOSTAT database (http://www.fao.org/corp/statistics/en/ updated January 2009) and *World Development Indicators* (2009: 40–2).

Notes

a Land area is given in square kilometres (km^2) while agricultural area is given in thousand hectares (000 ha). Figures for agricultural area as percentage of land area were calculated by converting hectares to square kilometres (1 km^2 = 100 ha).

b The agricultural area percentages for SSA are averages for 1990–92 and 2003–05.

c Population figures are from *World Development Indicators* (2009).

The chapter is organised as follows. Section 4.2 provides a brief overview of the land resources in the region, highlighting the potential land for arable use as well as the factors that affect land use. Section 4.3 discusses the various forms of land ownership, stressing the point that the larger portion of land resources in SADC is under customary tenure. Section 4.4 presents the dominant forms of land use noting that the biggest proportion of the land is under smallholder subsistence land use. This form of land use plays a critical role in the production of staple food in many countries contrary to views that see the commercial agricultural sector as a key food producer. This section also shows that, despite the available land resources, SADC is increasingly becoming food dependent/deficient, relying on food imports (commercial and food aid), thus increasing food insecurity for the poor households. Section 4.5 situates the current challenges of land ownership, management and use in the political economy history of the region, arguing that even many years after the end of colonial rule, most of the countries in the region have not radically transformed institutions, policies and approaches to land resource ownership and use. In this part it is argued that the liberalisation policy adopted in many countries since the 1980s has resulted in land policies largely being driven by small elite groups or the economically powerful who try to increase their political and social power. Section 4.6 provides concluding remarks.

While acknowledging that there are land challenges in the urban setting, the chapter focuses on the challenges around agricultural land ownership and use, linking this to the challenges of food security and sustainable livelihood, especially for subsistence land users. Central to this chapter is the view that challenges of land use cannot entirely be attributed to lack of capacity and creativity among smallholders. Unproductive land use, in its various forms, is largely a reflection of inappropriate policy choices and misplaced political priorities. Dominant policy views have tended to emphasise tenure security such as titling (fully developed property rights) or formalisation, and have paid lateral or no attention to the problem of land resource use.[6] Little attention is paid to the question of how those who currently have access to land (secure or insecure) are using land. Or what needs to be done to promote productive and sustainable land use for the people facing food insecurity year in and year out. Tenure security certainly has an influential bearing on land use, but land use goes beyond tenure concerns, especially in a region like SSA where majority of the people are not primarily concerned with tenure rights, but with deriving some meaningful subsistence from land.[7] Thus, the chapter emphasises the point that non-tenurial factors such as infrastructure, output and input markets, input support for subsistence producers, extension services and use of appropriate technology constrain land use far more than other factors.

Being an overview on land ownership and use, the chapter does not provide detailed land use for individual SADC countries, but highlights some of the common challenges that the region faces with regard to land ownership, management and use. The chapter identifies some of the key challenges for individual countries which can be the basis for empirical research on land use in the region.

4.2 SADC land and labour resources: an overview

The 14 countries which make up the SADC region have a total land area of 9.9 million km^2, slightly more than the size of mainland China (9.5 million km^2) or the land area of the US (9.6 million km^2), and just about the same size as Canada (9.93 million km^2).[8] In terms of population, the region is home to more than 256 million people, accounting for almost one-third of SSA's total population. As Table 4.1 shows, the distribution of this population in the region is highly uneven, ranging from an average of over 660 persons per km^2 in Mauritius to just three persons per km^2 in Botswana and Namibia.

On average, the region has a high percentage of land which can be utilised for agriculture production, higher than the average for SSA. Recent studies on land use show that the region has a relatively higher potential to expand the size of its agricultural land without disturbing forest land or other ecological systems.[9] However, over the last decade, SADC agricultural land has only changed marginally, by less than one percentage point, suggesting that agricultural land use has largely remained unchanged between 1997 and 2007, despite rapidly growing population and high levels of poverty. Agriculture land in the region grew only by 0.7 per cent which is less than half the average growth of agricultural land for SSA over the same period of time.

As regards use of land in SADC, the agricultural area indicator gives a rough idea of the proportion of land that is under agricultural use out of the total land.[10] However, this indicator does not reflect the potential land available in each country; the potential land resource is often larger than the land classified as agricultural. For the region as a whole, about half of the land area is designated agricultural land. For individual countries, the proportion of land under active use varies greatly from less than 1 per cent in DRC to over 88 per cent in Lesotho as Table 4.2 shows. Even countries such as Namibia and Botswana where a

Table 4.2 Percentage of potential arable land in use, 2007

Country	*2007*
Angola	4.0
Botswana	4.6
DR Congo	0.7
Lesotho	88.6
Madagascar	8.7
Malawi	25.1
Mauritius	49.5
Mozambique	5.0
Namibia	5.6
South Africa	46.9
Swaziland	23.7
Tanzania	5.2
Zambia	9.0
Zimbabwe	11.7
SADC	**51.0**

Source: FAOSTAT (2009), http://www.fao.org/corp/statistics/en.

significant part of the landmass is a desert, the proportion of agricultural land is comparatively high. Countries such as DRC, Zambia, Zimbabwe, Tanzania and Mozambique have huge proportions of untapped agricultural land.

As Table 4.2 shows, most of the countries in the region are underutilising their land. Countries such as DRC, Angola, Botswana, Madagascar, Mozambique, Tanzania, and Zambia, utilise less than 10 per cent of the potential arable land. Interestingly, all of these countries have relatively good soil, rainfall and other climatic factors. If these available land resources were effectively utilised, the region would reach comfortable levels of food sufficiency and sovereignty,[11] and substantially reduce chronic food insecurity which has plagued majority of the rural population in the region.[12] Thus, while land scarcity may be a major concern in some countries like Lesotho, Mauritius and South Africa, this need not be a major concern for countries like the DRC, Mozambique, Zambia, Zimbabwe and Tanzania.

If figures in Table 4.2 are anything to go by, the challenges around land resources in the region may have little to do with land resource paucity, but mainly with how the resource is distributed (ownership) and used. While the particular nuances of the challenges related to land may differ among these countries, there are a number of key challenges which are common to most of the countries, mainly how land is owned, utilised, managed and administered.[13] These common challenges regarding land resources are a result of a common historical, political and economic experience of colonialism, land dispossession, enclave economies and migrant labour, which most of these countries share to varying degrees.[14] Consequently, it can be argued that the persistent cases of chronic and transitory food crisis in the region can be largely attributed to the policy and institutional variables,[15] although climatic conditions play an important role.

4.3 Factors affecting SADC land resource availability

When looking at the land resource base and how it is used, it is crucial to look at what determines the availability of land for use.[16] There are a number of factors which influence what land is available for productive use including productive factor proportions such as the ratio of capital to labour. For southern Africa, climate and soil quality, farming systems, labour productivity and capital investments have significant impact on land use and food security. Here focus is on soil quality and climatic conditions.

Climate and soil type are crucial factors in determining whether land can be used for agricultural production in the wider sense of the term. Out of the land resource shown in Tables 4.1–2, it is only land with suitable climate and soil qualities which can be used productively and consequently for human settlement. Most soils in SADC have low content of macro-nutrients needed by plants such as nitrogen (N) and phosphorus (P), as well as micro-nutrients such as sulphur (S), zinc (Zn) and magnesium (Mg).[17] Similarly, land without sufficient moisture (rain, underground water or surface water) and suitable temperature may not be available for productive use. Almost half of the region's soils are 'sandy or coarse gravelly soils with low nutrient retention and moisture holding capacities'.[18]

With regard to climatic conditions, there are different climatic zones and soil types in SADC, which are divided into five agro-ecological zones: (1) humid, (2) moist sub-humid, (3) dry sub-humid, (4) semi-arid and (5) arid.[19] The large part of SADC is either arid, semi-arid or dry sub-humid with annual rainfall of below 600 mm. The humid and moist sub-humid zones receive rainfall of over 1,000 mm per year. However, different agricultural activities can take place in all the five zones ranging from rain-fed crops to pasturing and hunting. The region also suffers from recurrent droughts, on one hand, and severe flooding on the other. These climatic conditions negatively affect the availability and use of land, which in turn impact on the food security situation in the region.

4.4 Farming system

Because of its diverse climatic conditions, SADC countries have a total of 14 different farming systems.[20] A farming system is generally defined as 'a population of individual farm systems that have broadly similar resource bases, enterprise patterns, household livelihoods and constraints, and for which similar development strategies and interventions would be appropriate'.[21] Each farming system has a particular use of land, and is determined by the resource base where the unit is found. As shown below, the larger parts of SADC are occupied by smallholders or subsistence farmers involved in cereal-root food production (mainly maize, millet, cassava, sorghum and pulses). Most commercial farmers, though small in number, are largely involved in cash crop production. There are also a large proportion of smallholder land users with mixed crop–livestock production especially in arid and semi-arid areas of South Africa, Botswana, southern Namibia and Lesotho. The type of farming system influences both land use and demand. Agro-pastoral farming systems may require large chunks of land for crop cultivation and animal grazing, while the cereal-root crop systems may require relatively small, but more fertile pieces of land. For agrarian reforms in the region to be more effective, it is necessary to take into account the different dynamics in each of these systems.

4.5 Sectoral distribution of labour force

The other important factor that influences patterns of land use is population distribution and the level and nature of economic development. Low-income countries with a large share of the agricultural sector in Gross National Product (GNP) have more people involved in agriculture, mainly subsistence production, while middle-income countries with large and well developed industrial and services sectors have a small proportion of the population engaged in agriculture. In terms of sectoral composition of GNP, countries with large agriculture–GNP ratio such as Tanzania, Mozambique, Madagascar, Malawi, DRC and Zambia tend to have a relatively small size of industrial and/or manufacturing sectors as Table 4.3

Table 4.3 SADC: sectoral composition of GNP, 1995 and 2007 (%)

Country	*Agriculture*		*Industry*		*Manufacturing*		*Services*	
	1995	*2007*	*1995*	*2007*	*1995*	*2007*	*1995*	*2007*
Angola	7	9	66	70	4	5	26	21
Botswana	4	2	51	49	5	3	45	49
DR Congo	57	42	17	28	9	6	26	29
Lesotho	16	12	36	47	15	19	48	41
Madagascar	27	26	9	17	8	16	64	56
Malawi	30	34	20	20	16	14	50	45
Mauritius	10	5	32	28	23	20	58	67
Mozambique	35	28	15	26	8	15	51	47
Namibia	12	11	28	30	13	11	60	59
South Africa	4	3	35	31	21	18	61	66
Swaziland	12	7	45	49	39	44	43	43
Tanzania	47	45	14	17	7	7	38	37
Zambia	18	22	36	38	11	11	46	40
Zimbabwe	15	19	29	24	22	14	56	57
SADC	**21**	**18.9**	**30.9**	**33.8**	**14.3**	**14.5**	**48**	**46.9**
SSA	18	15	29	32	16	14	53	53

Source: author, based on data from *World Development Indicators* (2009).

shows. Conversely, countries such as Botswana, South Africa, Namibia, Mauritius and Swaziland with 10 per cent or less agriculture–GNP ratio, tend to have a relatively higher share of industrial and/or manufacturing sectors.

In these countries, small numbers of large-scale commercial farmers are responsible for almost 90 per cent of the agriculture output.[22] Likewise, the proportion of labour force in agriculture in such countries, tend to be smaller (at less than 10 per cent in 2006 for South Africa and Mauritius), compared to countries such as Malawi, Madagascar, Mozambique, Tanzania, Angola with more than two-thirds of the labour force engaged in agriculture. Though all the countries in the region experienced a decline in the labour force share of agriculture, the larger proportion of the labour force is still in agriculture as Table 4.4 shows.

In countries with high labour force in agriculture, majority of the people are in rural areas pursuing land-based livelihoods. For SADC as whole, almost two-thirds of the population are in rural areas relying on land resources directly or indirectly as Table 4.5 shows. In countries such as Malawi, DRC, Lesotho, Swaziland, Madagascar and Tanzania, more than two-thirds of the national population were reported to be living in rural areas in 2007.

Although the rural population seems to have declined in all the SADC countries over the last 17 years and the population growth rates for rural areas slowed down, many countries in the region, except South Africa, Angola and Botswana, still have more than half of the population in rural areas. In countries with large rural population, land is a crucial source of livelihood and therefore should be used and managed more effectively to be able to contribute to poverty reduction

Table 4.4 SADC: percentage of the labour force in agriculture, 1990–92, 2000–02 and 2004–06

Country	*1990–92*	*2000–02*	*2004–06*
Angola	74.3	71.6	70.5
Botswana	46.0	44.1	43.2
DR Congo	67.3	62.8	60.8
Lesotho	41.3	38.9	38.0
Madagascar	77.8	73.8	72.0
Malawi	86.3	82.5	80.8
Mauritius	16.2	11.4	09.9
Mozambique	83.2	81.0	80.0
Namibia	48.4	40.5	37.4
South Africa	13.0	9.2	08.0
Swaziland	39.3	33.3	31.0
Tanzania	84.0	80.0	78.2
Zambia	73.9	68.7	66.3
Zimbabwe	67.6	62.1	59.6
SADC	**58.5**	**54.3**	**52.6**

Source: author, based on data from *World Development Indicators* (2009).

and improved food security.[23] In this case, though land scarcity may not be a major problem in most of these countries, efficient land use and management is an urgent issue in the region since poverty levels are highest in the rural areas as shown in Table 4.6. Land issues become central to the fight against poverty, not just in the rural areas, but in urban areas as well.

Table 4.5 SADC: population, by type of residence, 1990–2007 (%)

Country	*Rural population*		*Average growth*	*Urban population*		*Average growth, 1990–2007*
	1990	*2007*	*1990–2007*	*1990*	*2007*	
Angola	63	44	0.7	37	56	5.2
Botswana	58	41	−0.1	42	59	3.9
DR Congo	72	67	2.5	28	33	4.0
Lesotho	86	75	0.5	14	25	4.7
Madagascar	76	71	2.4	24	29	4.1
Malawi	88	82	1.8	12	18	5.0
Mauritius	56	58	1.2	44	42	0.8
Mozambique	79	64	1.4	21	36	5.8
Namibia	72	64	1.5	28	36	3.8
South Africa	48	40	0.7	52	60	2.7
Swaziland	77	75	2.2	23	25	2.8
Tanzania	81	75	2.2	19	25	4.4
Zambia	61	65	2.6	39	35	1.6
Zimbabwe	71	63	0.8	29	37	2.9
SADC	**70.6**	**63.1**	**1.5**	**29.4**	**36.9**	**3.7**
SSA	72	64	1.9	28	36	4

Source: author, based on data from *World Development Indicators* (2009).

Table 4.6 SADC: levels of poverty, 1993–2005 (%)

Country	*Population below national poverty line*			*Survey year*	*Population below*		*Survey year*
	Rural	*Urban*	*National*		*$1/day*	*$2/day*	
Angola	n.a.	n.a.	n.a.		54.3	70.2	2000
Botswana	n.a.	n.a.	n.a.		31.2	49.4	1993–94
DR Congo	75.7	61.7	71.3	2004–05	59.2	79.5	2005–06
Lesotho	60.5	41.5	56.3	2002–03	43.4	62.2	2002–03
Madagascar	76.7	52.1	71.3	1999	67.0	89.6	2005
Malawi	66.5	54.9	65.3	1997–98	73.9	90.4	2004–05
Mauritius	n.a.	n.a.	10.6	1992	n.a.	n.a.	
Mozambique	55.3	51.5	54.1	2002–03	74.7	90.0	2002–03
Namibia	n.a.	n.a.	n.a.		49.1	62.2	1993
South Africa	n.a.	n.a.	n.a.		26.2	42.9	2000
Swaziland	75.0	49.0	69	2000–01	62.9	81.0	2000–01
Tanzania	38.7	29.5	35.7	2000–01	88.5	96.6	2000–01
Zambia	78.0	53.0	68	2004	64.3	81.5	2004–05
Zimbabwe	48.0	7.9	34.9	1995–96	56.1[a]	83.0[a]	1990–2005

Sources: author, based on data from *World Development Indicators* (2009). *a* Figures for Zimbabwe from UNDP (2008) *Human Development Report, 2007–08* (New York: UNDP), available on <http://hdr.undp.org> (accessed 17 February 2010).

Notes: national poverty lines differ from one country to another and in most cases use a lower threshold than the international poverty line of US$1 or US$2 per day. *n.a.* Figures not available.

In all the countries that had data, poverty is higher in rural areas, with most of the countries having more than two-thirds of the rural population below the national poverty line. Since in most of these countries, majority of the people reside in rural areas and derive their livelihood from land-related activities, land becomes a key resource which can be used to reduce poverty and food insecurity in particular.

4.6 Forms of land ownership in SADC

Broadly, there are three dominant forms of land ownership in the regions, namely customary, individual or group freehold/lease and state ownership.

In a research report on land profile in Africa, Bruce and others observe that, apart from South Africa and Namibia where private ownership of land is the dominant form of land tenure, customary tenure is *de facto* the most dominant form of land ownership in the rest of the region.[24] Mafeje also argues that despite frantic efforts to individualise land ownership rights by colonial administration and now through the 'pseudo' land reforms programmes, larger portion of land in Africa (including SADC) is still under customary tenure.[25] As may be evident from Table 4.7, private ownership of land (either freehold or/and leasehold) exist in almost all the countries, but the percentage of land under these forms of ownership is relatively small in most countries. In terms of proportion of land use under each of these categories, most of the land fall under smallholder subsistence farmers whose main form of land tenure is customary.[26] This fact is important in understanding the main land issues in SADC, but most importantly in designing and implementing appropriate land reform policies and programmes.

4.6.1 Customary tenure

As noted above, majority of the people in SADC reside in rural areas (64 per cent in 2007), and majority of these are smallholder land users, falling under the customary land system. Though there may be different shades and nuances to customary tenure in the different countries in SADC, the common feature of this system of land tenure is that the control over access and use of land is vested in the community, kinship structures or village authorities.[27] Authorities who hold the responsibility to allocate the 'rights' to access and use land range from chiefs, village headmen, elders to formal structures who form part of the local land institutional set-up.[28] Land boards and land committees in Botswana and Tanzania, respectively, are examples of some of these authorities.

One of the major debates around tenure reforms in Africa is understanding the nature of customary tenure rights.[29] The controversy is not so much about whether tenure security is important or not; there seems to be wide agreement on this, particularly in the literature.[30] Controversies arise more about whether customary tenure is secure, and whether security of tenure impacts on land use, productivity and investment. On one side of the debate is the view that customary land tenure is not secure and therefore, there is need to migrate to more secure forms of tenure.[31] The argument is that once tenure is secured this will provide an incentive to invest in land, utilise land more efficiently and productively, thereby unlocking the potential value or capital of land.[32] Formalisation or land registration has been seen by the international development agencies such as the World Bank, especially during the early 1980s through the 1990s, as the only way to promote growth and reduce poverty in Africa.[33] Secure land rights are seen to inhere mainly in some form of a private formal title to land as opposed to unwritten or unformalised systems of rights predominant in customary tenure. In addition, it is argued that secure tenure in the form of individual titles can enable the landholder to use land as collateral when borrowing investment capital from formal financial markets.

Recently work from a number of researchers challenge this view contending that the 'security' of tenure does not necessarily lie in having a private or statutory title to land. On this side of the debate, there is wide agreement that customary tenure systems do not entail insecurity, but can actually provide sufficient levels of security in land access and use.[34] Although many analysts acknowledge that security of tenure under customary system can be weak, especially for vulnerable groups such as widows and other power-voice-less groups in society,[35] there is growing consensus that many forms of customary land tenure can confer secure access to and use of land.[36] Recent studies[37] have shown that titling or formalisation of land rights does not necessarily lead to security of tenure or increased investment. In certain circumstances, creation of private title to land can, in fact, lead to conflict due to 'opportunistic behaviour' of some powerful

Table 4.7 SADC: percentage composition of land, by type of tenure

Country	*Customary*	*State*	*Freehold/lease*
Angola	n.a.	n.a.	n.a.
Botswana	70[a]	25	5
DR Congo	n.a.	n.a.	n.a.
Lesotho	95	5	n.a.
Madagascar	n.a.	n.a.	n.a.
Malawi	72	20	8
Mauritius	n.a.	n.a.	n.a.
Mozambique	80	14	3
Namibia	43	13	44
South Africa	14	14	72
Swaziland	60		40
Tanzania[b]	93.4	6.6	0
Zambia[c]	94	6	0
Zimbabwe	42	16	41

Sources: *Economic Commission for Africa* (ECA, 2003: 2); Mathuba (2003); Adams *et al.* (2003); Malope and Batisani (2008); *Tanzania Land Policy* (1997); *Zambia Land Administration and Management Policy* (2006, draft); Bruce *et al.* (2003). *n.a.* No data available.

Notes: These different sources give different figures, probably because of the difference in the periods they report on. In cases where there are two different figures, the later figure is preferred and is what is reported here. Similarly, official figures are preferred to other sources.

a This figure is reported in three different sources (Adams *et al.* 2003: 56; Mathuba 2003: 4; Malope and Batisani 2008), and is much higher than the figure (14%) reported by the ECA.

b The figures for Tanzania are from the national land policy document; no figures are given in the ECA report.

c Figures from the national land policy for Zambia are preferred to the ECA figures.

members of the community or the elite who may attempt to amass land at the expense of the poor and voiceless.[38] Thus, evidence from a number of empirical studies in Africa seem to suggest that:

> … land registration creates increased insecurity for vulnerable parts of the population; it does not activate the land market, and if it does, it is mainly for speculative reasons; it does not bring about a reversal in land fragmentation nor does it improve land allocation; it does not in significant ways improve smallholders access to credit; and there is no significant correlation between land titling and increased agricultural yield.[39]

With regard to the productivity and investment arguments, a case study on Madagascar reveals no significant relationship between titling and productivity or investment.[40] It is rather the provision of support to smallholder land users which tend to have a significant effect on productivity and eventually investment.[41] Thus, the 'old consensus' that titling of land increases investment, productivity and efficient use of land needs to be evaluated in the light of emerging empirical evidence from different parts of Africa. Current policy focus on titling as the first step towards a successful land reform is based on grave misreading of the actual situation on the ground, especially in Sub-Saharan Africa where such policies may be counterproductive given the inadequate state capacity to effectively accomplish such exercises. What is crucial at the moment is to establish how people are using the land that they have access to and what factors constrain their access and use of land, if any. Is it true that customary tenure system is a major constraint to land access and use in the region? Given the prevailing land-holding patterns in the region, what type of tenure would be more appropriate and how can that contribute to improved land access and use?

Evidence from smallholder/subsistence land users does bring out the fact that infrastructure, public services, input support, extension services and access to markets are some of the pressing issues for many smallholding land users. Without these enabling conditions, even if a person is given the most secure land rights, they will contribute little to improving the living conditions of the many smallholding land users who face food security problems. For instance secure rights to land in a place without roads, markets, agricultural services, will contribute little to the life of the right holder. Therefore, for majority of the people in SADC the key land issue is providing the enabling conditions for them to use land more productively and sustainably. In most countries, majority of the smallholder land users complain about lack of inputs, equipments and agriculture services, and far less about security of tenure.

4.6.2 State-owned land

For a number of countries in the region, there is some ambiguity with regard to what is referred to as state land. As indicated in Table 4.7, most countries in the region, except South Africa, Namibia and Zimbabwe, where freehold title is a significant proportion of the land, land has been nationalised *de jure* with all the land vested in the state or head of state. For instance the National Land Policy in Zambia stipulates that '*all* land is vested in the President who holds it absolutely in perpetuity in trust for and on behalf of the people of Zambia'.[42] Essentially, this means that land is owned by the state, including land under customary tenure or leasehold.[43] In countries that have adopted this principle, it is not only former 'Crown land' which has become state land, but the entire land base belongs to the state, though in practice, customary land enjoys 'almost' absolute autonomy. This applies to countries like Lesotho, Swaziland, Tanzania and Mozambique. In countries such as Angola, Mozambique, Zambia and Tanzania where socialist forms of governments were adopted at independence, freehold titles which were issued to European settlers during colonial rule were completely abolished, leaving leasehold as the only form of private land ownership. In countries such as Botswana, Malawi, Lesotho and Swaziland, freehold titles exist but they are a tiny fraction of the land.[44]

However, in practice state land 'proper' is actually reserve land: land consisting of national game reserves, national parks, national conservation sites and pieces of urban land which are often leased for a fixed period of time. In Botswana for instance, state land in urban or peri-urban areas is leased for 99 years for residential land and 50 years for commercial land.[45] Most of the countries have abandoned freehold titles and those that still have them are contemplating land nationalisation[46] which promotes leasehold as the common form of private land ownership. There are also cases in the region where customary land can be converted into leasehold via some form of land market. However, such occurrences are few. In countries such as South Africa, Zimbabwe and Namibia where redistributive land reform has taken place, a significant number of reform beneficiaries have acquired leasehold titles.[47]

4.6.3 Statutory/private land tenure

The two most common forms of individual private land ownership in the SADC region are freehold and leasehold, commonly referred to as statutory tenure. As highlighted earlier, most governments are moving away from freehold titles towards leasehold. In many countries, large-scale farming is often under either leasehold or freehold. Although in terms of population only a small fraction of the population is under this tenure system, land under this system tend to be the most productive due to the use of modern farming methods and advanced technology. In addition, the larger part of land under statutory tenure system is often the most fertile. In Botswana for instance, freehold titles are mainly farms acquired during colonial administration and are concentrated in the most fertile parts of the country (the south-east and north-east).[48]

4.6.4 Other forms of land ownership and access

Even though the three forms of land ownership discussed above are the most dominant in the region, there are also other forms of access to land. In general, there are various forms of land tenancy. This is common in countries where there is pressure on land due to high population such as Mauritius, Lesotho, Malawi, Swaziland and South Africa. In these countries, land tenancy has been either labour tenancy or sharecropping. These are actually crude forms of land market, and in southern Africa they are a minor occurrence today compared to West Africa and East Africa (Rwanda, Ethiopia, Burundi).[49] Although these are not in any way forms of land ownership, they constitute important ways in which the land-needy households acquire access to and use of land. There are also situations where the poor household leases out land to those in need, including the well-off, as a source of income.[50] For some analysts, this is confirmation of the theory of 'induced innovation'.[51] These forms of land access occur on both customary and privately owned land and are usually informal arrangements. It is not just poor land-needy households who engage in this form of land access, well-off people who do not wish to buy land or who want a short-term use of land may acquire access to land in this way. This is preferred because it is a less risk form of engagement for the lessee and the lessor. Existence of such practices, however, points to the unequal distribution of land and need to be addressed through policy.

In southern Africa, land renting appears to be the most common arrangement. Often this occurs between well-resourced land users who enter into a formal contract to use land with agreed rent rates for a specific period. Often land renting occurs on privately owned land or state land, with land contracted for a short period of time which is not suitable for a lease. In countries where this practice is common, such as Swaziland, South Africa, Namibia and Malawi, it is often among livestock owners, in need of more land for their livestock who rent land from other landholders. In South Africa, this is common in the arid areas of the Eastern Cape where livestock is the dominant agricultural occupation.

In addition, some people do invade land as a form of accessing land. Land invasions can occur on private and state-owned land. Cases of land invasions often occur in many countries[52] in southern Africa, though it is Zimbabwe's land invasions which have hit headlines in mainstream media.[53] Land invasions occur in the region, though more often in peri-urban areas for residential purposes. There are of course different reasons why invasions occur, but where they do, this points to gaps in the administration and management of land.

4.6.5 Land policy, management and administration in SADC

Land ownership and use are inextricably linked to land administration and management. Debates on land ownership in southern Africa, more than anywhere else, have generated complex issues with far reaching social, economic, political and cultural effects. One of the reasons cited for the complex nature of land in the region is the extensive and extended white settlement in most of the countries, which resulted in massive land dispossession during colonial rule and apartheid.[54] As a result of colonial rule, most of the countries at independence were faced with the difficult task of addressing the legacy of centuries of discriminatory land policy. For countries with large numbers of settlers such as South Africa, Zimbabwe and Namibia, the problem of land is further complicated by the fact that long periods of colonial occupation have left skewed ownership patterns along racial lines, which if not resolved carefully, can result in huge social and economic costs.[55] This situation does threaten the political and economic stability of the region as a whole.[56]

While many countries in the region had the opportunity to address the land issue immediately after independence, most countries have not effectively addressed the pressing land issues.[57] Often land has low priority on the 'real' agenda, and is frequently ignored or is manipulated by politicians and the economic elite.[58] This is clearly evident when one looks at the major policies and pieces of legislation on land in the different countries of the region. Even if a good number of the countries attained independence during the 1960s, land policy came on the agenda only during the second half of the 1990s. Prior to that, the colonial policy and institutional framework continued to guide land administration, use, ownership and management.

This is in spite of the fact that most of these countries framed the liberation struggle around land issues.[59] For countries that attempted to reform the land administration and policy framework, little was done to radically reform the colonial land institutions, distribution patterns, policy and legal framework. As Bruce and others have noted, it is surprising how little has changed since independence.[60] In some countries, land policy is not even on the agenda. Even in countries where land policies and legislation have been updated, weak institutional capacity has left most of these policies just mere documents without any concrete programme to implement them. A report on the establishment of the Regional Land Reform Support Facility (RLRSF) notes that the 'major constraint facing Member States is the lack of capacity for implementing land and agrarian reforms in an efficient and comprehensive manner'.[61]

But as with other policies, it may not even be lack of capacity which is a problem, instead, it is lack of commitment. Where there is commitment from the politicians, capacity can be built to ensure that programmes are developed and implemented. To a large extent, the failure or slow progress of land reform in the region is not due to lack of policies or models, but mainly due to lack of political commitment.[62] This is re-echoed by the participants of the consultative workshop on land policy in SADC who observed that the national policies, where they exist, have touched on major and urgent land issues, but this has only remained on paper.[63]

It is often easy for governments to put the blame on lack of capacity within state institutions when in actual fact the main problem is that the policy under consideration has not received enough political support. Prolonged inadequate capacity may be an indication of a deeply underlying lack of commitment. As indicated above most policies that have been developed so far have largely remained on paper, revisited only on the eve of the trumpeted 'land crisis' in Zimbabwe.[64] Although most countries have rightly acknowledged that land is a key factor not only in economic growth and poverty reduction, but also in promoting food security, social stability and sustainable development, yet countries that have tried to address the land issue have often done so in an uncoordinated manner resulting in little impact on poverty and food security.[65] Unfortunately, today land reform agenda in many SADC countries is being driven and often captured by the elite who use it to enrich themselves by taking advantage of the weak policy and administrative environment.

4.6.6 SADC Land Reform Support Facility

At the regional level, commendable efforts have been made to provide support and encouragement to member countries to begin to address land issues in a more integrated way. The establishment of the SADC Land Reform Support Facility (SADC LRSF, initiated in 2006)[66] is expected to provide some encouragement to member countries in their effort to implement reforms seriously. However, as an advisory body, SADC LRSF's role and influence is limited by the very nature of the body, since it can only provide support when asked. No doubt, the establishment of the facility is likely to make positive contributions, but this contribution will in the end depend on how responsive each member state will be to the issues at hand. Though the initial setting up of the facility has been based on wide consultation of stakeholders including governments, civil society organisations, private sector, academic institutions and development partners, the absence of key stakeholders such as traditional leaders, smallholder land users, landless people and farm workers/labourers may weaken its support base.

4.7 Forms of land use in SADC

Land as a basis for human existence is used in many ways to satisfy various interests of different groups of people. In southern Africa land is used for different purposes ranging from the simplest food gathering and hunting to the sophisticated game farming and agro-tourism. However, as mentioned earlier the most dominant forms of land use are smallholder subsistence and commercial agriculture both of which may include crop production, livestock rearing, fishing, hunting and forestry.[67]

4.7.1 Smallholder/subsistence land use

In terms of both land size and population, smallholder subsistence farming is the most widespread form of land use in the region. Here it is important to note that smallholders or subsistence land use is not a homogeneous group;[68] what is referred to as smallholder differs from one context to another even within the same country. This term is, nonetheless, generally applied to land users with roughly between 0.5 ha up to 10 ha.[69] Similarly, while the term subsistence refers to producers for domestic consumption, this group is not homogeneous; most land users in this category produce for the market at one time, while at another only producing for home consumption. However, most of the smallholder subsistence land users are predominantly involved in the production of staple food, primarily for home consumption without precluding sale of the surplus on the market.

For the SADC region, the main staple food produced by small land holders includes maize, sorghum, millet, cassava, yam and pulses. In some cases, smallholder land users combine arable agriculture with livestock production, especially in areas where the soil has limited potential for crop production. In more arid zones, cattle, sheep, goat, pigs, and local chickens are the major livestock reared. Although smallholder land use is the largest in terms of numbers, in some countries such as South Africa, Namibia, Swaziland (and Zimbabwe before the controversial land reform), the largest proportion of agriculture output mainly comes from a small number of commercial farms.[70] For example even in countries such as Zambia where commercial farming is limited, the 545,000 smallholder farmers produce 60 per cent of the total food, while the 400 large commercial farms produce the remaining 40 per cent. However, in countries such as Malawi, Mozambique, Tanzania and Lesotho, it is the smallholder land users who produce the bulk of the food on the domestic market. In Malawi for instance, up to 80 per cent of the food is produced by smallholder land users,[71] though productivity among smallholders is comparatively low. Some of the reasons for the low productivity in the smallholder category include poor quality of soil, poor farming methods, poor tools and inadequate access to inputs and unfavourable climatic conditions. In many countries, smallholder land users have been pushed into poorer areas either by colonial discriminatory land policy or the elite in the post-independence period. Most of the smallholder land users rely on rain-fed crop and livestock production, and depend primarily on family labour.

Although majority of the people in this category of land use depend on agriculture for their livelihoods, there has been reported diversification of livelihood strategies, ranging from petty trading, fishing, wood fuel harvesting, honey production, local beer production, remittances, and farm and non-farm employment.[72] Notwithstanding the reported processes of 'de-agrarianisation' and 'depeasantisation' in rural Africa,[73] majority of the people still pursue land-based livelihoods, and for them land is a springboard from which they can launch other livelihood strategies. Even in areas where diversification of income strategies has taken place for a sizable section of the population, still many smallholder land users in rural areas simply add these different forms of income generating activities without completely abandoning the use of land, contrary to the de-agrarianisation/de-peasantisation theory.[74]

4.7.2 Commercial land use

This category of land use, though present in most countries in the region, is dominant in countries which had large settler populations during colonial rule, such as South Africa, Namibia, Zimbabwe. In most cases, commercial land use involves capital intensive activities, applying modern methods of farming together with the latest technology, and relying mainly on hired labour. Like the smallholder group, this is also not a homogeneous group. But most of the land users in this group have access to the most fertile land and they are usually individual freehold or leasehold titles. This group of land users combine rain-fed and irrigated crop production. Though rainfall patterns are usually precarious in the region, irrigation has remained only a small proportion of arable land use as Table 4.8 shows.

Another common feature of commercial land use is the focus mainly on cash crop as opposed to food crop production. This has been noted to be one of the legacies of the colonial agricultural policy that encouraged and supported production of cash crops such as cotton, tea, tobacco, cocoa and coffee while ignoring or even indirectly discouraging production of staple food for the local market through unfair pricing mechanism, subsidies, and sometimes directly limiting the growing of certain food crops.[75]

Since colonial times, there has been a strong bias in most governments towards cash crop (and commercial) farmers, resulting in what some authors have referred to as the 'African agrarian paradox'.[76] Unfortunately, these policies have continued today in many countries with commercial farmers and those engaged in cash crop production receiving state support of various kinds[77] while smallholder farmers who are the main food producers continue to be ignored.[78] This is apparently justified by arguing that cash crops bring in the foreign currency and therefore play an important role in macro-economic stabilisation via the foreign exchange market. But the opposite is also true; a country that is able to produce enough food (especially staple food) to feed its population can build a healthy foreign currency reserve which can play a significant role in stabilising the economy. Evidence from various countries in the region shows that both foreign reserves and the exchange rates deteriorate when there is a poor harvest due to food imports. In countries such as Zambia, Malawi, Mozambique, Swaziland, Lesotho and Tanzania, a good harvest often means stable exchange rates and low inflation, and a healthy foreign currency reserve. In Zambia, both the monthly and annual inflation rates gravitate around the average movement in staple food prices.[79]

With regard to cereal production, although the yield per unit of land for the SADC region was higher than that of SSA in both 1990–02 and 2005–07 periods, the region's cereal yield per hectare remained relatively low when compared to other regions such as Latin America and South Asia as Table 4.9 shows.

In countries such as Angola, Botswana, Lesotho, Namibia and Zimbabwe, the yield per hectare has remained lower than a third of the region's average over the reference period. Although the yield per hectare increased in a number of countries between 1990 and 2007, it declined in DRC, Lesotho, Swaziland, Tanzania and Zimbabwe. It is also interesting to note that while some countries that have reduced the land under cereal production have recorded an increase in cereal yield per hectare (South Africa, Mauritius, and Botswana), there are also countries that have increased land under cereal production and yet have recorded decline in yield per hectare (Tanzania, DRC and Zimbabwe). There are many reasons to account for this, but adoption of technology and intensive agriculture methods are two of the main factors. Declining in cereal production in some countries has largely contributed to the worsening food security situation in the region.[80]

Uncoordinated use of land together with inappropriate policy choices make the SADC region increasingly becoming food-deficient or dependent (relying on food imports). The food deficit situation has worsened as indicated by the growing net food import in the region. As Table 4.10 shows, although there were some improvements in terms of self-sufficiency in food in a number of countries from 1990 to 2000, there are a number of countries whose proportion of food consumption is increasingly imported through the market or food aid. Food aid as a proportion of total food consumption increased in DRC, Lesotho, Malawi, Swaziland, Zambia and Zimbabwe over the last decade.

Most of these countries have sufficient land and other natural resources to produce enough food to meet domestic needs and even for export. What seems evident from Table 4.10 is that the region has been suffering from food shortfalls up to the value of 2 per cent of the region's GDP and this deficit is growing since

Table 4.8 SADC: irrigated land as a percentage of cultivated land, 1990–92 and 2003–05

Country	*1990–92*	*2003–05*
Angola	2.3	2.2
Botswana	0.2	0.3
DR Congo	0.1	0.1
Lesotho	0.6	0.9
Madagascar	30.7	30.6
Malawi	1.2	2.2
Mauritius	16.0	20.8
Mozambique	2.8	2.6
Namibia	0.7	1.0
South Africa	8.3	9.5
Swaziland	24.1	26.0
Tanzania	1.4	1.8
Zambia	0.7	2.9
Zimbabwe	3.6	5.2
SADC	**6.6**	**7.6**
SSA	3.4	3.5

Source: FAOSTAT, http://www.fao.org/corp/statistics/en/ 2009.

the 1990s. Countries such as Lesotho, Madagascar, Malawi, Mozambique, Swaziland, Zambia and Zimbabwe experienced some shortfall in the supply of cereal between October 2009 and March 2010. The shortfall over this period was highest in Zimbabwe (over 66,000 t) and Mozambique (over 22,000 t).[81]

This is an indication of a declining ability of the region to produce enough food to meet domestic demand. What is more worrying is the fact that countries such as Madagascar, Namibia and Zimbabwe, which have been enjoying a surplus food balance, have now become net food importers. Though there are several reasons that account for the declining food balance in the region, inappropriate land policy, management and use have all contributed to this scenario. Improved access to and efficient use of land for majority of the rural population is crucial to improving the region's food supply and food security in the long run. Thus, addressing the outstanding land issues such as productive and sustainable land use and creating an enabling environment for smallholder producers in the regions remains central to food security and poverty reduction. There is also need for government in the region to revise the policy towards smallholder producers *vis-à-vis* commercial farmers.

4.7.3 Game farming

Game farming is another form of land use that is emerging in a number of countries in the region. This often involves the conversion of land used for conventional agriculture to the keeping of wild animals. Though it is not clear how much agricultural land is being converted to game farming, there is some evidence that this is a growing form of land use especially among commercial land

Table 4.9 SADC: land use and cereal production, 1990–92 to 2005–07

Country	*Land under cereal (000 ha)*		*Cereal yield (kg/ha)*	
	1990–92	*2005–07*	*1990–92*	*2005–07*
Angola	892.6	1,476.4	378	526
Botswana	140.1	84.3	312	508
DR Congo	1,867.6	1,972.9	794	772
Lesotho	177.6	160.7	703	546
Madagascar	1,321.0	1,590.9	1,935	2,493
Malawi	1,442.6	1,791.8	871	1,416
Mauritius	0.5	0.1	4,117	7,666
Mozambique	1,508.6	2,180.5	330	949
Namibia	206.4	284.0	388	420
South Africa	5,735.9	3,570.9	1,602	3,081
Swaziland	69.1	59.4	1,299	1,196
Tanzania	3,003.3	4,906.7	1,276	1,162
Zambia	813.4	837.2	1,003	1,228
Zimbabwe	1,430.8	2,095.0	1,125	674
SADC			**1,152.4**	**1,616.9**
SSA			1,003	1,228
South Asia			1,977	2,581
Latin America			2,234	3,308

Source: author, based on data from *World Development Indicators* (2009).

users.[82] The impact of this conversion of agricultural land to game farming on food security and livelihoods in general is not yet clear, but there are some concerns that this might actually worsen the current food crisis in the region. In some countries, it may be necessary to introduce legislation to lessen the impact this may have on food security. For instance, the former Minister of Agriculture in South Africa has intimated that 'given the threat game farming poses to food security in South Africa, the government would consider drafting legislation to curb their proliferation'.[83]

4.8 Political economy of land distribution and use in SADC

The forms of land ownership, access and use described above are largely a product of a common history that most of the countries in the region share. These current forms of ownership, access and use of land have been shaped by extended colonial domination which resulted in skewed ownership and use of land. Though different countries in the region have different experiences of colonial occupation and rule, there are certain underlying features which are common to most of the countries.[84] For the region as whole, land has been at the centre of social, economic and political struggle since the beginning of imperial occupation. During colonial rule, the establishment of large communities of European settlers created unique problems with regard to land ownership, access and use for southern Africa in particular.[85] When compared to other regions in Africa, southern Africa has experienced acute land challenges which have attracted a lot of attention over

Table 4.10 SADC food supply scenario, 1990–2006

Country	*Value of food imports as % of total imports*			*Net food trade as % of GDP*		
	1990–92	*2000–02*	*2004–06*	*1990–92*	*2000–02*	*2004–06*
Angola	21.3	−3.7	10.8	9.7	−3.7	−2.6
Botswana	10.5	−3.2	16.7	3.8	−3.2	−0.7
DR Congo	28.3	−2.1	24.6	16.3	−4.3	−5
Lesotho	13.9	−16.9	14.3	5.1	−14.1	−4.8
Madagascar	10.9	2.1	12.3	13.7	1.7	−1.1
Malawi	15.2	−3.6	12.8	8.7	−1.2	−0.2
Mauritius	10.6	7.3	11.4	11.1	1.2	0.7
Mozambique	25.3	−7.9	15.7	15.3	−4.3	−4.0
Namibia	9.2	2.4	11.9	7.8	−1.8	−0.8
South Africa	4.7	0.4	3.0	2.8	0.6	0.3
Swaziland	10.5	19.3	11.4	9.9	8	3.3
Tanzania	5.8	−0.7	17.1	11.7	−1.2	−1.7
Zambia	7.3	−1.5	8.2	6.8	−1.1	−0.4
Zimbabwe	7.0	0	7.1	20.5	0.3	−10
SADC	**12.9**	**−0.6**	**12.7**	**10.2**	**−1.7**	**−1.9**

Source: FAOSTAT, http://www.fao.org/corp/statistics/en/ 2009.
Note: the percentages are three-year averages.

the last four decades.[86] The presence of rich mineral wealth and a large population of Europeans created the dynamics which have affected land policy, institutions, ownership and use even today.

4.8.1 Land ownership in 'Africa of the Labour Reserves'

Strong European interest in land in southern Africa can be traced to the discovery of gold and diamonds in South Africa, resulting in increased fortune seekers from mainly Europe. Prior to the 'mineral revolution' most of the local African communities in the region had practised self-sufficiency, pre-capitalist relations and modes of production based on land[87] or what has been referred to as the 'redistributive economy'.[88] The second half of the nineteenth century saw the consolidation of the capitalist economy, and its modes of production became more entrenched, eventually dominating the 'natural economy'.[89] Though in the initial stages of capitalist development in the region (estimated from around 1870 to 1930), the two modes coexisted, but as the capitalist mode became dominant the result was the 'deterioration of the productive capacity' with increasing rapidity, leading to the destruction of the pre-capitalist societies.[90] Since the 'natural economy' relies almost entirely on land, in order to integrate the natural economy into the capitalist accumulation process, access to, and subsequently, use of land had to be limited.

As the demand for labour for the expanding mining and commercial agricultural sectors increased (and later on, manufacturing), restricting access to and use of land among the indigenous population became the only way to induce the supply of labour. In order to force the indigenous population engaged in pre-capitalist modes of production into wage labour, capital had to annihilate and dominate the redistributive economy by depriving the indigenous people of the means of production (mainly land) and sustenance.[91]

In effect, the massive dispossession of land that this process entailed resulted in the creation of 'labour reserves'. Since this process was more widespread in southern Africa than elsewhere in the continent, the region is sometimes referred to as 'Africa of the labour reserves'.[92]

Although this process of creating 'labour reserves' was more pronounced in countries with large settler populations such as South Africa, Zimbabwe and Namibia, a similar process was initiated in other countries in the region, resulting in fertile land being allocated and often preserved for the exclusive use of the settler population. While most of the political economy accounts of southern Africa have restricted the analysis to South Africa, Zimbabwe and Namibia, this process was introduced in other countries, either to induce cheap labour for the individual countries or to supply labour to the region's sub-imperial hub.[93] With the exception of present day DRC, Tanzania, Mauritius and Madagascar, the rest of the countries in the region supplied labour to the mines and farms in South Africa. Thus, creating a labour reserve was not only a peculiar experience of the Bantustans or native reserves of South Africa, but was extended to the rest of the region to varying degrees.

To distinguish the 'labour reserves' in South Africa from those in other countries in the region, Ntsabane has divided the region into two 'tier reserves' with South Africa's Bantustans (Transkei, Ciskei, Bophuthaswana, Gazankulu, Venda, KwaNgwane, KwaZulu Lebowa and Quaqua) constituting the first tier, while the other countries (such as Malawi, Botswana, Mozambique, Swaziland, Lesotho, Zimbabwe and Zambia) making up the second tier.[94] A complete appreciation of the capitalist development in the region needs to take account of similar processes induced elsewhere in the region and the role of South Africa in the region. For instance, during colonial times dispossession of land and supply of labour to South Africa was reported in most of the countries in the region. Available evidence suggest that by 1975 the second tier labour reserves provided up to 70 per cent of the total labour force to South Africa.[95] In many of these countries a number of well calculated strategies such as market restriction, unfair allocation of subsidy, differential taxation, differential access to public goods such as roads, credit, extension services, education, were employed on top of restrictions on land use.[96] In all this the state played an important role through regulation and sometimes the open use of force.[97] Access to and use of land was used as a key policy instrument by the state.

4.8.2 SADC land policy in context

Themes of access to, use and ownership of land are subjects of public policy. Land policy in particular, can address various issues related to land ranging from the unequal distribution to rules specifying land ownership, use and management. As such, land reform is a complex and context-specific social and political process, which can be influenced by various considerations including social, economic, cultural, administrative factors and power relations. In southern Africa, as is the case elsewhere, land reforms are rarely induced by a single factor, but by a combination of many factors and actors who influence the policy that is finally adopted. Thus, an analysis of any reform must take cognisance of the state as a key role player in the reforms.[98]

Often analysis of land reforms takes the state to be an uninterested actor whose main interest is to redistribute land or increase access to land among the population. For example, market-aided reform approaches often assume the state to be a disinterested party whose main objective is to regulate the other actors and create a level playing field to achieve equitable and efficient land distribution and use. But often, a state is not a disinterested party. Various state actors have a deep-rooted interest in embarking on reform of land policy, administration and practice.[99] Although these interests are often hidden behind the rhetoric and bureaucratic formulations in policy documents, they influence and shape policy and the subsequent programmes, and how these are implemented. Understanding some of the key underlying interests or motives is essential to appreciating the current forms of land reform, their achievements and failures in the region.

Clearly, land policy and reforms are undertaken for different reasons some of which may include promoting equal access to land, addressing past injustices, economic growth, addressing ownership types, cultural injustice, poverty reduction, promoting sustainable and efficient use of land, increase food security, employment growth, achieve social stability and peace, build capacity to administer land more effectively, etc. Choosing what to focus on is often not a democratic process where citizens or even affected parties cast their ballot to determine which issue is in the 'public interest'. Often such decisions are taken at policy level and translated into implementable programmes by various state institutions. In this way, any policy making is a political process through which state (and often the political elite) express their interest, power and inclinations.[100] As such, land policy, like any other public policy, can be seen as an outcome of a process of choosing from, sometimes, competing interests, alternatives, goals and players. The state as one of the players may have interests or goals different from other players on the policy platform. For example, the decision to adopt redistribution of land in Zimbabwe or South Africa may not have been a unanimous decision; there have always been interest groups opposed to land redistribution while other groups lobby for land redistribution.

The policy arena therefore is a space where different actors contest and express their interests, views, ideologies, aspirations and power. Hence, policy formulation is often not a product of a neutral, disinterested 'benevolent state' performing the Pareto optimal calculus with the aim of maximising individual and social good. In reality policy is determined by actors with unequal powers, different knowledge and interests.[101] Similarly, public policy choices are not entirely a product of a self-interested bureaucracy, calculating what is in it for them, as public choice theorists have claimed. Rather to understand the public policies, including land policy, requires knowledge of the nature of states, type of current social and political institutions, how they function, and whether various interest groups including media, civil society groups, professional organisations, trade unions, financial institutions, religious institutions, traditional authorities and social movements play a role in the formulation and implementation of policy programmes.

4.9 Concluding remarks

Southern Africa is a large regional group of countries rich in natural resources including land. Access to, use and ownership of land in this region are important given that more than two-thirds the population depend on land for their livelihoods. As such, the way land is owned, redistributed and used forms an important part of public policy and administration in all the countries. In some countries, addressing issues of land ownership, use and management has necessitated implementing land reforms.

In recent years, the democratisation process that is on-going in the region has begun to open up spaces where a more robust debate on the appropriate forms of land reform needed can be held. Reports from countries such as Zambia, Mozambique, Tanzania, and Malawi, show that the policy reform process has been built around wide consultation, with recognisable effort to decentralise land management and administration.[102] For a long time, most states have been ignoring the views of other actors on the land issues such that land policy has been a monopoly of the state often manipulated by elite interests. Similarly, the role of financial institutions such as the World Bank and the IMF, which have dominated the policy arena since the debt crisis, have tended to adopt policies that are far removed from the realities on the ground. The dominant views of the World Bank on land such as favouring market option against state-led interventions have often left no room for other actors including various state agencies to make contributions to the policy process. Often this has resulted in more pressing issues being sidelined.

One of the reasons why some of the reform policies have not performed well in terms of achieving their intended goals is particularly because the processes are largely generated from a very narrow constituency. In addition, the anti-agriculture scepticism which has its roots in mainstream economic theory that sees a diminishing contribution of agriculture to economic growth has done more harm, not just to land reform but to agriculture policy, food security and poverty reduction.[103] Although there has been sufficient evidence[104] showing that agriculture-based growth has more poverty-reducing impact in countries with large population dependent on agriculture, policy advice has continued to be sceptical of the role that agrarian reforms can play in the fight against poverty.

Worse still, land has often been equated to agriculture; and since agriculture's contribution to economic growth has been declining, there has been a tendency to underplay the economic significance of agrarian reforms. Such views have been reinforced by claims of diversification of rural livelihoods leading to de-agrarianisation and de-peasantisation. There has often been a failure to realise that land is much broader than agriculture, and that diversification of the rural economy does not imply that land issues nor agriculture have less social and economic significance. Land still remains a key asset (and the only asset for the rural poor) for many people even those who have diversified into non-farm income generating activities.[105]

Southern Africa has a large land resource base with diverse agro-ecological and farming systems. Land ownership, access and use have been greatly shaped by colonial experience and the current political and economic environment. Although most of the countries in the region gained independence between 30 and 45 years ago, many have not resolved the land problems created by colonial rule. Extensive unequal distribution of land in countries which had large settler populations continue even today, while tenure, administration and management of land have not significantly changed in most of the countries. Reliance on foreign policy advice has resulted in misplaced land policies which have failed to address some of the urgent problems. For instance, insistence on individual titling in countries where majority of the land is under customary tenure and where state capacity to conduct such an exercise is weak, has left some of the state agencies almost paralysed. In addition to this, weak institutions and lack of political commitment to the land question in the region have left most of the land-related problem brilliantly described on paper, but little done to transform this into concrete programmes. Often this has resulted in ignoring the more pressing issues of ensuring that the poor have the means to use land productively to meet their basic food needs.

Consequently, inappropriate land policies and lack of genuine commitment to land issues, have affected agricultural policy and compromised the region's ability to produce sufficient food to meet the growing demand. As illustrated above, although the region has sufficient land and labour resources, it is increasingly finding it difficult to use these resources to reduce food insecurity, evident by the growing food deficit in a number of countries.

Land reforms which should be addressing some of these challenges are severely underdeveloped, underfunded, uncoordinated, resulting in delays in implementing necessary programmes. Though there is hope that the regional support facility for land reform may highlight the land issue on the region's agenda, there is little hope that this will be realised in a number of countries, since the regional facility, being a support instrument, can provide support only where it is needed or asked for. However, there are encouraging signs of an increasing political attention to the land issues in the region, especially after the impact of the 'land crisis' in Zimbabwe. Despite countries in the region acknowledging that land has an important role to play in promoting economic growth, regional stability, reducing poverty and improving the situation of food security, land continues to be a secondary issue which is often exploited for political gains by the political elite.

Notes

* Senior Researcher, Land Reform and Democracy NRF Chair, University of Cape Town, Republic of South Africa.
1 Others are the East African Community (EAC), Economic Community of West African States (ECOWAS), Common Market for Eastern and Southern Africa (COMESA), Community of Sahel-Saharan States (CEN-SAD), Economic Community of Central African States, Arab Maghreb Union and Intergovernmental Authority on Development (IGAD).
2 Southern African Development Community (2007a, 2007b).
3 Havnevik (1997).
4 Kalibwani (2005); Maunder and Wiggins (2006); Moyo (nd).
5 Southern African Development Community (2007a, 2008).
6 Mafeje (2003); Havnevik (1997).
7 Mafeje (2003); Shipton and Goheen (1992).
8 World Bank (2009), pp 333–34.
9 Fischer, Shah, Velthuizen and Nachtergaele (2006).
10 According to FAO, agricultural area includes arable land under temporary crops or pasture, land under permanent long-term crops which are not planted annually, and permanent meadows and grazing land. Abandoned land due to shifting cultivation is excluded if the land is fallow for more than five years within the reference period (see FAOSTATS Glossary for details at <http://www.fao.org/corp/statistics/en/>). Thus arable land is not a reflection of potential cultivatable land.
11 Moyo (2010).
12 Maunder and Wiggins (2006); Overseas Development Institute (2004), <http://www.odi.org.uk/food-security-forum> (accessed 23 February 2010); SADC (2008).
13 SADC (2007a).
14 Roth (2002); Ntsabane (2003).
15 Maunder and Wiggins (2006); Kalibwani (2005).
16 Sombroek (1997).
17 Food and Agriculture Organisation (2003).
18 Ibid, p 9.
19 Ibid, p 6; Dixon, Gulliver and Gibbon (2001).
20 Dixon, Gulliver and Gibbon (2001), p 8.
21 Ibid, p 2.
22 Economic Commission for Africa (2005).
23 Kalibwani (2005); SADC (2008).
24 Bruce, Jansen, Kloeck-Jenson, Knox, Subramanian and William (1998), p 205.
25 Mafeje (2003), p 8.
26 Ibid, p 14; Deininger (2003).
27 Mafeje (2003); Shipton and Goheen (1992); Akuffo (2009).
28 Ntsebeza (2006).
29 Place (2009).
30 Chimhowu (2006); Van den Brink, Thomas, Bruce and Byamugisha (2006); Platteau (1996); Bruce, Migot-Adholla and Atherton (1994).
31 Deininger (2003); Deininger and Binswanger (1999).
32 De Soto (2000).
33 Havnevik (1997).
34 Shipton and Goheen (1992); Platteau (1996); Adams, Kalabamu and White (2003); Mafeje (2003); Van den Brink, Thomas, Bruce and Byamugisha (2006); Place (2009).
35 Economic Commission for Africa (2003); Havnevik (1997).
36 Bruce and Migot-Adholla (1994); Platteau (1996); Akuffo (2009).
37 Van den Brink, Thomas, Bruce and Byamugisha (2006); Jacoby and Minten (2007); Sender and Johnston (2004); Place (2009).

38 Moyo (2010); Mafeje (2003); Shipton and Goheen (1992).
39 Havnevik (1997), p 8.
40 Jacobs and Minten (2007), p 477.
41 Ibid; Moyo (2010).
42 Republic of Zambia (2006), p 10.
43 Ibid, p 12 (emphasis added).
44 Bruce, Jansen, Kloeck-Jenson, Knox, Subramanian and William (1998), p 206.
45 Adams, Kalabamu and White (2003), p 62; Mathuba (2003), p 8.
46 A good example is the South African Green Paper on land which was rumoured to have embraced land nationalisation, although the document has not been yet made public, mainly due to 'louder voices' from influential sectors of society.
47 Chimhowu (2006).
48 Mathuba (2003), p 8.
49 Place (2009).
50 Ibid, p 1329.
51 Platteau (1996); Demsetz (1967).
52 In South Africa, the 'Bredell Land Occupation' in 2001 was one of the highly publicised land invasions. Some of the invasions in KwaZulu-Natal since 2004 have gone on without much publicity.
53 Sihlongonyane (2003).
54 Bruce and others (2003), p 202; Mafeje (2003); SADC (2007a, 2007b).
55 Binswanger-Mkhize and Deininger (2007).
56 Wily (2000); Moyo (nd); ECA (2003).
57 Havnevik (1997).
58 Chimhowu (2006), p 17.
59 Havnevik (1997); Patnaik (2003).
60 Bruce, Jansen, Kloeck-Jensen, Knox, Subramanian and William (1998).
61 SADC (2007a), p 2.
62 Bruce, Jansen, Kloeck-Jenson, Knox, Subramanian and William (1998).
63 SADC (2007b).
64 Chimhowu (2006); Sihlongonyane (2003).
65 Kalibwani (2005); ODI (2004).
66 Recommendation to establish the regional land reform support facility was made in 2001 by the Heads of State and Government meeting. The proposal to establish the facility was approved in 2003, and the initial work to set up the facility started in 2006 with a feasibility study which was finalised in 2007. A stakeholder consultative workshop was held in 2008 to set up the facility (see SADC 2008 for details).
67 ECA (2005).
68 Cousin (2010).
69 ECA (2005); FAO (2003); Dixon, Gulliver and Gibbon (2001).
70 Baiphethi and Jacobs (2009).
71 Ibid, p 469.
72 ECA (2005).
73 Bryceson (2000).
74 ECA (2005), p 33; World Bank (2008), p 72.
75 Mafeje (2003); ECA (2005); Kalibwani (2005).
76 Lofchie (1975), cited in Kalibwani (2005), p 11. The paradox lies in the fact that while the continent is unable to produce sufficient food to meet the growing demand, production of cash crops for export markets has been increasing sharply.
77 Binswanger-Mkhize and Deininger (nd).
78 Mafeje (2003); Smith (1989).
79 Republic of Zambia (2007).
80 ODI (2004).
81 United States Agency for International Development (2009).

82 Cousin, Sadler and Evans (2008); Langholz and Kerley (2006); Luck (2003).
83 Luck (2003), p 3.
84 SADC (2007a).
85 Mafeje (2003).
86 Bruce and others (2003); Hammond, Antwi and Proverbs (2006).
87 Ntsabane (2003).
88 Polanyi (1944); Wolpe (1972).
89 Luxemburg (1913).
90 Wolpe (1972).
91 Legassick and Wolpe (1976); Hyden (1986); Smith (1989); Luxemburg (2003).
92 Amin (1972), pp 105, 114.
93 Ntsabane (2003), p 107.
94 Ibid, p 107.
95 Ibid, p 109.
96 Binswanger-Mkhize and Deininger (1995).
97 Legassick and Wolpe (1972), Amin (1972), Luxemburg (2003).
98 Platteau (1996), p 50.
99 Ibid, p 39.
100 Parson (2003).
101 Hammond, Antwi and Proverbs (2006).
102 Wily (2000).
103 Hazel and Diao (2005).
104 Thirtle, Lin and Piesse (2001); ECA (2005).
105 World Bank (2009).

Bibliography

Adams, Martin and Palmer, Robin (2007) *Independent Review of Land Issues in Eastern and Southern Africa*, Vol. 11, <http://www.oxfam.org.uk/what_we_do/issues/livelihoods/landrights/downloads/independent_review_land_issues_2004_5_vol_3_number_1_southern_africa_dec_2005_final.pdf (accessed 21 January 2010).

Adams, Martin, Kalabamu, Faustin and White, Richard (2003) 'Land Tenure Policy and Practice in Botswana: Governance Lessons for Southern Africa', *Austrian Journal of Development Studies*, 19(1): 55–74.

Adams, Martin, Sibanda, Sipho and Turner, Stephen (1999) 'Land Tenure Reforms and Rural Livelihoods in Southern Africa', *Natural Perspectives*, No. 39.

Akuffo, Kwame (2009) 'The Conception of Land Ownership in African Customary Law and Its Implications for Development', ACTS Conference Report.

Amin, Samir (1972) 'Underdevelopment and Dependency in Black Africa: Historical Origin', *Journal of Peace Research*, 9(2): 105–20.

Baiphethi, M. and Jacobs, P. (2009) 'The Contribution of Subsistence Farming to Food Security in South Africa', *Agrekon*, 48(4): 459–82.

Binswanger-Mkhize, Hans and Deininger, Klaus (nd) 'History of Land Concentration and Land Reforms', paper prepared for the workshop 'Land Redistribution in Africa: Towards a Common Vision'.

Bruce, John (1998) 'Tanzania Country Profile', in John Bruce (ed) *Country Profiles of Land Tenure: Africa, 1996* (Madison, WI: Land Tenure Center, University of Wisconsin), pp 260–69.

Bruce, J. W., Migot-Adholla, S. E. and Atherton, J. (1994) 'The Findings and their Policy Implications: Institutional Adaptation or Replacement?' in J. W. Bruce and S. E. Migot-Adholla (eds) *Searching for Land Tenure Security in Africa* (Dubuque, IA: Kendall Hunt).

Bruce, John, Jansen, Eva, Kloeck-Jenson, Scott, Knox, Anna, Subramanian, Jyoti and William, Michael (1998) 'Synthesis of Trends and Issues Raised by Land Tenure Country Profiles of Southern African Countries, 1996', in John Bruce (ed) *Country Profiles of Land Tenure: Africa, 1996* (Madison, WI: Land Tenure Center, University of Wisconsin), pp 202–08.

Bryceson, F. Deborah (1999) 'Sub-Saharan Africa Betwix and Between: Rural Livelihood Practices and Policies', Working Paper No. 43 (De-agrarianisation and Rural Employment, DARE, and Afrika-Studiecentrum, ASC), available at <http://www.asc.leidenuniv.nl/general/dare.htm> (accessed 13 May 2009).

Bryceson, Deborah (2000) 'Rural Africa at the Crossroads: Livelihood Practices and Policies', *Natural Resources Perspectives*, No. 52.

Centre for Land Economy and Rights of Women (CLEAR) (2005) *Land Policies in Sub-Saharan Africa* (Nairobi: CLEAR).

Chimhowu, Admos (2006) 'Tinkering on the Fringes? Redistributive Land Reforms and Chronic Poverty in Southern Africa' (Working Paper No. 58, Manchester: Chronic Poverty Research Centre).

Cousin, Ben (2010) 'What is a "Smallholder"? Class-analytic Perspectives on Small-scale Farming and Agrarian Reforms in South Africa' (Working Paper No. 16, Belville: PLAAS).

Cousin, Jenny, Sadler, Jon and Evans, James (2008) 'Exploring the Role of Private Wildlife Ranching as a Conservation Tool in South Africa: Stakeholder Perspectives', *Ecology and Society*, 13(2), available at <http://www.ecologyandsociety.org/vol13/iss2/art43/> (accessed 5 February 2010).

De Soto, Hernando (2000) *The Mystery of Capital: Why Capitalism Triumphs in the West and Fails Everywhere Else* (London: Transworld).

Deininger, Klaus (2003) *Land Policies for Growth and Poverty Reduction* (New York: Oxford University Press).

Deininger, Klaus and Binswanger, Hans (1999) 'The Evolution of the World Bank's Land Policy: Principles, Experiences and Future Challenges', *World Bank Research Observer*, 14(2): 247–76.

Demsetz, Harold (1967) 'Towards a Theory of Property Rights', *American Economic Review*, 57(2): 347–59.

Dixon, J., Gulliver, A. and Gibbon, D. (2001) *Farming Systems and Poverty* (Rome: Food and Agriculture Organisation; Washington, DC: World Bank).

Economic Commission for Africa (ECA) (2003) *Land Tenure Systems and Sustainable Development in Southern Africa* (Lusaka: ECA Regional Office), available at <http://www.uneca.org> (accessed 3 February 2010).

Economic Commission for Africa (ECA) (2005) *Land Tenure Systems and their Impact on Food Security and Sustainable Development in Africa* (Addis Ababa: ECA), available at <http://www.uneca.org> (accessed 3 February 2010).

FAOSTAT (2009) <http://www.faostat.org> (last update 12 October 2009, accessed 21 January 2010).

Fischer, G., Shah, M., van Velthuizen, H. and Nachtergaele, F. (2006) 'Agro-ecological Zones Assessment', *Encyclopaedia of Life Support Systems* (EOLSS) (Oxford: Institute for Applied System Analysis).

Food and Agriculture Organisation (FAO) (1999) *Land Resources Information Systems for Food Security in SADC Countries* (Proceedings of a Sub-regional Workshop, Harare: FAO, 3–5 November).

Food and Agriculture Organisation (FAO) (2003) *A Perspective on Water Control in Southern Africa: Support to Regional Investment Initiatives* (Rome: FAO).

Hammond, Felix, Antwi, Adarkwah and Proverbs, David (2006) 'The Political Economy of Sub-Saharan Africa Land Policies', *American Review of Political Economy*, 4(1–2): 19–35.

Havnevik, Kjell (1997) 'Land Question in Sub-Saharan Africa,' in Nils-Ivar Isaksson (ed) *Land Question in Sub-Saharan Africa* (Uppsala: Department of Rural Development Studies, Swedish University of Agricultural Sciences).

Hazel, P. and Diao, X. (2005) 'The Role of Agriculture and Small Farms in Economic Development' (Washington, DC: International Food Policy Research Institute, IFPRI).

Hyden, Goran (1986) 'The Anomaly of the African Peasantry', *Development and Change*, 17: 677–705.

Jacoby, H. and Minten, Bart (2007) 'Is Land Titling in Sub-Saharan Africa Cost-effective? Evidence from Madagascar', *World Bank Economic Review*, 4(3): 461–85.

Jensen, Eva (1998) 'South Africa Country Profile', in John Bruce (ed) *Country Profiles of Land Tenure: Africa, 1996* (Madison, WI: Land Tenure Center, University of Wisconsin), pp 253–60.

Kalibwani, Fred (2005) 'Food Security in Southern Africa: Current Status, Key Policy Perspectives and Key Players at Regional Level' (Background paper, Southern African Regional Poverty Network, SARPN, Overseas Development Institute, ODI, Food and Natural Resources Policy Analysis Network, FANRPAN).

Kloeck-Jenson, Scott (1998) 'Mozambique Country Profile', in John Bruce (ed) *Country Profiles of Land Tenure: Africa, 1996* (Madison, WI: Land Tenure Center, University of Wisconsin), pp 238–46.

Knox, Anna (1998) 'Malawi Country Profile', in John Bruce (ed) *Country Profiles of Land Tenure: Africa, 1996* (Madison, WI: Land Tenure Center, University of Wisconsin), pp 230–37.

Langholz, J. A. and Kerley, G. I. H. (2006) 'Combining conservation and development on private lands: an assessment of ecotourism-based private game reserves in the Eastern Cape' (Ecology Report No. 56, Port Elizabeth: Centre for African Conservation, Nelson Mandela Metropolitan University).

Legassick, M. and Wolpe, H. (1976) 'Bantustans and Capital Accumulation in South Africa', *Review of African Political Economy*, 3(7): 87–107.

Leisz, Stephen (1998) 'Madagascar Country Profile', in John Bruce (ed) *Country Profiles of Land Tenure: Africa, 1996* (Madison, WI: Land Tenure Center, University of Wisconsin), pp 223–29.

Luck, Kelly (2003) 'Farm Workers and Land Tenure Reform: The Case of Game Farming in Hope Fountain in the Eastern Cape' (Working Paper No. 58, East London: Fort Hare Institute of Social and Economic Research).

Luxemburg, Rosa (2003/1913) *The Accumulation of Capital* (New York: Routledge).

Mafeje, Archie (2003) 'The Agrarian Question: Access to Land and Peasant Response in Sub-Saharan Africa' (Civil Society and Social Movement Programme, Paper No. 6, Geneva: United Nations Research Institute for Social Development).

Malope, Patrick and Batisani, Nnyaladzi (2008) 'Land Reform that Excludes the Poor: the Case of Botswana', *Development Southern Africa*, 25(4): 383–97.

Mathuba, M. B. (2003) 'Botswana Land Policy', paper presented at the International Workshop on Land Policies in Southern Africa, Berlin, 26–27 May.

Maunder, Nick and Wiggins, Steve (2006) 'Food Security in South Africa: Changing the Trend?' Review of Lessons Learnt on Recent Responses to Chronic and Transitory Hunger and Vulnerability, Final Report (Washington, DC: IFPRI).

Michael, W. (1998) 'Angola Country Profile', in John Bruce (ed.) *Country Profiles of Land Tenure: Africa, 1996* (Madison, WI: Land Tenure Center, University of Wisconsin), pp 209–17.

Moyo, Sam (1995) *The Land Question and Land Reform in Southern Africa* (Harare: SAPES).

Moyo, Sam (2010) 'Prospects for Agrarian Reform in Southern Africa', *Opening Society Through Advocacy* (Johannesburg: Open Society Initiative for Southern Africa).

Ntsabane, Tidimare (2003) 'Comparative Analysis of Two Labour Reserves in Early 20th Century Southern Africa', *Journal of African Studies*, 17(2): 105–14.

Ntsebeza, L. (2006) *Democracy Compromised: Chiefs and the Politics of Land in South Africa* (Cape Town: HSRC Press).

Overseas Development Institute (ODI) (2004) 'Achieving Food Security in Southern Africa: Policy Issues and Options' (Synthesis Paper, Forum for Food Security in Southern Africa), <http://www.odi.org.uk/food-security-forum>.

Parson, W. (2003) *Public Policy: An Introduction to the Theory and Practice of Policy Analysis* (Northampton, MA: Edward Elgar).

Patnaik, U. (2003) 'Global Capitalism, Deflation and Agrarian Crisis in Developing Countries' (Social Policy Paper Series, Geneva: UNRISD).

Place, Frank (2009) 'Land Tenure and Agricultural Productivity in Africa: A Comparative Analysis of the Economics Literature and Recent Policy Strategies and Reforms', *World Development*, 37(8): 1326–36.

Place, Frank and Hazell, Peter (1993) 'Productivity Effects of Indigenous Land Tenure System in Sub-Saharan Africa', *American Journal of Agricultural Economics*, 75(1): 10–19.

Platteau, Jean-Philippe (1992) 'Land Reform and Structural Adjustment in Sub-Saharan Africa: Controversies and Guidelines' (Economic and Social Development Paper No. 107, Rome: Food and Agriculture Organisation).

Platteau, Jean-Philippe (1996) 'The Evolutionary Theory of Land Rights as Applied to Sub-Saharan Africa: A Critical Assessment', *Development and Change*, 27(1): 29–86.

Polanyi, Karl (1944) *The Great Transformation: The Political and Economic Origins of our Times* (Boston, MA: Beacon Press).

Republic of Zambia (2006) 'Zambia Land Policy' (Draft, Lusaka: Ministry of Lands).

Republic of Zambia (2007) *The Month: July*, vol. 52 (Lusaka: Central Statistical Office), available at <http://www.zamstats.gov.za>.

Roth, Michael (2002) 'Integrating Land Issues and Land Policy with Poverty Reduction and Rural Development in Africa' (Synthesis paper prepared for the World Bank Regional Workshop on Land Issues in Africa and the Middle East, Kampala, 29 April–2 May).

Sender, John and Johnston, Deborah (2004) 'Searching for a Weapon of Mass Production in Rural Africa: Unconvincing Arguments for Land Reform', *Journal of Agrarian Change*, 4 (1–2): 142–64.

Shipton, Parker and Goheen, Mitzi (1992) 'Understanding African Land-holding: Power and Meaning', *Journal of the International African Institute*, 62(3): 307–25.

Sihlongonyane, F. Mfanisen (2003) 'Land Occupation in South Africa' (Monitoring Paper, Land Research Action Network), available at <http://www.landaction.org> (accessed 19 March 2010).

Smith, D. Charles (1989) 'Did Colonialism Capture the Peasantry? A Case Study of the Kagera District, Tanzania' (Research Report No. 83, Uppsala: Scandinavian Institute of African Studies).

Sombroek, W. G. (1997) 'Land Resources Evaluation and the Role of Land-related Indicators', in *Land Quality and their Use in Sustainable Agriculture* (Workshop proceedings, Rome: FAO).

Southern African Development Community (SADC) (2007a) 'Establishing the SADC Land Reform Support Facility and Inception Activities, Final Report' (Gaborone: Food, Agriculture and Natural Resources Directorate, FANR).

Southern African Development Community (SADC) (2007b) 'Report of the Proceedings of a Consultative Workshop on Land Policy in Southern Africa, 29–31 August' (Windhoek: SADC).

Southern African Development Community (SADC) (2008) 'Land Reform for Poverty Reduction in Southern Africa' (Proceedings of a Multi-stakeholder Conference held in Gaborone, 18–19 June).

Subramanian, Jyoti (1998) 'Lesotho, Namibia, Swaziland, Zambia and Zimbabwe Country Profiles,' in John Bruce (ed) *Country Profiles of Land Tenure: Africa, 1996* (Madison, WI: Land Tenure Center, University of Wisconsin), pp 218–22, 247–52, 261–65, 270–75, 276–82.

Thirtle, C., Lin, L. and Piesse, J. (2001) 'The Impact of Research-led Agricultural Productivity Growth on Poverty Reduction in Africa, Asia, and Latin America' (Research Paper No. 016, London: Management Centre Research Papers, King's College).

United Republic of Tanzania (1997) *National Land Policy* (2nd edn, Dar es Salaam: Ministry of Lands and Human Settlement Development).

United States Agency for International Development (USAID) (2009) 'Southern Africa Food Security Update', September, available at <http://www.fews.net/south> (accessed 12 October 2009).

Van den Brink, Rogier, Thomas, Glen, Bruce, John and Byamugisha, Frank (2006) 'Consensus, Confusion and Controversy: Selected Land Reform in Sub-Saharan Africa' Washington, DC: World Bank), available on <http://www.worldbank.org> (accessed 13 February 2009).

Van Donge, Jan Kees (2005) 'Land Reform in Namibia: Issues of Equity and Poverty' (Land, Poverty and Public Action Policy Paper No. 8, The Hague: Institute of Social Studies).

Wily, A. Liz (2000) 'Land Tenure Reform and the Balance of Power In Eastern and Southern Africa', *Natural Reserve Perspectives*, No. 58.

Wolpe, H. (1972) 'Capitalism and Cheap Labour Power in South Africa: From Segregation to Apartheid', *Economy and Society*, 1(4): 425–56.

World Bank (2008) *World Development Report 2008: Agriculture for Development* (New York: World Bank).

World Bank (2009) *World Development Indicators 2009* (New York: World Bank).

5 Land issues before the Southern African Development Community Tribunal

A case for human rights?

*Oliver C. Ruppel**

5.1 Introduction

Over the past few decades, land issues have climbed to the top of the agenda in many African countries. These issues are a highly sensitive topic as they reflect African history, on the one hand, and are an indicator for the future development of African States and the African people on the other. The *status quo* of land distribution still shows the imprints of colonial powers that have left their indelible mark in African history over the past few centuries. This is probably why, whenever land issues are being discussed, emotions run high – more often than not culminating in violence and even cold-blooded murder.

Member States of the Southern African Development Community (SADC) have experienced the whole range of difficulties attached to land issues, with Zimbabwe being an extreme and sad example. In the latter country, a government programme of land redistribution in 2000 resulted in the invasion of largely white-owned farms, accompanied by massive violence tolerated and even encouraged by the Zimbabwean government.

Of course, such developments are of both national and international concern, especially when the issue of land distribution goes hand in hand with human rights violations – as was and is the case in Zimbabwe. Undoubtedly, the issue of land distribution needs to be addressed in a manner that rectifies colonial land distribution and other social injustices such regimes spawned. However, this should not be allowed to justify the neglect of national and international human rights standards; in particular, supranational organisations cannot turn a blind eye to States where land redistribution is undertaken in an inhuman and illegal manner. In this context, the concept of *regional integration* plays a vital role in that it strives to harmonise law and jurisprudence, also with regard to human rights.

The case of Zimbabwe has come to the attention of SADC and its judicial organ, the SADC Tribunal, and will continue to be of national and international interest in the near future. Therefore, this chapter intends to introduce SADC, the SADC Tribunal, and their relevance for the protection and promotion of human rights. One specific case (*Mike Campbell (Pvt) Ltd v The Republic of Zimbabwe*[1]) that relates to the land question and the protection of human rights will be discussed in detail. To put this case in context, the history of land distribution in

Zimbabwe will be outlined, with a special emphasis on the legal background to the land reform process that began in 2000. The most recent developments relating to the dispute will be highlighted before showing the legal, political and social consequences that sub-regional jurisdiction may unfold.

It is hoped that land-related human rights violations, such as those that occurred in Zimbabwe, will remain singular instances. Even though the land question always evokes strong passions,[2] other SADC countries have shown that inequities related to land issues can indeed be addressed in a more moderate manner to secure peace, stability, democracy, and the rule of law. Albeit far from perfect, land reform in Namibia has the potential to serve as one such example and will, therefore, be sketched for comparative reasons.

Africa has taken various steps towards enhancing the process of economic and political integration on the continent.[3] For example, several Regional Economic Communities (RECs) have been established on the continent.[4] At the Seventh Ordinary Session of the African Union's (AU's) Assembly of Heads of State and Government in Banjul, The Gambia, in July 2006, the AU officially recognised eight such communities[5] and all AU member States as being affiliated to one or more such RECs.[6] Alphabetically listed, the RECs are as follows:

- The Arab Maghreb Union (AMU)
- The Community of Sahel-Saharan States (CEN-SAD)
- The Common Market for Eastern and Southern Africa (COMESA)
- The East African Community (EAC)
- The Economic Community of Central African States (ECCAS)
- The Economic Community of West African States (ECOWAS)
- The Intergovernmental Authority on Development (IGAD), and
- The Southern African Development Community (SADC).

Even though it might seem that the protection of human rights is not within the RECs' focal range, it has been established that such rights do indeed play an important role in RECs and in the integration process in general.[7] Human rights are integrated into the RECs' legal frameworks as well as their daily practice, as many have implemented provisions in their mandate that have an impact on human rights and good governance. The reasons for integrating human rights into the structure of RECs are manifold. One is certainly that States have committed themselves to respecting human rights by virtue of their binding or non-binding obligations under specific human rights treaties, conventions or declarations on the international, regional and sub-regional level, including the Universal Declaration of Human Rights; the International Covenants on Civil and Political Rights and on Economic, Social and Cultural Rights; the Convention on the Elimination of Racial Discrimination; and the African Charter on Human and Peoples' Rights. The obligations and commitments resulting from human-rights-related legal instruments such as these are also reflected in the conceptualisation of RECs. One further aspect of incorporating human rights into the legal regimes of RECs is that such rights and good governance – the latter being 'an effective democratic form of government relying on broad public engagement (participation), accountability (control of power) and transparency (rationality)'[8] – play an essential role in economic development. The extent of good governance can be regarded as the degree to which the promise of civil, cultural, economic, political and social rights is realised. For example, human rights and good governance have an impact on the investment climate, which contributes to growth, productivity, and the creation of jobs – all essential for economic development and sustainable reductions in poverty. The furtherance of economic development and the promotion of human rights should, thus, go hand in hand. Indeed, there is no need to choose between economic development and respecting human rights: an analysis of the legal structure of RECs with regard to human rights shows that a peaceful environment which recognises and promotes human rights is regarded as a fundamental prerequisite for economic development.

The interrelationship between human rights and economic development has become closer over the past few years due to increasing international debate on the issue.[9] This interconnection is also displayed in the Zimbabwean land question.

5.2 The Southern African Development Community – SADC

SADC currently counts 15 States among its members, namely Angola, Botswana, the Democratic Republic of Congo (DRC), Lesotho, Madagascar, Malawi, Mauritius, Mozambique, Namibia, the Seychelles,[10] South Africa, Swaziland, Tanzania, Zambia, and Zimbabwe. SADC[11] was established in Windhoek in 1992 as the successor organisation to the Southern African Development Co-ordination Conference (SADCC), which was founded in 1980. SADC was established by signature of its constitutive legal instrument, the SADC Treaty. SADC envisages:[12]

> ... a common future, a future in a regional community that will ensure economic well-being, improvement of the standards of living and quality of life, freedom and social justice and peace and security for the peoples of southern Africa. This shared vision is anchored on the common values and principles and the historical and cultural affinities that exist between the peoples of southern Africa.

The Regional Indicative Strategic Development Plan (RISDP) approved by the SADC Summit in 2003, has defined the following ambitious targets for regional integration within SADC:

- A Free Trade Area by 2008,[13]
- Completion of negotiations of the SADC Customs Union by 2010,
- Completion of negotiations of the SADC Common Market by 2015,
- SADC Monetary Union and SADC Central Bank by 2016, and
- Launch of a regional currency by 2018.

SADC's overall objectives include the achievement of development and economic growth; the alleviation of poverty; the enhancement of the standard and quality of life; support of the socially disadvantaged through regional integration; the evolution of common political values, systems and institutions; the promotion and defence of peace and security; and achieving the sustainable utilisation of natural resources and effective protection of the environment.[14]

5.3 Human rights protection within SADC

It might appear that the promotion and protection of human rights are not SADC's top priority as an organisation that furthers socio-economic co-operation and integration as well as collaboration in respect of politics and security among its 15 southern African member States. However, the protection of human rights plays an essential role in economic development as it has an impact on the investment climate, which in turn contributes to growth, productivity and employment creation, all being essential for sustainable reductions in poverty.

A ministerial workshop in 1994 called for the adoption of a SADC Human Rights Commission as well as for a SADC Bill of Rights. In 1996, a SADC Human Rights Charter was drafted, albeit by non-governmental organisations (NGOs) of several SADC member States. In the course of establishing the SADC Tribunal in 1997, a panel of legal experts[15] considered the possibility of separate human rights instruments such as a Protocol of Human Rights or a separate Southern African Convention on Human Rights. None of these proposals was realised, however.[16] Nonetheless, many human-rights-related provisions can be found within SADC's legal framework.

The SADC Treaty itself refers to *regional integration* and *human rights* directly or indirectly at several stages. In its Preamble, the Treaty determines, *inter alia*, to ensure, through common action, the progress and well-being of the people of southern Africa, and recognises the need to involve the people of the SADC region centrally in the process of development and integration, particularly through guaranteeing democratic rights, and observing human rights and the rule of law. The Preamble's contents are given effect within the subsequent provisions of the SADC Treaty. Chapter 3, for example, which deals with the Treaty's principles, objectives, the common agenda, and general undertakings, provides that SADC and its member States are to act in accordance with the principles of human rights, democracy and the rule of law.[17] Moreover, the objectives of SADC[18] relate to human rights issues in one way or another. For instance, the objective of alleviating and eventually eradicating poverty contributes towards ensuring, *inter alia*, a decent standard of living, adequate nutrition, health care and education – all these being human rights.[19] Other SADC objectives such as the maintenance of democracy, peace, security and stability refer to human rights, as do the sustainable utilisation of natural resources and effective protection of the environment – known as *third-generation* human rights.[20]

Besides the aforementioned provisions and objectives, the SADC legal system offers human rights protection in many legal instruments other than the SADC

Treaty. One category of legal documents constitutes the SADC Protocols. The Protocols are instruments by means of which the SADC Treaty is implemented; they have the same legal force as the Treaty itself. A Protocol comes into force after two-thirds of SADC member States have ratified it. A Protocol legally binds its signatories after ratification. It has been argued that, because there is no particular SADC Protocol on human rights, such issues cannot be brought to the attention of the Tribunal.[21] However, most SADC Protocols[22] are either directly or indirectly relevant to human rights and, in accordance with Article 4(c) of the SADC Treaty, the Tribunal has made it clear that it has jurisdiction in respect of any dispute concerning human rights, democracy and the rule of law.[23] Notably, each of these instruments gives guidance to the various SADC institutions within the manifold decision-making processes. In the legal sense, however, only provisions of a binding nature can be enforced.

5.4 The SADC Tribunal and its mandate

5.4.1 The Tribunal

The SADC Tribunal is the judicial institution within SADC. The establishment of the Tribunal was a major event in SADC's history as an organisation as well as in the development of its law and jurisprudence. The Tribunal was established in 1992 by Article 9 of the SADC Treaty as a SADC institution. The legal provisions governing the SADC Tribunal are contained in the SADC Protocol on the Tribunal and the Rules of Procedure thereof (the *Protocol*), which entered into force in 2001. The Protocol comprises 39 Articles[24] and, among other things, establishes the Tribunal and clarifies its functions. According to Article 23 of the Protocol, the Rules of Procedure (the *Rules*) form an integral part of the Protocol. These Rules comprise 90 regulations governing, *inter alia*, the constitution and functions of the Tribunal; representation before the Tribunal; written, oral and special proceedings; and decisions.

Article 16(3) of the SADC Treaty and Article 4 of the SADC Protocol provide for the appointment of judges. Ten judges are appointed for five years renewable, by the common accord of the SADC member States' governments. For obvious practical reasons, the number of judges cannot equal that of the member States. However, Article 3(5) of the Protocol provides that, if it eventually becomes apparent that there is a need for an increase in the ten judges initially chosen, the Council of Ministers may increase the number if the Tribunal so proposes. Once the ten judges have been appointed, the Council has to designate five as regular members who have to sit regularly. The remaining five constitute a pool from which the President may invite a member to sit on the Tribunal whenever a regular member of the Tribunal is temporarily absent or otherwise unable to carry out his or her functions.[25] The Tribunal is to be comprised of three members at all times: this constitutes an ordinary sitting. In cases where the Tribunal decides to constitute a full bench, the members should be five in number.[26]

The Tribunal is not permitted to include more than one national from the same member State.[27] At most, a judge may only serve for two consecutive terms, after which he or she ceases to qualify for holding office.[28]

Article 6(1) of the Protocol provides, amongst other things, that–

> … of the Members initially appointed, the terms of the two (2) of the regular and two (2) of the additional Members shall expire at the end of three (3) years. The Members whose term is to expire at the end of three (3) years shall be chosen by a lot to be drawn by the Executive Secretary immediately after the first appointment.

It is submitted that the above provision was included in order to ensure a certain measure of continuity. Two-fifths of the court – i.e. four judges – are elected every three years, while the other three-fifths remain until their five-year terms expire.[29]

Member States have great latitude in choosing who to nominate for the Tribunal. All States parties to the Treaty have the right to propose a candidate. The only limitation is that such candidates should qualify for appointment to the highest offices in their respective States, or are jurists of recognised competence.[30]

The Summit of Heads of State or Government, which is the Supreme Policy Institution of SADC pursuant to Article 4(4) of the Protocol on the Tribunal, appointed the first members of the Tribunal during its Summit in Gaborone, Botswana, on 18 August 2005. The inauguration of the Tribunal and the swearing in of its members took place on 18 November 2005 in Windhoek, Namibia. The Council also designated Windhoek as the Seat of the Tribunal. Article 22 of the Protocol on the Tribunal provides that its working languages are to be English, French and Portuguese. The Tribunal began hearing cases in 2007.

5.4.2 Jurisdiction

The Tribunal was primarily set up to resolve disputes arising from closer economic and political union, rather than human rights.[31] However, the Tribunal has demonstrated that it can also be called upon to consider the human rights implications of economic policies and programmes. The legal provisions governing the Tribunal's jurisdiction are Article 16 of the SADC Treaty and Articles 14–20 of the Protocol. Article 16(1) of the SADC Treaty provides for the following primary mandate:

> The Tribunal shall be constituted to ensure adherence to and the proper interpretation of the provisions of this Treaty and subsidiary instruments and to adjudicate upon such disputes as may be referred to it.

Article 14 of the Protocol provides for the subject-matter jurisdiction (*ratione materiae*) of the Tribunal, stating that the latter has jurisdiction over all disputes and all applications referred to it in accordance with the Treaty and the Protocol which relates to the interpretation and application of the Treaty; the interpretation and application or validity of the Protocols and subsidiary instruments adopted within SADC as well as acts of community institutions; and all matters specifically provided for in any other agreements that member States may conclude among themselves or within SADC and which confer jurisdiction on the Tribunal.[32]

According to Article 15(2) of the Protocol, the Tribunal has the mandate to adjudicate disputes between States, and between natural or legal persons and States. Thus, one prerequisite for an application to the Tribunal is that the dispute at hand involves the State's obligations under community law. Only disputes between natural or legal persons do not fall under the jurisdiction of the Tribunal.[33] The Protocol further grants the Tribunal jurisdiction over all matters provided for in any other agreements that member States may conclude among themselves or within the community and that confer jurisdiction to the Tribunal. Articles 18 and 19 of the Protocol provide that the Tribunal has exclusive jurisdiction in disputes between organs of the community or between community personnel and the community.[34] Apart from jurisdiction in contentious proceedings, according to Article 20 of the Protocol the Tribunal also has an advisory jurisdiction at the request of the Summit or the Council of Ministers.

One further prerequisite for bringing an application to the Tribunal is that the applicant must have exhausted all available remedies under domestic jurisdiction.[35] The rule of exhaustion of local remedies is not peculiar to the SADC Tribunal: one will find a similar clause in most instruments pertaining to supranational legal bodies.[36]

The Tribunal's admissibility stage, according to Article 15(2), requires litigants to have exhausted local remedies or to be unable to proceed under domestic jurisdiction. The latter clause refers to instances in which domestic remedies are unduly prolonged, ineffective or unavailable. A failure to exhaust local remedies will, therefore, not constitute a bar to a claim if it is clearly established that, in the circumstances of the case, an appeal to a higher municipal legal body would have had no effect. Nor is a claimant against another State required to exhaust justice in that State where there is no justice to exhaust. Where the local remedies are futile or provide no reasonable possibility of effective redress, there is also no need to attempt to exhaust them.[37] As a rule, it is for the applicant (claimant) to prove that there are no effective remedies to which recourse can be had; however, no such proof is required if legislation exists which, on the face of it, deprives the private claimants of a remedy.[38] It is contended that the requirement of exhaustion of local remedies leads one to conclude that the SADC Tribunal can be considered as a *final court of appeal* rather than a court of first instance.

The Protocol does not explicitly require that an applicant demonstrate a vested interest in the matter brought before the Tribunal. However, the question whether the Tribunal will also recognise and apply public complaint, the so-called *actio popularis*, has not yet plagued this SADC body, but it could become important in the long run.

5.4.3 Community law

The core function of the Tribunal is to ensure adherence to law within SADC in the application and interpretation of the SADC Treaty, and to adjudicate disputes that fall under the Tribunal's jurisdiction. Unlike the EAC Treaty law,[39] the SADC Treaty law contains no provisions dealing with the relationship between community law and domestic law. In addressing this issue, the SADC Tribunal can, however, resort to Article 21 of its Protocol, which requires the Tribunal to apply the SADC Treaty, its Protocols and all subsidiary instruments adopted by the Summit, by the Council, or by any other institution or organ of the community pursuant to the Treaty or Protocols. While the Tribunal has the mandate to develop its own jurisprudence, it is also obliged to give due regard to applicable treaties, the general principles and rules of public international law, and any rules and principles of the law applicable in member States. With regard to the regional integration process, Article 21 reflects a clear desire to create a supranational law applicable to community member States. It is assumed that the Tribunal can also apply general principles and rules of public international law and any rules and principles of the law of its member States, including jurisprudence of other regional or international courts or tribunals.

A corollary to the issue of applicable law is the interrelationship between (SADC) community laws and municipal laws. Put another way, the question is what law will prevail in the event of a conflict or inconsistency between community law and member States' domestic laws. The answer also depends on the various national constitutions and the status (legal force) of conventional law in member States, as well as on the relationship between domestic laws and conventional law in particular (e.g. whether the relationship is determined by a monist or dualist approach to law[40]). In any case, the Tribunal has made it very clear that a SADC member State cannot rely on its national law if it is attempting to avoid its legal obligations under the Treaty.[41]

5.4.4 Judicial independence and impartiality

For the SADC Tribunal to effectively fulfil its functions, it is essential that the culture of judicial independence is sustained by procedures for appointment which are fair, transparent and reasonable.[42] Certainly, a proper and concrete assessment of the judicial independence and impartiality of the SADC Tribunal is not easy without reference to its jurisprudence. This, however, is not possible given that the Tribunal is still in its infancy. Several provisions have been included in the Protocol to guarantee the independence and impartiality of the judges. Before taking up their duties, all members of the Tribunal are required to make a solemn declaration in open session that they will exercise their powers independently, impartially and conscientiously.[43] The implication and essence of this solemn declaration is that, in the exercise of its judicial function entrusted to it alone by the SADC Treaty and the Protocol, the Tribunal should only act on the basis of the law, independent of any outside influence or intervention whatsoever.

It should be emphasised that, once elected, a member of the Tribunal is neither a delegate of the government of his/her own country nor of any other State. Unlike most other organs of international organisations, the Tribunal is not composed of representatives of various governments. Members of the Tribunal reach their decisions with complete independence and impartiality. However, in some way or other, they do in fact represent their respective legal systems: the judges' professional experience and background obviously have a way of showing in their decisions. This is in no way a weakness, however; in fact, this has the valuable consequence that the Tribunal operates as a comparative law jurisdiction, merging the experience and understanding of lawyers skilled in a wide range of different legal (civil and common law) systems and, indeed, families of law.

In order to guarantee judicial independence, no member of the court can be dismissed unless it is done in accordance with the rules.[44] Members of the Tribunal may not hold any political or administrative office in the service of a State, community, or any other organisation.[45] This provision seeks to protect the judges from the influences of member States and other institutions. In addition, it fosters the general public's confidence in the Tribunal as a separate and independent judicial entity.

While the European Court of Justice (ECJ) forbids its judges from engaging in any occupation, whether gainful or not, the judges of the SADC Tribunal, for practical reasons, are employed on a part-time basis and can, therefore, hold other judicial offices.[46] With regard to the well-known principle of *nemo judex sua causa est*, Article 9(2) of the Protocol stipulates that no member of the Tribunal may participate in the decision of any case (dispute) in which he was previously involved.[47]

Another feature relevant to the independence of the Tribunal is the fixed five-year renewable term of office of its judges. It has been argued that the possibility of renewal of their appointment could encourage judges to try to please their governments in order to get another renewal nomination.[48] While this might pose a problem with the ECJ, where each member State nominates one candidate, this does not apply to the SADC Tribunal. The selection process is such that not all member States can have a candidate sitting on the bench. The result is that the Summit is forced to consider the qualifications of the candidates recommended by the Council in order to make their choice. In the end, the judge on the bench will not feel compelled to please his/her government to ensure another term in office. Furthermore, when engaged in the business of the Tribunal, the judges enjoy privileges and immunities to ensure that their decisions are not tainted with the fear of being held accountable at the end of their tenure.[49]

5.4.5 Effect, review and enforcement of judicial decisions

Article 16(5) of the SADC Treaty and Article 24(3) of the Protocol clearly state that the decisions of the Tribunal are final and binding. At this stage, however, one major challenge for the SADC Tribunal lies with the enforcement of its judgments and non-compliance by member States. As to the finality of decisions, the aforementioned provisions imply that there is no instance of appeal within the legal regime of SADC to review a decision or ruling issued by the Tribunal. Article 26 of the Protocol merely provides as follows:

> An application for review of a decision may be made to the Tribunal if it is based upon the discovery of some fact which by its nature might have had a decisive influence on the decision if it had been known to the Tribunal at the time the decision was given, but which fact at the time was unknown to both the Tribunal and the party making the application.

Were the Tribunal's decisions not binding, i.e. enforceable and executable by member States, the whole purpose becomes questionable. The primary responsibility to enforce and execute the SADC Tribunal's decisions and rulings lies with member States to the SADC Treaty and the Protocol. This is buttressed by the well-rooted principle of *pacta sunt servanda* under public international law, i.e. obligations undertaken in international or regional treaties or conventions have to be honoured in good faith. Article 32 of the Protocol specifically provides for the enforcement of the Tribunal's decisions.[50] According to this provision, the enforcement and execution of judgments are governed by the law and rules of civil procedure for the registration and enforcement of foreign judgments in force in the territory of the State in which the judgment is to be enforced. Furthermore, member States are obliged to take all measures necessary to ensure the decisions of the Tribunal are executed. In the event that a State fails to comply with a decision, such failure can be referred to the Tribunal by any party concerned; and if the Tribunal is satisfied that such failure of compliance exists, the latter is to be reported to the SADC Summit[51] to take appropriate action. These are the theoretical steps in terms of enforcing the Tribunal's decisions. However, these steps may be considered inadequate and ambiguous because they are ineffective: member States can escape their international obligations by invoking rulings of domestic courts in their favour.[52]

5.4.6 The role of the Summit

Whether or not the SADC dispute resolution mechanism is a toothless tiger is ultimately for the SADC Summit to decide. According to Article 33(1) and (2) of the SADC Treaty, the Summit is the institution within SADC that has to decide on a case-by-case basis whether and which sanctions are to be imposed against a member State where a State fails to comply with its obligations. Article 33 does not, however, mention any possible sanctions that may be imposed. It would seem appropriate to include a provision containing at least a non-exhaustive list of possible coercive measures. In the style of the United Nations legal framework, such a list could include complete or partial interruption of economic relations; interruption of rail, sea, air, postal, telegraphic, radio, and other means of communication; and the severance of diplomatic relations.[53] Further possible measures could be the freezing of any assets belonging to the defaulting State that are to be found in the territory of the State which is the successful party, as well as in that of third States, or the suspension of voting rights or other rights and privileges.[54]

It is incumbent upon the SADC Summit to ensure respect for its legal instruments. Clearly, the Council's activities in this regard are closely connected to political and economic issues, and diplomacy plays a significant role in these cases[55] and it is hoped that the SADC Summit will in current and future cases be progressive enough to take appropriate initiatives where necessary in order to guarantee an effective mechanism to ensure stability in the SADC region.

5.5 The Zimbabwean land question

Since its independence in 1980 and until 2000, Zimbabwe was a relatively peaceful, stable and generally tolerant country.[56] However, since 2000, in the Zimbabwe government's redress of unequal land situation, white farmers found – and are still finding – themselves being victims of farm invasions and farm seizures that mirror the land seizures of the colonial period. Under the Lancaster House Constitution, the Zimbabwean government was constrained to protect white property ownership through the 'willing seller – willing buyer' principle, and compensation for land had to be paid in foreign currency. In those days, the only underutilised land was permitted to be expropriated, subject to compensation at full market value. After the expiry of the Lancaster House guarantees in 1990, the Zimbabwean government was prepared to make its land reform programme more effective. Thus, the Land Acquisition Act 1992 was promulgated and various amendments were made to the Constitution to allow for the acquisition of land by government for resettlement purposes. This Act empowered the President of Zimbabwe to acquire any land where it was reasonably necessary for purposes set out in it. The process led to a new elite of black farmers, with little or no improved access to land for the majority of the population.[57]

At the beginning of 2000, the ruling ZANU-PF[58] party found its popularity declining rapidly due to a deteriorating economic situation which, in turn, was due largely to the government's reckless economic policies and rampant corruption. As a result, the party suffered a resounding defeat in the constitutional referendum held on 11 and 12 February 2000. The referendum defeat triggered a spate of violent farm occupations. From mid-March 2000 onwards, hundreds of commercial farms were invaded by "war veterans", i.e. people who were alleged to be veterans of Zimbabwe's liberation war, but who were in fact mostly unemployed youths not old enough to have been part of that war. Indeed, these farm invasions were not a spontaneous demonstration by landless people against inequitable land distribution in Zimbabwe. There is overwhelming evidence that high-ranking ZANU-PF members were actively involved in implementing the invasions, together with intelligence and army personnel, and that they formed part of a political strategy to combat the growing influence of the opposition MDC[59] party and to win back rural support by using the promise of land resettlement and crude violence.[60]

The 2000 referendum defeat led to the radical process of land occupation by means of governmental exploitation of the racial divide in land distribution. The historical incidents of the fight for political freedom and the aggravating rhetoric of 'they stole our land'[61] was paired with the peasant's legitimate need for land and the failure of the British government and other donors to live up to their compensation promises.[62] Justified under nationalist dogma, the Zimbabwean government from then on supported violent farm invasions that occurred in negligent (if not intentional) violation of the law. Farm invasions were accompanied by the compulsory acquisition of commercial farms, which was increasingly unfair and arbitrary. The land programme itself has been accompanied by considerable violence, leading to the unlawful eviction of farmers and their workers. Approximately 95 per cent of commercial farms have been seized or are in the process of being seized. Moreover, as stated previously, many beneficiaries of the land programme are not landless peasants but Ministers, other senior government officials, and prominent supporters of the ruling party.[63]

Section 23 of the Constitution of Zimbabwe states as follows:

> No law shall make any provision that is discriminatory either of itself or in its effect; and no person shall be treated in a discriminatory manner by any person acting by virtue of any written law or in the performance of the functions of any public office or any public authority.

In 2005, however, the Constitution was amended. The Constitutional Amendment (No. 17) Act 2005 allows the government to seize or expropriate farmland without compensation, and it bars courts from adjudicating over legal challenges filed by dispossessed and aggrieved farmers. Section 2(2) of the Amendment Act provides that –

> ... all agricultural land – [a description is given here of such agricultural land identified by the government] ... is acquired by and vested in the State with full title therein ... ; and ... no compensation shall be payable for land referred to in Paragraph (a) except for any improvements effected on such land before it was acquired.

The practical implications of the Amendment Act resulted in farm seizures, where the majority of the approximately 4,000 white farmers were forcibly ejected from their properties with no compensation being paid for the land. The only compensation the government paid was for developments on the land such as dams, farm buildings and other improvements.

Apparently, at this stage, Zimbabwean land reform programme has gone into reverse gear. It has been revealed that some beneficiaries of the land reform programme – including traditional and political leaders – are reengaging white farmers as farm managers or even leasing out their farms to the farms' white former owners. Zimbabwe's President Robert Mugabe himself has openly criticised new farmers for taking land when they knew they could not farm.[64] Thus, in

March 2010, Zimbabwean Government has confirmed that it will re-demarcate land allocated to farmers who are failing to attain optimum production owing to resource constraints by way of rationalising the allocations so that people have pieces of land they can fully use.[65]

5.6 *Mike Campbell (Pvt) Ltd v The Republic of Zimbabwe*

On 11 October 2007, Mike Campbell (Pvt) Ltd,[66] a Zimbabwean-registered company, instituted a case with the SADC Tribunal to challenge human rights violations by the expropriation of agricultural land in Zimbabwe by that country's government.[67] Mike Campbell had purchased the farm in question on the open market in 1980 – after Zimbabwe's Independence. In 1997, the property was listed for acquisition as part of the government's land reform programme.

In July 2001, the government made an initial attempt to seize the Campbell farm without paying compensation. At first, the High Court of Zimbabwe declared such acquisitions to be invalid.[68] However, in September and October 2001, the property was invaded by so-called war veterans – ZANU-PF's informal paramilitary wing – for the first time. The aforementioned Amendment Act eliminating judicial recourse or remedy for farmers who wished to object to the acquisition of their farms came into effect on 14 September 2005. In 2006, Campbell opposed an attempt to allocate the farm to the former Minister for Land, Land Reform and Resettlement, Nathan Shamuyarira. On 15 May 2006, Campbell instituted legal proceedings in the Supreme Court of Zimbabwe in order to halt his eviction from the farm by way of challenging the constitutional validity of the Amendment Act. As the Supreme Court did not rule on the matter within a reasonable period of time, on 11 October 2007, the applicants approached the SADC Tribunal. Thus, the *Campbell* case became a benchmark of the SADC Tribunal's key role in the integration of legal and institutional systems in its region of jurisdiction.

5.6.1 The 2007 interim order

In 2007, an application was brought before the SADC Tribunal in terms of Article 28 of the SADC Protocol for an interim measure to prohibit the Zimbabwean government from evicting Mike Campbell (Pvt) Ltd and others from the land in question until the main case had been finalised.

In one of the Tribunal's first hearings, the issue of non-exhaustion of local remedies was raised. In this context it is worth noting that the new section 16B of the Zimbabwean Constitution, which is the creation of the said Amendment Act, deprives affected landowners of their right to seek remedy within domestic courts.[69] In fact, when the applicants in this case approached the SADC Tribunal seeking an interim order in terms of Article 28 of the Protocol as read with Rule 61(2) and (5) of its Rules of Procedure, the respondent State argued that the application had not been properly placed before the Tribunal in that the applicants had not exhausted local remedies in terms of Article 15(2) of the Protocol.[70]

When the matter was filed with the Tribunal in October 2007, the Supreme Court of Zimbabwe, sitting as a Constitutional Court, was still dealing with the constitutional challenge of section 16B of the Zimbabwean Constitution brought by the same applicants as in the *Campbell* case.[71] The relief being sought from the highest court in Zimbabwe was similar to that which the applicants sought from the SADC Tribunal. However, the Tribunal held as follows:

> Referring to the issue of failure to exhaust local remedies by applicants, we are of the view that the issue is not of relevance to the present application but that it may only be raised in the main case. It may not be raised in the present case in which applicants are seeking an interim measure of protection pending the final determination of the matter.[72]

The claimant argued that the Zimbabwean land acquisition process was racist and illegal by virtue of Article 6 of the SADC Treaty and the African Union Charter, both of which outlaw arbitrary and racially motivated government action. Article 4 of the SADC Treaty requires SADC and its member States to, among other things, act in accordance with the principles of human rights, democracy, and the rule of law, as well as with the principles of equity, balance and mutual benefit, and the peaceful settlement of disputes. According to Article 6(2) of the SADC Treaty, 'SADC and Member States shall not discriminate against any person on grounds of gender, religion, political views, race, ethnic origin, culture or disability'.

It was put forward by Campbell that the constitutional amendments behind the farm seizures were contrary to SADC statutes, and that the Supreme Court of Zimbabwe had failed to rule on an application by Campbell and 74 other Zimbabwean white commercial farmers to have the race-based acquisition declared unlawful.[73]

On 13 December 2007, the SADC Tribunal ruled that Campbell should remain on his expropriated farm until the dispute in the main case had been resolved by the Tribunal:

> The Tribunal grants the application pending the determination of the main case and orders that the Republic of Zimbabwe shall take no steps, or permit no steps to be taken, directly or indirectly, whether by its agents or by its orders, to evict from or interfere with the peaceful residence on and beneficial use of the farm known as Mount Campbell in the Chetugu District in Zimbabwe, by Mike Campbell (Pvt) Ltd and William M Campbell, their employees and the families of such employees and of William Michael Campbell.[74]

On 22 January 2008, the Zimbabwean Supreme Court dismissed the application by the white commercial farmers challenging the forcible seizure and expropriation of their lands without compensation. The court ruled that 'by a fundamental law, the legislature has unquestionably said that such an acquisition shall not be challenged in any court of law. There cannot be any clearer language by which the jurisdiction of the courts is excluded'.[75] The court further ruled that the 2005 Constitutional Amendment was valid and, therefore, constitutional in that its purpose was to acquire the land for public use.

On 23 January 2008, the Zimbabwean government announced that it would seize the farm. Land Reform Minister Dydimus Mutasa said the farm would be handed over to a black owner as part of State land reforms, and in accordance with the ruling by the Zimbabwean Supreme Court.[76]

5.6.2 The 2008 urgent application and application for intervention

The main hearing before the SADC Tribunal originally scheduled for 28 May 2008 was postponed until 16 July 2008. In the meantime, the claimant, Campbell, and members of his family were brutally beaten up on their farm in Zimbabwe and allegedly forced to sign a paper declaring that they would withdraw the case from the SADC Tribunal.[77] On 18 July 2008, applicants and other interveners in the *Campbell* case made an urgent application to the Tribunal seeking a declaration to the effect that the respondent State was in breach and contempt of the Tribunal's orders. After hearing the urgent application, the Tribunal found that the respondent State was indeed in contempt of its orders. Consequently, and in terms of Article 32(5) of the Protocol, the Tribunal decided to report the matter to the Summit for the latter to take appropriate action.

Meanwhile, a significant number of recently resettled indigenous farmers had filed an application seeking an order to allow them to intervene in the main case.[78] This more recent application was, however, dismissed with costs. In the Tribunal's view, the latter applicants/interveners could not be allowed to intervene in the main case for the following reasons: the application had been filed out of time and no good reason had been advanced to justify the inordinate delays;[79] the alleged dispute in the present application was between present applicants and applicants in the main case (*Campbell* case), and not between persons (either natural or juristic) and a State;[80] and the applicants had failed to demonstrate any legal right or interests which were likely to be prejudiced or affected by the Tribunal's decision in the *Campbell* case.[81]

5.6.3 The 2008 final ruling

The hearing of the *Campbell* case was finalised on 28 November 2008. The SADC Tribunal in its final decision ruled in favour of the applicants Mike and William Campbell and 77 other white commercial farmers.[82] In conclusion, the Tribunal held that the Republic of Zimbabwe was in breach of its obligations under Articles 4(c) and 6(2) of the SADC Treaty and that the applicants had been denied access to the courts in Zimbabwe;[83] the applicants had been discriminated against on the ground of race;[84] and fair compensation had to be paid to the applicants for their lands compulsorily acquired by the Republic of Zimbabwe.

The Tribunal further directed the Republic of Zimbabwe to take all necessary measures to protect the possession, occupation and ownership of the lands of those applicants who had not yet been evicted from their lands, and to pay fair compensation to those who had already been evicted. The ruling is considered to be a landmark decision which will, without any doubt, influence the legal landscape in the SADC region.[85]

5.6.4 The 2009 urgent application

Despite the rule that the Tribunal's decisions are final and binding,[86] at the beginning of 2009 the Zimbabwean government announced that it would not accept the Tribunal's judgment in the *Campbell* case.[87] Subsequently, the farm of Michael Campbell, who had won the case at the SADC Tribunal, was invaded.[88] This raised the question of how the Tribunal's judgments were to be enforced. Sanctions for non-compliance may be imposed by the Summit, according to Article 33 of the SADC Treaty, and are determined on a case-by-case basis. However, no specific sanction is outlined for non-compliance with judgments issued by the Tribunal.[89] The Tribunal itself can only refer cases of non-compliance to the Summit for the latter to take appropriate steps.

On 7 May 2009, an urgent application was filed with the Tribunal, seeking, in substance, a declaration to the effect that the respondent was in breach and contempt of the Tribunal's decision of 28 November 2008 in the *Campbell* matter. In its decision on 5 June 2009,[90] the Tribunal noted 'that the respondent has not taken part in the proceedings since, as learned Counsel for the respondent has put it, he lacks instructions from the respondent'. The Tribunal further held that 'the applicants have adduced enough material to show that the existence of a failure on the part of the respondent and its agents to comply with the decision of the Tribunal has been established'. In this regard, the Tribunal referred, among other things, to the Deputy Attorney-General's letter addressed to Messrs Gollop and Blank, Legal Practitioners, dated 18 December 2008, which states that ' … the policy position taken by the Government to the judgment handed down by the SADC Tribunal on the 28th November, 2008 is that all prosecutions of defaulting farmers under the provisions of the Gazetted Lands (Consequential Provisions) Act should now be resumed'; to the speech delivered on 12 January 2009 in Bulawayo, Zimbabwe, by the Deputy Chief Justice at the opening of the 2009 legal year, in the course of which speech he stated, among other things, that the Tribunal lacked jurisdiction to hear and determine the *Campbell* case; and to the fact that President Robert Mugabe, in the course of his birthday celebrations, qualified the Tribunal's decision as 'nonsense' and 'of no consequence'.[91]

The Tribunal, presided over by the newly appointed Justice Ariranga Govindasamy Pillay,[92] the former Chief Justice of Mauritius, concluded that all of the above statements had been followed by invasion of the applicants' lands, and their intimidation and prosecution. Consequently, pursuant to Article 32(5) of the Protocol, the Tribunal decided to report its finding to the Summit for the latter to take appropriate action.[93] To date, Zimbabwe has not been censured by the Summit over its controversial land reform programme.

5.6.5 Aftermaths and current legal developments

It has been demonstrated, that the issue of land reform in Zimbabwe has been subject to the SADC Tribunal's jurisdiction. The Tribunal has declared that Amendment 17 is in breach of Article 4(c) and 6(2)[94] of the SADC Treaty. However, the issue is far from being closed as will briefly be outlined in the following. Despite the Tribunal's rulings in the *Campbell* case, seizures of white-owned farms have continued. The Campbell farm has been robbed on numerous occasions and in August and September 2009, the homesteads of Mike Campbell and his son-in-law Ben Freeth, respectively, were destroyed by fire.[95]

Despite Zimbabwe's refusal to adhere to the Tribunal's ruling, white farmers have continued to take all necessary legal steps to enforce it. An application to have the ruling registered in Zimbabwe as a prerequisite for enforcement on a national level was dismissed by Judge Barack Patel of the Zimbabwean High Court. He argued that the decisions were not registrable or enforceable in terms of Chapter 8:02 of the Civil Matters (Mutual Assistance) Act, which contains the relevant statutory provisions presently in force in Zimbabwe for the registration of foreign civil judgments, as 'the Tribunal had not been specifically designated under the Act'.[96] Furthermore, registration and consequent enforcement of the Tribunal's judgment would be fundamentally contrary to the Zimbabwean Constitution and public policy, and that, compared with the number of applicants before the Tribunal, a much greater number of Zimbabweans shared –

> … the legitimate expectations that the Government will effectively implement the land reform programme and fulfil their aspirations thereunder. Given these countervailing expectations, public policy as informed by basic utilitarian precept would dictate that the greater public good must prevail.[97]

On 25 February 2010, the North Gauteng High Court in Pretoria, with respect to the same matter, however, ordered that the rulings by the Tribunal delivered on 28 November 2008 and 5 June 2009 against the seizure of farms in Zimbabwe were declared to be registered, i.e. recognised and enforceable in terms of Article 32 of the Protocol on the SADC Tribunal by the High Court of South Africa.[98] The latter order will obviously put severe political pressure on both the governments of South Africa and Zimbabwe as it opens the door to the seizure of Zimbabwean government assets. Zimbabwe's farmers intend to seize Zimbabwean property in South Africa[99] to recover their legal costs, which constitutes a precedent as such.[100] As the Zimbabwean government had not contested in the aforementioned High Court ruling, there seems no way for that government to appeal against the order. On 26 November 2009, the same High Court had already made an order in terms of which the South African government undertook to respect and honour the judgments by the Tribunal in favour of commercial farmers in Zimbabwe, and to uphold the rights and remedies of victims of Zimbabwe's unlawful land expropriation exercise.

On 12 February 2010, Zimbabwean farmers who had lost their farms, the Zimbabwe Commercial Farmers' Union and the Southern African Commercial

Farmers' Union instituted an urgent legal action at the SADC Tribunal claiming that the Zimbabwean government was in continued breach, defiance and contempt of the SADC Treaty and of the Tribunal's rulings. The applicants seek that the Zimbabwean Government be referred to the SADC Summit to be held in August 2010 for possible suspension or expulsion from SADC. At the time of writing,[101] the judgment for this application was still outstanding. Whatever the case may be, one thing has to be pointed out very clearly: only if the SADC Summit stands behind the decision of its Tribunal will the latter be in the position to develop legally relevant jurisprudence halting ongoing human rights violations in the region. Thus, SADC has a number of options,[102] namely to:

- ignore human rights issues, leaving it to the domestic or regional legal system to redress violations,
- use the limited human rights mandate in its Treaty as a basis to cultivate a better human rights environment in the member States concerned,
- adopt own sub-regional charters on human rights, or
- fully incorporate the African Charter on Human and Peoples' Rights into the sub-regional treaty.

5.7 A comparative perspective: land reform in Namibia

For good reason, the land question in Namibia – as in other African countries – has been subject to debate since the country gained Independence in 1990.[103] The Republic of Namibia, as the country is known today, was declared a German Protectorate in 1884 and a Crown Colony in 1890; thereafter it variously became known as *Deutsch-Südwestafrika*, *South West Africa*, *South West Africa/Namibia*, and *Namibia*. The territory remained a German colony until 1915, when it was occupied by South African forces. In 1920, it was declared a protectorate, i.e. a mandated territory under the protection of South Africa in terms of the Treaty of Versailles. Significant local and international resistance to South Africa's subsequent colonial domination of the country emerged in the late 1950s and early 1960s.[104] In the wake of the substantial repression of an incipient nationalist movement within South West Africa, the South West African People's Organisation (SWAPO) was formed in exile in 1960 under the leadership of Sam Nujoma. The organisation committed itself to ongoing efforts to work through international bodies such as the UN to pressure the South African government, and took up an armed struggle against the latter. Political and social unrest within Namibia increased markedly during the 1970s, and was often met with repression at the hands of the colonial administration. In 1978, the UN Security Council passed Resolution 435 and authorised the creation of a transition assistance group to monitor the country's transition to independence. In April 1989, the UN began to supervise this transition process, part of which entailed monitoring elections for a Constituent Assembly to be charged with drafting a constitution for the country. After more than a century of domination by other countries and after a long struggle on both diplomatic and military fronts, Namibia finally achieved its independence in 1990.[105]

Germany's comparatively short period of colonial rule in the territory was marked by massive violence against the local people. In 2004, the German Minister of Economic Co-operation and Development, Heidemarie Wieczorek-Zeul, apologised for the treatment of the Herero people during the colonial period,[106] when the majority of the Herero population were killed during the years 1892–1905 in an orchestrated attempt by the Germans to seize their land. Today, large parts of this land are still in the hands of white Namibians.[107] This as yet unresolved issue of inequitable land distribution – itself a consequence of both German colonial rule and the subsequent apartheid government under South African rule – has shaped one aspect of current development co-operation from Germany, in the sense that it provides substantial support for just and peaceful land reform. Dialogue between the government, landowners and farmers is encouraged, and support is given for community development.[108] In this context and contrary to the situation in Namibia's neighbouring countries, specifically as experienced in Zimbabwe[109] and to some extent currently in South Africa,[110] the Namibian government and its people have so far been able to address the land issue in a sensitive and peaceful manner. This can be seen as a major achievement, considering that about half of the agricultural land in Namibia is in the hands of about 3,500 whites, while almost a million blacks live on subsistence farms on communal lands.[111] Communal land areas vest in the State in trust for the benefit of the traditional communities living in those areas; and customary land rights such as farming or residential rights and rights of leasehold may be allocated to applicants by the Chief or Traditional Authority of a traditional community.[112]

As Namibia's supreme law is its Constitution, all measures with regard to land redistribution are required to be in line with Article 16 in particular, which recognises the right to property,[113] but permits expropriation of land subject to the payment of just compensation.[114] In 1991, the first independent Namibian government held a national land conference which formulated 24 consensus resolutions.[115] These paved the way for land legislation in an independent Namibia, namely the Agricultural (Commercial) Land Reform Act 1995.[116] Since the process of land reform began, major principles guiding it have included the 'willing seller – willing buyer' principle, which holds that those in the possession of land retain full discretion on whether or not to sell such land, with a possibility of expropriation[117] of un- and underutilised of the following group of landowners: foreign landlords, commercial farmers with excessive land, and absentee landlords. The Land Reform Act reserves government's preferential rights to buy land from willing sellers. In 1998, the Ministry of Lands and Resettlement launched Namibia's National Land Policy, followed in 2001 by the National Resettlement Policy.

Within the last 20 years, the Namibian government has, through its Ministry of Lands and Resettlement, acquired 234 farms (almost 1.5 million ha) for land reform purposes.[118] In 1,007 cases (1,007 farms, 4.2 million ha), the government has waived its option rights in favour of formerly disadvantaged Namibians who could acquire such farms through an Affirmative Action Loan Scheme. Five farms have so far been expropriated. The government's resettlement and expropriation procedures have been subject to public debate[119] and judicial proceedings.[120] Resettlement as well as expropriation mechanisms are sensitive issues with high relevance for human rights – not only for the owners of expropriated land in terms of their right to property, but also, and especially, with regard to the fate of farm workers: at this stage, they are still on the losing side when it comes to expropriation or resettlement.[121] However, Namibia and its people are to be commended for the fact that, despite the sensitivity of the issue, the land reform process has so far not gone hand in hand with violent crimes to the extent that has been experienced in other African countries and in the SADC region as a whole.

5.8 Challenges reflected

SADC's objectives include the achievement of development and economic growth; the alleviation of poverty; the enhancement of the standard and quality of life; support of the socially disadvantaged through regional integration; the evolution of common political values, systems and institutions; the promotion and defence of peace and security; and achieving the sustainable utilisation of natural resources and effective protection of the environment.[122] However, several challenges have to be tackled in order to fulfil these objectives, and this applies to human rights as well.[123]

The Summit of SADC Heads of State and Government of SADC held in Sandton, South Africa, on 16–17 August 2008 launched the SADC Free Trade Area (FTA), which is the first milestone in the regional economic integration agenda. During the same meeting, the Summit recognised that –[124]

> … the region had managed to consolidate peace and democracy in SADC. With regard to the challenges in Zimbabwe, [the] Summit noted the outcomes of the Extraordinary Summit of the Organ held in the course of the Summit and reaffirmed its commitment to work with the people of Zimbabwe in order to overcome the challenges they are facing. [The] Summit called for the acceleration of interventions to further deepen the regional integration agenda through the development of a programme of co-operation aimed at expanding regional production capacity which entails [the] provision and rehabilitation of regional infrastructure to facilitate [the] efficient movement of goods and people in a more open regional economy.

Yet, the fear of loss of State autonomy, the fear of loss of identity, socio-economic disparity among SADC members, historical disagreement, lack of vision, and unwillingness to share resources are among the obstacles envisaged when it comes to regional integration. The lack of legal harmonisation is another challenge for the integration process. The heterogeneity of SADC member States is not only reflected by surface area, population figures, size of the domestic markets, per capita incomes, endowment with natural resources and the social and political situation, but also by the variety of legal systems applied in these States.

Instead of radically equalising the legal systems applied in the community, the SADC Tribunal can contribute towards integration if its decisions are properly enforced on the national level and if they serve as guidelines for national courts when deciding on questions that might also be relevant on the regional level. This, in turn, enhances the harmonisation of SADC relevant jurisprudence. Harmonisation, however, can only take place if the application of law by national courts in comparable cases leads roughly to the same results – because only in cases of comparable results do the same competitive conditions prevail for all member States.

National courts, therefore, have to consider community law when ruling on community-relevant issues. One essential precondition for such considerations by national courts is that there should be a common understanding of community law in order to guarantee legal certainty in terms of the predictability of legal decisions. With the SADC Tribunal, a central institution was created that can give impulses and provide impetus for a community-wide common understanding of community law. In the light of the integrative effect of its function, the Tribunal can become similar to the ECJ – a 'motor of integration'.[125]

The fact that many African States are members of various regional economic communities can be regarded as another hurdle in respect of the integration process.[126] Except for Mozambique, all SADC countries are at the same time members of at least one other trade agreement in the region. Thus, eight SADC members are simultaneously members of the Common Market of Eastern and Southern Africa (COMESA); four are members of SADC and the Southern African Customs Union (SACU); Swaziland is a member of SADC, SACU and COMESA; and Tanzania is a member of SADC and the East African Community (EAC). Various bilateral free-trade agreements as well as the membership of all SADC countries in the African Union may be regarded as obstacles to deeper integration in many respects. Such overlapping memberships are not only problematic in terms of duplication of work and costs, but also because a sub-regional customs union is envisaged by both COMESA and SADC, and it is legally and technically impossible to be a member of more than one such union.[127] The question of concurrent jurisdiction of different judicial organs is also closely related to multiple memberships.[128] Thus, SADC not only provides for a Tribunal, but SACU intends to establish a SACU Tribunal,[129] COMESA established the COMESA Court of Justice,[130] and the East African Court of Justice is the EAC's judicial arm,[131] not to mention the African Court on Human and Peoples' Rights (ACHPR).[132]

From this it is clear that, in the near future, the issue of the conflicting jurisdictions of regional courts on the African continent will become a prominent one. For the time being, the consequence of overlapping jurisdiction is that a claimant may in fact choose to which judicial body a case is to be submitted,[133] as a competent court may not decline jurisdiction – the argument being that another court may also be competent. In this context, factors such as the cost of litigation, the organisational context in which the dispute would be decided, the entity that would decide the dispute, the advantages of the applicable law, who can initiate a complaint against whom, procedural advantages, the possibility of appeal, the remedies that can be obtained, the parties who are bound by an eventual ruling, and the consequences of non-compliance will be decisive.[134] In terms of regional integration, the absence of a judicially integrated Africa is undeniably a problem: there will be divergent interpretations of one normative source by different judicial bodies.[135]

Moreover, the controversy around sovereignty is often encountered, especially when it comes to concepts of regional integration. In the so-called Sutherland Report,[136] *sovereignty* is described as one of the 'most used and also misused concepts of international affairs and international law'. Acceptance of almost any treaty involves a transfer of a certain amount of decision-making authority away from States, and towards some international institution. Generally, this is exactly why 'sovereign nations' agree to such treaties: they realise that the benefits of co-operative action that a treaty enhances are greater than the circumstances that exist otherwise.[137] It is undeniable that discrete, territorially bound State units no longer have exclusive control over the process of governance pertaining to the societies that live in their respective territories. In this context, governance has come to be conceptualised in multilevel terms, as power has become widely dispersed amongst a range of institutions and actors. The dispersion of power and the increase in integration activities leading to multiple levels of governance are further challenges faced by SADC.[138]

With their Regional Indicative Strategic Development Plan (RISDP), SADC member States committed themselves to good political, economic and corporate governance entrenched in a culture of democracy;[139] full participation by civil society; transparency; and respect for the rule of law. With regard to monitoring the RISDP's implementation, the Summit is expected to exercise continuous oversight using progress reports from the Secretariat.[140] Unfortunately, the RISDP is only indicative in nature: it merely outlines the necessary conditions to be realised. Furthermore, although the RISDP is a strategic plan that can be adapted, it is not binding on member States, and it makes no specific reference to the SADC Tribunal.[141]

5.9 Conclusion

Amendment 17 of the Zimbabwean Constitution has been challenged before the SADC Tribunal. On the one hand, the Zimbabwean constitutional amendments shifted the responsibility for the payment of compensation for compulsorily acquired farms to Britain as the former colonial power.[142] Arbitrarily, on the other hand, Zimbabwe fails to take the full responsibility for its actions by way of not recognising the SADC Tribunal's rulings, claiming the country has been fully recognised as a sovereign State.

The Zimbabwean land issue is not only a reflection of the unresolved question of 'how States resolve past and continuing social injustices that are rooted in colonial or some such other similar experience … ':[143] it is also a reflection of land reform per se being understood as the transfer of land from one owner or group of owners to another for political, social, or ideological purposes.

If one looks at Europe, for example, it was thought throughout the nineteenth century and most of the twentieth that land reform would solve an array of political and social problems. The main argument for land reform has always been that the unequal distribution of land was the root of many social problems. Twentieth-century Europe saw several periods in which the politics of land reform wrought vast changes on the Continent. All of these periods were times of economic crisis and political transformation. Although these ideas of land reform essentially disappeared in the 1950s and 1960s with the development of the European Union's common market, they have not entirely died – especially since large parts of continental Europe are still owned by aristocratic elites, meaning that the imbalances of the past that were caused through privileges granted and acquired under imperial rule prevail to the present day.[144]

In respect of political stability in southern Africa, one of the greatest threats undoubtedly lies in unequal land ownership patterns, where poor people's livelihoods mostly depend on farming. Redressing historical problems and social justice through land redistribution is, thus, a crucial ingredient of reconciliation and development in the sub-region. However, this must be done through appropriate land reform policies that are not merely motivated by political power play, but respond to the very historical issues they aim to rectify, and in so doing, solve contemporary problems of equity, poverty reduction and economic growth as well. When it comes to land issues, it is irrelevant whether one tends to argue for or against 'eternal land rights':[145] human rights abuses in this context strongly depend on political will, procedural fairness, and the rule of law. Land ownership always goes hand in hand with power; and, although power structures change during the course of history, it is important to acknowledge that such changes are always in the hands of a few, and affect the fate of others. Having said this, the *Campbell* case not only demonstrates that the SADC Tribunal can be called upon to consider human rights implications of economic (land) policies and programmes; the fact that the first cases before the Tribunal deal with land-related human rights issues also sends a very specific message. This needs further exploration because it tells us other things about the state of integration (or lack of it) in southern Africa: that the internal rule of law is being neglected, and that more effective inter-State mechanisms for protecting human rights are absent.

So far, the SADC Tribunal's position is considered to be rather weak, especially due to its lack of enforcement mechanisms and – perhaps more importantly – a lack of protest by other SADC member States against Zimbabwe's persistent non-compliance with the Tribunal's judgments.

Notes

* Professor of Law at the Faculty of Law of the University of Stellenbosch, South Africa and an adjunct Professor at the Pupkewitz Graduate Business School at the Polytechnic of Namibia.

1 Cf. section 5.6 herein.

2 B. Chigara (2004), p xv.

3 On various initiatives by African leaders to carry out the integration process in Africa, cf. R. N. Kouassi (2007).
4 The number of RECs varies depending on the definition of REC and on whether or not specific subgroups or monetary unions such as the Central African Economic and Monetary Community or certain free trade areas such as the Euro-Mediterranean Free Trade Area (with Egypt, Morocco, Tunisia, and certain States around the Mediterranean) are counted. Viljoen states that at least 14 sub-regional integration groupings exist in Africa; cf. F. Viljoen (2007).
5 Cf. the decision relating to the recognition of RECs, namely Assembly/AU/Dec.112 (VII) Doc. EX.CL/278 (IX); text in French available at <http://www.africa-union.org/Official_documents/Assemblee%20fr/ASS06b.pdf> accessed 18 April 2010.
6 For a list of REC State members, cf. O. C. Ruppel (2009a), p 278.
7 Ibid.
8 N. Kersting (2007), p 69.
9 O. C. Ruppel (2009a), p. 279.
10 The Seychelles was a member of SADC from 1997 to 2004; it rejoined SADC in 2008.
11 For more details on SADC, cf. <http://www.sadc.int/>.
12 Cf. SADC's Vision, at <http://www.sadc.int/>.
13 Common Market for Eastern and Southern Africa–East African Community–Southern African Development Community (2008) *Final Communiqué of the COMESA–EAC–SADC Tripartite Summit of Heads of State and Government, held in October 2008 in Kampala, Uganda: Towards a Single Market – Deepening COMESA–EAC–SADC Integration*, section 14, <http://about.comesa.int/attachments/078_Final_Communique-Kampala_22_10_08.pdf> (accessed 18 April 2010).
14 These are some of the SADC objectives laid down in Article 5 of the SADC Treaty.
15 This panel consisted of the late Professor W. Kamba (founding Dean of the Faculty of Law at the University of Namibia) and Justice F. Jacobs (Judge at the Court of Justice of the European Communities). Cf. F. Viljoen (1999), p 200.
16 For more details on these historical developments, cf. ibid, pp 200 ff.
17 Article 4(c), SADC Treaty.
18 Article 5, SADC Treaty.
19 United Nations Development Programme (2000), p 8.
20 O. C. Ruppel (2008a).
21 As argued by the Respondent in *Mike Campbell (Pvt) Ltd v Republic of Zimbabwe* SADC (T) Case No. 2/2007 pp 23 ff.
22 For a list of all SADC Protocols, cf. O. C. Ruppel (2009a), p 293.
23 *Campbell*, above, n 21, p 25.
24 It has to be noted, however, that Articles 35 and 36 (ratification and accession, respectively) of the Protocol have been repealed by the Agreement Amending the Protocol on the Tribunal. The latter Agreement entered into force in October 2002; hereafter *SADC Protocol*.
25 SADC Protocol, Article 3(2).
26 Ibid, Article 3(3).
27 Ibid, Article 3(6).
28 Ibid, Article 6(1).
29 The same method was also adopted by the International Court of Justice: their judges run for a maximum term of nine years, but a third of them are elected every three years. Cf. A. S. Muller *et al* (1997), p 67.
30 SADC Protocol, Article 3(1).
31 F. Viljoen (2007), p 503.
32 Cf. O. C. Ruppel and F.-X Bangamwabo (2008), p 188.
33 Cf. the ruling in *Albert Fungai Mutize v Mike Campbell (Pvt) Ltd* 2008, p 4.

34 It is on this ground that the Tribunal exercised its jurisdiction in the case of *Ernest Francis Mtangwi v SADC Secretariat* 2007. The dispute in the case arose between the SADC Community Secretariat and one of its staff members.
35 O. C. Ruppel and F.-X Bangamwabo (2008), p 189.
36 In fact, all major human rights instruments (both regional and international) provide for the rule on the exhaustion of local remedies. Examples include Article 35(1) of the Convention for the Protection of Human Rights and Fundamental Freedoms (European Convention on Human Rights, as amended; ECHR); Article 46(1) of the American Convention on Human Rights, 1969; Articles 50 and 56(5) of the African Charter on People's and Human Rights (adopted 27 June 1981, entered into force 21 October 1986; 1982, 21 ILM 58, African Charter); and Articles 2 and 5(2)(b) of the Optional Protocol to the International Covenant on Civil and Political Rights, 1966. With regard to the Rome Statute of the International Criminal Court (ICC), the principle of exhaustion of domestic remedies is substituted by the complementarity principle as laid down in Article 17(a) of the ICC Statute. The latter article makes it clear that the ICC will only accept a case where a State which has the required jurisdiction is unwilling or unable to carry out the investigation and/or prosecution.
37 J. Dugard (2003), p 293.
38 Ibid.
39 EAC Treaty, Articles 8(4) and 33(2).
40 For more on the Namibian approach in respect of the incorporation of international law in the national legal system, cf. G. Erasmus (1991), pp 81 ff.
41 *Campbell*, above, n 21, p 25.
42 Cf. O. C. Ruppel (2008b).
43 SADC Protocol, Article 5.
44 Ibid, Article 8(3).
45 Ibid, Article 9.
46 Cf. N. M. Hunnings (1996), pp 52 ff.
47 This may happen in many ways, e.g. where the judge has acted previously in the dispute at hand as an agent, attorney/advocate, or legal adviser, or as a judge at domestic level.
48 Hunnings (1996), p 53.
49 SADC Protocol, Article 10.
50 Cf. O. C. Ruppel and F.-X. Bangamwabo (2008).
51 Consisting of the 'Heads of State or Government of all Member States'; cf. Article 10(1) of the SADC Treaty.
52 The High Court of Zimbabwe has for instance ruled that a decision of the SADC Tribunal cannot be enforced at the national level as such would be in contradiction to the Constitution of Zimbabwe. See *Gramara (Pvt) Ltd and Colin Bailie Cloete v Government of the Republic of Zimbabwe*, High Court of Zimbabwe decision, 26 January 2010; available at <http://www.kubatana.net/docs/landr/high_court_patel_gramara_goz_100126.pdf> accessed 8 June 2010.
53 Those are the measures that the United Nations (UN) Security Council may impose with respect to threats to peace and acts of aggression; cf. Article 41 of the UN Charter.
54 An example of an effective enforcement mechanism is the World Trade Organisation (WTO) system of imposing limited trade sanctions in the form of the suspension of concessions or other obligations, as provided for in Article 22 of the Dispute Settlement Understanding. Due to the great political and economic significance, such sanctions are appropriate for ensuring compliance with the rulings of the WTO's judicial organ, the Dispute Settlement Body (DSB).
55 G. Erasmus and G. Coleman (2008).
56 Save for the massacres in Matebeleland in 1980–87, in which the Zimbabwean government caused the death of 20,000 civilians and the disappearance of thousands more.
57 'Crisis in Zimbabwe Coalition', *Zimbabwe Report* (2002).

58 Zimbabwe African National Union–Patriotic Front.
59 Movement for Democracy and Change.
60 'Crisis in Zimbabwe Coalition', *Zimbabwe Report* (2002).
61 W. H. Shaw (2003).
62 M. Dube and R. Midgley (2008).
63 'Crisis in Zimbabwe Coalition', *Zimbabwe Report* (2002).
64 T. Mudiwa (2010).
65 In an interview with the Zimbabwean newspaper *The Herald* the Mashonaland Central Provincial Governor, Advocate Martin Dinha, said some farms were too big for occupiers to cope with. Cf. *The Herald* (Harare), 19 March 2010, <http://cfuzim.org/index.php?option=com_content&view=article&id=449:govt-to-rationalise-farm-sizes&catid=51:newspaper-clippings&Itemid=92 (accessed 10 April 2010).
66 *Campbell*, above, n 21.
67 For more information, cf. O. C. Ruppel (2009a); O. C. Ruppel (2009b); O. C. Ruppel (2009c); O. C. Ruppel (2009d); O. C. Ruppel and F.-X. Bangamwabo 2008).
68 *Commercial Farmers' Union v Minister of Lands, Agriculture and Resettlement* 2001 (2) SA 925 (ZSC).
69 Section 16B(3) of the Zimbabwean Constitution reads as follows: ' … a person having any right or interest in the land [expropriated land] shall not apply to court to challenge the acquisition of the land by the State, and no court shall entertain such challenge … '.
70 *Campbell*, above, n 21; Interim order dated 13 December 2007, p 6.
71 *Mike Campbell (Pvt) Ltd v Minister of National Security responsible for Land, Land Reform and Resettlement and the Attorney-General*, Constitutional Application No. 124/06 (unreported case: Supreme Court of Zimbabwe).
72 *Campbell*, above, n 21; Interim order dated 13 December 2007.
73 D. Grebe (2008a).
74 Cf. *Campbell*, Interim order 13 December 2007. This interim relief was also applied for by and granted to other applicants/interveners on 28 March 2008; cf. cases SADC (T) 03/08, 04/08 and 06/08.
75 Cf. <http://www.thezimbabwean.co.uk/index.php?option=com_content&view=article&id=13001:campbell-case-heads-of-argument-summary&catid=31:top%20zimbabwe%20stories&Itemid=66 (accessed 10 April 2010).
76 Cf. also M. Dube and R. Midgley (2008).
77 D. Grebe (2008b).
78 Cf. *Nixon Chirinda v Campbell (Pvt) Ltd and Republic of Zimbabwe* SADC (T) 1, 17 September 2008.
79 Rule 70(2) of the Tribunal provides that an 'application in terms of this Rule (application to intervene) shall be made as soon as possible and not later than the closure of the written proceedings in the main case … '.
80 The Tribunal based its reasoning on the content of Article 15(1) of the Protocol, which reads as follows: 'The Tribunal shall have jurisdiction over disputes between States, and between natural or legal persons and States.' Thus, where a dispute involves only persons (either natural or juristic), the Tribunal is not competent to adjudicate it.
81 The Tribunal further held that the applicants/interveners had failed to adduce any evidence showing that they had indeed been denied access to justice and had suffered racial discrimination or loss. Cf. *Nixon Chirinda.*
82 *Campbell*, above, n 21.
83 *Campbell*, above, n 21, pp 57 ff.
84 The issue of racial discrimination was decided by a majority of four to one. Judge O. B. Tshosa, in his dissenting opinion, concluded that 'Amendment 17 does not discriminate against the applicants on the basis of race and therefore does not violate the respondent obligation under Article 6(2) of the Treaty'. He argued that 'the target of Amendment 17 is agricultural land and not people of a particular racial group and that –

although few in number – not only white Zimbabweans have been affected by the amendment'. Cf. *Campbell*, dissenting opinion of Hon. Justice Dr Onkemetse B. Tshosa.

85 Cf. O. C. Ruppe (2009d).

86 SADC Treaty, Article 16(5).

87 On 28 February 2009, Zimbabwe's President, Robert Mugabe, said that '[t]here is no going back on the land reforms', and that '[s]ome farmers went to the SADC tribunal in Namibia but that's nonsense, absolute nonsense, no one will follow that … We have courts here in this country, that can determine the rights of people. Our land issues are not subject to the SADC tribunal' ('Mugabe says Zim land grabs will continue', *The Namibian*, 2 March 2009).

88 On 25 February 2009, Michael Campbell and his wife had to leave the farm in fear for their safety after a group of two vehicles led by Peter Chamada, nephew of Cabinet Minister Nathan Shamuyarira, claiming to be from the Lands Office, came to the farm and said that they did not care about the law or the police, and that they had come to take over the land. Cf. 'Campbell flees farm invasion in Zimbabwe', *The Namibian*, 27 February 2009.

89 Interestingly, a draft SADC Human Rights Charter drawn up by NGOs of SADC Member States in 1996 contained a provision according to which any State 'which does not comply with an order of the Court interpreting this Charter shall be suspended from SADC for the duration of its non-compliance with such order'. This proposal, although it appears very effective, has not, however, been realised. Cf. F. Viljoen (1999) 'The Realisation of Human Rights through Sub-regional Institutions', *African Yearbook of International Law* 7: 185–216.

90 *Campbell v Republic of Zimbabwe*, SADC (T) 03/2009 [2009] SADC (T) 1 (5 June 2009).

91 Ibid. On 26 January 2010 the Zimbabwean High Court ruled that the Tribunal's decision could not be enforced at national level as this would be in contradiction to the Constitution of Zimbabwe. See *Gramara (Pvt) Ltd and Colin Bailie Cloete v Government of the Republic of Zimbabwe*, High Court of Zimbabwe decision dated 26 January 2010.

92 Hon. Justice A. G. Pillay is also the Vice-chairperson of the Committee on Economic, Social and Cultural Rights (CESCR); cf. <http://www.unhchr.ch/tbs/doc.nsf/bf12f8158bdd1ce4c1256a4d002dfbc7/80256404004ff315c12563ef002df626?OpenDocument> (accessed 15 June 2009). The CESCR is a body of independent experts that monitors implementation of the International Covenant on Economic, Social and Cultural Rights (ICESCR) by its States Parties. The CESCR was established under United Nations Economic and Social Council (ECOSOC) Resolution 1985/17 in 1985 to carry out the monitoring functions assigned to ECOSOC in Part IV of the Covenant. Within two years of having acceded to the ICESCR, all States Parties are obliged to submit an initial report to the committee on how these rights are being implemented. Regular reports are also required every five years after that. The committee examines each report and addresses its concerns and recommendations to the State Party in question in the form of 'concluding observations'. With regard to individual complaints, on 10 December 2008 the General Assembly unanimously adopted an Optional Protocol (GA Resolution A/RES/63/117) to the ICESCR which empowers the Committee to receive and consider communications. The General Assembly took note of the adoption of the Optional Protocol by the Human Rights Council by its Resolution 8/2 of 18 June 2008. For more information, cf. <http://www2.ohchr.org/english/bodies/cescr/> (accessed 15 June 2009).

93 D. Grebe (2008).

94 It must be noted that different views exist on this issue. The decision that Amendment 17 is in breach of Article 6(2) of the SADC Treaty was not a unanimous decision. Cf. the dissenting opinion in the *Campbell* case by Hon. Justice Dr Onkemetse B. Tshosa.

95 Cf. J. Raath (2009).

96 See *Gramara (Pvt) Ltd and Colin Bailie Cloete v Government of the Republic of Zimbabwe*, High Court of Zimbabwe decision dated 26 January 2010 at p 6. Text available at

<http://www.kubatana.net/docs/landr/high_court_patel_gramara_goz_100126.pdf> accessed 8 June 2010.

97 *Gramara (Pvt) Ltd and Colin Bailie Cloete v Government of the Republic of Zimbabwe*, High Court of Zimbabwe decision dated 26 January 2010. Text available at <http://www.kubatana.net/docs/landr/high_court_patel_gramara_goz_100126.pdf> accessed 8 June 2010.

98 *Louis Karel Fick v Government of the Republic of Zimbabwe* Case No. 77881/2009. Order by Judge G. Rabie, High Court of South Africa (North Gauteng High Court, Pretoria).

99 Several properties owned by the Zimbabwean government have been identified, including houses in Cape Town. Unlike properties in Pretoria which are connected with the embassy, the Cape Town properties are thought not to be protected by diplomatic immunity. Cf. P. Thornycroft and S. Berger (2010) 'Zimbabwe's White Farmers Plan to Seize Government Property', *Telegraph* (Harare/Johannesburg), 7 March, <http://www.telegraph.co.uk/news/worldnews/africaandindianocean/zimbabwe/7386395/Zimbabwes-white-farmers-plan-to-seize-government-property.html> accessed 18 March 2010.

100 Ibid.

101 It has to be noted, that this Chapter was submitted for review and editing in June 2010. The author was, however, granted permission to include this postscript footnote shortly before publication: In August 2010, the SADC Committee of Justice Ministers and Attorney Generals was tasked to examine the role and functions of the SADC Tribunal and the implications of a Member State ignoring its rulings. Subsequently an independent legal opinion was commissioned to review the Tribunal. Although such review had been submitted in January 2011, the last SADC Summit meeting in May 2011 decided, that the SADC Tribunal may still not hear new cases until August 2012 'until the role, functions and terms of reference of the Tribunal and its regulatory framework have been reviewed and amended'. Several applications have been filed before the SADC Tribunal to set aside 'its suspension' – without success. In April 2011 Mike Campbell died in Harare. It was said that he never recovered from the abduction and brutal beatings meted out to him in 2009.

102 Cf. F. Viljoen (1999) 'The Realisation of Human Rights through Sub-regional Institutions', *African Yearbook of International Law*, 7: 185–216, 206 ff.

103 For further reference, cf. e.g. S. L. Harring (2002); S. L. Harring and W. Odendaal (2002, 2007); J. Hunter (2004); C. Sasman (2010).

104 S. K. Amoo and I. Skeffers (2008).

105 Ibid.

106 During the 2004 remembrance ceremony, Wieczorek-Zeul asked for forgiveness 'of our trespasses, in the words of the Lord's Prayer that we share'.

107 Cf. O. C. Ruppel (2009c).

108 Cf. <http://www.bmz.de/en/countries/partnercountries/namibia/index.html> accessed 10 April 2010.

109 As described in the above paragraphs.

110 The murder of Eugene Terre'blanche on 4 April 2010, who led the Afrikaner resistance movement (Afrikaner Weerstandsbeweging, AWB) that pushed to preserve apartheid in the 1990s, has once again exposed the racial divide between white farmers and the indigenous population in South Africa that remains 16 years after the end of apartheid. Although the murder allegedly did not have a political background, the situation for white farmers in South Africa has worsened over the past few years. Since 1991, approximately 2,000 farmers have been killed in the course of violent attacks, and the number of white commercial farmers has decreased from 62,000 in 1994 to 40,000 today. Yet it is said that only 2 per cent of violent crimes against farmers in South Africa are politically or racially motivated. Cf. W. Drechsler (2010).

111 S. L. Harring and W. Odendaal (2007).

112 On the concept of *communal land* and the question of ownership, cf. M. O. Hinz (1998).

113 Article 16(1).
114 Article 16(2).
115 Cf. Ministry of Lands, Resettlement and Rehabilitation (1991).
116 Hereafter Land Reform Act.
117 The expropriation mechanism was introduced in 2004; cf. Sasman (2010), p 12.
118 Cf. E. Hofmann (2010).
119 Cf. e.g. B. Weidlich (2007a, 2007b). The first expropriations and their impacts have been discussed in detail by S. L. Harring and W. Odendaal (2007). Cf. also S. L. Harring and W. Odendaal (2008).
120 Cf. e.g. the following in the High Court of Namibia: *Kessl v Ministry of Land and Resettlement*, Case Nos (P) A 27/2006 and (P) A 266/2006; *Heimaterde CC v Ministry of Lands and Resettlement*, Case No. (P) A 269/2005; and *Martin Joseph Riedmaier v Ministry of Lands and Resettlement*, Case No. (P) A 267/2005; judgments delivered on 6 March 2008.
121 It is estimated that land reform processes could leave many farm workers unemployed. About 222,000 people have been displaced so far, which has not been considered by relevant land reform legislation. Cf. S. L. Harring and W. Odendaal (2007), p 27.
122 These are some of the SADC objectives laid down in Article 5 of the SADC Treaty.
123 Cf. further references in O. C. Ruppel (2009b, 2009c) 213–38.
124 Final Communiqué of the Twenty-eighth Summit of SADC Heads of State and Government Text, available at <http://www.sadc.int/fta/index/browse/page/203> (accessed 8 June 2010).
125 This term was coined by Schwarze; cf. S. J. Schwarze (1988).
126 Cf. O. C. Ruppel (2009a, 2009b).
127 C. Jakobeit, T. Hartzenberg and N. Charalambides (2005).
128 For a more detailed discussion, cf. O. C. Ruppel (2009a).
129 Cf. <http://www.sacu.int/main.php?include=about/tribunal.html (accessed 28 August 2009).
130 Cf. <http://www.comesa.int/institutions/court_of_justice/Multi-language_content.2003-08-21.2608/view> (accessed 28 May 2009).
131 Cf. <http://www.aict-ctia.org/courts_subreg/eac/eac_home.html> (accessed 28 March 2010).
132 M. Hansungule (2009).
133 Referred to as 'forum shopping': cf. F. Viljoen (2007), p 502.
134 J. Pauwelyn (2004).
135 F. Viljoen (2007), p 502.
136 P. Sutherland (2005).
137 Ibid. The concept of *sovereignty* and its relevance to the WTO is discussed in depth in the Sutherland Report.
138 O. C. Ruppel (2009c), pp 216 ff.
139 For an analysis of the state of democracy in the SADC region, cf. W. Breytenbach (2002).
140 Cf. <http://www.sadc.int/index/browse/page/106> (accessed 19 October 2009).
141 Cf. T. Hartzenberg (2008); O. C. Ruppel (2009c).
142 Cf. Section 16A(2) of the Constitution of the Republic of Zimbabwe. For further references, cf. M. Dube and R. Midgley (2008), p 313.
143 B. Chigara (2004), p 1.
144 J. Hari (2005).
145 B. Chigara (2004), pp 33 ff.

Bibliography

Amoo, S. K. and Skeffers, I. (2008) 'The Rule of Law in Namibia' in N. Horn and A. Bösl (eds) *Human Rights and the Rule of Law in Namibia* (Windhoek: Macmillan) 17–38.

Assembly/AU/Dec.112 (VII) Doc. EX.CL/278 (IX); text in French available at <http://www.africa-union.org/Official_documents/Assemblee%20fr/ASS06b.pdf> (accessed 18 April 2010).

Breytenbach, W. (2002) 'Democracy in the SADC Region: A Comparative Overview', *African Security Review*, 11: 4, <http://www.iss.co.za/Pubs/ASR/11No4/Breytenbach.html> (accessed 20 April 2009).

Chigara, B. (2004) *Land Reform Policy: The Challenge of Human Rights Law* (Burlington, VT: Ashgate).

Crisis in Zimbabwe Coalition (2002) *Zimbabwe Report*, <http://ocha-gwapps1.unog.ch/rw/RWFiles2002.nsf/FilesByRWDocUNIDFileName/OCHA-64DB46-czc-zim-20jun.pdf/$File/czc-zim-20jun.pdf> (accessed 5 April 2010).

Drechsler, W. (2010) 'Südafrikas Farmer leben gefährlich', *Allgemeine Zeitung* (Windhoek), 7 April.

Dube, M. and Midgley, R. (2008) 'Land Reform in Zimbabwe: Context, Progress, Legal and Constitutional Issues and Implications for the SADC Region', in A. Bösl, W. Breytenbach, T. Hartzenberg and others (eds) *Monitoring Regional Integration in Southern Africa: Yearbook*, Vol. 8 (Stellenbosch: Trade Law Centre for Southern Africa), pp 303–42.

Dugard, J. (2003) *International Law: A South African Perspective* (3rd edn, Juta: Lansdowne).

Erasmus, G. (1991) 'The Namibian Constitution and the Application of International Law in Namibia', in D. van Wyk, M. Wiechers and R. Hill (eds) *Namibia: Constitutional and International Law Issues* (Pretoria: Verloren van Themaat Centre for Public Law Studies).

Erasmus, G. and Coleman, G. (2008) 'Regional Dispute Resolution: The SADC Tribunal's First Test', <https://www.givengain.com/cgi-bin/giga.cgi?cmd=cause_dir_news_item&news_id=45435&cause_id=1694 (accessed 18 April 2010).

Final Communiqué of the 28th Summit of SADC Heads of State and Government Text available at <http://www.sadc.int/fta/index/browse/page/203> (accessed 8 June 2010).

Final Communiqué of the COMESA–EAC–SADC Tripartite Summit of Heads of State and Government (2008) *held in October 2008 in Kampala, Uganda: Towards a Single Market – Deepening COMESA–EAC–SADC Integration*, section 14, <http://about.comesa.int/attachments/078_Final_Communique-Kampala_22_10_08.pdf> (accessed 18 April 2010).

Grebe, D. (2008a) 'Klägerschar vervielfacht. 74 simbabwische Farmer dürfen mit Campbell Enteignung anfechten', *Allgemeine Zeitung* (Windhoek), 31 March.

Grebe, D. (2008b) 'Simbabwe. Brutaler Überfall auf Campbell. Schlägertrupps misshandeln Farmerfamilie schwer und erpressen Verzichtserklärung für Prozess am SADC Tribunal', *Allgemeine Zeitung* (Windhoek), 1 July, <http://www.az.com.na/afrika/simbabwe-brutaler-berfall-auf-campbell.69175.php> (accessed 10 April 2010).

Grebe, D. (2009) 'Zweiter Sieg für weiße Farmer. SADC-Tribunal: Simbabwe missachtet Urteil. Gipfel soll Konsequenzen prüfen', *Allgemeine Zeitung* (Windhoek), 9 June.

Hansungule, M. (2009) 'African Courts on Human Rights and the African Commission', in A. Bösl and J. Diescho (eds) *Human Rights in Africa* (Windhoek: Macmillan), pp 233–68.

Hari, J. (2005) 'Britain's Land is Still Owned by an Aristocratic Elite – But it Doesn't Have to be This Way', *The Independent* (London), 2 February, <http://www.independent.co.uk/opinion/commentators/johann-hari/britains-land-is-still-owned-by-an-aristocratic-elite–but-it-doesnt-have-to-be-this-way-483131.html> (accessed 10 April 2010).

Harring, S. L. (2002) 'The "Stolen Lands" under the Constitution of Namibia: Land Reform under the Rule of Law', in M. O. Hinz, S. K. Amoo and D. van Wyk (eds) *The Constitution at Work: Ten Years of Namibian Nationhood* (Pretoria: VerLoren van Themaat Centre), pp 269–84.

Harring, S. L. and Odendaal, W. (2002) *'One day we will all be equal': A Socio-legal Perspective on the Namibian Land Reform and Resettlement Process* (Windhoek: Legal Assistance Centre).

Harring, S. L. and Odendaal, W. (2007) *No Resettlement Available: An Assessment of the Expropriation Principle and its Impact on Land Reform in Namibia* (Windhoek: Legal Assistance Centre).

Harring, S. L. and Odendaal, W. (2008) *Kessl: A New Jurisprudence for Land Reform in Namibia* (Windhoek: Legal Assistance Centre).

Hartzenberg, T. (2008) 'Comments on the SADC Free Trade Area to be Launched at SADC Summit, 2008', <http://www.givengain.com/cgi-gin/giga.cgi?cmd=cause_dir_news_item&cause_id=1694&news_id=50552&cat_id= (accessed 19 May 2009).

Hinz, M. O. (1998) 'Communal Land, Natural Resources and Traditional Authority', in F. M. d'Engelbronner-Kolff, M. O. Hinz and J. L. Sindano (eds) *Traditional Authority and Democracy in Southern Africa* (Windhoek: Centre for Applied Social Sciences, University of Namibia).

Hofmann, E. (2010) 'Interview with Minister of Land and Resettlement Alpheus Naruseb', *Allgmeine Zeitung* (Windhoek), 26 March.

Hunnings, N. M. (1996) *The European Courts* (London: Catermill).

Hunter, J. (ed) (2004) *Who Should Own the Land?* (Windhoek: Namibia Institute for Democracy).

Jakobeit, C., Hartzenberg, T. and Charalambides, N. (2005) *Overlapping Membership in COMESA, EAC, SACU and SADC* (Eschborn: Gesellschaft für Technische Zusammenarbeit).

Kersting, N. (2007) 'SADC and Good Governance: Regional Integration and Electoral Reform', in A. Bösl, W. Breytenbach, T. Hartzenberg and others (eds) *Monitoring Regional Integration in Southern Africa: Yearbook 7* (Stellenbosch: Trade Law Centre for Southern Africa).

Kouassi, R. N. (2007) 'The Itinerary of the African Integration Process: An Overview of the Historical Landmarks', *African Integration Review*, 1: 1–23.

Ministry of Lands, Resettlement and Rehabilitation (1991) *National Conference on Land Reform and the Land Question: Conference Brief* (Windhoek: Ministry of Lands, Resettlement and Rehabilitation).

Mudiwa, T. (2010) 'Mugabe Attacks Zimbabwe's Land Reform Again', *ZimDaily* (Harare), 23 March, <http://www.zimdaily.com/beta/news271338.html> (accessed 10 April 2010).

Muller, A. S., Raic, A. and Thuranzky, H. (1997) *The International Court of Justice: Its Future Role after Fifty Years* (The Hague: Nijhoff).

Pauwelyn, J. (2004) 'Going Global, Regional or Both? Dispute Settlement in the Southern African Development Community (SADC) and Overlaps with the WTO and other Jurisdictions', *Minnesota Journal of Global Trade*, 13: 231–304.

Raath, J. (2009) 'Activists Mike Campbell and Ben Freeth's Farms "Set Alight by Henchmen"', *Times online* (Harare), 3 September, <http://www.timesonline.co.uk/tol/news/world/africa/article6819284.ece> (accessed 25 March 2010).

Ruppel, O. C. (2008a) 'Third-generation Human Rights and the Protection of the Environment in Namibia', in N. Horn and A. Bösl (eds) *Human Rights and the Rule of Law in Namibia* (Windhoek: Macmillan), pp 101–20, <http://www.kas.de/proj/home/pub/8/2/-/dokument_id-16045/index.html> (accessed 28 November 2009).

Ruppel, O. C. (2008b) 'The Role of the Executive in the Promotion of the Independence of the Judiciary', in N. Horn and A. Bösl (eds) *The Independence of the Judiciary in Namibia* (Windhoek: Macmillan), pp 207–28, <http://www.kas.de/proj/home/pub/8/2/dokument_id-15058/index.html> (accessed 22 December 2009).

Ruppel, O. C. (2009a) 'Regional Economic Communities and Human Rights in East and Southern Africa', in A. Bösl and J. Diescho (eds) *Human Rights in Africa* (Windhoek: Macmillan), pp 275–319, <http://www.kas.de/upload/auslandshomepages/namibia/Human_Rights_in_Africa/9_Ruppel.pdf> (accessed 24 March 2010).

Ruppel, O. C. (2009b) 'The Southern African Development Community (SADC) and its Tribunal: Reflexions on Regional Economic Communities' Potential Impact on Human Rights Protection', *Verfassung und Recht in Übersee* (Baden-Baden: Nomos), 2: 173–86.

Ruppel, O. C. (2009c) 'The SADC Tribunal, Regional Integration and Human Rights: Major Challenges, Legal Dimensions and Some Comparative Aspects from the European Legal Order', *Recht in Afrika*, 2: 213–38.

Ruppel, O. C. (2009d) 'Das SADC Tribunal: Eine Juristische Zwischenbilanz', *Allgemeine Zeitung* (Windhoek), 5 February, <http://www.az.com.na/afrika/das-sadc-tribunal-eine-juristische-zwischenbilanz.80234.php> accessed 9 September 2009.

Ruppel, O. C. (2009e) 'Koloniale Altlasten in Namibia und die Grenzen des Völkerrechts', *Allgemeine Zeitung* (Windhoek), 12 August, <http://www.az.com.na/politik/koloniale-altlasten-in-namibia-und- die-grenzen-des-vlkerrechts.90808.php> accessed 4 January 2010.

Ruppel, O. C. (2010) 'SACU 100: The Southern African Customs Union turns 100', in *Namibia Law Journal* (*NLJ*), 2010(2) (Windhoek: Macmillan), <http://www.namibia-lawjournal.org/pnTemp/downloads_upload/Journal_Vol2_Iss2/NLJ_section_7.pdf> (English).

Ruppel, O. C. and Bangamwabo, F.-X. (2008) 'The Mandate of the SADC Tribunal and its Role for Regional Integration', in A. Bösl, W. Breydenbach, T. Hartzenberg and others (eds) *Yearbook for Regional Integration* (Stellenbosch: Trade Law Centre for Southern Africa), pp 179–221, <http://www.tralac.org/cause_data/images/1694/MRI2008-WithCover20090415.pdf> (accessed 25 November 2009).

Sasman, C. (2010) 'Large Country, Little Land: Land Reform 20 Years on', *Government Information Bulletin* (Windhoek), March, pp 12–13.

Schwarze, S. J. (1988) *The Role for the European Court of Justice in the Interpretation of Uniform Law among the Member States of the European Communities* (Baden-Baden: Nomos).

Shaw, W. H. (2003) '"They stole our land": Debating the Expropriation of White Farms in Zimbabwe', *Journal of Modern African Studies*, 41: 75–89.

Sutherland, P. (2005) *The Future of the WTO: Addressing Institutional Challenges in the New Millennium* (Geneva: WTO Consultative Board), <http://www.wto.org/english/thewto_e/10anniv_e/future_wto_e.htm> (accessed 20 October 2009).

Thornycroft, P. and Berger, S. (2010) 'Zimbabwe's White Farmers Plan to Seize Government Property', *Telegraph* (Harare and Johannesburg), 7 March, <http://www.telegraph.co.uk/news/worldnews/africaandindianocean/zimbabwe/7386395/Zimbabwes-white-farmers-plan-to-seize-government-property.html> (accessed 18 March 2010).

United Nations Development Programme (2000) *Human Rights and Development: Human Development Report, 2000* (New York: United Nations).

Viljoen, F. (1999) 'The Realisation of Human Rights through Sub-regional Institutions', *African Yearbook of International Law*, 7: 185–216.

Viljoen, F. (2007) *International Human Rights Law in Africa* (Oxford: Oxford University Press).

Weidlich, B. (2007a) 'Farmworkers at Odds with Former Police General', *The Namibian* (Windhoek), 7 June, <http://www.namibian.com.na/index.php?id=28&tx_ttnews%5Btt_news%5D=36413&no_cache=1 (accessed 28 March 2010).

Weidlich, B. (2007b) 'Forgotten Farmworkers Still Waiting', *The Namibian* (Windhoek), 24 August, <http://www.namibian.com.na/index.php?id=28&tx_ttnews[tt_news]=32255& no_cache=1 (accessed 28 March 2010).

Part 2

Juridical and regulatory challenges around SADC land issues

6 Indigenous land rights and claims under international law

Ilias Bantekas

6.1 Introduction

Indigenous land rights are not merely a sub-category of indigenous rights under international law. Rather, they are the cornerstone of indigenous wellbeing because of the inextricable connection between the indigenous psyche with its ancestral land. This chapter explores the historical roots of indigenous land rights and claims from the time of the early colonisers to the present day. It seeks to assess the current position in international law on the most acceptable form of legal title over land. This is by no means an easy task because indigenous land tenure is recognised through a variety of forms throughout the world and this fact alone renders the reaching of any definitive conclusions next to impossible. I have relied on positive sources, particularly state practice as this is reflected through domestic laws and judicial pronouncements and have generally refrained from giving legal credence to state practice that violates its own laws and regulations. In order to make this study as representative as possible I have drawn from laws and practices in developed and developing countries as well as from nations in the Americas, Asia, Africa and Australia. Hopefully, as a result of this exercise the reader will be in a better position to ascertain whether the various international instruments dealing with indigenous land rights reflect the current state of play or whether in fact they are more progressive than that actual law on-the-ground. In a study of this nature I have been mindful of focusing on my particular subject matter and I have thus refrained from assessing indigenous rights in general. It is assumed that the reader possesses at least a basic understanding of the topic.[1]

6.2 The historical justifications for the *terra nullius* and discovery doctrines: their contemporary effect on indigenous land rights

There is an inherent tension and incongruence between land rights granted to, or claimed, by indigenous groups in contemporary States and the understanding of the concept of land by such groups. States view land as a commodity with a fixed commercial value that is moreover a *sine qua non* component of their national economies. The value of land and the real property attached to it provides the

State with a significant amount of tax revenue, whether in the form of sales tax, annual tax on property, lease tax and community (council) tax. Moreover, arable land is the cornerstone of a country's feeding needs and its obvious breadbasket. The right cultivation of land minimises reliance on imports but also gives rise to the export of produce, which in turn entails profits for the exporting State. One should not also forget the riches found in the subsoil beneath the land. Whether these consist of hydrocarbons, minerals or simply building materials, subsoil resources are capable of giving States a significant amount of wealth. Finally, land is a living space for people and the natural environment controls man's subsistence conditions, whether for nourishment or for breathing purposes. All these considerations justify putting a price in the form of commodity on land that one, for example, cannot place on the atmosphere. The tension alluded to above materialises because indigenous communities view their relation to land as anything but a commodity. In the indigenous legal literature this relationship is typically described as naturalistic, religious, social and spiritual in nature, among others.[2] Modern man, in the majority of capitalist societies, cannot fully grasp this attachment to land because real property has not fully been associated with the notion of 'home', but as a commodity whose price fluctuates and which at any time when the price is right may be sold or otherwise invested. This approach is further augmented by the fact that few people fully own their houses and most usually pay lengthy instalments on the basis of a hefty mortgage. Moreover, in contemporary societies it is natural for family members to leave the family home in order to study or seek employment in other cities within the same country or elsewhere. As a result, attachment to a particular land or living area is less important today than it was in past times where family members did not migrate but inherited the land and laboured on it through successive generations.

Placing a monetary value on land is not achieved in a vacuum; rather, it requires the existence of an organised society, namely a State. In turn, the protection of the monetary value of land by the State is necessarily premised on law, usually promulgated formally, although informal land law is no less valid and binding. Before the advent of law to regulate the economics of land, it is not true to say that individuals or groups thereof do not assert entitlements to land they occupy. History, from the time of the Old Testament, is replete with wars fought for grazing and pastoral rights, notwithstanding the religious or other attachments people may have had with the contested lands. There is no record in history indicating that any one people simply lived on a land without utilising its natural resources for their sustenance and survival. Therefore, people have always attached a commercial value to land in one way or another. The advent of law did not only concretise this commercial underpinning, it also gave land a fixed monetary value. In addition, law changed the existing commercial relationships to land and it is this manifestation of law that is repugnant to indigenous people. By way of example, if indigenous group X traditionally cultivated and inhabited its ancestral land it did so on the implicit assumption of a tacit 'ownership'. This would have extended to the natural resources of the land (e.g. its water, soil, animals and adjacent sea), as well as its subsoil. Moreover, group X would have relied on an internal land tenure system whereby the land would be inheritable and subject to good and continuous use. The coming of the European colonisers and the application of law would have turned indigenous 'ownership' on its head. The colonisers would typically transplant their own land laws to the colonies, subject to certain notable exceptions, and proceed to re-distribute all land on the basis of these laws. As a result, the implicit indigenous ownership would be removed and replaced with the granting or purchase of formal ownership, land leases, subsoil concessions and others. The obvious problem here is not so much whether the discovery and annexation of new lands was lawful and legitimate, but whether the various forms of indigenous ownership could validly be suspended by the colonising power.

The lawfulness of the annexation will be assessed on the basis of the principle of inter-temporal law; i.e. that part of international law which was applicable at the time.[3] Indeed, all discoveries and annexations that took place at, or prior to, the middle of the nineteenth century, whether by war or peaceful means, were considered legitimate. This is true, for example, in respect of North and South America and Australia. It is certainly unfortunate and lamentable that millions of indigenous peoples died in the process, albeit this does not diminish the title to territory of the colonisers.[4] This result is true irrespective of the fact the law of discovery was created by the very entities that employed it to serve their own interests.[5] International relations are not premised on multiple legal regimes depending on the attributes (e.g. weak, powerful, rich, poor) of the parties or the past injustices they may have suffered. Moreover, there is nothing in international law and practice that purports to annul and invalidate its past precepts because by today's standards they are cruel, unjust, immoral, or only served the dictates of the powerful contrary to the rights of self-determination of the local population.

Discovery should be distinguished from the annexation of territory that belonged to a sovereign State and which was either ceded or taken as a result of force by the annexing State. Although both were traditionally permissible, the annexation that followed discovery was justified by the fact that the territory in question lacked formal ownership by another sovereign State. The discovering State was therefore entitled to claim this newly 'discovered' land as its own, subject to a continuous, effective and uninterrupted period of occupation. This doctrine of *terra nullius* (empty land or land belonging to no one) was predicated on the absence of exercise of sovereign powers by third States and not on the existence of an indigenous population that was otherwise opposed to a new sovereign rule. A people lacking sovereign identity in the community of nations at the time was incapable of making territorial entitlements, even in respect of its own ancestral lands. With today's standards the international law of occupation not only prohibits annexation but moreover renders any changes to local laws unlawful, unless they promote the health and safety of the occupied population.[6] The majority of human rights scholars criticise the Euro-centric and Christian-dominated colonial approach to discovery, which generally viewed indigenous populations as 'heathens' and backward, primarily because they were not baptised.[7] While many manifestations of this approach are unfortunate even with the standards of their era, this was not generally inconsistent with the dictates of their time and it should also be remembered that the colonisers did encounter a number of indigenous groups that treated their own members in atrocious ways.

The leading case in US legal history that endorsed the doctrine of discovery in the sense that it nullifies indigenous land claims of absolute ownership is *Johnson v McIntosh*,[8] which concerned the validity of a land purchase contract between two Native American nations and private land purchasers. Despite the accusations of bias and personal conflicts rightly (most probably) directed against Chief Justice Marshall, the US Supreme Court ruled that:

> Discovery gave title to the government, by whose subjects, or by whose authority it was made, against all other European governments, which title might be consummated by possession … While the different nations of Europe respected the rights of the natives, as occupants, they asserted the ultimate dominion to be in themselves; and claimed and exercised, as a consequence of this ultimate dominion, a power to grant the soil, while yet in possession of the natives. These grants have been understood by all, to convey a title to the grantees, subject only to the Indian right of occupancy.[9]

The right of discovery was therefore deemed to have extinguished full and complete ownership and sovereignty of the Indian tribes. This consideration was not a mere remnant of a distant past, but was sustained more than a century later in *Tee-Hit-Ton Indians v USA*.[10] In that case the Tee-Hit-Ton Alaska natives sued the US government for granting a timber concession to a private company in respect of a national forest over which they claimed to be its sole owners. The Supreme Court referred back to the doctrine of discovery, adding that the advent of colonial rule granted merely a right of occupancy to the indigenous groups, which is potential termination by the government without any legally enforceable obligation to compensate.[11]

This line of thinking should not be viewed as wholly unnatural or contrary to contemporary notions of human rights. Indeed, were indigenous peoples to enjoy full and uninterrupted sovereignty over their ancestral lands and subsoil thereof they would in effect enjoy a species of autonomy by reason of that very land tenure. This result is, however, absurd, because the granting of autonomy encompasses the explicit session of sovereign entitlements by the incumbent government; autonomy, therefore, cannot constitute a mere side effect stemming from the enjoyment of particular land rights. Rather, it must be explicitly granted as a political entitlement. This does not mean, however, that other more suitable land rights cannot be granted to indigenous peoples, such that would satisfy land tenure for future generations without giving rise to unnecessary tensions. The validity of the *terra nullius* doctrine has been sustained in practice in at least one contemporary respect; in order to explain and assess sovereignty claims. The International Court of Justice in the *Western Sahara* case dismissed legal title on the basis of the *terra nullius* doctrine on the following grounds:

> Whatever differences of opinion there may have been among jurists, the state practice of the relevant period [from 1884 onwards] indicates that territories inhabited by tribes or peoples having a social and political organisation were not regarded as *terrae nullius*. It shows that in the case of such territories the acquisition of sovereignty was not generally considered as effected unilaterally through 'occupation' of *terra nullius* by original title but through agreements concluded with local rulers. On occasion, it is true, the word 'occupation' was used in a non-technical sense denoting simply acquisition of sovereignty; but that did not signify that the acquisition of sovereignty through such agreements with authorities of the country was regarded as an 'occupation' of a *terra nullius* in the proper sense of these terms. On the contrary, such agreements with local rulers, whether or not considered as an actual 'cession' of the territory, were regarded as derivative roots of title, and not original titles obtained by occupation of *terrae nullius*.[12]

A closer reading of the judgment clearly suggests that not only was the indigenous population sufficiently well organised to constitute a *de facto* State, but that more importantly the Court considered that Spain proclaimed sovereignty over the contested territory on the basis of its agreements with the local chiefs and not on the grounds of *terra nullius*.[13] As a result, the Court refused to further entertain discussion of this doctrine. Clearly, however, it did not rule out the possibility that title premised on *terra nullius* was valid prior to 1884, as would be the case with indigenous populations – who were not sufficiently well organised it should be added – in North America and Australia. In fact, the Court would not, and could not doubt the validity of such titles and its discussion demonstrates that it perceived *Western Sahara* to constitute a very exceptional case. That indigenous peoples should enjoy exclusive or full ownership rights, as opposed to a sovereignty-type of ownership akin to full or partial autonomy has been confirmed by seminal judgments and progressive legislation rendered in developed nations. In *Mabo v Queensland* the High Court of Australia ruled that although the *terra nullius* doctrine could no longer be applied to deny aboriginal Australians rights to land, these were of an occupancy nature and the Australian government could in any event extinguish or remove these only under strict grounds.[14] Similarly, in *Delgamuukw v The Queen* the Supreme Court of Canada accepted that indigenous Canadians enjoyed a *sui generis* title to land, but that this consisted of a right to use and occupy it. This right was further restricted by the fact that said land could not be used for purposes other for which the Crown had designated it and can only be sold back to the Crown.[15] Naturally, these forms of ownership are *sui generis* and are far more enhanced than mere possession in that they constitute common law interests in land that cannot easily be extinguished. In the section dealing with indigenous land as a right to property it will be shown that the practice of most States with indigenous populations is to treat the granting of land as involving full and unimpeded communal ownership, although in practice evictions and eminent domain are frequent occurrences.

These developments demonstrate that whatever the feelings against the morality of discovery and *terra nullius* they have validly transferred title to the occupying powers as a matter of international law. What this means is that *vis-à-vis* third States the occupying power's sovereignty over the occupied land is absolute as it is over any claims of secession of the land's indigenous populations. The condemnation of the *terra nullius* doctrine for countries such as Australia and Canada merely means an internal re-distribution of property rights and a legal acknowledgment of the validity of indigenous customary law, expressed through the institution of native title. Let us now examine in what way this limited entitlement is entrenched in international law.

6.3 Indigenous land rights in contemporary international law

We have already briefly examined one of the sources of international law on this subject, that is, state practice, although we will come back to it with more examples in a following section. Such state practice provides evidence of a customary rule, which in the case at hand serves to demonstrate that States are willing to grant particular rights of use, occupation or ownership to indigenous populations that have occupied the contested land prior to colonisation. Indigenous occupation is both a matter of fact and a matter of law. A group has to provide evidence as to the duration of its occupation, the standard for which will be analysed subsequently in this chapter. From the point of view of law indigenous rights of occupancy or communal ownership are typically reflected in domestic constitutions and, or, in specific statutes. In the *Mayagna* case before the Inter-American Court of Human Rights the government of Nicaragua had granted a timber concession to a private company in respect of land occupied by an indigenous group that had not sought a title for its occupation, nor had the government demarcated the land. The Nicaraguan government argued that because the law required registration and titling, which the Mayagna had not undertaken, they possessed no valid native title. Nonetheless, evidence furnished showed that the group had occupied the land for at least three hundred years and moreover the right of 'communal ownership of lands' was guaranteed under Articles 5, 89 and 180 of the Nicaraguan Constitution. The Court and the Commission agreed that Nicaragua could not expect indigenous groups to undertake all the legal formalities associated with titling and that it had an obligation to demarcate their land, particularly since it had recognised the indigenous nature of the Mayagna. It thus affirmed their right to property under Article 21 of the Inter-American Convention on Human Rights as follows:

(a) the Mayagna Community has communal property rights to land and natural resources based on traditional patterns of use and occupation of ancestral territory. Their rights 'exist even without state actions which specify them'. Traditional land tenure is linked to a historical continuity, but not necessarily to a single place and to a single social conformation throughout the centuries. The overall territory of the Community is possessed collectively, and the individuals and families enjoy subsidiary rights of use and occupation;

(b) traditional patterns of use and occupation of territory by the indigenous communities of the Atlantic Coast of Nicaragua generate customary law property systems, they are property rights created by indigenous customary law norms and practices which must be protected, and they qualify as property rights protected by Article 21 of the Convention. Non-recognition of the equality of property rights based on indigenous tradition is contrary to the principle of non-discrimination set forth in Article 1(1) of the Convention;

(c) the Constitution of Nicaragua and the Autonomy Statute of the Regions of the Atlantic Coast of Nicaragua recognise property rights whose origin is found in the customary law system of land tenure which has traditionally existed in the indigenous communities of the Atlantic Coast. Furthermore, the rights of the Community are protected by the American Convention and by provisions set forth in other international conventions to which Nicaragua is a party;

(d) there is an international customary law norm which affirms the rights of indigenous peoples to their traditional lands.[16]

This Inter-American jurisprudence suggests that indigenous peoples may possess an inherent right under international law to communal ownership – subject, I should add, to non-discriminatory restrictions that serve public social interests – other than by official conferral by the apparatus of the State. The essence of this observation is that native title is deemed to exist irrespective of official recognition. Such recognition serves merely to demarcate indigenous land and guarantee all the rights over it against third parties. Communal indigenous rights 'encompass a broader and different concept [of territorial rights] that relates to the collective right to survival as an organised people, with control over their habitat as a necessary condition for reproduction of their culture, for their own development and to carry out their life aspirations. Property of the land ensures that the members of the indigenous communities preserve their cultural heritage'.[17] This line of thinking supports the exceptional nature of indigenous land ownership, as opposed to other forms of ownership within the same country. What this means is that although the State cannot discriminate between indigenous and other ownership, in cases of necessary expropriation, for example, it should adopt measures that take into consideration the particular relationship of indigenous peoples with their land, if indeed such exists in a particular case. The Inter-American Court succinctly noted that:

> This does not mean that every time there is a conflict between the territorial interests of private individuals or of the State and those of the members of the indigenous communities, the latter must prevail over the former. When States are unable, for concrete and justified reasons, to adopt measures to return the traditional territory and communal resources to indigenous populations, the compensation granted must be guided primarily by the meaning of the land for them.[18]

It is worth analysing two international instruments in order to assess the precise nature of the communal land rights pertaining to indigenous communities. These are the 2007 UN Declaration on the Rights of Indigenous Peoples[19] and ILO Convention No. 169 concerning Indigenous and Tribal Peoples in Independent Countries. This does not mean that the more generic human rights treaties do not cater for indigenous land rights. The opposite is in fact true. Rather, because these are very specific matters that could not have been negotiated and agreed in the context of an all-encompassing treaty they have subsequently been taken up by relevant treaty monitoring bodies or otherwise became the subject of progressive or evolutionary interpretation. By way of example, Article 27 of the 1966 International Covenant on Civil and Political Rights (ICCPR) guarantees the protection of minority group members and makes no explicit reference to indigenous rights. Nonetheless, it is evident that Article 27 may protect indigenous peoples where these also constitute a minority in a particular State. Moreover, given that minority protection encompasses some element of land tenure, it was not a far leap for the Human Rights Committee to assert that the enjoyment of rights under Article 27 'may consist in a way of life which is closely associated with territory and use of its resources. This may particularly be true of members of indigenous communities constituting a minority … With regard to the exercise of the cultural rights protected under Article 27, the Committee observes that culture manifests itself in many forms, including a particular way of life associated with traditional activities such as fishing or hunting and the right to live in reserves protected by law'.[20] This right to communal ownership is made explicit in Article 26 of the UN Declaration, which provides as follows:

1 Indigenous peoples have the right to the lands, territories and resources which they have traditionally owned, occupied or otherwise used or acquired.
2 Indigenous peoples have the right to own, use, develop and control the lands, territories and resources that they possess by reason of traditional ownership or other traditional occupation or use, as well as those which they have otherwise acquired.
3 States shall give recognition and protection to these lands, territories and resources. Such recognition shall be conducted with due respect to the customs, traditions and land tenure systems of the indigenous peoples concerned.

Article 26 of the UN Declaration is in my opinion more reflective of state practice than Article 14(1) of ILO Convention No. 169. The latter obliges member States to recognise the rights of ownership and possession of indigenous peoples over the lands which they traditionally occupy. This wording is much broader than its UN Declaration counterpart, which subdues all rights over land to 'traditional ownership or traditional occupation'. It may turn out that both provisions convey the same legal meaning in situations where traditional ownership is translated into legislation that vests indigenous peoples with indefinite and uninterrupted land tenure, which is otherwise not termed ownership. Moreover, it is practically impossible to ascribe ownership rights to a nomadic group that moves across territories in which it does not establish a permanent settlement. Equally, it probably makes more sense for traditional hunting groups to endow them with exclusive and uninterrupted use of their traditional hunting grounds rather than ownership of a limited territory. In any event, although most States have granted collective ownership rights, which are deemed absolute, in reality they are not. Concessions based on community interests, eminent domain justifications and prohibitions against selling traditional lands to any entity other than the territorial State entail a species of ownership that is subject to a web of possible limitations.

6.4 Indigenous ownership as a right to property

A recent study by the World Bank documented the precise content of land rights afforded to indigenous groups in 33 client countries.[21] It is instructive to iterate these results in order to assess state practice in this area of law and whether it conforms to the standards set in the aforementioned international instruments. As far as Asia is concerned, in China,[22] Thailand and Vietnam all land is owned fully by the State. In the Philippines, in accordance with Article 7 of the Indigenous Peoples Rights Act 1977, such groups are entitled to claim ownership over ancestral lands and claim all benefits from their natural resources. In Malaysia, some native title is recognised,[23] but in most cases indigenous peoples do not possess title and are considered 'tenants-at-will'. Similarly, in Indonesia all land belongs to the State but indigenous people have some limited customary land tenure to the extent that it does not conflict with ordinary property or other law. In Cambodia indigenous groups are entitled to communal ownership rights over their lands, which is tantamount to private ownership rights.[24] In South America the situation is slightly more clear and coherent. In Argentina community ownership of ancestral lands is recognised, although generally hampered by bureaucratic procedural hurdles, and is not available to indigenous peoples that have relocated to urban areas. Communal ownership rights are equally recognised in Chile, Colombia, Peru, Ecuador, Bolivia and Venezuela. In Brazil indigenous persons retain exclusive possession and use but ownership is vested in the State. In Central America the situation is more or less equally consistent. With the exception of Mexico and El Salvador, which do not recognise communal rights of ownership, Honduras, Nicaragua, Panama and Guatemala extend such rights to their indigenous people, subject to minor limitations. Russia, the world's largest country does not recognise land ownership for its indigenous populations.[25] In India and Pakistan communal ownership is possible but is subject to the dictates of regional bodies and the decisions of customary council of elders and others. In the case of developed nations we have already seen that land ownership is not generally afforded to indigenous peoples. In Canada, Indian lands are held in the name of the Crown and only a right to occupy and possess is granted to indigenous persons. The Sami people in Norway equally only enjoy usufructary rights,[26] whereas in the United States Indian lands are held in trust by the federal government, in which case the Indians enjoy either beneficial interests or some limited communal ownership.[27] Exceptionally, New Zealand recognises communal freehold in respect of the Maori.[28] Finally, in sub-Saharan Africa the situation is somewhat confusing because post-colonial governments have recognised traditional customary tenure rights, albeit these are vested to all persons without distinction between indigenous and non-indigenous. The landmark decision in the *Endorois* case will most probably have an impact on African land laws in the near future.

Having determined the normative recognition of indigenous ownership by reason of state practice it is instructive to assess its legal nature under the protection afforded by international human rights law to property. In a landmark decision the African Commission on Human and People's Rights (ACHPR) in the *Endorois* case was faced with the eviction of the Endorois people in Kenya from their ancestral lands in order to construct a game reserve and tourist facilities. The contested land was home to a lake which the Endorois considered a part of their own particular religious belief as having been formed after God became angry with their ancestors and as punishment sank the ground, thus forming lake Bogoria. All their kinsmen are buried adjacent to the lake and it is evident that their traditional ceremonies are also inextricably linked to the lake. The ACHPR confirmed the Endorois' spiritual connection to their land[29] and hence found a violation of Article 8 of the African Convention on Human and People's Rights relating to the freedom of religion.[30] The ACHPR accepted that indigenous rights on traditional lands constitute 'property' and the rights thereto accordingly 'property rights'.[31] The Commission went on to explain the content of these rights by reference to the UN Declaration on the Rights of Indigenous Peoples, as follows:

> The jurisprudence under international law bestows the right of ownership rather than mere access. The African Commission notes that if international law were to grant access only, indigenous peoples would remain vulnerable to further violations/dispossession by the State or third parties. Ownership ensures that indigenous peoples can engage with the State and third parties as active stakeholders than as passive beneficiaries.[32]

In the view of the African Commission, the following conclusions could be drawn: (a) traditional possession of land by indigenous people has the equivalent effect as that of a State-granted full property title; (b) traditional possession entitles indigenous people to demand official recognition and registration of property title; (c) the members of indigenous peoples who have unwillingly left their traditional lands, or lost possession thereof, maintain property rights thereto, even though they lack legal title, unless the lands have been lawfully transferred to third parties in good faith; and (d) the members of indigenous peoples who have unwillingly lost possession of their lands, when those lands have been lawfully transferred to innocent third parties, are entitled to restitution thereof or to obtain other lands of equal extension and quality.[33]

The ACHPR is emphatically stating that indigenous people possess full property rights over their ancestral lands irrespective if the State has registered or titled such land or if the group has satisfied any formal property requirements.[34] The fact that they constitute property rights distinguishes them from mere access rights or privileges that can be withdrawn or sold to third parties at any time by the government. This is a development that is certainly far more progressive than legislation applicable in many industrialised nations such as those to which reference has been made in this and previous sections of this chapter. Although it is implicit in the material analysed thus far, it should be emphasised that the land rights afforded to indigenous peoples are not meant to grant them any kind of autonomy, let alone sovereignty.

Human rights treaties oblige member States not only to afford but also to protect the rights enshrined therein. In the case of indigenous peoples this obligation is of twofold nature. On the one hand the State is under a duty to protect the right to property, while on the other hand it has to do so within the particular context in which indigenous land rights are exercised. Hence, if an indigenous group enjoys the land for its hunting and fishing needs, as far as the State is capable it must preserve and sustain the relevant ecosystem. Equally, if a group believes in its spiritual attachment to a lake this must not be exploited in such a way as to deplete or pollute its waters. The Inter-American Court of Human Rights in the *Saramanka* case has held that indigenous groups are owed special measures of protection in order to guarantee the full exercise of their rights.[35]

6.5 Restrictions to indigenous land rights

We have already seen the greatest restriction to indigenous land rights, which is the lack of full and complete ownership in certain States. Lack of ownership entails insecurity in land tenure, which although not necessarily a human rights violation brings about a perpetual Damoclean sword over the head of successive indigenous generations. The other dangers facing indigenous land tenure, whether ownership or possession, concern the so-called extinguishment of existing rights, or their partial extinguishment through the granting of concessions or leases to third parties by the government.[36] Another possible restriction is the amendment to the land tenure in a way that although does not affect it against third parties it changes the legal relationships between the members of the indigenous groups *per se*. Finally, even if no alteration is to be made to indigenous land tenure, it is not certain whether the members of the group are entitled to the subsoil resources beneath their land.

It has already been determined that native title over land is subject to some form of state confirmation. This provides a degree of legal certainty, but where it has not been granted the indigenous group concerned may otherwise demonstrate its status as such and demand the occupation of its ancestral land. This is possible because every country with indigenous populations has enshrined this entitlement in its constitution. Native title should be distinguished from land rights. The former, although requiring some positive act of recognition by the State, is generally deemed to be proven by the mere existence and continuity of the group and its customary law pertinent to the contested land. Native title serves to confirm the various entitlements under the group's customary law against third persons and thus to invalidate any counter-demands and claims by government or private parties.[37] Any lawful entitlements emanating therefrom may be challenged by the State on grounds of necessity, urgency, public benefit or other of a similar nature. However, because such a taking is detrimental to the enjoyment of the holder's property right, it should only be exercised by the State as a means of last resort, it must be fully justified and the owners must be offered fair and adequate compensation. In the case of indigenous land tenure the concept of monetary compensation is alien to those communities that pursue a traditional lifestyle and to whom removal from their ancestral abodes cannot be otherwise compensated. It is evident therefore that there is a qualitative difference between commercial and indigenous ownership which national legislatures must take into account.[38] As a result, if the relevant prescriptions of international indigenous law and human rights is to have any significance the taking of property by institutions such as eminent domain must be fundamentally distinguished in case of indigenous lands.[39] The guiding criterion in each case must be whether displacement can be prevented through the adoption of alternative measures. Any taking solely intended for profit, which destroys a traditional way of life or a site that is sacred to a particular group, is contrary to international law. In practice, national law differs considerably from the writings of scholars and the few international instruments are sparsely ratified. For example, at the time of writing of this chapter ILO Convention No. 169 had only received twenty ratifications, none of which were from the United States, Canada, Australia or African nations. What this means is that the true litmus test of the state of the law rests in the actual practice of States. With minor exceptions all legislation dealing with indigenous lands expressly or implicitly permits takings subject to a pressing social or public need. In general terms communal ownership, let alone *sui generis* possession, cannot trump any contrary constitutional demands.

Indigenous law is a fast-changing sphere and is susceptible to deep amendments from time to time. Thus, the change of government in some cases may signal significant changes to local indigenous land laws in favour of their tenants, as was the case in Australia with the end of the Howard government, which remained in power through four successive terms.[40] Very indicatively one should note the passage of the Native Title Amendment Act 2007 in Australia, which despite not strengthening indigenous land rights *per se* gave rise to several presumptions in favour of native title. This was potently expressed by Kirby J as follows:

> Laws that appear to deprive or diminish the pre-existing property rights of indigenous peoples must be strictly interpreted. This is especially so where such laws were not made with the effective participation of indigenous peoples themselves. Moreover, where (as in Australia) there is a constitutional guarantee providing protection against acquisition of property unless just

> terms are accorded, development of international law will encourage the national judge to give that guarantee the fullest possible protective operation.[41]

In a subsequent case an aboriginal group opposed the granting of a mining concession which would have meant the destruction of a sacred lake. The group was willing to sacrifice the lake in return for permanent jobs and educational prospects for their children, which, however, the planned investment would not deliver. The court, although recognising that native title did not give the aboriginals a right of veto against projects of this nature, it did find that their views held considerable weight in respect of any final determination.[42] This is a significant development that is important in assessing the attitude of Australia in respect of the limits which government can impose on native title.

Native title, at least as this is guaranteed under international law and implemented in domestic laws, is a collective right.[43] It does not belong to any one individual, but belongs in common to all members of the indigenous group. Thus, if a State were to re-organise customary land tenure only between the members of the group but in a manner that is alien to them and potentially destructive of the communal right itself, such action may well constitute an indirect taking. By way of example, this situation would arise where State A retained native title in respect of the lands occupied by group X but proceeded to enact legislation by which it granted commercial ownership equally to each member of the group. This may seem as enhancing the group's ownership capacity, but in reality it is potentially destructive because it allows for the land to be appropriated under terms applicable for commercial property and it moreover gives monetary value to the land, which may later be used against the indigenous group to show that the land possesses no sentimental or religious value.

One of the most cumbersome restrictions on indigenous land ownership is the requirement of proof as to the group's continuous occupation of the contested land and of its specific uses. This may seem pretty straightforward but it is not, particularly since in the determination of evidence the authorities may well justify the employment of ordinary evidentiary principles, such as written testimonies, witness reports and others which indigenous peoples are unable to furnish. Indigenous peoples do not generally keep written accounts and are typically aware of their ancestors' historical accounts by means of hearsay and storytelling. If these were to be discounted in determining their relationship to a particular geographical area on the basis that they were contrary to common evidentiary rules and principles one would in effect be disregarding the value and distinctiveness of indigenous culture altogether. It is for this reason that the Inter-American Commission and Court of Human Rights allow the testimonies of anthropologists and most national laws equally provide for distinct evidentiary rules in order to establish the veracity of an indigenous claim to land.[44] Australia, for example, recently adopted its Evidence Amendment Act 2008 which exempted all evidence relating to traditional law and custom from its regular hearsay and opinion evidence rules. The law similarly permitted the courts to extract evidence wholly or partially in narrative form, rather than in the usual format of questions and answers.[45]

An additional restriction to the enjoyment of indigenous land rights concerns the precise scope of the lands over which such entitlement may be exercised. What is certain is that this right extends over lands that have traditionally been occupied or considered sacred by the group. It is not at all certain whether international law obliges States to extend the same property rights over territories merely associated with the life of the group, such as adjacent hunting grounds. Article 14 of ILO Convention No. 169 provides that in addition:

> measures shall be taken in appropriate cases to safeguard the right of the peoples concerned to use lands not exclusively occupied by them, but to which they have traditionally had access for their subsistence and traditional activities. Particular attention should be paid to the situation of nomadic peoples and shifting cultivators in this respect.

This is, no doubt, hard for many countries to accept. The Court of Appeal of Malaysia recently held that proof of continuous occupation of land in order to grant native title to indigenous peoples is restricted only to their settlements, not to areas where 'they used to roam to forage for their livelihood in accordance with their tradition'.[46] The best and most sensible solution is to allow access to and use of the natural resources of such areas to indigenous groups without however any native title.

Closely related to the latter restriction is the extent to which native title encompasses ownership over the subsoil resources of the occupied land. Subsoil resources are generally distinguished from natural resources in that the former concern minerals whereas natural resources consist of anything on the surface of the earth, such as water, soil, plants and trees.[47] Save for a very limited number of exceptions[48] States do not extend land ownership over subsoil resources to private individuals or indigenous peoples. These are vested in the State and not the landowner.[49] In fact, many States in the developing world have adopted legislation that vests all subsoil resources to the State under the guise of a trust for the benefit of all peoples.[50] Indigenous peoples may, at best, be given a proportion of the earnings or possess the right of prior consultation for the project. The State may extract these through its own means, although in practice extraction takes place either through a concession or a variety of other agreements in which the risk is passed to the investor, such as so-called production sharing agreements (PSAs). As far as I am aware no case has come before an international tribunal or quasi-tribunal through which an indigenous group has claimed a continuous exploitation of subsoil resources in the land over which it enjoys native title. If such a case were to arise the tribunal would have to assess whether current mining laws, which seem to put forward a general principle of law, are consistent with native title under international law. My personal opinion is that indigenous mining would only take place for non-commercial purposes, which is opposite to the purpose of mining laws, the pursuit of which is profit. Therefore, the State should be able to come to some agreement with the indigenous group whereby small-scale, non-commercial artisanal mining could take place alongside the extensive mining of the State. This arrangement would not be detrimental to the financial and political interests of the State and would certainly accommodate the needs of indigenous populations.

6.6 Land claims

Much of this chapter, although largely concentrating on the nature of the rights pertinent to native title, indirectly referred to mechanisms through which indigenous land claims may be brought. Some of these have been brought before national courts, while others were submitted to international tribunals, such as the African Commission of Human and People's Rights and the Inter-American Court of Human Rights. It may be the case that some countries have set up specialised tribunals to deal with indigenous matters, albeit any final appeal against their decisions must surely be submitted to the country's highest court, whether this is a supreme court or a court of cassation. In each case the pertinent legislation treats the case as a single claim because of the collective nature of indigenous rights. Therefore, no one indigenous person can lay claim to his or her ancestral land unless this is done through the entity of the group. One of the biggest obstacles to bringing native title claims relates to the very recognition of a group as being of an indigenous nature. We have already examined situations where although an indigenous group was recognised as such it was not granted native title because it could either not prove continuous occupation of the contested land or because it had failed to apply for the necessary permits and demarcation thereof. The most acute manifestation of non-recognition, however, concerns situations in which a group's indigenous status is not entertained at all. This is particularly prevalent in Africa where most African governments are adamant that all natives therein are indigenous and that therefore no special protection should be granted to any tribal people. The African Commission on Human and People's Rights disagreed with this notion, arguing that it is legally possible for some African groups to be classified as indigenous on the basis of the following four criteria:

> occupation and use of a specific territory; the voluntary perpetuation of cultural distinctiveness; self-identification as a distinct collectivity, as well as recognition by other groups; an experience of subjugation, marginalisation, dispossession, exclusion or discrimination.[51]

Besides national courts and international human rights tribunals, two further avenues are available to indigenous people through which to satisfy their claims against the government. The first concerns claims before the Inspection Panel of the World Bank, whereas the other relates to bilateral agreements between the disputing parties. Paragraph 12 of the Resolution setting up the Inspection Panel states that:

> The Panel shall receive requests for inspection presented to it by an affected party in the territory of the borrower which is not a single individual (i.e. a community of persons such as an organisation, association, society or other

> grouping of individuals) or by the local representative of such party or by another representative … The affected party must demonstrate that its rights or interests have been or are likely to be directly affected by an action or omission of the Bank as a result of a failure of the Bank to follow its operational policies and procedures with respect to the design, appraisal, and/or implementation of a project financed by the Bank (including situations where the Bank is alleged to have failed in its follow-up on the borrower's obligations under loan agreements with respect to such policies and procedures) provided in all cases that such failure has had, or threatens to have, a material adverse effect. In view of the institutional responsibilities of the Executive Directors in the observance by the Bank of its operational policies and procedures, an Executive Director may in special cases of serious alleged violations of such policies and procedures ask the Panel for an investigation.[52]

It is obvious that the Panel, or the Bank for that matter, does not pursue land or other claims on behalf of indigenous peoples. Rather, it is solely interested for the integrity of its own lending operations and that of its debtors and creditors. This integrity will be assessed on the basis of the Bank's institutional policies and procedures and more specifically those pertinent to indigenous peoples. The World Bank's Operation Directive 4.10 on Indigenous Peoples, as revised in July 2005, constitutes a Guide for the Bank's staff as well as its borrowers. Its scope and language is more conservative but in my opinion reflects current state practice. Articles 16 and 17 of the Directive demands that borrowers must pay particular attention to:

> 16. (a) the customary rights of the indigenous peoples, both individual and collective, pertaining to lands or territories that they traditionally owned, or customarily used or occupied, and where access to natural resources is vital to the sustainability of their cultures and livelihoods;
>   (b) the need to protect such lands and resources against illegal intrusion or encroachment;
>   (c) the cultural and spiritual values that the Indigenous Peoples attribute to such lands and resources; and
>   (d) Indigenous Peoples' natural resources management practices and the long-term sustainability of such practices.
>
> 17. If the project involves (a) activities that are contingent on establishing legally recognised rights to lands and territories that Indigenous Peoples have traditionally owned or customarily used or occupied (such as land titling projects), or (b) the acquisition of such lands, the IPP sets forth an action plan for the legal recognition of such ownership, occupation, or usage. Normally, the action plan is carried out before project implementation; in some cases, however, the action plan may need to be carried out concurrently with the project itself. Such legal recognition may take the following forms:
>   (a) full legal recognition of existing customary land tenure systems of indigenous peoples; or

(b) conversion of customary usage rights to communal and/or individual ownership rights.

If neither option is possible under domestic law, the IPP includes measures for legal recognition of perpetual or long-term renewable custodial or use rights.

The Directive is not meant to prejudice the indigenous land rights legislation of the Bank's client States. It is, however, aimed at informing both its debtors, borrowers and most of all the entities implementing projects financed by it to make a number of considerations when undertaking projects involving indigenous peoples. A complaint by an indigenous group that a project financed by the Bank failed to respect their rights under the Directive may cause the Bank to suspend the project or trigger contractual penalties under the terms of the contract. It is thus a potentially powerful mechanism.

It should not be thought, however, that all indigenous peoples wish to live in their ancestral lands abandoned from the rest of the world. This is a fallacy. In fact, a number of projects financed by the World Bank, particularly those requiring transit or access through indigenous lands, were faced with demands from indigenous people that included education and employment opportunities over and above any compensation for the loss of their lands. It is therefore necessary in every land dispute, demarcation or granting of native title for the relevant governments and international organisations to seek the consent and viewpoint of the indigenous groups concerned.[53]

6.7 Conclusion

The international law of indigenous peoples has always been rapidly changing, subject to political conflicts and intensive lobbying and is always in constant flux. No significant international treaty solely designated for indigenous peoples exist and most texts are premised on soft law and state practice. Nonetheless, mainly through the exhilarating struggle of NGOs, as well as regional and global international organisations the plight of indigenous peoples has come a long way in the last twenty years. Many of the seminal judgments throughout the globe have come about during this space of time. The issue of indigenous land rights is particularly acute because indigenous populations are traditionally attached to their ancestral lands in ways that people in contemporary societies cannot fully grasp or otherwise comprehend. Following the analysis in this chapter two conclusions can be drawn. Firstly, there exists sufficient state practice through a relatively safe representative sample of domestic legislation on the basis of which the veracity of soft law instruments can be assessed. Secondly, this state practice aptly demonstrates that two general models of indigenous land ownership are recognised; full ownership that is communal in nature and limited ownership, typically in the form of rights of possession and use, exclusive or not. Developed nations usually refrain from granting full ownership rights, although in practice the limited ownership offered offers a number of significant benefits to indigenous peoples and the latter are always consulted in respect of projects that may affect their livelihood on ancestral lands. While full ownership is typically offered in many developing nations its precise content and quality is not always sufficient to guarantee legal certainty and tenure safety. The greatest threat to both forms of tenure (i.e. communal ownership and possession or use) is extinguishment by governmental action. In fact, this author is not aware of any legislation that protects against partial or total extinguishment for reasons of public necessity.

The emerging trend is to secure tenure safety irrespective of the model of ownership ultimately adopted. Although this will never halt the imposition of some limitations, future international instruments can be more realistic and offer States the possibility of elaborating on measures of extinguishment which they feel very strongly about. In any event, indigenous people should be able to retain a decisive vote in respect of projects that affect their lands.

Notes

1 For a general reading the reader should consult either of the following: J. Anaya (2004); A. Xanthaki (2007).

2 UN Commission on Human Rights, 'Indigenous Peoples and their Relationship to Land', UN Doc E/CN.4/Sub.2/2001/21 (11 June 2001), 7–9. See also *Mayagna (Sumo) Awas Tingni Community v Nicaragua*, Inter-Am Ct HR, Ser C No 79 (31 August 2001), para 149, which held: 'Among indigenous peoples there is a communitarian tradition regarding a communal form of collective property of the land, in the sense that ownership of the land is not centred on an individual but rather on the group and its community. Indigenous groups, by the fact of their very existence, have the right to live freely in their own territory; the close ties of indigenous people with the land must be recognised and understood as the fundamental basis of their cultures, their spiritual life, their integrity, and their economic survival. For indigenous communities, relations to the land are not merely a matter of possession and production but a material and spiritual element which they must fully enjoy, even to preserve their cultural legacy and transmit it to future generations.'

3 *Western Sahara* (Advisory Opinion) 1975 ICJ Reports 12, para 79.

4 Unless, of course, it is contrary to, or impedes, the exercise of self-determination of the local population at a later date. This is too complex an issue to discuss in the limited confines of this chapter.

5 See S. Dodds (1998), who considers that as significant as the values and structures of indigenous peoples may be, they are unworkable in the contemporary framework of State institutions.

6 Hague Convention No IV (1907), Regulations Respecting the Laws and Customs of War on Land, Article 43, 1 *Bevans* 631.

7 See generally R. A. Williams (1990); A. Anghie (2007).

8 *Johnson's Lessee v McIntosh* [1823] 8 Wheat 543.

9 Ibid, pp 576, 574.

10 *Tee-Hit-Ton Indians v USA* (1955) 348 US 272.

11 Equally, in *City of Sherrill v Oneida Indian Nation of New York* (1957) 125 S Ct 1478, the doctrine of discovery was implicitly upheld in respect of a dispute over whether the Oneida Indian nation ancestral lands were sovereign and thus not subject to taxation.

12 *Western Sahara* (Advisory Opinion), above, n 3, para 89.

13 Ibid, para 81.

14 *Mabo v Queensland (No 2)* (1992) 175 CLR 1. It should, however, be noted that prior to *Mabo (2)* Australian courts had recognised the right of aboriginals to retain occupancy of their ancestral lands. See *Gerhardy v Brown* (1985) 159 CLR 70.

15 *Delgamuukw v The Queen in Right of the Province of British Columbia and the Attorney-General of Canada* [1997] 3 SCR 1010.
16 *Mayagna (Sumo) Awas Tingni Community v Nicaragua* judgment, above, n 2, para 140.
17 *Case of the Yakye Axa Indigenous Community v Paraguay*, Judgment, Inter-Am Ct HR Ser C No 125 (17 June 2005), para 146.
18 Ibid, para 149.
19 UNGA Res 61/295 (13 September 2007).
20 Human Rights Committee, General Comment No 23, UN Doc CCPR//C/21/Rev 1/Add 5 (1994), paras 3, 2 and 7.
21 See IBRD Operations Evaluation Department, *Implementation of Operational Directive 4.20 on Indigenous Peoples: An Independent Desk Review*, 5–38, <http://www.worldbank.org/oed/indigenouspeople/docs/IP1.pdf>.
22 China reserves special treatment for ethnic minorities and has set up autonomous regions, but these laws should not be viewed as also protecting indigenous peoples, despite some overlap.
23 That indigenous land rights are tantamount to normal property rights under Article 13 of the Constitution has been duly recognised by the Malaysian High Court in *Adong bin Kuwau and 51 Others v Government of Jahore* [1997] 1 MLJ 418, confirmed by the Malaysian Court of Appeal [1998] 2 MLJ 158.
24 Cambodian Land Law 2001, Articles 25–27. The Cambodian government in April 2009 proceeded to adopt legislation through which the titling of customary title could be officially concretised. See ECOSOC Permanent Forum on Indigenous Issues, Information Received from Cambodia, UN Doc E/C.19/2010/12/Add.5 (16 February 2010). It should, however, be noted that the Cambodian government frequently flouts its indigenous laws by granting concessions on protected lands to foreign investors.
25 See A. Shapovalov (2005), where the author argues that Russia adheres to the *terra nullius* doctrine.
26 See H. Minde (2000).
27 See generally, N. J. Newton, R. Anderson *et al* (2005).
28 For a survey of the Waitangi Treaty and its reinvigoration and the work of the Waitangi Tribunal in securing Maori land and resource rights see P. McHugh (1991).
29 *Centre for Minority Rights Development (Kenya) and Minority Rights Group International on behalf of Endorois Welfare Council v Kenya* [*Endorois* case], Case No 276/2003, Decision on Merits (4 February 2010), paras 156, 166.
30 Ibid, para 173.
31 Ibid, para 187.
32 Ibid, para 204.
33 Ibid, para 209.
34 Canadian courts distinguish between title and rights and hold that a right may exist independently of title. See *R v Van der Peet* (1996) 137 DLR 289 and *R v Adams* [1996] 138 DLR 657, confirmed in *Delgamuukw v British Columbia* (1997) 153 DLR, para 138.
35 *Case of the Saramanka People v Suriname*, Judgment (28 November 2007).
36 In *Wik Peoples v Queensland* (1996) 187, CLR 1 the High Court of Australia held that pastoral leases granted by the government on indigenous land occupied under native title did not extinguish such native title where the lease was not exclusive. In situations, however, where the lease gave the leaseholder exclusive possession native title was necessarily extinguished. This judgment led to the adoption of Native Title Amendment Act 1998, which provided guarantees to non-indigenous leaseholders that their lease would not be nullified by the operation of native title.
37 In some countries it is not unlikely that native title – in the sense of recognition of pre-existing customary law – is indistinguishable from land rights validated by the State. In Australia, for example, the two are distinct.
38 See *Griffiths v Minister for Lands, Planning and Environment* (Northern Territory) [2008] HCA 20, *per* Kirby J.

39 In *Wurridjal v Commonwealth* (2009) 237 CLR 309, the High Court of Australia held that intervening legislation through which the compulsory acquisition of five-year leases in aboriginal land and the abrogation of relevant permits in order to enter such lands was just because it allowed for recovery of reasonable compensation.
40 Australian Human Rights Commission (2009) 'The State of Land Rights and Native Title Policy in Australia in 2009', in *Native Title Report*, 2–7, where the Commissioner undertakes an account of the anti-aboriginal policies of the Howard administration in order to emphasise the progress achieved through the new developments.
41 *Wurridjal v Commonwealth*, above, n 39, 413.
42 *Western Desert Lands Aboriginal Corporation (Jamukurnu – Yapalikunu) Western Australia Holocene Pty Ltd* [2009] NNTTA 49.
43 Exceptionally, in some countries, such as Australia, it is possible for native title to be conferred on an individual, provided that his or her particular customary law vested in that person traditional land tenure.
44 In *Nor Anak Nyawai and Three Others v Borneo Pulp Plantation Sdn Bhd and Two Others* [2001] 6 MLJ 241, para 29, the Malaysian High Court admitted oral tradition evidence of native customary rights as hearsay, rejecting the arguments of the defendants.
45 Australian Human Rights Commission (2008) *Native Title Report* (Sydney: Australian Human Rights Commission), pp 19–20.
46 *Sagong bin Tasi and Others v Kerajaan Negeri Selangor and Others* [2002] 2 MLJ 591. See P. Crook (2005) for an analysis of other appellant decisions confirming this result.
47 See J. C. Tresierra (1999).
48 In Canada, some Aboriginal nations were given rights in various treaties or statutes, while in the United States native tribes usually have the right to exploit oil and minerals on their lands. In New Zealand, however, the Maori have a certain level of control over the exploitation of non-renewable resources on their lands. See IBRD Operations Evaluation Department, 'Implementation of Operational Directive 4.20 on Indigenous Peoples: An Independent Desk Review' (Washington, DC: IBRD), p 42.
49 H. Hannum (1996), p 93.
50 This is the case, for example, with section 1 of Nigeria's 1978 Land Use Act, which 'vests all the lands (and mineral oils) comprised in the territory of the state in the governor of the state in trust for the common benefit of all Nigerians'. Given its trust status the Act distinguishes the title to land vested in the State from the beneficial ownership that remains with the community. M. Banire (2002) at p 18. This result was confirmed in *Gamba Abioye v Sa'adu Yakubu* (1991) 5 NWLR 130 SC, where it was held that the bare trust established must be executed by the governor in accordance with the provisions of the Act, thus giving legitimacy to the view that the local communities possess a residual right of ownership in the land and its minerals.
51 *Endorois* Decision, above, n 29, para 150.
52 IBRD Res 93–10 and IDA Res 93–96 (22 September 1993).
53 See I. Bantekas (2005), where I discuss the plight of the Bakola tribe in Cameroon.

Bibliography

Anaya, J. (2004) *Indigenous Peoples in International Law* (Oxford: Oxford University Press).

Anghie, A. (2007) *Imperialism, Sovereignty and the Making of International Law* (Cambridge: Cambridge University Press).

Banire, M. (2002) *The Nigerian Law of Trusts* (Caldwell: Caxton Press).

Bantekas, I. (2005) 'Sociological Concerns arising from World Bank Projects and their Impact on Sub-Saharan Indigenous Peoples', *International Journal of Law in Context*, 1: 143.

Crook, P. (2005) 'After Adong: The Emerging Doctrine of Native Title in Malaysia', *Journal of Malaysian and Comparative Law*, 3: 71.

Dodds, S. (1998) 'Justice and Indigenous Land Rights', *Inquiry*, 41: 187.

Hannum, H. (1996) *Autonomy, Sovereignty and Self-determination: The Accommodation of Conflicting Rights* (Pittsburgh, PA: University of Pennsylvania Press).

McHugh, P. (1991) *The Maori Magna Carta: New Zealand Law and the Treaty of Waitangi* (Oxford: Oxford University Press).

Minde, H. (2000) 'Sami Land Rights in Norway: A Test Case for Indigenous Peoples', *Indigenous Law Bulletin*, 8(2–3): 107–25.

Newton, N. J., Anderson, R. *et al.* (2005) *Cohen's Handbook of Federal Indian Law* (London: Lexis Nexis).

Shapovalov, A. (2005) 'Straightening out the Backward Legal Regulation of Backward Peoples' Claim to Land in the Russian North: The Concept of Indigenous Neo-modernism', *Georgetown International Environmental Law Review*, 17: 435.

Tresierra, J. C. (1999) 'Rights of Indigenous Groups over Natural Resources in Tropical Forests' (Working Paper, Washington, DC: Inter-American Development Bank).

Williams, R. A. (1990) *The American Indian in Western Legal Thought: The Discourses of Conquest* (Oxford: Oxford University Press).

Xanthaki, A. (2007) *Indigenous Peoples and United Nations Standards: Self-determination, Culture and Land* (Cambridge: Cambridge University Press).

7 The new scramble for Africa

Towards a human rights-based approach to large-scale land acquisitions in the Southern African Development Community region

Jérémie Gilbert and David Keane**

... and that has increased; this unappeasable hunger for land.

John B. Keane, 'The field' (1965)

7.1 Introduction

Large-scale land acquisitions are a direct result of the vagaries of the global food market, seriously compromised by the 2007–08 crisis which led to food riots in over twenty States.[1] In what has been labelled a 'land grab', there has been a sharp acceleration in acquisition of lands in Africa, and globally, by foreign investors in developing countries seeking to produce crops for export. This rush for land has been generated by several factors but reflects concerns of States for their food security, as well as the increasing demand for biofuels globally.[2] Generally, while large-scale land acquisitions have been predominantly associated with the recent strive to acquire land for food production, other forms of agribusiness are affected such as mining, petroleum, forestry and tourism. However, the present chapter focuses on food as the central concern emerging from the phenomenon.

Investment in foreign farms is not new, but what distinguishes the recent acquisitions is their scale – worth up to US$30 billion and involving some 20 million ha of farmland in poor countries in Africa, Cambodia, Pakistan and the Philippines, according to the International Food Policy Research Institute.[3] Africa is particularly touched, to the extent that the rush to acquire farming land has been referred to as the 'new scramble for Africa'.[4] This makes direct reference to the colonial 'scramble for Africa' when five European powers divided most of the land in Africa amongst themselves, with total disregard for the rights of the local populations.[5] The first parallel is that foreign companies, investors and States are taking control of large areas of land, with the 'scramble' for food production and access to natural resources rather than political control. A further parallel is the haste inherent in the word 'scramble'; it should be recalled that in just half a generation Europe controlled virtually the whole continent of Africa, and it is feared that the contemporary process could be similarly swift.

A further distinguishing feature of large-scale land acquisitions is the involvement of governments. Foreign farming investment in the past was conducted by firms, but present acquisitions can also be governments. The complexity of the land deals is enhanced by the fact that 'there is no single dominant model for financial and ownership arrangements but rather a wide variety of locally specific arrangements among governments and the private sector'.[6] Foreign Direct Investment (FDI) is cited by host governments as the reason why they are inviting land acquisitions, with the bargaining power on the side of the investors, especially given the support of the host State or local elites.[7] Hence the July 2009 meeting of the G8 promised a code of conduct based on principles of best practice to provide greater regulation, with support from the African Union.[8] Grassroots protests are pointing to 'neo-liberal policies of transnational corporations, the WTO and large-scale corporatisation of farming' as directly responsible for an alarming, unregulated process.[9]

The best-known example of a large-scale land acquisition was the proposed land lease by Daewoo Logistics Corporation in Madagascar of 1.3 million ha, about half of Madagascar's arable land, to grow half of South Korea's corn, which received significant media attention.[10] The project finally collapsed due to the heavy civil society backlash against the lease, causing the resignation of the country's president.[11] But this is only the beginning, it seems. For example the Gulf States, 'pioneers of this agri-colonialism', have found that they can no longer rely on regional and global markets to feed their populations and have hastened to secure food supplies.[12] Qatar, with only one percent of its land suitable for farming, has purchased 40,000 ha in Kenya for crop production. China has purchased 101,171 ha in Zimbabwe in June 2008 and invested 800 million dollars in Mozambique to modernise agriculture for export rice production.

The chapter seeks a rights-based approach to large-scale land acquisitions. Section 7.2 will examine the right to food, and in particular the mandate of the Special Rapporteur on the Right to Food, Olivier de Schutter, who has produced a report examining the issues surrounding acquisitions with a proposed set of minimum principles for negotiations between States and corporations. Section 7.3 analyses the right to land as a human right, positing that the system of communal land ownership in the SADC region is endangered by the rush to generate FDI through land leases. It also raises the question of indigenous and pastoralist land rights. Section 7.4 examines the right to development, which is used as a justification for leasing lands. The section highlights the concurrent obligations on States to fulfil the right to development through recognition of interlinking rights of peoples to control decisions which affect their economic and social development. Section 7.5 isolates transnational corporations as non-state actors who must be accountable for the process. The difficulties in the home–host state dynamic, and the potential extraterritorial jurisdiction of the International Covenant on Economic, Social and Cultural Rights, are mooted.

Overall the aim is to signal the alarming move towards large-scale land acquisitions in the SADC region, and the potential for human rights to provide a regulatory framework. It is suggested that the issue could galvanise the international movement towards non-state actor accountability, which has been evolving for several decades.

7.2 The right to food

Colin Gonsalves writes: 'there can be no more fundamental right for all people than the right to food'.[13] It is a volatile issue that transcends hunger and involves nations and large corporations.[14] The 2008 global food crisis has accelerated the process of large-scale acquisitions, with major food-importing and capital-exporting States losing confidence in the global market as a stable and reliable source of food.[15] The right to food discourse has directly engaged with the question of large-scale land acquisitions through a recent report by the present UN Special Rapporteur on the Right to Food, Olivier de Schutter.[16]

The right is found in a range of international instruments and has its origins in Article 25 of the Universal Declaration of Human Rights (UDHR).[17] That provision declared that everyone has the right to an adequate standard of living, 'including food'. This proclamation was realised in the 1966 covenants, with the right to food considered an implied corollary of the right to life under the International Covenant on Civil and Political Rights (ICCPR).[18] The right has its strongest legal basis in Article 11 of the International Covenant on Economic, Social and Cultural Rights (ICESCR).[19] According to Article 11(1), States Parties expressly recognise the right of everyone to an adequate standard of living 'including adequate food'. Article 11(2) proclaims the 'fundamental right of everyone to be free from hunger', with Article 11(2)(a) requiring States 'to improve methods of production, conservation and distribution of food', in particular reforming agrarian systems to achieve the most efficient use of natural resources; and Article 11(2)(b) implementing 'an equitable distribution of world food supplies'.

The Committee on Economic, Social and Cultural Rights characterises the provision as the human right to *adequate* food, and its General Comment 12 in 1999 sets out the Committee's expectations for the fulfilment of this right.[20] The General Comment was the result of a request by Member States during the 1996 World Food Summit for a better definition and understanding of the principles inherent in the right. It is premised on the belief that the roots of the problem of hunger and malnutrition are not lack of food but lack of access to available food.[21]

The right is realised when 'every man, woman and child, alone or in community with others, has the physical and economic access at all times to adequate food or means for its procurement'.[22] The concept of 'adequacy' is particularly significant as it underlines that the right must not be interpreted in a narrow restrictive sense, equivalent to a minimum package of calories, proteins and other nutrients. The meaning of 'adequacy' is determined by prevailing social, economic, cultural, climatic, ecological and other factors, which involves the idea of long-term availability and accessibility.[23] Thus the Committee considers that the core content of the right implies:

> The availability of food in a quantity and quality sufficient to satisfy the dietary needs of individuals, free from adverse substances, and acceptable within a given culture; The accessibility of such food in ways that are sustainable and that do not interfere with the enjoyment of other human rights.[24]

The right to adequate food imposes three levels of obligations on States Parties, the obligation to respect, protect and fulfil.[25] 'Respect' is negative in that States Parties are obliged not to take any measures resulting in the prevention of access to adequate food. 'Protect' requires positive measures to ensure enterprises or individuals do not deprive individuals of their access to adequate food. 'Fulfil' is the widest obligation, meaning States must actively engage in activities intended to strengthen access to resources and means to ensure their livelihood, including food security. It also implies the direct provision of the right.[26] However, the Committee recognises that the right 'will have to be realized progressively'.[27]

Violations of the right occur when a State Party is unwilling to comply, and has demonstrated that every effort has been made to use all the resources at its disposal in an effort to satisfy these minimum obligations. The State has the burden of proof in this regard.[28] Examples include the 'adoption of legislation or policies which are manifestly incompatible with pre-existing legal obligations relating to the right to food; and failure to regulate activities of individuals or groups so as to prevent them from violating the right to food of others'.[29] States must regulate the activities of the private business sector and civil society to ensure conformity with the right to food.[30] The right must be especially fulfilled for vulnerable population groups.[31] The Committee emphasises the need for 'the adoption of a framework law as a major instrument in the implementation of the national strategy concerning the right to food.'[32] Effective judicial remedies at the national or international level must be provided.[33] The World Bank and International Monetary Fund (IMF) are included as addressees in the General Comment.[34]

In 2002, the UN Special Rapporteur on the Right to Food elaborated the definition of the right as follows:

> to have regular, permanent and unrestricted access, either directly or by means of financial purchases, to quantitatively and qualitatively adequate and sufficient food corresponding to the cultural traditions of people to which the consumer belongs, and which ensures a physical and mental, individual and collective fulfilling and dignified life free of fear.[35]

In 2004, the Food and Agricultural Organisation (FAO) issued its Voluntary Guidelines to Support the Progressive Realisation of the Right to Adequate Food in the Context of National Food Security.[36] These do not establish legally-binding obligations but rather act as a human rights-based practical tool addressed to all States.[37]

The present Special Rapporteur, Olivier de Schutter, has issued a recent study on the question of large-scale land acquisitions, which proposes a series of principles and measures to ensure human rights standards are protected.[38] He signals that the right to food framework is important for the debate on large-scale land acquisitions or leases, arguing in terms of potential violations:

> The human right to food would be violated if people depending on land for their livelihoods, including pastoralists, were cut off from access to land,

> without suitable alternatives; if local incomes were insufficient to compensate for the price effects resulting from the shift towards the production of food for exports; or if the revenues of local smallholders were to fall following the arrival on domestic markets of cheaply-priced food, produced on the more competitive large-scale plantations developed thanks to the arrival of the investor.[39]

In using the language of violations, the Special Rapporteur is addressing all States and not only those that have ratified the ICESCR and have a concurrent obligation under Article 11. Thirteen out of the fifteen SADC States have ratified the Covenant; Angola, Democratic Republic of the Congo, Lesotho, Madagascar, Malawi, Mauritius, Namibia, Seychelles, South Africa, Swaziland, United Republic of Tanzania, Zambia and Zimbabwe.[40] The Special Rapporteur's mandate expressly mentions co-operation with the Committee on Economic, Social and Cultural Rights, emphasising the link between his office and the rights and obligations under the ICESCR.[41] However, the 2000 Commission on Human Rights resolution that founded the mandate also recalls the UDHR, the Universal Declaration on the Eradication of Hunger and Malnutrition and the Rome Declaration on World Food Security and the Plan of Action of the World Food Summit, emphasising the universality of the Special Rapporteur's recommendations.[42] Paragraph 2 of the resolution reaffirms 'the right of everyone to have access to safe and nutritious food, consistent with the right to adequate food, and the fundamental right of everyone to be free from hunger'.[43]

Hunger is considered 'an outrage and a violation of human dignity', requiring the adoption of urgent measures, while States are encouraged to 'achieve progressively the full realization of the right to food', in line with the prevailing philosophy of the ICESCR.[44] The ICESCR distinction between the right to adequate food and the *fundamental* right to be free from hunger was repeated in Human Rights Council resolution 6/2, which extended the period of the Special Rapporteur's mandate.[45] Therefore the mandate quite clearly distinguishes between hunger and adequate food. The fundamental right of everyone to be free from hunger is granted to all persons and is an obligation on all States, through a link with the universal concept of human dignity. The obligation to progressively realise the right to adequate food falls on States that have ratified the ICESCR, however the thematic special procedures apply to all States and the Special Rapporteur's recommendations to realise this right need to be followed in the entire SADC region.

According to Smita Narula, there is a question as to whether the right to food could be said to be a norm of customary international law, which has not been sufficiently analysed.[46] It would seem that an argument could be made that the fundamental right to be free from hunger has achieved this status, as indicated by its inclusion in the Millennium Development Goals which saw universal participation and support of States.[47] It is more difficult to extend this argument to the broader right to adequate food.

Nevertheless the right to food has been viewed as an essential means of upholding other rights. In particular, the African Commission's decision on the harm caused by Shell and the Nigerian government in Ogoniland emphasises that the right to food is implicit in the African Charter.[48] The African Commission found: 'the right to food is inseparably linked to the dignity of human beings and is therefore essential for the enjoyment and fulfilment of such other rights as health, education, work and political participation.'[49] The decision is significant in that the link to human dignity is attributed to the broader right to food, rather than freedom from hunger.

The Special Rapporteur's study on large-scale land acquisitions can at a minimum be characterised as an authoritative interpretation of: States Parties' obligations to uphold the right to adequate food under the ICESCR; universal obligations stemming from Article 25 UDHR and related declaratory instruments on the right to food; and international human rights standards. As well as presenting the potential for violations of Article 11, a number of conditions are proposed under which investments should be made. The study is therefore not *prima facie* against such acquisitions; it is arguing instead for a more structured approach which places human rights standards at the centre of negotiations between investors and States. If large-scale land acquisitions and leases are to benefit all of the parties concerned, and the study is quite certain that they can,[50] an appropriate institutional framework before the arrival of investors is essential. If States Parties wait until such investments arrive, this will make it less likely that such a framework will be implemented effectively. This is because large investors may gain sufficient influence to avoid regulation that would impact on their interests. Eleven minimum principles are given, which are addressed to investors, home States, host States, local peoples, indigenous peoples and civil society. They can be summarised as follows:

1. Negotiations leading to investment agreements must be transparent, with the full and effective participation of local communities whose access to land may be affected by the agreement;
2. Transfer of land-use or ownership can only take place with the free, prior and informed consent of the local communities. This is particularly relevant to indigenous communities given their historical experience of dispossession;
3. States should adopt legislation protecting land rights including individual titles or collective registration of land use in order to ensure full judicial protection;
4. Local populations should benefit from the revenues generated by the investment agreement;
5. Host States and investors should promote farming systems that are sufficiently labour-intensive to secure employment;
6. Modes of agricultural production must respect the environment and not accelerate climate change, soil erosion and depletion of freshwater reserves;
7. Obligations of the investor should be defined in clear, enforceable terms, with the potential inclusion of pre-defined sanctions which fully compensate for potential violations of terms;
8. A certain minimum percentage of the produce should be sold on local markets with the potential for increases dependent on international market prices;

9 Impact assessments on vulnerable groups should be conducted prior to the arrival of investors, notably women, ethnic groups and pastoralists or itinerant farmers;
10 Indigenous peoples' right to land, as recognised under international law, will be upheld by obtaining their full, free and informed consent, in particular in relation to the exploitation of minerals, water or other resources; and
11 Labour rights of waged agricultural labourers will be respected and promoted, consistent with relevant ILO standards.[51]

The study emphasises that all of these principles are based on contemporary human rights law, and while they are designed to inform current initiatives including efforts by regional and international organisations to frame further guidelines, States should not wait until these are adopted to act in accordance with existing human rights obligations. Home States are required to regulate the activities of investors abroad if host States are unable or unwilling to do so. The World Bank and its private sector arm, the International Finance Corporation, are bound by international human rights law and should make support for such large-scale investments contingent on compliance with these minimum principles.[52] They are 'not optional; they follow from existing international human rights norms'.[53]

7.3 Land rights as human rights

As outlined in the introduction, one of the important impacts of the acquisition of land by foreign companies is on the right to land of local communities. On the surface, most of the lands that have been leased to foreign companies have thus far been State-owned lands.[54] However, these lands are in fact customarily owned and used by local communities who are directly affected, since they are losing access and enjoyment of the lands they are living on. For most of the concerned communities, the land leases have meant losing their rights to use or own their lands from which they are usually evicted. These large-scale land acquisitions cause land expropriation, which in most situations has not given rise to compensation to smallholders given that they do not hold formal rights to the land they farm. While companies and governments are agreeing on long-term leases over agricultural lands, the local populations are being pushed off the plot in favour of foreign investors, in most situations without consultation or compensation.

While individual farmers are sometimes involved in the land leases, it is mainly the local communities, whose rights are poorly protected, that are affected. Generally, with some few exceptions, private land ownership tends not to be widespread in the SADC region (and the African continent). The World Bank estimates that across Africa, only between two and ten percent of the land is held under formal land tenure; this mainly concerns urban land.[55] Consequently, the governments have huge control over land ownership, and most of the lands allocated to land leases for food or biofuel production is formally in the hands of the State. However, such lands are mainly used and controlled by customary land-holders. Despite the emergence of national legislation recognising land rights for local communities, large-scale land acquisitions are ignoring the existence of such rights. For example, recent studies have shown that lands allocated to investors in Tanzania and Mozambique ignored pre-existing land-use and claims.[56] Commonly using the smokescreen of State ownership, the land leases granted to foreign companies bypass the customary land rights of the local communities. One of the central issues in the SADC region has been the non-recognition, or the ignorance, of customary land-holders. This has happened either by allocation of State land that ignores customary rights (Madagascar) or the legal allocation of customarily-held land (Tanzania and Mozambique).

The general perception of foreign companies and government is that land in the SADC region (and in Africa generally) is abundant and available for food or agribusiness production. This viewpoint is counter to the fact that most of these lands are actually occupied and being used by land users, which are marginalised from formal land rights and access to the law and institutions recognising their right to these lands. The position often cited by both private investors and governments is that the concerned lands are not properly 'used' or, if they are, they are being used in an 'unproductive' fashion. This reference to the productivity of the land is not new, and is reminiscent of the 'agricultural argument'. Traditionally, the 'agricultural argument' implies that only cultivation of the land can be regarded as a 'proper' occupation of land, and only agriculture can be considered a basis of a real land tenure system.[57] From this perspective, the most affected communities are usually pastoralist or hunter-gatherers societies who are seen as epitomising the use of land in an 'unproductive' manner.[58] Potentially, the land deals could threaten the survival of local communities' customary land rights, as well as undermine customary land usage of the pastoralist livestock herders and indigenous peoples.

In many ways the continuing 'land grab' is undermining the current movement of land reforms which are finally starting to recognise the land of the local communities.[59] While there is a movement towards ensuring access to land and security of tenure, the land leases granted to foreign companies are hindering this evolution by undermining customary land rights of the local communities. The acquisition of lands by foreign companies is predominantly taking place in areas where local communities are suffering from a lack of secured land rights, which makes them vulnerable to dispossession. Hence, indirectly, the acquisition of lands by foreign companies is impacting negatively on the recognition and protection of the land rights of local communities. International human rights law can play an important role since most of the national legal frameworks in the SADC do not provide adequate recognition for customary land rights-holders.

Historically, international law has been a predominately negative force regarding customary land rights in Africa. During colonisation, international law was used as a tool to justify the dispossession of communities by the colonial States.[60] However, with the more recent development of international human rights law, this approach has drastically changed. By focusing on the rights of individuals and also communities, international law has become more supportive of the promotion and protection of communities' rights to land, and also the recognition of their customary rights. Strictly speaking, land rights are not protected under international human rights law; as such there are no established human rights to land (with the exception of indigenous peoples and women). Nonetheless, several of the rights enshrined in the International Bill of Human Rights (UDHR, ICCPR and ICESCR) contain provisions which are tied to the respect of land rights. The UDHR and ICESCR protect the right to an adequate standard of living; the UDHR and ICCPR protect privacy and property rights. Access to land is also an important element to fulfil the right to adequate housing. In the words of the UN Special Rapporteur: '[l]and is often a necessary and sufficient condition on which the right to adequate housing is absolutely contingent for many individuals and even entire communities.'[61] However the main recognition of land rights comes through the right to property.

Under the general universal framework, land rights are usually protected under the heading of property rights.[62] While Article 17 of the UDHR does not specifically mentions land rights, it states that:

1 Everyone has the right to own property alone as well as in association with others.
2 No one shall be arbitrarily deprived of his property.

The recognition that property can be held collectively, or 'in association with others', is an important statement in a system predominately dedicated to the rights of individuals. This collective aspect of the right to property is a vehicle for the recognition of local communities' land rights, which are traditionally held collectively. While the right to property was not reproduced in any of the two Covenants, its content was included in the International Convention on the Elimination of All Forms of Racial Discrimination (ICERD).[63] Article 5(d)(v) ICERD holds that States should guarantee: 'the right to own property alone as well as in association with others'. On the basis of this provision, the Committee on the Elimination of Racial Discrimination (CERD) has developed an important jurisprudence regarding indigenous peoples' land rights, including customary land rights.[64] The focus of this jurisprudence is non-discrimination, based on the idea that the non-recognition of indigenous peoples' land rights could be discriminatory since it is based on the notion that their legal system is inferior to other land-holding systems. While such jurisprudence concerns indigenous peoples, the same argument could be extended to all traditional local communities whose land rights are based on customary land-holding systems. Of the fifteen SADC Member States, only Angola has not ratified the ICERD.[65]

The human rights approach to the right to property could be interpreted to mean that people have a right to possess legal title to lands which they have traditionally occupied. Arguably, the important focus on non-discrimination also supports the fact that governments should support customary land rights of both individuals and communities, since it would be discriminatory to recognise only 'formal' individual land rights. The rights to equality and non-discrimination are probably the most important rights which underlie the whole international human rights edifice. As such, the non-recognition of the customary land rights of local communities affected by the 'land grab' could be seen as violating some of the most fundamental principles of human rights law.

Another relevant aspect of international human rights law comes from the development of specific norms to protect minorities and indigenous peoples. While this aspect of international law would not be relevant to all rural communities, several of these communities who are especially marginalised find themselves in need of special measures of protection. International law has established a clear connection between the cultural rights of minorities and customary land rights. The Human Rights Committee has stated: 'with regard to the exercise of the cultural rights protected under Article 27, the Committee observes that culture manifests itself in many forms, including a particular way of life associated with the use of land resources, especially in the case of Indigenous peoples.'[66] The law in this area is directly engaged with customary land rights since it has been recognised as an important factor for indigenous peoples. For example, CERD highlights in its General Recommendation XXIII that States should: ' … recognize and protect the rights of indigenous peoples to own, develop, control and use their communal lands, territories and resources',[67] and additionally urges restitution or compensation where required. The view of the Committee is that the non-recognition of customary land rights would equate to a discriminatory practice on the part of the government.

The International Labour Organisation's Convention (No. 169) Concerning Indigenous and Tribal Peoples in Independent Countries (ILO 169),[68] outlines the special rights of such peoples regarding activity on their customary lands. More precisely, Article 14 states that:

> the rights of ownership and possession of the peoples concerned over the lands which they traditionally occupy shall be recognised. … Governments shall take steps as necessary to identify the lands which the peoples concerned traditionally occupy, and to guarantee effective protection of their rights of ownership and possession.

While most of the States in the SADC region have not yet ratified this Convention, the recently adopted Declaration on the Rights of Indigenous Peoples (2007) adopts similar or even stronger language.[69] Most of the States in the region voted in favour of the adoption of the Declaration which is by far the most explicit as to collective property rights. The Declaration notably states in its Article 26:

> Indigenous peoples have the right to own, use, develop and control the lands, territories and resources that they possess by reason of traditional ownership or other traditional occupation or use, as well as those which they have otherwise acquired. States shall give legal recognition and protection to these lands, territories and resources. Such recognition shall be conducted with due respect to the customs, traditions and land tenure systems of the indigenous peoples concerned.

Another element of the Declaration is the affirmation of the right to Free, Prior and Informed Consent (FPIC) in Article 32. This affirmation of FPIC is a notable development that is particularly relevant in the context of land acquisitions. FPIC is a composite concept which requires participation in decisions to lease or sell the lands of any indigenous communities living on the concerned lands. It implicates a process of consultations which have to be free from manipulation and coercion, respect traditional decision-making processes, and be held in sufficient time in advance of project execution with adequate information provided to enable informed decisions to be taken. In the end, FPIC means that the concerned communities have to give their consent before any development takes place on their traditional territories.[70] In the context of large-scale land acquisitions in the SADC region, it means that before leasing or selling land governments have an obligation to obtain the consent of the concerned indigenous communities.

At the regional level, the African Commission on Human and Peoples' Rights is increasingly calling upon States to pay specific attention to the customary land rights of their indigenous populations.[71] This is notably visible through the establishment of a specific Working Group on Indigenous Peoples/Communities, which has highlighted the importance of the recognition and promotion of customary interests.[72] Importantly, in a recent decision against Kenya, the African Commission has clearly stated that governments should respect the customary land rights of indigenous communities, and that non-recognition of such customary land rights would be a violation of Article 14 protecting property rights.[73] This is the first legal decision directly related to customary land rights for indigenous peoples and could have important consequences for the SADC region. The concerned community was a pastoralist community, and as such the decision applies to the need to recognise customary land rights of pastoralist communities when land leases are signed between States and foreign companies.

7.4 Investment and the right to development

One of the central justifications for the current movement of land grabs is that such large-scale land acquisitions promote development. Unquestionably, African leaders recognise that improvements in standards of living are predicated on greater and sustained economic development. This requires capital, of which direct private foreign investment provides a ready vehicle.[74] In turn the developed world relies on African raw materials to sustain high standards of living. Generally, the acquisitions are taking place within the context of increased Foreign Direct Investments (FDI) in Africa. Kwame Nkrumah describes current direct investment as taking the form and structure of neo-colonialism, meaning a nation State that is theoretically independent and sovereign but whose economic system, and therefore political system, is externally directed.[75] It implies increased impoverishment through a process described by Andre Gunder Frank as 'the development of underdevelopment'.

The study undertaken by IIED, FAO and IFAD highlights: '[T]rends in large-scale land acquisitions for agricultural investments must be placed within the broader context of expanding economic relations between Africa and the rest of the world.'[76] In this regard, the argument put forward to defend land acquisitions in developing countries has often been that in the end it is a 'win-win' situation for both the investors and the host country.[77] The main focus is thus on the potential benefits that investment in the agricultural sector can bring to the host country. The investment of foreign corporations is seen as a way to support the growth of agriculture in developing countries, which finally will bring benefits to the general infrastructure as well as support for the dissemination of new agricultural technologies. As such, States, investors and intergovernmental organisations have usually been supportive of such investments which are seen as generating development for the region.

Legally, it is interesting to note that this simplified 'win-win' argument relies on the notion of development. In recent years, development has become an integral part of the human rights legal framework.[78] This is visible through the increased relevance and recognition of the right to development as a human right. The clearest expression of the rights-based approach to development is found in the UN Declaration on the Right to Development adopted in 1986.[79] Article 1 of the Declaration provides:

> The right to development is an inalienable human right by virtue of which every human person and all peoples are entitled to participate in, contribute to, and enjoy economic, social, cultural and political development, in which all human rights and fundamental freedoms can be fully realized.

Focusing on the 'human aspect' of development, the Declaration affirms the rights of people to participate in the development decisions that affect their lives. Article 2(3) holds that States should: 'formulate appropriate national development policies that aim at the constant improvement of the well-being of the entire population and of all individuals, on the basis of their active, free and meaningful participation in development and in the fair distribution of the benefits resulting therefrom'. The emphasis on the participation of people in the process of development is important in the context of large-scale land acquisitions. This means that when developments are taking place on their lands, the concerned communities should be consulted. Furthermore it implies that these communities should participate in land-use zoning, property rights reforms, and other decisions regarding the management of the natural resources found in these lands. Another angle of the human rights-based approach to development is access to the benefits of developmental projects by the local communities. The preamble of the Declaration recognises that development: 'aims at the constant improvement of the well-being of the entire population and […] all individuals on the basis of their active, free and meaningful participation in development and in the fair distribution of benefits resulting therefrom.' The UN Special Rapporteur on the Right to Food has concluded that the human rights-based approach to development: 'requires that States ensure the adequate participation of the local communities concerned by land leases or purchases, and that the decision-making process is fully transparent.'[80]

Legally, there has been some debate regarding the binding value of the Declaration, which some commentators argue represents guiding principles rather than strictly binding obligations.[81] This position is not relevant in the context of Africa since the right to development is enshrined in the African Charter of Human and Peoples' Rights, to which all SADC States are a party, and which is therefore legally binding on the region.[82] Article 22 of the African Charter states that: 'All peoples shall have the right to their economic, social and cultural development with due regard to their freedom and identity and in the equal enjoyment of the common heritage of mankind.'

This reflects the rights-based approach to development inherent in the UN Declaration. Significantly, this article was central to the complaint of the Endorois pastoralist community in their case against Kenya before the African Commission on Human and Peoples' Rights.[83] The pastoralist community argued that Kenya had violated their right to development by its failure to adequately involve them in the development process taking place on their customary lands, as well as failing to ensure the continued improvement of the community's well-being. In this case, Kenya had allocated the land to tourism and mining. The Endorois also argued that their exclusion from the benefits emerging from the exploitation of their land violated their right to development. Finally, the Endorois highlighted that the government: 'did not embrace a rights-based approach to economic growth, which insists on development in a manner consistent with, and instrumental to, the realisation of human rights and the right to development through adequate and prior consultation.'[84]

The African Commission found that Kenya violated the right to development of the pastoralist community. This case is being recognised as a landmark decision, since it is the first time that a violation of the right to development has been formally recognised, regionally and internationally. An important aspect of the decision is the emphasis placed on the State's obligation to ensure the participation and informed choice of the concerned communities before embarking on a developmental project. In the words of the African Commission, States have the duty: 'to conduct the consultation process in such a manner that allowed the representatives to be fully informed of the agreement, and participate in developing parts crucial to the life of the community.'[85] The Commission concluded: 'the result of development should be empowerment of the Endorois community. It is not sufficient for the Kenyan Authorities merely to give food aid to the Endorois. The capabilities and choices of the Endorois must improve in order for the right to development to be realised.'[86] Finally, the Commission highlighted that governments bear 'the burden for creating conditions favourable to a people's development'.[87]

While the case involved development taking place through tourism, mining and wildlife protection, the decision is evidently of relevance to large-scale land acquisitions. Any forms of development, including agribusiness, would fall under the obligations inscribed in Article 22 of the African Charter. The important lesson from this jurisprudence is that prior to leasing lands for development, States have a duty to ensure that the concerned local communities take part and benefit from the development. In the context of land deals between States and foreign investors, the right to development means that governments have the obligation to ensure the participation of directly affected peoples in the planning, approval and establishment of large-scale agricultural projects.

The human rights based-approach to development is also based on the right to self-determination. More particularly, the rights of peoples to self-determination found in common Article 1 ICCPR and ICESCR includes the right not to be deprived of their own means of subsistence. In the case of land acquisitions this could be interpreted as meaning that rural local communities cannot be denied access to their traditional sources of food, medicine or fuel. States and other actors involved in land acquisitions have the obligation to ensure that the leasing of lands would not deprive local communities of their means of subsistence.

Overall, for large-scale land acquisitions the right to development framework works two ways. It provides a *prima facie* justification to governments who are entering into contracts with foreign corporations or governments. The pressing need for capital ensures that governments in the SADC region and throughout Africa are beginning to actively seek investment, citing development needs as justification. However the right to development is not enjoyed by governments; it is an individual human right. In the regional African system, the right to development is being understood as a dynamic in which projects undertaken by governments must conform to certain agreed standards for the improvements of the people they affect. This means that for land acquisitions, there is a third party to the contract between a government and a corporation; the users of the land. The comprehensive set of measures for the development of the people concerned reveals a series of obligations which governments must conform to, if they are not to violate the right.

The discussion has focused on host State obligations. The final section explores the rights and responsibilities of home as well as host States with regard to transnational corporations, as well as the growing internal and external regulation of non-state actors.

7.5 Accountability of transnational corporations

As highlighted throughout the chapter, transnational corporations (TNCs) are playing a central role in large-scale land acquisitions. The growth of TNCs has far exceeded expectations, with some fifty corporations controlling US$4 trillion by the turn of the century, leading to intense influence on world resources.[88] African States by contrast experienced general decline until the early 1990s, and while capital flows to the developing world increased from the 1990s, African States were generally not the beneficiaries. Many are still not even listed for consideration by TNCs for locational decisions for FDI, despite offering many attractions for investors.[89] There is a prevailing viewpoint that 'Africa is the great exception to the defining and otherwise global economic trend of recent decades: steady improvement in people's lives.'[90]

While traditionally international human rights law has been concerned with the relationship between States and their citizens, its reach is changing and there are significant developments regarding the impact of human rights on corporations. The Special Representative of the UN Secretary-General (SRSG), Professor John Ruggie, has developed a framework that seeks to capture the responsibilities of various parties in the field of business and human rights. The three pillars of the SRSG's framework are the following: first, the state duty to protect against human rights abuses by third parties, including business, through appropriate policies, regulation and adjudication; secondly, the corporate responsibility to respect human rights, which means to act with due diligence to avoid infringing on the rights of others; and thirdly, greater access by victims to effective remedy, both judicial and non-judicial.[91]

Using the three levels of protection identified in General Comment 12 – to respect, protect and fulfil the right to adequate food – the Special Rapporteur identifies the second level, to protect, as placing an obligation on States to prevent others, in particular private actors such as firms, from encroaching on the ability of individuals and groups to feed themselves.[92]

These developments have impacted on the right to food, as evidenced in the Committee on Economic, Social and Cultural Rights' General Comment 12, which states:

> Violations of the right to food can occur through the direct action of states or other entities insufficiently regulated by states. These include … failure to regulate activities of individuals or groups so as to prevent them violating the right to food of others, or the failure of a State to take into account its international legal obligations regarding the right to food when entering into agreements with other States or with international organisations.[93]

According to Clapham, the Committee is here suggesting that non-state actors are capable of violating the right to food.[94] The General Comment further emphasises that 'the private business sector [has] responsibilities in the realisation of the right to adequate food.'[95] Thus the private sector, national and transnational, should pursue its activities within the framework of a code of conduct conducive to the respect of the right to adequate food, agreed jointly by government and civil society.[96] A similar approach has been taken with the right to water.[97] Furthermore the decision of the African Commission in the Ogoniland case, highlighted above, also held that the right to food gives rise to an obligation to protection from non-state actors, with the requirement in the decision that the Nigerian government: 'should not allow private parties to destroy or contaminate food sources, and prevent peoples' efforts to feed themselves.'[98]

Narula notes that the right to food has been undermined by the state-centric system of rights obligations. She argues that the influence of TNCs on global access to the right to food has reached a level that necessitates obligations under international human rights law. These should be clearly defined in order to hold TNCs accountable, if the right to food is to be effectively realised.[99] There has been considerable discussion on the means of achieving this, with Clapham outlining the distinction between corporate responsibility and corporate accountability; the former refers to voluntary initiatives such as the UN Global Compact and Corporate Social Responsibility (CSR) self-regulation by TNCs, while the latter implies requiring TNCs to adhere to standards or face sanctions.[100] Corporate responsibility was the initial tool favoured by campaigners throughout the 1990s, but this has since given way to a harder approach which seeks binding legal obligations on TNC activities. Corporate accountability has seen incremental gains, such as the successful use of the *Alien Tort Claims Act* 1789 in the United States.[101] In particular, where acts involved constitute international crimes, the appropriate international criminal law on complicity may be invoked.[102] Thus tort law and criminal law are providing potential avenues for responsibility and redress.

Commentators are increasingly suggesting that corporations and businesses have to respect the Universal Declaration of Human Rights.[103] The Declaration is regularly referred to by corporations as being part of their remit. Yet there is no international jurisdiction to try a corporation. Nevertheless, they evidently bear certain international duties. Clapham writes: 'The absence of an international jurisdiction to try corporations does not mean that transnational corporations cannot break international law.'[104] He signals the growing relationship between human rights agencies and businesses, concluding that a shift is underway towards human rights accountability in the private sector; 'in fact, many of us imagine we are already there'.[105] By contrast Narula finds that 'international legal accountability for TNCs remains virtually nonexistent'.[106]

Host States in the SADC region can hold TNCs accountable for human rights standards under the ICESCR. Evidently, the Committee on Economic, Social and Cultural Rights has interpreted Article 11 as applying to non-state actors such as corporations, and States' duties to protect the right to adequate food include private entities. Therefore it is reasonable to apply the Special Rapporteur's minimum framework to acquisitions involving host States in southern Africa and foreign enterprises, and indeed not to do so would represent a violation of the Covenant, as interpreted. SADC States that have ratified the ICESCR are required to implement the eleven principles in the context of land acquisitions, otherwise they could legitimately be held to be in violation of their obligations under Article 11. Those SADC States that have not ratified the Covenant should look to international human rights standards and African regional standards, which argue that the right to adequate food, implicit in the Banjul Charter, has universal application under the concept of protecting human dignity.

However can home States, for example South Korea or the Gulf States, also be held responsible for violations of the right to adequate food in the SADC region? In general home State liability for TNCs is not a settled question. In 2003, former Special Rapporteur on the Right to Food, Jean Ziegler, reported that governments have extranational obligations which extend to a duty to avoid actions which have a negative impact on the right to food for people in other States.[107] While the duty to protect the right to adequate food implies host State regulation of TNCs, as highlighted above in the de Schutter report, it can also require home State obligations, in that States have a duty to prevent violations by their companies and corporations operating abroad.[108] Hence Narula argues that the extraterritorial application of States' obligations under the ICESCR to uphold the right to food has been expanded.[109] While morally laudable, this is problematic in terms of international law in particular given that the ICESCR, unlike other treaties, has no provision specifying its jurisdictional scope.[110]

In sum, there are three problems: first, States are only responsible for human rights obligations in their own jurisdictions, or where they exercise 'effective control'; second, despite advances, non-state actors are not full subjects of international law and the indirect regulation of TNCs by States is fraught with difficulties; third, States have obligations under multiple legal regimes, including international financial institutions.[111] Narula notes that 'under international law, the home State is generally not liable for the conduct of non-state actors unless the non-state actors are *de facto* agents of the state'.[112] Citing the *Draft Articles on the Responsibilities of States for Internationally Wrongful Acts* (2001), non-state actors must be acting 'on the instruction of, or under the direction and control of, that State in carrying out the [wrongful] conduct'.[113] Her argument is that while an argument for the extraterritoriality of the ICESCR can be made where a State is exercising 'effective control', this concept is too narrow to realise the right to food given that it is primarily interpreted in relation to the exercise of control over armed forces.[114]

Yet according to the IIED, large-scale land acquisitions which have accelerated in the past year involve support from governments, or indeed 'significant levels of government-owned investments'.[115] There is certainly evidence that States such as Saudi Arabia and South Korea are in control of corporations that are buying or leasing land. Nevertheless removing this concept from its largely humanitarian framework to argue for extraterritorial jurisdiction of the ICESCR, even in cases of direct government acquisition of lands, is unrealistic. International human rights jurisprudence indicates that a State can exercise 'effective control' in situations of occupation or armed conflict, but 'the majority of extraterritorial violations of the right to food under globalisation are committed outside these limited scenarios.'[116] Effective control does not extend to effective economic control, even in the case of government acquisition of land. To admit as much would be to recognise that this is indeed a situation of *de facto* colonisation akin to occupation, with obvious political difficulties.

There is considerable resentment at the unequal relationship and a perception that there can be no reciprocity between rich and poor nations.[117] Bobo writes:

> It is an unlikely proposition, as some observers of the African situation propose, that black Africa will be able to arouse any significant growth and development without the kind of assistance multinationals can offer. But whether black Africa will elect to maintain and/or expand the presence of multinational corporations in its economies may depend on how successful it is in finding solutions to the several problems that have emerged in its recent relationship with multinational firms.[118]

The paramount need to establish an equitable relationship between TNCs and the developing world has seen a strong movement towards accountability of non-state actors for human rights standards. Remarkably, five corporations control the global trade in grain, while ten corporations control thirty-two per cent of the global commercial seed market.[119]

Imposing economic and social rights obligations on TNCs is a challenge, and to the extent that such bodies are held accountable, responsibility normally attaches to the host State.[120] Meanwhile home States, which provide extensive political and economic support, and in the case of land acquisitions are heavily involved in the transfers, remain largely beyond the regulatory sphere. In home States, a combination of soft law norms such as codes of conduct replace binding standards. Thus the focus must be on TNC regulation by host States, despite the economic inequality of arms. The state-centric nature of economic and social rights is undermining the full implementation of the ICESCR. The right to food requires accountability of TNCs, in the short term in host States, and in the long-term in home States.

The SADC region should implement the Special Rapporteur's eleven minimum principles, given that his mandate applies to all States in the region. Regulation of TNCs by host States is a growing area, and the region has an opportunity to use large-scale land acquisitions as a blueprint for forceful regulation and accountability of TNC activity. Thirteen SADC States can cite Article 11 ICESCR obligations in support of TNC regulation. The growing political nature of large-scale land acquisitions indicates that civil society is prepared to use these developments as a means of finally drawing real accountability of corporations from governments. A movement that has been evolving since the 1970s could crystallise around this issue.

7.6 Conclusion

A human rights-based approach to large-scale land acquisitions is central to preventing exploitation. The discourse on neo-colonialism has been readily applied, with Biney describing the haste to acquire land as 'another scramble for Africa', fuelled by fears of global food insecurity. It is supposed that food will become the next major geopolitical commodity, after oil.[121] The head of the FAO, Jacques Diof, has also attached the label 'neo-colonialism' to the process, although the organisation has engaged in studies which also emphasise the potential benefits.[122] Governments have had to defend their actions against these accusations, with the Ethiopian ambassador to Japan stating in the *Japan Times* that his government, while encouraging large-scale agricultural investment by Japan in the State, 'has never been colonized … and neither would it succumb to any form of neo-colonialism'.[123]

The aim of the present chapter has been to analyse whether human rights law could act as regulatory framework to control the ever expanding large-scale acquisition of lands by foreign corporations and governments. As suggested throughout the chapter, this 'land grab' is touching on three fundamental human rights of the local rural communities: their right to food, right to land and right to development. Adopting the eleven minimum principles set out by the Special Rapporteur on the Right to Food, it is submitted that human rights law must play a central role in regulation and accountability of the state and non-state actors involved in the leases.

The right to food is an evolving area of human rights law that distinguishes between the fundamental freedom from hunger, considered sufficiently basic to potentially constitute customary international law, and the broader right to adequate food. The combination of ICESCR obligations and settled international human rights standards ensures that host States are accountable for a regulatory framework governing land acquisitions. These standards apply to state and non-state actors. Non-state actors are increasingly coming under the remit of international human rights, and home States have a concomitant duty to hold corporate representatives responsible. At present, however, the primary responsibility is on host States to ensure TNCs do not violate the right to adequate food.

On the question of land rights, States' land reforms should prioritise the recognition of customary land rights of all local communities and provide adequate legal protection to such rights. In the case of pastoralist and hunter-gathering communities, States should recognise their use of the land as providing legal entitlement and reject the notion of 'unproductive' land usage. For indigenous peoples, States have the duty to ensure their free, prior and informed consent before undertaking any developmental project on their lands.

The right to development is raised as a defence by governments to justify land acquisitions, but the standards implied in the right to development are strongly weighted towards the benefit of peoples affected by large-scale investments. Negotiations leading to investment agreements must be transparent, with the full and effective participation of local communities whose access to land may be affected by the agreement. Local populations should benefit from the revenues generated by the investment agreement. Furthermore, impact assessments on vulnerable groups should be conducted prior to the arrival of investors, notably women, ethnic groups and pastoralists or itinerant farmers, as well as indigenous peoples.

Human rights law is proposing to act as a potential platform for negotiations between the local rural communities, governments, investors and corporations. By putting the right to food, land rights and the right to development to the fore of any land acquisition, this framework will ensure that local people benefit from the investment taking place in the region. There is evidence that civil society in the SADC and throughout Africa is organising around opposition to what is perceived as neocolonial practices and policies, as evidenced in Madagascar. While the chapter has focussed on the SADC and Africa, large-scale land acquisition is becoming a global practice. Global opposition is evolving at a similar pace.

Notes

* PhD, Senior Lecturer in Law, Middlesex University, London.

1 Ama Biney (2009), available at <http://pambazuka.org/en/category/features/58809>.

2 Daniel Shepard and Anuradha Mittal (2009) *The Great Land Grab: Rush for World's Farmland Threatens Food Security for the Poor* (Oakland, CA: Oakland Institute), available at <http://www.oaklandinstitute.org/pdfs/LandGrab_final_web.pdf>.

3 Ama Biney, above, n 1.
4 Thomas Pakenham (1991: xxvii) notes that the term 'Scramble for Africa' was apparently coined in 1884. Modern historians do not agree what period it covers, but he uses it to embrace the final hectic phase of partition, from 1876 to 1912.
5 Ibid, p xxiii.
6 Cotula, Vermeulen, Leonard and Keeley (2009), p 35, available at <http://www.ifad.org/pub/land/land_grab.pdf>.
7 Ruth Meinzen Dick, International Fund for Agriculture Development, quoted in Ama Biney, above, n 1.
8 Ama Biney, above, n 1.
9 See for example the Asian Peasant Coalition, <http://www.asianpeasant.org>.
10 See for example BBC News, 'Madagascar Leader Axes Land Deal', 19 March 2009, available at <http://news.bbc.co.uk/1/hi/world/africa/7952628.stm>.
11 Ibid.
12 Ama Biney, above, n 1.
13 Colin Gonsalves (2004), p 317.
14 Ibid, p 310.
15 Report of the Special Rapporteur on the Right to Food, Olivier de Schutter (2009), para 2.
16 Ibid.
17 Universal Declaration of Human Rights, GA Res 217A (III), UN Doc A/810 at p 71 (1948).
18 International Covenant on Civil and Political Rights, GA Res 2200A (XXI), 21 UN GAOR Supp (No. 16) at p 52, UN Doc A/6316 (1966), 999 UNTS 171, entered into force 23 March 1976. See further Smita Narula (2006) at p 706.
19 International Covenant on Economic, Social and Cultural Rights, GA Res 2200A (XXI), 21 UN GAOR Supp (No. 16) at p 49, UN Doc A/6316 (1966), 993 UNTS 3, entered into force 3 January 1976.
20 Committee on Economic, Social and Cultural Rights, 'General Comment 12: The Right to Adequate Food (Article 11)', UN Doc E/C.12/1999/5, 12 May 1999.
21 Ibid, para 5.
22 Ibid, para 6.
23 Ibid, para 7.
24 Ibid, para 8.
25 These three levels were developed by Asbjorn Eide in an influential study for the then UN Sub-commission. See UN ECOSOC Sub-commission on the Prevention of Discrimination and Protection of Minorities, 'The New International Economic Order and the Promotion of Human Rights: Report on the Right to Adequate Food as a Human Right', UN Doc E/CN.4/Sub.2/1987/23, 7 July 1987.
26 General Comment 12, para 15.
27 Ibid, para 6.
28 Ibid, para 17.
29 Ibid, para 19.
30 Ibid, para 27.
31 Ibid, para 28.
32 Ibid, para 29.
33 Ibid, para 32.
34 Ibid, para 41.
35 Quoted in Food and Agricultural Organisation (FAO), 'The Human Right to Adequate Food: Guiding Principles', available at <http://www.fao.org/righttofood/principles_en.htm>.
36 Food and Agricultural Organisation (2004), available at <http://www.fao.org/docrep/meeting/008/J3345e/j3345e01.htm>.
37 Ibid, para 9.
38 Olivier de Schutter (2009), above, n 15.

39 Ibid, para 4. See also para 11.
40 UN Office of the High Commissioner for Human Rights, Table of Ratifications, available at <http://treaties.un.org/Pages/ViewDetails.aspx?src=TREATY&mtdsg_no=IV-3&chapter=4&lang=en>.
41 Special Rapporteur on the Right to Food, Overview of the Mandate, available at <http://www2.ohchr.org/english/issues/food/overview.htm>. See Human Rights Council, 'Mandate of the Special Rapporteur on the Right to Food', UN Doc A/HRC/Res/6/2, 27 September 2007, para 2(f).
42 Commission on Human Rights Res 2000/10, 'The Right to Food', 17 April 2000.
43 Ibid.
44 Ibid, paras 1 and 5.
45 Human Rights Council, 'Mandate of the Special Rapporteur on the Right to Food', UN Doc A/HRC/Res/6/2, 27 September 2007. The resolution notes that the fundamental right to be free from hunger is found in Millennium Development Goal No. 1, which commits to halving the proportion of people who suffer from hunger by 2015.
46 Smita Narula (2006), p 780.
47 See Road Map towards the Implementation of the UN Millennium Declaration, UN Doc A/56/326, 6 September 2001.
48 Comm. 155/96, *The Social and Economic Rights Action Centre and the Centre for Economic and Social Rights v. Nigeria*.
49 Ibid, para 65.
50 Olivier de Schutter (2009), above, n 15, Conclusion, para 33.
51 Ibid, Annex.
52 Ibid, para 5.
53 Ibid, para 5.
54 See IIED report (Cotula *et al*, 2009), above, n 6.
55 Klaus Deininger (2003).
56 Emmanual Sulle (2009) 'Biofuels, Land Access and Tenure, and Rural Livelihoods in Tanzania' (Arusha: Tanzania Natural Resources Forum, and London: International Institute for Environment and Development), unpublished report; Isilda Nhantumbo and Alda Salomao (2009) 'Biofuels, Land Access and New Business Models for Rural Livelihoods in Africa: The Mozambican Case' (Maputo: Centro Terra Viva and London: International Institute for Environment and Development), unpublished report.
57 T. Flanagan (1989) 'The Agricultural Argument and Original Appropriation: Indian Lands and Political Philosophy', *Canadian Journal of Political Science*, 22: 589; see also William Bassett (1986).
58 See J. Gilbert (2007).
59 Generally, on the importance of customary land rights in the land reforms process, see: Liz Alden Wily (2006); Pauline E. Peters and Daimon Kambewaa (2007); E. Lahiff (2003) 'The Politics of Land Reform in Southern Africa' (Sustainable Livelihoods in Southern Africa, Research Paper 19, Brighton: Institute of Development Studies); A. Chimhowu and P. Woodhouse (2006) 'Customary versus Private Property Rights? Dynamics and Trajectories of Vernacular Land Markets in Sub-Saharan Africa', *Journal of Agrarian Change*, 6(3): 346–71.
60 See Joshua Castellino and Steve Allen (2003).
61 Commission on Human Rights, Report of the Special Rapporteur on Adequate Housing as a Component of the Right to an Adequate Standard of Living, Miloon Kothari, UN Doc E/CN.4/2005/48 (3 March 2005), para 41.
62 Robert Plant (1993).
63 International Convention on the Elimination of All Forms of Racial Discrimination, GA Res 2106 (XX), Annex, 20 UN GAOR Supp (No. 14) at 47, UN Doc A/6014 (1966), 660 UNTS 195, entered into force 4 January 1969.
64 For example, see: Committee for the Elimination of Racial Discrimination, Early Warning and Urgent Action Procedure Decision 1 (68) – United States of America

(Sixty-eighth session, Geneva, 20 February–10 March 2006). Generally, see Patrick Thornberry (2005, 2002).

65 UN Treaties Collection, Table of Ratifications, available at <http://treaties.un.org/Pages/ViewDetails.aspx?src=TREATY&mtdsg_no=IV-2&chapter=4&lang=en>.

66 Human Rights Committee (1994), General Comment No. 23: 'The Rights of Minorities' (Article 27), UN Doc CCPR/C/21/Rev.1/Add.5.

67 Committee on the Elimination of Racial Discrimination, General Comment XXIII: 'Rights of Indigenous Peoples' (Fifty-first Session, 1997), UN Doc A/52/18, annex V at p 122 (1997).

68 International Labour Organisation, Convention concerning Indigenous and Tribal Peoples in Independent Countries, entered into force 5 September 1991.

69 United Nations Declaration on the Rights of Indigenous Peoples, Human Rights Council, Report to the General Assembly on the First Session of the Human Rights Council, at p 58, UN Doc A/HRC/1/L.10 (2006).

70 Marcus Colchester and Maurizio Farhan Ferrari (2007).

71 Kealeboga N. Bojosi and George Mukundi Wachira (2006).

72 Resolution on the Adoption of the Report of the African Commission's Working Group on Indigenous Populations/Communities, ACHPR/Res 51 (XXVII).

73 *Centre for Minority Rights Development (Kenya) and Minority Rights Group International on behalf of Endorois Welfare Council v Kenya* (2010) Communication 276/2003.

74 Bobo Benjamin (2005), p 26.

75 Cited in Bobo Benjamin (2005).

76 IIED Report, above, n 6.

77 See Oakland Report, above, n 2.

78 See Philip Alston (1988); Daniel Aguirre (2008); Koen de Feyter (2001).

79 Declaration on the Right to Development, GA Res 41/128, annex, 41 UN GAOR Supp (No. 53) at 186, UN Doc A/41/53 (1986).

80 Ibid, para 5.2.

81 For references, see: Russel Lawrence Barsh (1991); Arjun Sengupta (2002).

82 See list of ratifications, available at <http://www.achpr.org/english/ratifications/ratification_african%20charter.pdf>.

83 *Endorois* case, above, n 73. The decision was adopted by the African Commission in May 2009 and approved by the African Union at its January 2010 meeting.

84 Ibid, para 135.

85 Ibid, para 237.

86 Ibid, para 238.

87 Ibid, para 298.

88 Bobo Benjamin (2005), p 12.

89 Ibid, p 15.

90 Clive Crook (2002) 'When Economic Development just isn't Enough', *National Journal*, p 2436, cited in Bobo Benjamin (2005), p 140. Crook points out that, region by region, poverty has dropped everywhere, except in Africa, where it continues to rise.

91 Report of the Special Representative of the Secretary-General, Olivier de Schutter (2009).

92 Olivier de Schutter, above, n 15, para 3.

93 General Comment 12, above, n 20, para 19.

94 Andrew Clapham (2006), p 325.

95 General Comment 12, above, n 20, para 20.

96 Ibid.

97 See further Andrew Clapham (2006).

98 Comm. 155/96, *The Social and Economic Rights Action Centre and the Centre for Economic and Social Rights v. Nigeria*, para 65, quoted in Andrew Clapham (2006), p 435.

99 Smita Narula (2006), p 694.

100 Andrew Clapham (2006), p 195.

101 Ibid, p 252.
102 Ibid, p 265.
103 Ibid, p 264. Although Clapham emphasises that the complicity tests cannot substitute the corporation for the government, with the corporation responsible only for its own acts of assistance.
104 Ibid, p 267.
105 Ibid, p 270.
106 Smita Narula, above (2006), p 750.
107 UN Commission on Human Rights, 'Report Submitted by the Special Rapporteur on the Right to Food in Accordance with the Commission on Human Rights Resolution 2002/25, UN Doc E/CN.4/2003/54, 10 January 2003, p 29.
108 Smita Narula, above (2006), p 725.
109 Ibid, p 725.
110 Ibid, p 728.
111 Ibid, p 726.
112 Ibid.
113 Draft Articles on the Responsibilities of States for Internationally Wrongful Acts, UN Doc A/56/10 (2001).
114 Smita Narula (2006), p 728.
115 IIED Report (Cotula *et al*, 2009), above, n 6, p 4.
116 Smita Narula (2006), p 734.
117 Bobo Benjamin (2005), p 29.
118 Ibid, p 28. He identifies in particular technology transfer, transfer pricing, taxation and conduct and ethics as being the greatest areas in need of regulation to move towards a more equitable relationship.
119 Smita Narula (2006), p 722.
120 Ibid, p 751.
121 Ama Biney, above, n 1.
122 IIED Report (Cotula *et al*, 2009), above, n 6.
123 Abdirashid Dulane (2010), available at <http://farmlandgrab.org/12069>.

Bibliography

Books

Aguirre, Daniel (2008) *The Human Right to Development in a Globalized World* (Aldershot: Ashgate).

Bobo, Benjamin (2005) *Rich Country, Poor Country: The Multinational as Change Agent* (Westport, CT: Praeger).

Castellino, Joshua and Allen, Steve (2003) *International Law and Title to Territory: A Temporal Analysis* (Aldershot and Burlington, VT: Ashgate).

Clapham, Andrew (2006) *Human Rights Obligations of Non-state Actors* (Oxford: Oxford University Press).

De Feyter, Koen (2001) *World Development Law* (Mortsel, Belgium: Intersentia).

Gonsalves, Colin (2004) *The Right to Food* (Delhi: Human Rights Law Network).

Pakenham, Thomas (1991) *The Scramble for Africa* (London: Weidenfeld & Nicolson).

Thornberry, Patrick (2002) *Indigenous Peoples and Human Rights* (Manchester: Manchester University Press).

Journal articles

Alston, Philip (1988) 'Making Space for New Human Rights: The Case of the Right to Development', *Harvard Human Rights Yearbook*, 1: 3.

Barsh, Russel Lawrence (1991) 'The Right to Development as a Human Right: Results of the Global Consultation', *Human Rights Quarterly*, 13: 322.
Bassett, William (1986) 'The Myth of the Nomad in Property Law', *Journal of Law and Religion*, 4: 133.
Bojosi, Kealeboga N. and Wachira, George Mukundi (2006) 'Protecting Indigenous Peoples in Africa: An Analysis of the approach of the African Commission on Human and Peoples' Rights', *African Human Rights Law Journal*, 6: 382.
Gilbert, Jérémie (2007) 'Nomadic Territories: A Human Rights Approach to Nomadic Peoples' Land Rights', *Human Rights Law Review*, 7(4): 681–716.
Narula, Smita (2006) 'The Right to Food: Holding Global Actors Accountable under International Law', *Columbia Journal of Transnational Law*, 44: 691–800.
Peters, Pauline E. and Kambewaa, Daimon (2007) 'Whose security? Deepening Social Conflict over "Customary" Land in the Shadow of Land Tenure Reform in Malawi', *Journal of Modern African Studies*, 45: 447–72.
Plant, Robert (1993) 'Land Rights in Human Rights and Development: Introducing a New ICJ Initiative', *International Commission of Jurists Review*, 51: 17.
Sengupta, Arjun (2002) 'On the Theory and Practice of the Right to Development', *Human Rights Quarterly*, 24: 837.
Thornberry, Patrick (2005) 'Combating Racial Discrimination: A CERD Perspective', *Human Rights Law Review*, 5: 239–69.

Reports

Colchester, Marcus and Ferrari, Maurizio Farhan (2007) 'Making Free, Prior and Informed Consent Work: Challenges and Prospects for Indigenous Peoples' (Moreton in Marsh: Forest Peoples Programme).
Cotula, Lorenzo, Vermeulen, Sonja, Leonard, Rebeca and Keeley, James (2009) 'Land Grab or Development Opportunity? Agricultural Investment and International Land Deals in Africa' (London: International Institute for Environment and Development with Food and Agriculture Organisation and International Fund for Agriculture Development).
Deininger, Klaus (2003) 'Land Policies for Growth and Poverty Reduction' (Washington, DC: World Bank).
Food and Agriculture Organisation (2004) 'Voluntary Guidelines to Support the Progressive Realization of the Right to Adequate Food in the Context of National Food Security', 24 November.
Ruggie, John (2008) 'Report of the Special Representative of the Secretary-General on the Issue of Human Rights and Transnational Corporations and other Business Enterprises', UN Doc A/HRC/8/5, 7 April.
Schutter, Olivier de (2009) Report of the Special Rapporteur on the Right to Food, 'Large-scale Land Acquisitions and Leases: A Set of Minimum Principles and Measures to Address the Human Rights Challenge', UN Doc A/HRC/33/13/Add.2.
Sub-commission on the Prevention of Discrimination and Protection of Minorities (1987) 'The New International Economic Order and the Promotion of Human Rights: Report on the Right to Adequate Food as a Human Right', UN Doc E/CN.4/Sub.2/1987/23, 7 July.
Wily, Liz Alden (2006) 'Land Rights Reform and Governance in Africa: How to Make it Work in the 21st Century?' (Oslo: UNDP Drylands Development Centre and UNDP Oslo Governance Centre).

Newspaper articles

Biney, Ama (2009) 'Land Grabs: Another Scramble for Africa', *Pambazuka*, 448, 17 September.

Dulane, Abdirashid (2010) 'No Land Grab in Ethiopia', *Japan Times*, 11 April.

8 The land crisis in southern Africa

Challenges for good governance

Hany Besada and Ariane Goetz†*

8.1 Introduction

With the publication of an alarming report by the international non-governmental organisation (NGO) GRAIN,[1] entitled 'Seized! The 2008 Land Grab for Food and Financial Security', a new topic has come to the fore of public and international attention: international investments in and acquisitions of land by foreign investors, primarily in Africa (GRAIN 2008).

While hard data is largely unavailable at this point, the Washington, DC-based International Food Policy Research Institute (IFPRI) has estimated that these deals, located mainly in Africa, totalled US$20 billion to US$30 billion between 2006 and 2009 and were made by foreign investors from China, South Korea, India and the Gulf States (Bahrain, Jordan, Libya, Qatar, Saudi Arabia, United Arab Emirates) (Von Braun and Meinzen-Dick 2009). Increasing scarcity of land and water as well as export restrictions (e.g. export taxes, export bans)[2] by major global food producers[3] during times of high food prices have resulted in a 'growing distrust in the functioning of regional and global markets' (Von Braun and Meinzen-Dick 2009: 1). Land deals have become a national security strategy for states facing environmental scarcity or preparing for future energy shortages. At the same time, the increase in agricultural commodity prices in 2007–08[4] increasingly attracted private companies (agrifood business, bioenergy corporations, investment funds) and/or government–private sector arrangements to invest in land acquisitions in times of financial crisis.

These developments come at a time when most sub-Saharan African countries are still trying to come to terms with a land crisis involving a number of obstacles and challenges, such as their colonial legacy, structural inequality, land tenure insecurity, communal impoverishment, and environmental stress. Since the end of colonialism in much of Africa in the 1950s and 1960s and demise of Apartheid in South Africa in 1994, land reforms have been at the very core of southern African societies' aspirations towards democratisation and socio-economic reconstitution.

Definitively, international investments in land are nothing new.[5] It is, however, the massive scale of the new investments in and acquisitions of land at a time of a global triple crisis (in form of food, energy and financial insecurity), together with the prevalent problem of land tenure insecurity in most 'recipient' countries, which calls for greater scrutiny of why and how these investments and land deals are taking place, and what their local[6] and global repercussions might resemble.

In the southern African region alone, deals have mushroomed on an unprecedented scale. In 2008, China signed a US$800 million investment deal with the government of Mozambique that aims to increase rice production from 100,000 t to 500,000 t.[7] There has been significant local opposition to the deal. Another 100,000 ha were acquired by the Swedish bio energy company Skebab for biofuel crops. Additionally, the British Sun Biofuels company secured land (size unknown) in Mozambique (in 2008–09) for the production of similar crops. In Zambia, an inquiry was placed by China over 2 million ha for biofuel crops. In Tanzania, the Chinese Chongqing Seed Corporation leased 300 ha for rice production; and British corporations CAMS Group and Sun Biofuels secured 45,000 ha and 5,500 ha respectively for biofuel production in 2008–09.[8]

Meanwhile, in Madagascar, a 1.3 million ha deal for US$6 billion by the South Korean Daewoo Logistics Corporation for corn and palm oil production was discontinued in March 2009 after the collapse of the government under President Marc Ravalomanana. In fact, the Daewoo land deal had fuelled public protests over insecure land rights and worsening living conditions, and strengthened the position of President Ravalomanana's political rival and opposition leader, Mr. Andry Rajoelina. Mr. Rajoelina was a leading figure in a political crisis, which started out as several anti-government demonstrations in January 2009, and then – with the support of the military – yielded the accession of Andry Rajoelina to the presidency. Upon his assumption of the presidential office in March 2009, Rajoelina proclaimed the land deal unconstitutional.[9]

Assessments of the potential impact of these investments differ greatly. While the IFPRI claims that land acquisitions could have the potential 'to inject much-needed investment into agriculture and rural areas in poor developing countries', it also warns about the potential negative repercussions for the rural poor in recipient countries (Von Braun and Meinzen-Dick 2009: 1).

Given the broad range of actors and interests involved, it seems that the study by the Food and Agriculture Organisation (FAO), the International Institute for Environment and Development (IIED) and the International Fund for Agricultural Development (IFAD) on the issue, titled 'Land Grab or Development Opportunity', should be rephrased into 'whose land and what kind of development?' (Cotula, Vermeulen, Leonard and Keeley 2009).[10]

In the following, this chapter will focus on developments in southern Africa. It will begin by characterising the historical evolution of the land crises to provide a better understanding of the domestic context in recipient countries. Against this background, the chapter will then proceed to analyse the global context in which and due to which land leases and acquisitions are taking place. In particular, the issues of economic liberalisation and food and energy security will be assessed, as well as how the notion of investment opportunities on the international level corresponds to issues of unclear land tenure, rural poverty, and the desperate need for state and community revenue at the local level. Concluding, it will provide policy recommendations on how to best mitigate the negative repercussions expected to be felt across African farming communities while maximising the perceived benefits that have accompanied these international investments.

8.2 Historical evolution of the land crisis in southern Africa (Namibia, Botswana, Zimbabwe, South Africa)

Southern African societies share a historical legacy of land dispossession and inequality that can be traced back to their colonial past which recent reforms have not been able to resolve adequately or justly. The complex problem of structural inequality in the form of skewed land ownership, access and socio-economic opportunity is closely linked to rural poverty, food insecurity and environmental degradation, all of which continue to haunt these states since post-independence (e.g., Namibia, Botswana) or post-apartheid (e.g., South Africa) (Kariuki 2007: 99–100, and Mutangadura 2007: 176–78).

In fact, it has been argued that the colonial legacies, including land inequity and pluralistic or dual land tenure systems, are the very source of the agrarian and environmental problems that southern African societies are facing today (Clover and Eriksen 2009: 53–56). On the one hand, the dual land tenure systems, legal uncertainty and the land and resource distributional inequalities minimized peoples' options to mitigate or adapt 'to risks to their human, environmental and social rights', limiting the mobility and choices of already impoverished communities (Clover and Eriksen 2009: 53). In Botswana and Mozambique, for instance, commercial farming by white settlers took place on appropriated land that was mostly arable and was largely held under freehold tenure, while communal farming was restricted to low potential conservation areas.

In South Africa and Zimbabwe, the denial of any form of land property rights to the indigenous majority resulted in an 'extreme concentration of people on small lands' (e.g., homelands and tribal reservoirs) (Clover and Eriksen 2009: 59). Thus, in all of these countries, skewed land tenure systems enhanced environmental degradation (e.g., in South Africa, the high concentration yielded a decrease in soil quality and thus utility); undermined subsistence farming efforts (due to land alienation, rapid degradation, and the bias of existing land administration systems towards large-scale (commercial) farming); and/or forced peasants into exploitive labour relationships (Clover and Eriksen 2009: 59–60).

Since independence, governments across southern African countries have attempted to reconcile the above outlined injustices and problems (Kariuki 2007: 99–102). In fact, the historical legacy of land dispossession and inequality has placed land reforms high on the agenda of democratic reform efforts led by post-independence African governments. In theory, two models of land reform are most common: the state-led (i.e. the resettlement of people on land acquired by the respective state, as was done in Zimbabwe and Namibia) and the market-led (i.e. the state provides financial support for people to acquire land). The latter is the current blueprint underpinning the programmes of international financial institutions (e.g., Foreign Investment Advisory Service and organisations such as the World Bank).[11] In practice, however, land reforms are hybrids, whereas countries lean to one of the two models, while encapsulating still elements of both.

The pressure to follow democratic land reforms has played out differently across the region. Considering that the distribution of land ownership was closely linked to control over South African workers, in South Africa, for instance, the post-apartheid land reform fulfilled the function of 'economic reconstitution' (Wellington 2003), and officially aimed to achieve an overhaul of the racially defined and discriminatory legal framework (Mutangadura 2007: 182). The country opted for a market-led and World Bank-supported land reform approach according to the 'willing seller, willing buyer' principle (Lahiff 2007: 1577). The approach consists of three elements: the market-facilitated redistribution of land, the restitution and protection of formerly (i.e. under apartheid) disposed people and tenure reform aimed to enhance tenure security across the multiple tenure systems in place (Mutangadura 2007: 182).

Yet, the implementation of the land redistribution programme has shown little success. The government's track record fell short of its promise to redistribute 30 per cent of the country's land before the 1999 national elections. A large proportion of this land was located in the dry and harsh terrain of the Northern Cape Province. Moreover, little post-settlement support was actually provided by the provincial government (Lahiff *et al* 2006). Consequently, shack dwellers from surrounding areas moved into these areas, having little practical farming experience, which resulted in low agricultural output, indebtedness and unsecured loans. Few believed in the government's ability to fulfil its commitment of redistributing up to 30 per cent of agricultural land to black owners by the new deadline of 2015. While evictions continued unabated, farm labour remained an insecure source of income and highly vulnerable to fluctuations in the price of agricultural exports.

By 2005, the redistribution programme had succeeded in transferring only an area of approximately 3.5 million ha, including state land, or roughly 4.3 per cent of commercial agricultural land to blacks (Centre for Development and Enterprise 2005). According to the South African Department of Land Affairs, the government would need to redistribute an additional 20.6 million ha of commercial agricultural land to reach their new deadline. With a delivery averaging 0.38 million ha a year, this would mean that it would take approximately 54 years for the South African government to meet their target. White South Africans (predominantly 60,000 farmers) and the state continue to effectively own approximately 87 per cent of the country's agricultural land, while approximately 19 million impoverished blacks living in rural areas are restricted to the remaining 13 per cent. Besides, land security has hardly improved for farm workers or labour tenants, who often do not know even about their (new) rights (UNECA 2003: 17–18).[12]

The fact that only minor improvements towards restitution and increased tenure security have been achieved is largely related to the domestic political economy and the market-led approach to agrarian reform. First, the reform process is influenced and supported by a group of conservative landowners, the World

Bank and individual policy makers from the ruling African National Congress (ANC). Power in the reform process is vested in those who, for different reasons (such as securing one's own advantage, international competitiveness, or food security concerns), are clearly in favour of sustaining the large-scale, capital-intensive farming model of the past, counter-acting restitution efforts (UNECA 2003: v). Second, in view of beneficiary selection, the market-led reform approach has itself contributed to discrimination against the poor who lack the resources to fully participate in the process, and it has been failing in its objective to achieve a transfer of land due to a small number of willing sellers.

Overall, the reforms have resulted in a beneficiary selection process for loans or land acquisition procedures that is biased towards moneyed participants and large-scale farming projects. The very low degree of mobilisation among the landless and rural poor in pushing for progress in reform implementation adds to this situation where reforms have not performed well, neither with regard to equity nor efficiency (Lahiff 2007: 1577, 1591).

Against this background, some scholars such as Edward Lahiff[13] have argued that the market-led reforms have mainly achieved two outcomes. Firstly, large-scale commercial farmers and entrepreneurs have become the main profiteers, despite promises by politicians to finally tackle the issue of land restitution and societal equity. In fact, the current system allows land owners to sell their low potential land at prices above the market level by using the formal system administering land acquisitions. Secondly, the system in place allows the profiteers to purport support for the democratic reform process while in reality there has been little change in the political-economic structure and economic wealth redistribution since post-apartheid[14] (Lahiff 2007: 1591).

At the same time, and in spite of the promotion of large-scale commercial farming, the agricultural sector as a percentage of gross domestic product (GDP) has experienced a sharp decline, from 23 per cent of GDP in 1920 to 3.4 per cent of GDP in 2005. These changes are related to rising costs and, most importantly, the significant reduction of subsidies to commercial farmers (Kariuki 2007: 101).

Unlike South Africa, where small-scale farming provides an important but mostly complementary source of income and food, in Namibia roughly half of the population depends primarily on subsistence agriculture (Kariuki 2007: 101). The subdivision of arable land follows a dual tenure system, with commercial farming under freehold tenure and land for communal farming owned by the state (Adams and Palmer 2007: 25, and Kariuki 2007: 100). Upon independence in 1990, Namibia pursued a mixed (state-led and market-led) land reform approach that was similar to South Africa in that it built upon the 'willing seller, willing buyer' principle (Kariuki 2007: 103).

However, the government has a preferential right to buy and engages in redistribution through the resettlement on re-bought, and therefore state-owned, land (Kariuki 2007: 101). The mandate of the Ministry of Lands and Resettlements, which is the responsible political actor for the planning and administration of land, is to render 'services to eradicate the vast disparities in respect of land distribution, social reintegration, and rehabilitation of people with disabilities and resettlement of disadvantaged Namibians'. According to its 'Vision 2030',[15] the ministry aims at the following results by 2030: the resettlement of about 68,882 to 70,000 people (based on the present annual resettlement rate of 2,222 people); the formal employment of approximately 400 people with disability; the provision of support to 1,000 people with disabilities in seeking self-employment and other economic resources; the provision of access to 200 children with learning difficulties to schooling facilities; the provision of access to 300 people with disability to vocational education; the creation of security of tenure in communal areas; to process 95 per cent of topographical and cadastral products/services as required by the market; and to establish topographical and cadastral information countrywide.[16] The focus on national reconciliation however forbids a 'forceful seizure of land' for the purpose of redistribution (Okafor 2006: 3, 13).

Namibia did not incorporate restitution as a reform component (Kariuki 2007: 101). Rather, the agrarian reform concentrates on land redistribution, tenure reform, a better utilisation of neglected communal land and the creation of the Affirmative Action Loan Scheme (AALS), which offers loans to communal farmers for land acquisition via the state-owned Agricultural Bank in order to increase black ownership of land (Kariuki 2007: 106–7).[17]

Yet, critics have argued that the two resettlement programmes, including state-led resettlement and the AALS, are suffering from a lack of sustainability, as there is no post-settlement support for resettled farmers in place who, when starting out, mostly lack the resources and knowledge needed to maintain existing farming enterprises.[18] Moreover, the programme in many cases did not create the desired self-sufficiency of settlers within the first five years of resettlement, and the majority of programme participants remain dependent on government provisions for food and clothing (Ministry of Environment and Tourism 1999: 7). In particular, the subdivision of ranches for resettlement purposes did not turn out to be an economic success, and the fencing of small farms has made it difficult for small-scale herders to manage their livestock in dry areas (Adams and Palmer 2007: 28).

Further points of critique were that clear criteria for the expropriation of commercial land have not been created due to a lack of communication between the National Agricultural Union (NAU)[19] and commercial farms, and the lack of a clear outline by the Government about the amount and type of land 'identified for expropriation' and the criteria used to 'identify the land required'.[20] Both prospective buyers and commercial farm owners were scared off by this lack of clarity. Another point of critique is that the overall agrarian reform efforts have not been directly linked to poverty alleviation efforts so far, but rather focused on strengthening export-led agricultural production as a means of income generation (Adams and Palmer 2007: 28).

As of 2006, the government had succeeded in purchasing 201 commercial, white-owned farms and had managed to resettle 1,561 families on the newly acquired land as part of the land redistribution efforts (Adams and Palmer 2007: 25–26). Yet according to the Ministry of Land and Resettlement, the problem remains that the market-led land reform approach is primarily dependent on the willingness of commercial farm owners to sell. Even after the Government's declaration in 2004 to make use of the expropriation provision under the Land Reform Act (enacted in 1995) that allows for the expropriation of white-owned commercial farms through compulsory purchase by the state for resettlement of landless people, ex-combatants, the marginalised San community, and retrenched farm workers, the redistribution efforts move at a very slow pace due to slow legal process for farm sales and the fact that there are only few farms offered for sale (Peterson and Garland 2010: 9). The government's target to acquire 15 million ha in order to resettle 240,000 landless people by 2020 remains a long way in the future.[21] In 2006, only three out of 18 farm businesses that had received Government letters of intent for expropriation had actually become state property available for resettlement purposes (Adams and Palmer 2007: 26).

At the same time, similar to South Africa, the political economy of agrarian reform clearly is biased towards large-scale farming projects, with the loan scheme targeted towards middle-class farmers (Adams and Palmer 2007: 25–26). This has led to a subdivision of farmers in 'progressive' and 'poor and less able' categories, the latter of which are largely targeted by the moderately successful resettlement programme (Kariuki 2007: 108).

Even in the case of Botswana, a country often portrayed by the international community and international organisations such as the World Bank[22] as a 'role model' for economic development in the region, land reforms look rather disappointing. The country pursued a gradual, publicly negotiated evolutionary approach to land reform, which deliberately integrated the traditional tenure system into the statutory land administration system. Upon independence, Botswana soon changed a 'large portion of state land (formerly Crown Land) back to customary land' and adopted new forms of land rights (Kalabamu 2000: 308). Subsequently, by 1992 land under customary tenure rose from 47 per cent to 71 per cent, and the fraction of state land dropped from 48 per cent to 28 per cent of the country's land area. Moreover, land under freehold tenure only increased modestly (from 5 per cent to 6 per cent of the country's total land area), and since 1978 no new areas have been allotted to freehold tenure in order to avoid land concentration in the hand of few investors (Kalabamu 2000: 308).

In addition to converting state-owned land back into communal tenure, the Tribal Land Act of 1968 was a central part of the country's land reforms. It aimed to achieve the modernisation of customary land management by 'providing a written law for easy reference', based on the idea to improve instead of alter customary land administration (Kalabamu 2000: 308). Moreover, the Tribal Land Act created subnational and decentralised land boards, governed by elected government representatives that replaced 'chiefs, sub-chiefs and headmen in the administration and allocation of customary land rights', which were put in place to manage the new land tenure system and related functions (Kalabamu 2000: 310).[23] For the process of land reform, mineral revenues provided funding, and during the reform process itself it was community consultations, adherence to the rule of law, and democratic and transparent procedures which contributed to its successful undertaking.

Overall, these land reforms have focused on revising the land tenure system in view of 'access, ownership, administration and transfer of land rights' to the sub-national and local level (Kalabamu 2000: 305). However, they did not have redistribution as primary goal. Unlike neighbouring countries and their colonial experience (e.g., South Africa, Namibia or Zimbabwe), Botswana had been a peripheral British protectorate, and colonial dispossession and the settlement of white farmers had been restricted 'to a few border areas'.[24] This meant that the country, upon gaining independence in 1966, did not face the problem of highly skewed land distribution, as was the case in South Africa or Namibia. Instead, land reforms in Botswana were intended to foster agricultural productivity, contribute to reduced range degradation, and decrease the social inequity in rural areas (Malope and Nnyaladzi 2008: 383–84).

While from the beginning it was controversial whether the reforms actually yielded improvements in view of productivity and range conservation (Arntzen, Ngcongco and Turner 1986) (primarily through the Tribal Land Grazing Policy[25] and the National Policy on Agricultural Development[26]), they seemingly failed to improve the livelihood of poor households. This is largely due to the low level of assets available to impoverished communities, as well as the lack of loans or other programmes that would support the participation of these communities in the land reform process (Malope and Nnyaladzi 2008: 305–10).

Moreover, the integration of traditional land tenure into the modern system has created 'land-related tensions and localized conflicts', often along ethnic lines, as current customary institutions actually form an ethnic-based lands rights system according to the Twsana customary system of land tenure (Clover and Eriksen 2009: 63). This has contributed to the fact that particular ethnic minority groups such as the Dobe Ju and other San groups have been marginalised in the land re-allocation process, as either they do not fit the specifications for land allocations (e.g., hunter and gatherer rights are not recognised under customary or statutory land law) (under the Tribal Land Grazing Policy (TLGP)) (Adams, Kalabamu and White 2003: 6–7; Clover and Eriksen 2009: 63).

According to a study by the United Nations Economic Commission for Africa (UNECA), all of these countries' land use and tenure reform efforts have suffered from 'inappropriate and exploitative administrative practices' (UNECA 2003: v). Common concerns today include unclear or overlapping land rights, the insecurity of farm workers and farm labour tenants, and administrative procedures that clearly favour wealthy landowners and large-scale commercial farming (e.g., South Africa) (UNECA 2003: v). Moreover, the problem of overcrowding remains unresolved as there are too many households in relation to the available land.[27] For instance, the majority of Malawi's rural population suffers from the small size of farms, which together with the lack of upgraded agricultural technology undermines the possibility of improved yields and enhances the environmental stress on the available arable land. As of 2004, the majority of farming activities in Malawi took place on less than one hectare of land, which is not only too little to cover household needs, but also undermines food security. Overall, it was estimated that approximately 1.26 million people in southern and some parts of central Malawi depended on food aid due to a series of poor harvests over the last years.[28]

Some states are also facing tenure security problems in the form of arbitrary customary land alienation into leasehold without compensation (e.g., Malawi, Mozambique, and Zambia). In Malawi, for instance, since the 1960s small-scale farmers were alienated from their land held under customary tenure without compensation. Until the late 1980s, over 700,000 ha of land were taken away and rights transferred to statutory leaseholders. In Mozambique, small-scale farmers lost their land held under customary tenure to investors and wealthy individuals that acquired it in a legal process following the statutory leasehold tenure system (UNECA 2003: 9). Against this background, studies on land reforms in southern Africa actually come to the rather gloomy conclusion that the biggest challenge to success might be the lack of political will to really address structural conditions of socio-economic inequity and provide for economic reconstitution.[29]

While it is difficult to point the finger at any single cause for these reform outcomes, it nevertheless can be put on record that small-scale farming, 'which provides a precarious living to millions of poor rural households', tends to be disregarded by policy makers, domestically as well as internationally (Lahiff 2003: i). Only in Zimbabwe has a substantial redistribution of land taken place, albeit in a chaotic, disruptive and violent manner;[30] yet, this has not led to better conditions for local right holders, and small-scale farmers remain vulnerable. In the ongoing anarchic and frequently violent redistribution of land, the winners, often so-called war veterans, have had little or no farming experience, while up to two million farmhands and their dependents, constituting 15 per cent of the population, have faced internal displacement and unemployment, worsening still further the country's political and economic turmoil.

The failure of current land reforms in addressing the land crisis prolongs human insecurity and heightens environmental pressures in the region. Instead of bringing about change in terms of altered asset distributions, land reforms have consolidated the dual or pluralistic structures of the colonial agricultural system and weakened traditional rights and local influence over livelihood conditions and choices (Clover and Eriksen 2009: 66). This has taken place 'first by deliberate state policies and, more recently, by the forces of deregulated capitalism' (Lahiff 2003: i).

In this context, it is important to consider that the domestic land crisis in southern African societies is embedded in an international and global context. Apart from domestic political vote catching and rallying activities undertaken by African government and policymakers, the matter is clearly influenced by issues related to global environmental scarcity, international trade, international organisations, and conflicting interests to grow cash crops or engage in subsistence farming (Adams and Palmer 2007: 74).

8.3 Land grab in southern Africa

Land deals (including sales and rent) covered an estimated 15 million ha to 20 million ha of farm land in 2006 (*Economist* 2009: 65).[31] The IFPRI Policy Brief '"Land Grabbing" by Foreign Investors in Developing Countries'[32] clarifies that this is equivalent to 25 per cent of all farmlands in Europe.[33] However, due to a lack of transparency amongst actors involved, these numbers are only a rough estimate. While these deals were originally taking place mainly on the African continent, GRAIN has recently published another report that shows that similar deals are on the rise across Latin America, and that these deals are about to exceed investments on the African continent (GRAIN 2010: 1–2). Investors claim that compared to the African continent, investments in Latin America are 'more secure and less controversial' (GRAIN 2010: 1–2). The Brazilian government has, for instance, begun to finance the construction of infrastructure in neighbouring Guyana's Rupununi Savannah to grow export crops such as rice in the medium-term (GRAIN 2010: 1–2).

The joint report 'Land Grab or Development Opportunity', published by the FAO, the IFAD and the IIED, a UK-based think tank, acknowledges this striking increase in agricultural investment and international land deals and observes that these take place in times when other forms of foreign direct investment (FDI) are decreasing due to the financial crisis. The report identifies several causes: the rise in global food prizes and concerns over food security, the global energy crisis and the expected rise in demand for biofuels and the expectation of rising rates of return in agriculture due to agricultural commodity price spikes (Cotula *et al* 2009: 4–6).

Already in 2008, a GRAIN report had argued that there was an actual link between the food and financial crises, both of which together were driving forces behind the 'new global land grab' (GRAIN 2008: 1). On the one hand, countries such as China, Saudi Arabia, India, Japan, Malaysia, South Korea, Egypt, Libya, Bahrain, Jordan, Kuwait, Qatar and the United Arab Emirates were acquiring farmland all over the world, trying to enhance their long-term food supply (GRAIN 2008: 3–4).[34] Between 2006 and 2009, Bahrain secured a 10,000 ha deal in the Philippines (according to *Bahrain News Agency*, February 2009); Saudi Arabia reportedly requested to acquire 500,000 ha in Tanzania (according to Reuters Africa, April 2009); and South Korea managed to secure 690,000 ha in Sudan for food crop production (*Korea Times*, June 2008) (Von Braun and Meinzen-Dick 2009: 2). On the other hand, the private sector had identified investments in land deals as a new basis for revenue which promised increasing returns (GRAIN 2008: 1–4).

The FAO/IFAD/IIED report identifies two types of land deals: land purchases, which are most common in Latin America and Eastern Europe; and land leases, which are most common in Africa, partly due to national law that forbids foreign land ownership. Most land deals are the result of intergovernmental negotiations or state–private sector arrangements. At the same time, there are also cases of land deals with local leaders, and sometimes even inter-governmentally negotiated deals necessitated contractual agreements between the host government and these leaders. For instance, a deal in Madagascar contained lease and contract farming arrangements, 'including a direct deal with 13 associations of local landholders' (Cotula 2009: 2).

Moreover, lease duration and content specificities vary greatly. Lease duration can be from short-term of less than five years up to 99 years, and lease content can go as far as to transfer water rights. Due to the latter phenomenon, the 'land grab' has also been called the hidden 'water grab'. On the one hand, host countries such as Ethiopia, often transfer land rights together with water rights, with the latter free of charge.[35] On the other hand, investor countries such as Saudi Arabia, which is one of the largest investors in food crops around the world, have so far negotiated land deals that also include the equivalent of hundreds of millions of gallons of water a year. In fact, the government of Saudi Arabia has openly declared the investments in agriculture abroad to be part of a plan to 'decrease its domestic cereal production by 12 per cent per year to conserve its water'.[36] Currently, US$5 billion is put into loans for Saudi companies which invest in agricultural projects abroad.[37]

Financially, the investments and land deals take place through state-owned enterprises (SOEs), bilateral investment treaties (BITs) or sovereign wealth funds (SWFs) (Cotula *et al* 2009: 27–34). So far it is primarily private sector actors, such as agribusiness and biofuel companies that are investing in land but intergovernmental arrangements are on the rise and often investments are backed by governments. For instance, the government of Saudi Arabia created a 'King Abdullah Initiative for Saudi Agricultural Investment Abroad' which assists Saudi Arabian companies investing in agriculture (Cotula *et al* 2009: 38–39) and negotiations have been taking place with Brazilian government officials over the creation of export-oriented food crop plantations (GRAIN 2010: 1–2).

Underpinning these land deals and investments are negotiations over the provisions of co-operation between the host government and investor. These include profit repatriation, as well as technical and legal concerns. The FAO/IIED/IFAD report highlights the weak negotiation position of African governments: in most cases, land fees, taxes and other costs to investors tend to be rather low, as host governments or communities hope to attract investment and consequently improve state revenue, job creation, or infrastructure development (Cotula 2009: 2). At the same time, weak and underfinanced legal institutions in these host countries make it difficult to hold investors accountable to the terms of reference of their contracts. All of these conditions have made host country legal systems an easy target for the promotion of legal changes in domestic law that serve to shield private investors from state action (Cotula *et al* 2009: 59, 102–7). In particular, national-level policy reforms have bettered the conditions for foreign investors. Numerous examples of these improved conditions exist, including the development of investment codes in Mali in 1991 and 2005, Mozambique in 1993, and Tanzania in 1997, as well as reform efforts in form of sectoral legislation on land, banking, taxation and customs (Cotula *et al* 2009: 59).

In addition, the majority of stakeholders, including land users, local rights holders, civil society associations, small-scale farmers and the local labour force are marginalised in two ways: first, they hardly ever participate in these negotiations, as investors and governments seldom make use of community co-operation strategies in the planning and implementation process of investments projects. Second, the domestic and international bias of policy makers towards large-scale farming projects further reduces the opportunities and choices available to small-scale farmers.

While these contractual conditions clearly challenge the 'win-win' narrative of international investments in land, it is also the broader context of food insecurity and dependence on food aid in host countries that makes these deals questionable. The FAO/IIED/IFAD report suggests that, in view of global security, it would be instead advisable to assess domestic agricultural productivity challenges and co-operate with communities to improve the situation of rural households. Moreover, a global strategy detailing how to deal with resource scarcity would need to be discussed as a point of orientation. However, this seems highly unlikely as states tend to see it as a threat to their sovereignty.

At the moment, there are several main policies and institutional arrangements that have served to create the institutional context for these land deals: firstly, government consumption targets on bioenergy in the European Union and government-backed financial incentives including subsidies and tax breaks have created a market for biofuel-related investments, such as export-led land deals. For example, the United Kingdom's CAMS Group secured 112,000 acres in Tanzania, and Sun Biofuels secured 13,500 acres in Tanzania for jatropha (biofuel). Trans4mation Agric-tech, also from the United Kingdom, has leased 25,000 acres in Nigeria. Sweden's Skebab Corporation has secured 247,000 acres in Mozambique, and Germany's Flora EcoPower secured 32,000 acres in Ethiopia.[38] In 2006, about 14 million ha were estimated to be used for the production of biofuels and their by-products, which accounts for about 1 per cent of globally available arable land (Cotula, Dyer and Vermeulen 2008: 19). Concerns over the impact of biofuel policies for food security and food price hikes have been neglected so far (Cotula *et al* 2009: 5).

Secondly, international financial institutions such as International Finance Corporation (IFC)[39] and Foreign Investment Advisory Service (FIAS)[40] have worked hard to overcome investment obstacles within potential recipient countries. In fact, these institutions have been negotiating with host governments to improve the business environment and thereby increase the likelihood of investment (Shepard and Mittal 2009: 7). As a result, simple investor regulations and foreign ownership laws were adopted in potential recipient countries.[41]

Thirdly, some donor countries and international organisations, such as the World Bank, have pushed a number of governments into a policy of titling under the assumption that this will yield private sector-led development (Clover and Eriksen 2009: 61). For instance, the Integrated Programme of Land Redistribution and Agricultural Development (IPLRAD) in South Africa contributed to a change of the target group for redistribution from the landless and poor towards commercial farmers (Clover and Eriksen 2009: 61, and Hall 2010: 189–90). Finally, international financial institutions as well as governments have created financial incentives by providing loans to private investors for agricultural investment purposes, such as Saudi Arabia's 'King Abdullah Initiative for Saudi Agricultural Investment Abroad', which was mentioned above.

With regard to implications for the domestic and local development of these global trends, prognoses differ. According to the Oakland Institute,[42] current land acquisitions have the potential to threaten the food security of the rural poor, as investments by corporate agribusiness mostly result in 'driving independent farmers off their land' or turning farmers into contract workers, which seems to be also a very likely scenario for the cases discussed before (Shepard and Mittal 2009: 11). In all scenarios, the effect is that access to land and other natural resources, such as water, will be more restricted. In addition, these large-scale commercial projects are likely to decrease biodiversity. Moreover, while land is definitively cheap, estimates that land is underutilised need to be seriously questioned. The predominant problem of land tenure insecurity on the ground, as well as the existence of internationally unacknowledged forms of communal tenure and farming practices, including dry-season grazing and shifting cultivation, might easily yield a incorrect assessment of land utility (Clover and Eriksen 2009: 54–55, and Cotula *et al* 2009: 59–61).

Overall, the example of South Korea's Daewoo Logistics Corporation's attempt to secretly negotiate a 99 years lease on 1.3 million ha of farmland in Madagascar, which amounts to about half of the arable land, reveals how these deals can undermine domestic security.[43] In this particular case, it not only encouraged political unrest but also led to the collapse of the host government (Shepard and Mittal 2009: 13). Even though Daewoo promised jobs, Madagascar's citizens, 70 per cent of which live in rural areas, feared displacement, and the Fekritana farmers confederation highlighted issues of social justice in a country where 'local farmers do not have enough land' (Shepard and Mittal 2009: 7).

While the Daewoo example perfectly illustrates the conflict potential that arises at the interface of domestic socio-economic marginalisation and tenure insecurity and internationally negotiated land deals, it also directs attention to geopolitical issues underpinning the alarm demonstrated by international media on the issue of land grab. In the case of Madagascar, the UK's *Financial Times* had published an article that included false allegations and information about the Daewoo deal. A South Korean newspaper therefore released an editorial questioning the *Financial Times*: 'why [was] the paper … turning a blind eye to British Jatropha farms in Madagascar (used for biodiesel fuel) and French plantations on the island while going after a Korean company only'?[44] As for Western media news coverage, a bias seems to persist as there is an irritation about the fact that largely states and corporations from the 'South' are undertaking these investments.

At the same time, and contrary to the large number of mostly negative articles on, for instance, China in Africa, there has been little coverage about 'Western' based agri-businesses or investment funds investing in land deals (Bräutigam and Tang 2009: 697–98).[45] For example, New York-based BlackRock has created a US$200 million agricultural hedge fund and aims to use US$30 million thereof to secure farmland, but this deal has garnered little international attention (Shepard and Mittal 2009: 4).

Currently international and regional organisations including World Bank, FAO and African Union are working on a set of voluntary guidelines for land deals that provide a benchmark of best practices. They will provide advice for host country governments, investors and international institutions on how to behave to enhance the (assumed) positive potential of these investments to contribute to a country's economic development. Yet, the impact of this codex framework is likely to be limited. In the absence of a monitoring and enforcement mechanism, two factors seem to be particularly adverse for such a voluntary guideline framework to work: firstly, the fact that many of these investments are done in the name of national food or energy security; and secondly, the fact that in most cases so far, the private sector as well as governments have tried to withhold information about land deals out of fear over public and political backlash (GRAIN 2008: 6–7).

Finally, and in addition to the lack of monitoring and enforcement mechanisms, the basic difficulty in bridging international and national regulations or practices will reduce the impact of these guidelines. Studies, focusing on the tourism sector in Namibia, have shown how efforts by the state to mediate legal differences between traditional domestic forms of customary law and international Western notions of private property rights might be to the disadvantage of communal organisation (Massyn 2007: 381–83). The principles at the core of Namibia's undertaking to formalise and integrate traditional systems of land tenure into the modern tenure administration gave decision-making leeway to traditional authorities, thereby undermining the trust of investors in legal certainty.

8.4 Foreign investors (South Korea, India, United Kingdom, Gulf States, China)

The amount of untapped resources in Africa is no surprise to anyone. For years foreign governments and companies have been looking for a way to break into these markets. However, with the food and oil prices having reached an all-time high in 2008, the desire to control or have access to the abundance of resources has been growing.

Foreign investment into Africa is nothing new. What is new is the rampant levels at which foreign investors have decided to invest in land in Africa. More specifically, foreign investors have increased dramatically the level of foreign investment in agricultural land in Africa. This has become somewhat of a hot topic for reasons noted above; mainly because of the sole fact that all of this investment has been coined as a 'land grab' or 'neo-colonialism'. The land grab is 'literally emerging as a race for securing food supply for the future to meet the growing need of food, by countries that are running out of arable land' (Chinafrica.asia 2009). Regardless of the term preferred in this situation, it is important to understand who is investing, where the investment is going, and what the terms are of contracts being signed.

Although hard numbers are hard to come by, here are some estimates of how much land has been acquired with the intention of exporting the goods to the investing country. The acquired area has been estimated at 20 million ha (and possibly as much as 100 million ha) of land. This accounts for 0.5–4 per cent of arable land in the world (Saunders 2010). Of the estimated 20 million ha,

Mozambique has leased or sold 600,000 ha, accounting for 1.9 per cent of its arable land; Tanzania has leased or sold 2,728,000 ha, accounting for 3.1 per cent of its arable land; Madagascar has leased or sold 800,000 ha which account for 2.3 per cent of its arable land; and lastly Zambia has leased or sold 3,150,000 ha which accounts for an astounding 4.2 per cent of its arable land (Anseeuw 2010). On average a hectare of land is being sold for only $800. This number is outrageous considering the price of arable land in the United States can range anywhere from US$100 to US$100,000 per acre; with US$500 per acre as an extremely low price in the United States.[46]

Over the past several years there have been many different countries investing in agricultural land and agribusiness in Africa. Typically, these countries are capital abundant countries. The most notable in Africa are South Korea, India, United Kingdom, Gulf States (most notably Saudi Arabia and the United Arab Emirates) and last and most important is China.

As mentioned above, South Korea's biggest acquisition was in Madagascar. It attempted to lease 1.3 million ha of land (approximately half of the country's arable land) for 99 years. Although it was promised that this investment would create jobs for local people, there was still a fear that locals would become displaced. This contract was later deemed unconstitutional after Andry Rajoelina overthrew Ravalomanana with the help of the military. This is an important example because although these countries are investing millions and millions of dollars, at the end of the day these countries can turn around and deem it unconstitutional and on the basis of sovereignty these contracts would become invalid. Therefore, foreign investors should take a hard look at the political stability of a country and ensure contracts are fair because if a country finds itself unable to feed its own people and the food security of its country is threatened, these countries will have no choice but to eliminate these contracts on the grounds that these contracts infringe on its national sovereignty.

Although less controversial in the media, India has become another big investor. India is a land with a large and dense population. Therefore, arable land in India is a scarce resource. Because of this dilemma India has sought land in Africa; most notably in Ethiopia, Kenya, Madagascar, Senegal and Mozambique. In each of these countries India has either bought or leased hundreds of thousands of hectares of land to grow rice, sugar cane, maize and lentils to feed their domestic country (Vidal 2010). However, the FDI coming from India appears that it is not solely being used for land grabbing. India has developed a collective engagement in Africa which also promotes agribusiness and infrastructure necessary to have a functioning agricultural sector. Jorge Heine (2008) has expressed that India's dealings with African countries are more of a reciprocal relationship because 'Indian companies are more willing to invest in infrastructure and in the downstream of facilities needed to bring products to part than western ones'. Regardless of the 'noble' stipulations in Indian contracts, the sharing ratio remains to be 70:30. That is, 70 per cent of total produce is reserved for export and the industry while only 30 per cent is to be used for domestic consumption (ibid.).

It has been argued that because 80 per cent of Africa's land is still uncultivated and that 7 per cent of its land is irrigated with low production yields, if it plays its cards right, this could benefit African countries as well (Mullin 2010). There are plenty of economic opportunities to be gained if African leaders play their cards right. Therefore, the real issue becomes ensuring these deals are structured in a fair and correct manner. International investors need to 'respect principles of responsible investment, [and] governments need to be more accountable, transparent and strategic in how they structure deals' (ibid). This is theoretically a nice thought, but those who argue this are forgetting one thing. The governments in Africa already struggle with becoming more transparent and accountable in general. There are many corrupt governments and African leaders who have no intention of following the recommendations made by scholars worldwide. There are leaders and African administrations that choose to do what is best for them and their own pockets and have a total disregard and lack empathy for the individuals in the country who are suffering. Furthermore, even if the leaders in some of these African countries are neither self-seeking nor corrupt, they do not necessarily have the tools or infrastructure in place to become more accountable or transparent. These African countries, for the most part, are very poor and as the administration of these countries and the leaders of these countries it becomes difficult to turn down investments and deals that will essentially give the country money no matter what the long-term repercussions may be. Therefore, although there are economic opportunities for these countries, if during negotiations African leaders push too hard, they could lose the contract as these foreign investors can easily go to another country that is willing to make a deal on these terms.

One of the more shocking elements of everything that is occurring is that it is mostly other developing nations that are exploiting African countries for their land. It is rare for such an outburst to be written in the media about developed nations. The one major foreign investor in land in the southern Africa region is the United Kingdom. The major tracts of land that have been secured by British firms reside mostly in Angola, Ethiopia, Mozambique, Nigeria and Tanzania.

The fourth group of foreign investors is the Gulf States. The most predominant foreign investors of the Gulf States of land in Africa are Saudi Arabia and the United Arab Emirates (UAE). In a report by the World Bank, 'Food production in Arab countries is limited by scarce land and water resources … Arab countries are highly exposed to international food commodity price shocks … because they are heavily dependent on imported food' (UPI 2010). Similar to the reasons India has invested in agricultural land, Gulf States have had no choice but to look elsewhere in order to secure food supply for their growing populations.

In Saudi Arabia, there has been the establishment of the King Abdullah Initiative for Saudi Agriculture Investment Abroad which 'supports agricultural investments by Saudi companies in countries with high agricultural potential, with a view to promoting national and international food security' (Cotula *et al* 2009). Strategically, the crops being grown on the land acquired in Africa include rice, wheat, barley, corn, sugar as well as some animal and fish resources. This initiative also states that only 'reasonable percentages' of goods is to be exported, 'so as not to exacerbate food insecurity in host countries' (Cotula *et al* 2009). Similar to the King Abdullah Initiative, the Abu Dhabi Fund for Development has financed the development of agricultural land to grow alfalfa (to use as animal feed), maize, beans and potatoes all for export back to the UAE (Cotula *et al* 2009).

Lastly and most controversial is the investments that China has been making in Africa. China's economy is quite sizable and depends on the help of outside resources to keep it running. For instance it relies on Angola, Sudan and Nigeria for its oil and South Africa, Zambia and Liberia for its minerals. To date, China has acquired 2.8 million ha in the Democratic Republic of the Congo for oil palm production and it is in the process of negotiating an additional 2 million ha in Zambia (Dyer 2009). China has also invested millions of dollars in Mozambique in rice production (Chinafrica.asia 2009).

Although it appears that China has really just started investing in 2006, the rampant level at which it is doing so is of great concern to scholars and practitioners alike. Between 1995 and 2005, China provided approximately US$12.5 billion in aid to Africa as well as cancelled billions of dollars' worth of debt and implemented infrastructure programmes across the continent. In exchange, Africa is the supplier of nearly one-third of China's oil supply (Rubinstein 2009). During 2008 and 2009, despite the financial crisis China was investing at significant rates. During the first half of 2009, investments in non-financial sectors (which include agriculture) grew 78.6 per cent to US$875 million (*China Daily* 2010). In comparison to developed nations and other nations who have invested in the region, the dollar figure appears insignificant. However the real concern is the pace at which the amount of investment in the region has increased significantly in such a short period of time.

Because of the vast amount of investment going into Africa from China, combined with the lax records being kept by China, it is difficult to estimate how much Chinese companies have infiltrated the African markets. Also, as a result of these two combined factors, it is difficult to determine if the deals being reached between China and its African counterparts are in fact fair or if China is exploiting the lack of transparency and accountability of African leaders and their administrations as noted above. Although the argument has been made that China's investments in Africa are purely self-serving, Chinese officials are insistent that this is not the case (Rubinstein 2009).

Not only is China investing in agricultural land, but it is also investing in agricultural schools. It has sent over at least 100 Chinese agricultural specialists who are working to find ways to improve agricultural conditions in Africa which includes development of canals and other methods of irrigation (Chinafrica.asia 2009). Whether or not this is a stunt to show the international community that there is more to its investments in Africa than self-seeking behaviour, there are a number of projects being done throughout the continent to improve the infrastructure to help African farmers and agribusinesses as well as the Chinese counterparts.

All of these countries who have contributed to the most thus far all have two things in common: large dense populations and a small portion of the world's arable land. It is a problem that will continue to get worse as food security continues to be threatened by growing populations, high food prices and thousands of failed crops a year due to weather conditions. Although this appears to be a solution for some, at the end of the day this solution has astronomical long-term effects that will not only impact the 1 billion people who live on the African continent, but also the 2.5 billion or so who reside in the countries discussed above. Although the World Bank and UN have started to compile standards for land acquisitions such as these, many argue that it is too little too late (UPI 2010).

8.5 Lessons learned and policy options to consider

Several lessons can be learned, and policy options considered, from the above analysis on attempts made to address the historical legacies dealing with land reforms which have undoubtedly influenced the debate surrounding land acquisitions by foreign governments and enterprises in the region and vice versa.

- The primary objectives of the land reform programmes in southern Africa have been essentially sought to redress colonial legacies associated with displacement and marginalisation of small-scale farmers and herders while reducing overgrazing and environmental degradation.
- To a large degree, the major outcomes of these land reforms have been the privatisation of land, social stratification and continued alienation of herders and small-scale farmers and landless peasants who do not possess the capital or credit to invest in large-scale agricultural development projects of commercial farms.
- It has been argued that regardless of the system of land tenure (customary or statutory), insecure land tenure has been one of the major problems of land reform in southern Africa. Secure tenure increases productivity and incentivises long-term agricultural improvements (including environmental sustainability), while insecure tenure can lead to an exploitative depletion of land because households are not able to produce optimally and sustainably.
- African governments need to build strong, accountable and representative rural institutions with democratically-elected land boards, in order to introduce democracy and accountability into land administration.
- Building in more procedural safeguards, provisions for community consultations and regulations to ensure that land administration decisions reflect the will of the community is another way to improve democratic accountability by governments in the region.
- Across southern Africa, the goal of land reform has shifted from poverty alleviation to privatisation and economic efficiency. Reforms have not made small-scale agriculture economically viable, and there have not been sufficient institutional support nor extension services to assist resettled farmers.
- African governments have found it difficult to mediate traditional systems of land tenure with Western notions of private property rights. Attempts to maintain the essence of customary laws, while at the same time providing a secure system in which partnerships between local communities and private investors can operate have been problematic.

- The carrying out of land policy involving translation of new land policies into government legislation and the advancement of achievable institutional foundations for implementation constitutes one of the most important policy challenges facing African governments.
- Any discussion surrounding land reforms in southern Africa need to take place within the discourse of human security and environmental sustainability. The focus should be on how land reform has affected the socio-economic rights of certain groups and disrupted the sustainability of their human–environment relations.
- Land grab is an outcome of both global food and financial insecurities. Resource pressures, water scarcity and soil depletion have compelled many governments to be concerned about future food production.
- For transnational firms, land has become a strategic asset and expanding the productive capacity is a potential source of profit because markets are predicted to remain very tight. The ongoing land grab is evidence that many countries are losing faith in the market as a provider of food security.
- Land deals involving foreign corporations and governments involved a number of financial partnerships and mechanisms, such as foreign state-owned enterprise (SOEs), sovereign wealth funds (SWF), and bilateral investment treaties (BIT).
- Although intergovernmental arrangements have increased in recent years, the majority of land deals that take place in southern Africa involve private consortiums.
- Land acquisitions have presented their own set of challenges and concerns for African governments and populations. Lack of transparency is a major issue, with many allegations of corruption and a shortage of available public information on contracts.
- African laws are generally weak, lacking the capacity to hold investors accountable on the agreed-upon terms, and in fact investment deals have often influenced changes to domestic legislation that protect investment against state action.
- Civil society, local rights holders and land users have been excluded from participation in planning and implementing projects because the requirements for mandatory community consultations have been poorly designed and tailored to produce favourable outcomes for foreign investors.
- Concerns have been levelled both against foreign investors and African governments arising from land investments, particularly with regards to food security.
- The legitimacy of having food and agricultural products departing host African countries which are food importers and often dependent on food aid has been called into question.

8.6 Concluding remarks

In recent years there has been a sharp rise in the purchase and lease of vast tracts of African agricultural lands by foreign countries and companies. The spike in global food prices and uncertainties about global food supply; nations finally facing the negative environmental externalities of decades of intensive production, (such as soil depletion and water scarcity); changes in world oil prices and the associated effects on transportation costs and fertilisers; and emerging economies, particularly China needing to acquire land for the production of non-agricultural commodities and for high-value food and livestock production to satisfy the growing consumer demands of the middle class have been blamed for the increase in agricultural investments. Indeed, southern Africa is a particularly prized location for land acquisition because land is relatively cheap, and estimates show that much of the cultivable land is underutilised.

The popular argument in favour of these land deals is that in exchange for their lease or purchase the foreign interests agree to build badly needed infrastructure including roads, bridges, wells and schools. Employment for the local inhabitants would also be a benefit. Proponents of the foreign land acquisitions portray it as a development opportunity for poor nations in the region.

Critics, however, point out that the lands that are acquired by foreign interests mostly affect the poorest inhabitants in the subcontinent. In an increasing number of cases, these inhabitants are subsistence farmers that are removed from the land by their own government without any or adequate consultation or compensation. They question the legitimacy of the export-oriented model that this process is promoting. Studies have shown that the displacement of small farmers and the loss of food sovereignty are too big a cost – the compensation in the form of capital inflows, job creation and increased incomes has either not materialised or increased inequalities. While the land deals are also being used as a positive example of South–South co-operation, particularly in the case of Chinese and other Asian investments, questions have risen about where the profits and products are being distributed.

African governments need to enhance the benefits they derive from the land deals they sign with foreign corporations and governments. In doing so, more needs to be done to ensure clearer assessment of how agricultural productivity gains could be achieved, with legally binding instruments on environmental protection, infrastructure development and job creation; ensuring that local land rights are secured so that communities aren't disposed; an opening up of negotiations to public scrutiny. African governments need to be accountable to their populations in ensuring that allegations of corruption and embezzlement arising from these land deals at the expense of poor farming communities are addressed while manifestations of neocolonialism are not repeated. With governments in southern Africa still battling to resolve the contentious issues surrounding land reforms that threaten to exacerbate the existing inequalities and deepen rural poverty, the recent land grabs threaten to derail and complicate them even further.

Notes

* Hany Besada is Program Head, Governance of Natural Resources and Senior Researcher, Development Cooperation, at the North–South Institute (NSI). Previously, he was Senior Researcher and Program Leader at the Centre for International Governance Innovation (CIGI). He would like to thank Shanna Scarrow, a Balsillie Fellow at

the Centre for International Governance Innovation, for research assistance provided towards this work. She holds a Master's degree in International Public Policy from Wilfrid Laurier University in Waterloo, Ontario.

† Ariane Goetz is a Balsillie Doctoral Fellow at the Centre for Governance Innovation.

1 GRAIN is an international NGO that works on and supports 'community-controlled and biodiversity-based food systems'. See the web site at <http://www.grain.org/front/> (accessed 11 March 2010).

2 See IMF information about 'Impact of High Food and Fuel Prices on Developing Countries [-] Frequently Asked Questions' (last updated 11 February 2010) under <http://www.imf.org/external/np/exr/faq/ffpfaqs.htm> (accessed 18 April 2010).

3 Data from the World Bank shows for instance that a total of 18 countries from Latin America, Eastern Europe, Central Asia, Africa, and Latin America imposed export restrictions during the food crisis. See <http://siteresources.worldbank.org/NEWS/Resources/risingfoodprices_chart_apr08.pdf> (accessed 18 April 2010); also see the Testimony of Arvind Subramanian (Peterson Institute for International Economics) at the US House of Representatives, Committee on Financial Services, Hearing on Contributing Factors and International Responses to the Global Food Crisis, 14 May 2008. Retrieved under <http://www.iie.com/publications/papers/paper.cfm?ResearchID=931 (accessed 18 April 2010).

4 For instance, as of March 2008, wheat and maize prices were 130 per cent and 30 per cent higher, respectively, than they were the year before. See the International Fund for Agricultural Development (IFAD) online report under <http://www.ifad.org/operations/food/ceb.htm> (accessed 18 April 2010).

5 Agribusiness corporations from the 'North' have engaged in land deals in poorer countries for a long time. For instance, Dole Foods is the owner of 88,000 acres and leaseholder of 66,000 acres of land. See Von Braun and Meinzen-Dick (2009): 2.

6 To 'recipient' countries, farming communities and national economies.

7 So far, it remains unclear whether the rice production by China is meant as an export platform, or whether the rice produced will be sold (at least partially) on the (local and regional) market.

8 See IFPRI data map under <http://maps.google.com/maps/ms?hl=en&ie=UTF8&oe=UTF8&msa=0&msid=100237997621038330776.000468b0a95f89721a96e> (accessed 11 March 2010). Also see BBC News under <http://news.bbc.co.uk/2/hi/africa/7952628.stm>.

9 Ibid.

10 In the following, this report will be referred to as FAO/IFAD/IIED (2009).

11 See bibliography under <http://www.met.gov.na/publications/research/rdp_0032.pdf> (accessed 10 April 2010).

12 See also Lahiff (2007).

13 Senior researcher at the Land and Agrarian Studies Department, University of the Western Cape.

14 Since 1994 little has changed for the majority of its black population, who comprise approximately 79 per cent of the country's population. Today, more than 48 per cent of its black population continue to live in abject poverty. On the health front, the ANC government has been battling the disastrous effects of the HIV/AIDS epidemic in the country. Today, more than 5.5 million South Africans are thought to be living with the virus. Having one of the highest HIV prevalence rates in the world, one of the most unequal societies, a spiralling crime rate, and a looming land crisis, South Africa's leaders are on a hasty gallop to try and avert the social crisis that threatens its fragile democratic institutions, as well as its ethnic cohesiveness and the stability that it has fought so hard to achieve since the end of apartheid.

15 Vision 2030 was begun in 2005.

16 See the Namibian Ministry of Lands and Resettlements web page under <http://www.op.gov.na/Decade_peace/lands.htm> (accessed 10 April 2010).

17 The Loan Scheme (AALS) amounts to N$25 million per year, subsidised by the government of Namibia, whereas no loans are being granted to individuals whose income is above N$400,000 per year. The AALS is targeted to support disadvantaged communities to buy and own land for farming purposes. The loans are granted for a period of 25 years, whereas the first three years are free of interest. Success of the AALS remains ambiguous: On the one hand, it has contributed to the transferral of land and farm businesses into black ownership. On the other hand, it has not proven to be successful with regard to productivity or poverty alleviation. Also, the opposition party Congress of Democrats (CoG) has claimed the AALS is 'a self-enrichment programme' for the government and individuals affiliated to it. See *The Namibian* (online newspaper), 'More Questions Arise on Pros and Cons of Affirmative Action Loan Scheme', 20 July 2004; *The Namibian*, 'Government, Agribank Defending Affirmative Action Loan Scheme', 12 August 2003; the Agribank of Namibia web page under <http://www.agribank.com.na/admin/news/Affirmative%20Action%20Loan%20Scheme%20%28AALS%29.pdf>.

18 See Irin News under <http://www.africaspeaks.com/blog/?p=2223 (accessed 10 April 2010).

19 The NAU is a 'national organization [that] has established itself well as the mouthpiece and mediator of the commercial farmer'. See web page under <http://www.agrinamibia.com.na/index.php?module=Pages&func=display&pageid=4> (accessed 10 April 2010).

20 *The Namibian*, 'RP slams Gobabis Farmers' Meeting as "unfortunate"', 11 June 2004, retrieved under <http://www.namibian.com.na/index.php?id=28&tx_ttnews[tt_news]=8134&no_cache=1 (accessed 10 April 2010).

21 See <http://www.africaspeaks.com/blog/?p=2223.

22 See for instance the World Bank's Country Brief on Botswana under <http://web.worldbank.org/WBSITE/EXTERNAL/COUNTRIES/AFRICAEXT/BOTSWANAEXTN/0,contentMDK:20183107~pagePK:141137~piPK:141127~theSitePK:322804,00.html> (accessed 10 April 2010).

23 These functions included the development and maintenance of customary law grants and leases, and the administration and allocation of state land.

24 See Botswana history under <http://ubh.tripod.com/bw/bhp1.htm> (accessed 10 April 2010).

25 The Tribal Land Grazing Policy (TLGP) was outlined in the government White Paper No. 2 of 1975 as a response to the growing number of cattle in Botswana on tribal land in the 1970s. Its goal is to prevent the over-utilisation of grazing land as well as to moderate the related environmental degradation (in the form of sheet erosion and bush encroachment). At the core, the TLGP changed land ownership from communal/tribal-based ownership to private tenures. Land was administered by Land Boards (with elected and mandated government representatives), and transferred to individuals on leases with low rental fees for a period of fifty years. Some ethnic groups such as the San were marginalised in this process of land allocation that focused on 'tribes', as they had been displaced from their lands earlier on and did not meet the 'tribal' requirements. In fact, the related 'Tribal Land Act' entrenched a fairly uniform system of Tswana land tenure. It did not accommodate other forms deviating from the Tswana patterns of land holding and use. The San are not the only minority marginalised in this way. See Adams, Kalabamu and White (2003: 55–74); Frimpong (1995: 1–16).

26 The National Policy on Agricultural Development is outlined in the government's White Paper No. 1 of 1991: 'The policy sought to improve agricultural production through provision of secure and productive environment for agricultural producers. The fencing component of the policy provided for extended determination of land for cattle ranching … ' (see web page of the Ministry of Land and Housing under <http://www.mlh.gov.bw/index.php?option=com_about&id=23) (accessed 10 April 2010). Overall, the National Policy on Agricultural Development expanded the privatisation efforts of the Tribal Grazing Land Policy (1975), according to which exclusive rights 'to

specific areas of grazing land were given to individuals and groups for commercial ranches with boreholes and fencing. Leases were granted and rents paid to the land boards. Tenure conditions in unfenced communal grazing areas remained unchanged.' See Adams, Kalabamu and White (2003): 55–74.

27 This issue is particularly apparent in South Africa, Malawi and Lesotho.

28 See for instance Irin News (online, 7 July 2004) under <http://www.irinnews.org/report.aspx?reportid=50528 (accessed 10 April 2010).

29 See for instance Lahiff (2007); Clover and Eriksen (2009).

30 In 1998, Zimbabwe took part in a donor conference to establish the ground rules for the redistribution of land in a legal, transparent, orderly and just manner. Many agreed that there was inequity in the ownership of land in Zimbabwe and that land reform was a matter of social justice. Mugabe stressed that Zimbabwe would be able to realise economic development for its people only if land were redistributed fairly. The international community felt, however, that land reform should be conducted on the basis of the willing seller, willing buyer principle. In April 2000, when it became clear that the land reform process agreed to in 1998 had broken down because of illegal land occupation and continued lawlessness on farms, the donor nations first suspended, then, in September, terminated, their support for the process. Two months later, the Mugabe government provided the political framework for the Land Ministry to confiscate 70 per cent of the best farming land owned by whites, who represented approximately 0.7 per cent of the population, and redistribute it to landless blacks without compensation. In October 2000, as a new report described, the veterans marched on to some 2,000 farms, threatening white farmers and assaulting their black workers. Local courts twice ruled that farm occupation was illegal and ordered government to drive off veterans and their supporters. As a result, Mugabe's land grabbing effectively crippled Zimbabwe's commercial industry, which was once dominated by 4,500 mainly white farmers and which, in the past, had constituted some 20 per cent of the country's GDP and 40 per cent of its export earnings.

31 Estimates are based on data provided by the International Food Policy Research Institute (IFPRI).

32 Land grabbing is defined by large-scale international land acquisitions by states, private sector (corporations) or investment funds.

33 See <http://www.worldmission.ph/index.php?option=com content&view=article&id=261%3Aland-grab-for-the-worlds-farms& catid = 80%3Ajuly-2009&Itemid=71 (accessed 11 March 2010).

34 However, the specific strategies of main investors vary, depending on their particular motivation, as a look at the biggest players reveals. China pursues a long-term food supply strategy to account for the heightening agricultural and water-related scarcity that is related to industrialisation and climate change (e.g. desertification) at home; the Gulf States – all net importers of food due to scarce soil and water conditions – aim to ensure sufficient food supply and stabilise costs of food imports. During the 2008 food crisis, and due to the fact that their currencies are pegged to the US dollar, the food import costs had exploded for these states from US$8 billion to US$20 billion, as the increase in food prices happened at the time of the depreciation of the US dollar.

35 See *The Guardian*, 7 March 2010, under <http://www.guardian.co.uk/environment/2010/mar/07/food-water-africa-land-grab> (accessed 10 April 2010).

36 Ibid.

37 Ibid.

38 See <http://solveclimate.com/blog/20090521/biofuels-watch-african-land-grab-deals-questioned> (accessed 10 April 2010).

39 IFC co-ordinates its activities with the other institutions of the World Bank Group but is legally and financially independent. See <http://www.ifc.org/ifcext/about.nsf/Content/Organization>.

40 FIAS is part of the IFC, and also co-ordinates with the World Bank Group: 'FIAS assists governments of developing countries and transition economies in reforming their business environments, with emphasis on regulatory simplification and investment generation. FIAS relies on close collaboration with its donors and World Bank Group partners to leverage value and deliver tangible results.' From FIAS web page, under <http://www.fias.net/ifcext/fias.nsf/Content/AboutFIAS>.

41 Malawi's Investment Promotion Act (Act No. 28 of 1991, assented to by the President on 24 January 2003 and effective on 16 March 1992) is an example of this (Shepard and Mittal 2009: 7).

42 The Oakland Institute is a 'policy think tank whose mission is to increase public participation and promote fair debate on critical social, economic and environmental issues in both national and international forums.' See <http://www.oaklandinstitute.org/> (accessed 11 March 2009).

43 See IFPRI data map, above, n 8, and BBC News, above, n 8.

44 See online report on the Madagascar controversy under <http://www.groundreport.com/World/Madagascar-South-Korean-Land-Deal-Sparks-Controver_1/2873670> (30 March 2010).

45 Deborah Bräutigam claims that most assessments and media coverage of China's land deals do not match the reality on the ground (Bräutigam and Tang 2009).

46 There are approximately 2.471 acres in a hectare.

Bibliography

Adams, M., Kalabamu, F. and White, R. (2003) 'Land Tenure Policy and Practice in Botswana: Governance Lessons for Southern Africa', *Austrian Journal of Development Studies*, 19(1): 55–74.

Adams, M. and Palmer, R. (eds) (2007) *Independent Review of Land Issues*, Vol. III, *2006–07, Eastern and Southern Africa* (Oxford: Mokoro).

Anseeuw, W. (2010) 'Large Scale Land Acquisitions in Southern Africa: Analysis, Perspectives and Regulations', report, 29–30 March (Paris: CIRAD; Pretoria: PGSARD-UP).

Arntzen, J. W., Ngcongco, L. D. and Turner, S. D. (eds) (1986) *Land Policy and Agriculture in Eastern and Southern Africa* (Tokyo: United Nations University Press).

Bräutigam, D. and Tang, X. (2009) 'China's Engagement in African Agriculture: Down to the Countryside', *China Quarterly*, 199: 686.

Centre for Development and Enterprise (2005) 'Land Reform in South Africa: A 21st Century Perspective' (Johannesburg: Centre for Development and Enterprise).

Chinafrica.Asia (2009) 'China Africa Agriculture', <http://www.chinafrica.asia/china-shows-substantial-interest-in-african-agriculture> (accessed 15 November 2010).

China Daily (2010) 'Chinese Firms boost African Investment', *China Daily*, 21 April, <http://english.peopledaily.com.cn/90001/90778/90861/6957843.html> (accessed 5 September 2010).

Clover, J. and Eriksen, S. (2009) 'The Effects of Land Tenure Change on Sustainability: Human Security and Environmental Change in Southern African Savannas', *Environmental Science and Policy*, 12: 53.

Cotula, L. (2009) *Land Grab or Development Opportunity? International Farmland Deals in Africa* (Bogotá: Colombia FDI Perspectives).

Cotula, L., Dyer, N. and Vermeulen, S. (2008) 'Fuelling Exclusion? The Biofuel Boom and Poor People's Access to Land' (London: IIED).

Cotula, L., Vermeulen, S., Leonard, R. and Keeley, J. (2009) 'Land Grab or Development Opportunity? Agricultural Investment and International Land Deals in Africa' (London and Rome: IIED/FAO/IFAD).

Dyer, G. (2009) 'African Land Grab', *Zimbabwe Independent* (Harare), 26 May, <http://yaleglobal.yale.edu/content/african-land> (accessed 5 September 2010).

Economist, The (2009) 'Buying Farmland Abroad: Outsourcing's Third Wave', *Economist* (London), 23 May.

Frimpong, K. A. (1995) 'A Review of the Tribal Grazing Lands Policy in Botswana, Pula: *Botswana Journal of African Studies*, 9(1).

Frimpong, K. (2009) 'A Review of the Tribal Grazing Land Policy in Pula', *Botswana Journal of African Studies*, 9(1): 1.

GRAIN (2008), 'Seized! The 2008 Land Grab for Food and Financial Security' (Barcelona: GRAIN).

GRAIN (2010) 'Land Grabbing in Latin America' (Barcelona: GRAIN).

Hall, R. (2010) 'Two Cycles of Land Policy in South Africa: Tracing the Contours', in W. Anseeuw and C. Alden (eds) *The Struggle over Land in Africa* (Pretoria: HSRC Press).

Heine, Jorge (2008) 'India and the New Scramble for Africa', available at <http:// www.militaryphotos.net/forums/showthread.php?137810-India-and-the-new-scramble-for-Africa> (accessed 2 May 2011).

Kalabamu, F. T. (2000) 'Land Tenure and Management Reforms in East and Southern Africa: The Case of Botswana', *Land Use Policy*, 17: 305.

Kariuki, S. (2007) 'Political Compromise on Land Reform: A Study of South Africa and Namibia', *South African Journal of International Affairs*, 14(1): 99.

Lahiff, E. (2003) 'The Politics of Land Reform in Southern Africa' (Sustainable Livelihoods in Southern Africa Research Paper, Brighton: Institute of Development Studies).

Lahiff, E. (2007) 'Willing Buyer, Willing Seller: South Africa's Failed Experiment in Market-led Agrarian Reform', *Third World Quarterly*, 28(8): 1577.

Lahiff, E., Manhenze, T., Quan, J., Aliber, M. and Wegerif, M. (2006) 'The Area Based Land Reform Initiative in Makhado, Limpopo Province' (Land and Territory Research Paper No. 4, Polokwane: Nkuzi Development Association).

Malope P. and Nnyaladzi, B. (2008) 'Land Reforms that Exclude the Poor: The Case of Botswana', *Development Southern Africa*, 25(4): 383.

Massyn, P. J. (2007) 'Communal Land Reform and Tourism Investment in Namibia's Communal Areas: A Question of Unfinished Business?' *Development Southern Africa*, 24(3): 381.

Microfinance Africa (2010) 'African Agriculture: An Abiding Investment Venue for India', <http://microfinanceafrica.net/microfinance-around-the-world/african-agriculture-an-abiding-investment-venue-for-india> (accessed 5 September 2010).

Ministry of Environment and Tourism (1999) 'A Preliminary Environmental Assessment of Namibia's Resettlement Programme' (Cape Town: University of Cape Town).

Mullin, K. (2010) 'African Agricultural Finance under the Spotlight', <http://blogs.reuters.com/africanews/2010/08/24/african-agricultural-finance-under-the-spotlight/> (accessed 5 September 2010).

Mutangadura, G. (2007) 'The Incidence of Land Tenure Insecurity in Southern Africa: Policy Implications for Sustainable Development', *Natural Resources Forum*, 31: 176.

Okafor, U. (2006) 'Computer-assisted Analysis of Namibian Land Reform Policy' (Master of Public Administration thesis, Stellenbosch: University of Stellenbosch).

Peterson, L. and Garland, R. (2010) 'Bilateral Investment Treaties and Land Reform in Southern Africa' (Report, Montreal: Rights and Democracy).

Rubinstein, C. (2009) 'China's Eye on African Agriculture', *Asia Times* (Hong Kong), 2 October, <http://www.atimes.com/atimes/China_Business/KJ02Cb01.html > (accessed 5 September 2010).

Saunders, D. (2010) 'China's "African Land Grab"', *Globe and Mail* (Toronto), 10 April <http://www.theglobeandmail.com/news/opinions/chinas-african-land-grab/article1529779/> (accessed 5 September 2010).
Shepard, D. and Mittal, A. (2009) 'The Great Land Grab: Rush for World's Farmland Threatens Food Security for the Poor', (Oakland, CA: Oakland Institute).
UNECA (2003) 'Land Tenure Systems and Sustainable Development in Southern Africa' (Lusaka: United Nations Economic Commission for Africa).
UPI (2009) 'Food and Water Drive Africa Land Grab', United Press International, 29 April, <http://www.upi.com/Science_News/Resource-Wars/2010/04/29/Food-and-water-drive-Africa-land-grab/UPI-11891272566080/ > (accessed 5 September 2010).
Vidal, J. (2010) '21st Century African Land Grab', *Observer* (London), 8 March, <http://www.countercurrents.org/vidal080310.htm> (accessed 5 September 2010).
Von Braun, J. and Meinzen-Dick, R. (2009) 'Land Grabbing by Foreign Investors in Developing Countries' (Washington, DC: International Food Policy Research Institute).
Wellington, T. D. (2003) 'Backgrounder: Land and Agrarian Reform in South Africa', Land Research Action Network, 21 January, <http://www.landaction.org/display.php?article=60> (accessed 11 March 2010).

9 The land question in Zimbabwe

The judiciary as an instrument of recovery?

*Alex T. Magaisa**

9.1 Introduction

The purpose of this chapter is to critically analyse the role of the judiciary in the land acquisitions in post-independent Zimbabwe and assess the extent to which it has been used by the executive arm of government as an instrument of 'recovery' of land rights expropriated during the colonial period. It is important, however, in considering the role of the judiciary in post-independent Zimbabwe to look into history, in particular, during the colonial period for purposes of setting the context. The chapter therefore draws some commonalities in the role of the colonial and the post-independent judiciary in the expropriation of land. A key point emerging from this analysis is that in the same way that the colonial judiciary was an instrument of expropriation of land rights, the post-independence judiciary in relation to the recent Fast Track Land Reform Programme (FTLRP) has also been used as an instrument of 'recovery' of land rights. Far from being an independent adjudicator for the protection of land rights, the history of the judiciary in Zimbabwe has been characterised by allegiance to prevailing political power interests and has therefore been either an instrument of expropriation or an instrument of recovery.

The chapter demonstrates that by and large, with limited exceptions, Zimbabwe's judiciary has, through the colonial to the independence era, generally been a critical political player, more so in relation to the expropriation of land rights. The impartiality of the judiciary in respect of the land question has been and continues to be influenced by political power so that its role is no more than to endorse the interests and demands of the dominant political players. This was the case with the colonial courts and continues to be the case with the post-independence judiciary.

At the heart of the problem for the judiciary is its role in the contestation between 'human rights' and 'human claims' in respect of land which were not effectively resolved at the Lancaster House Constitutional Conference (1979) through which Zimbabwe gained independence in 1980. As will be discussed in this chapter, in respect of the land question, it was always the view of the post-independence government that the Lancaster House Constitution sought to preserve the colonial order under which land had been expropriated but did little to address the claims of the black majority apart from permitting land acquisition under the 'willing seller, willing buyer' principle.

As the government sought to redress the colonial imbalances, it was left to the judiciary to adjudicate between the government and the landowners. An interesting feature is the transformation of the post-independence judiciary, from one that was fiercely independent of the executive to one that has become more aligned to the executive's interests. The independence of the judiciary in the early years must however be seen in the context of the politics of land and how this was perceived by the executive and nationalist politicians as a façade for serving the interests of the landowners and resisting the government's land reform programme. It is within this context that the role of the judiciary in the period of the FTLRP can be seen one of pursuing the 'recovery' of land rights under the direction of the government. In relation to land issue therefore, the judiciary in Zimbabwe can be characterised as an instrument of 'recovery' as much as it was an instrument of 'expropriation' in colonial Rhodesia.

9.2 Constitutional framework for the judiciary in Zimbabwe

9.2.1 Judicial structure

The Constitution of Zimbabwe makes provision under Chapter 8 for the establishment of the judiciary. The judiciary sits alongside the executive and parliament as one of the three arms of state. This arrangement is consistent with the principle of separation of powers dividing power between the lawmakers in parliament, the policymakers in the executive and the interpreters of the law in the judiciary.

The courts of Zimbabwe, led by the Supreme Court, are vested with judicial authority by virtue of section 79 of the Constitution.[1] Section 79A makes the Chief Justice the head of the judiciary assisted by the Deputy Chief Justice and other judges of the Supreme Court. It also consists of the judges of the High Court, which is headed by the Judge President.[2] Other courts include the Administrative Court, which deals with administrative matters, the Labour Tribunals, which handle labour disputes and also the Magistrates' Courts, which handle the majority of criminal and civil matters.

9.2.2 Judicial independence

The independence of the judiciary is guaranteed by section 79B of the Constitution.[3] It states that a member of the judiciary shall not be placed under the direction of any other person. The exception is where there is a specific written law which requires a member of the judiciary to be under the direction or control of another member of the judiciary. This is a limited exception necessary for administrative purposes to enable the proper functioning of the judiciary.

There are a number of other factors which are provided for under the Constitution such as appointment, remuneration, conditions of service, tenure of office and removal, etc which impact on the independence of the judiciary. However, as these issues are crucial to the exploration of the factors affecting the role of the judiciary in protecting human rights, they will be discussed later in this chapter.

9.2.3 Declaration of Rights

The Constitution contains in Chapter 3 a declaration of fundamental rights and freedoms of the individual. The Declaration of Rights follows the normal model adopted in the Universal Declaration of Human Rights.[4] These rights are also found in numerous international instruments such as the European Convention for the Protection of Human Rights and Fundamental Freedoms,[5] African Charter on Human and Peoples' Rights,[6] International Covenant on Civil and Political Rights.[7] Where differences occur, these are a circumstance of the different political and social conditions in Zimbabwe.

The rights covered under the Declaration of Rights are mainly of the civil and political type and, unlike the later constitutions in counties such as South Africa and Namibia, do not have much specifically on the socio-economic rights.[8] It is useful to note that these rights are subject to qualifications. The resulting derogations demonstrate where the rights may be affected without there being infringement, e.g. when a person's liberty is constrained through lawful imprisonment. Nevertheless the derogations are also qualified in many instances by the requirement that they must be judged to be 'reasonably justifiable in a democratic society'.[9]

9.2.4 Supreme Court as the constitutional court

The Supreme Court is the superior court of record and in practical terms most of the matters relating to human rights are decided in this forum. Although Zimbabwe does not have a specifically designated constitutional court the Supreme Court assumes this role when it deals with constitutional matters.

The Supreme Court has jurisdiction either on appeal or as a court of first instance to hear constitutional matters. In particular, section 24(1) of the Constitution gives the right of direct access to the Supreme Court in respect of matters relating to the Declaration of Rights under Chapter 3 of the Constitution.[10] Furthermore, section 24(3) permits constitutional issues to be raised where a matter has been brought to the Supreme Court on appeal.[11] In addition section 24(3) gives every court in Zimbabwe the power to make reference to the Supreme Court any matters that involve alleged breaches of human rights as provided for under the Declaration of Rights.[12]

The Supreme Court has wide powers under section 24(4) to make orders where a breach of the Declaration of Rights has been identified. It says that the Supreme Court may ' … make such orders, issue such writs and give such directions as it may consider appropriate for the purpose of enforcing or securing the enforcement of the Declaration of Rights'. In the case of *In re Mlambo*, the

Supreme Court stated that the language confers a very wide and unfettered discretion.[13] The result is that the Supreme Court has often made a wide range of orders in respect of constitutional matters brought before it.[14]

9.3 Conflict over the land question

This chapter argues that in order to create a meaningful and conclusive transitional justice mechanism over the land issue, the nature of the conflict must necessarily be understood in historical terms. That history is a critical part of the present-day conflict. As Sir Shridath Ramphal stated:

> It was about land in the beginning; it was about land during the struggle; it has remained about land today. The land issue in Zimbabwe (Rhodesia) is not ancient history.[15]

This indicates that an appreciation of the contestation over land is better achieved through an historical exploration and understanding of the land question. For purposes of this chapter what is important is the role of the judiciary both pre and post-independence in respect of the land question.

This section demonstrates how the law was used during the colonial era to legitimise the expropriation of land and the role of the judiciary in this process.

9.3.1 Law, expropriation and the colonial judiciary

The history of conflict over land in modern Zimbabwe commences with the colonisation in 1890 of the land between the Zambezi and Limpopo rivers by Great Britain via the agency of the British South Africa Company (BSAC) under the leadership of entrepreneur Cecil John Rhodes.[16] The BSAC was granted a Royal Charter in 1889 by the British Crown. Part of its mandate was to 'discharge and bear all the responsibility of government'.[17] Between 1894 and 1895, the BSAC created 'Native Reserves' for black Africans, the commencement of segregation and forced removals of black Africans from their ancestral lands.

After attempts to resist colonisation and expropriation of land were crushed by the new European settlers, the history of expropriation of land from Africans intensified.[18] The law played an important role in this process. During the course of colonialism, various legal instruments were enacted, giving legal control of the land to the new settlers. According to the International Commission of Jurists report (1976) (hereafter the ICJ Report):

> The initial expropriation of African land was consolidated by the subsequent Rhodesian land settlement legislation … its objective was to strengthen white dominion over the most fertile and economically important land and maintain the African population as a labouring class.[19]

An important event which demonstrates the critical role of the colonial judiciary in land expropriations is the seminal land case in which the courts held legal justification to expropriation of land from the Africans. In this case, *In re Southern Rhodesia*[20] the Privy Council of the House of Lords passed a significant judgment to the effect that all unalienated land in Southern Rhodesia belonged to the British Crown and not to the BSAC or anybody else, including the original African inhabitants.

Of great significance here is that it justified the expropriation of land from Africans on the basis that the lands were *terra nullius* (not owned by any person) because, according to the court, the local tribes were not sufficiently civilised to have developed any recognisable property rights over the land.[21] The Privy Council stated in justification of its position:

> Some tribes are so low in the scale of social organisation that their usages and conceptions of rights and duties are not to be reconciled with the institutions or legal ideas of civilised society … Such a gulf cannot be bridged. It would be idle to impute to such people some shadow of the rights known to our law and then to transmute it into the substance of transferable rights of property as we know them.[22]

According to Palmer, the case presented for the Africans in this case was summarily dismissed on the grounds that the Ndebele sovereignty, and with it all African rights to land, had been broken up and replaced by a new 'and, as their Lordships do not doubt, a better' system, as defined by the 1894 Order in Council.[23] The Privy Council came to the conclusion that 'whoever now owns the unalienated lands, the natives do not'.[24]

This decision, which set a precedent for justifying land expropriations from indigenous communities in various parts of the British Empire, shows the critical role played by the judiciary in the interpretation and enforcement of land expropriation rights. Not only did the judiciary consider the laws in African society antiquated and invalid, they provided judicial opinion to the effect that the new system, under which lands were expropriated was a better one. The fact that the original inhabitants were left with little land that was largely barren and not suitable for efficient farming did not register in the minds of the judges who decided the case. It was the victory of one legal order over another and the judiciary was interpreting the law through the lens of empire. The importance of this case is that it set a precedent and broader justification of all the expropriations that took place thereafter, including the legislation that was passed expropriating land from the Africans. For the purposes of this chapter it shows not only the condescending attitude of the colonial judiciary but illustrates the close links that existed between the colonising and expropriating forces, from which the judiciary cannot be excluded. Indeed, following the judicial confirmation of the legitimacy of expropriation, the legislature weighed in with new laws to legalise expropriation of more land.

9.4 Land Apportionment Act (1930) and the Land Tenure Act (1969)

One of the key pieces of legislation for land expropriation was the Land Apportionment Act of 1930. Palmer has written, about this law:

> For whites in Rhodesia, the Act has become something of a Magna Carta, guaranteeing the preservation of their way of life against encroachment from the black hordes, whereas for Africans the Act is seen as blatantly discriminatory and palpably unjust.[25]

The Land Tenure Act in 1969 extended the discriminatory effect of the Land Apportionment Act. Grievances over land among other issues of concern gave rise to the formation of resistance organisations among Africans and between 1965 and 1979, a protracted war of independence, known as the Second Chimurenga, after the original in the 1890s was fought between the Africans and the white settler forces. Linnington confirms the connection between the war and the land question in the following terms: 'the liberation struggle that followed the UDI in 1965 had its roots in the issue of land distribution'.[26]

The significance of this overview is that it locates the role of the judiciary and indeed the law in the process of expropriation of lands in Zimbabwe during the colonial period. A combination of the law and forceful means, legitimised by judicial orders, were employed to dispossess and evict the Africans from the land. The law left Africans at the periphery of economic activity, in geographically inferior lands far from the rail service and urban areas. Since however there were no effective rights to land for Africans under the colonial system, the courts simply enforced laws that perpetuated the segregation. There was no 'judicial activism' in the courts of Southern Rhodesia that enabled Africans to claw back any rights that they had lost through legislation. Indeed, in the seminal case of *Madzimbamuto v Lardner-Burke*,[27] that tested the independence of the judiciary, only two judges resigned in protest to the machinations of the Rhodesian government led by Ian Smith to defy a Privy Council judgment that effectively challenged the legality of the Smith regime.[28]

Nevertheless, the war did not solve the problem of the land question. It is important to demonstrate the effects of the settlement reached to end the war at the Lancaster House constitutional negotiations. It is this context that the role of the judiciary post-independence is located and probably explains the role that it has played in the expropriation of land. This, it must be stated boldly, does not necessarily justify this role – this chapter merely demonstrates the forces behind the judiciary's role post-independence and show that it is almost parallel to the role in the pre-independence period.

9.4.1 The land question at Lancaster House: continuity versus change

The Lancaster House Constitutional Agreement between the warring parties was signed in December 1979, paving way for independence the following year. It was largely a compromise, as exemplified by the agreement on the land question. Linnington has said that the final agreement:

> reflected to a large extent the fact that the various participants had had to make concessions on a number of issues. For example, the Patriotic Front (representing the nationalists) was obviously disappointed that its views on the land issue were not reflected in the text of the new constitution.[29]

The Patriotic Front[30] preferred provisions that would allow a new independence government to expeditiously carry out land reforms to satisfy the demands of their followers in the majority African population who had lost land rights to the settlers in the colonial period.

The Lancaster House Agreement did not deal with the land question conclusively. Rather, it simply postponed the problem and therefore its resolution. This view is echoed in the report of the Africa All Party Parliamentary Group of the UK parliament, which states that:

> The prime objective of Lancaster House was to achieve a political settlement and in order to do this it was necessary to defuse the land issue rather than solve it. There was no final agreement on land reform at Lancaster House. Given this, it is unsurprising that the land remains a thorn in both Britain and Zimbabwe's side 30 years later.[31]

Section 16 of the Lancaster House Constitution provided for a strong framework for the protection of property rights. As an entrenched part of the Bill of Rights its effect was that for the first decade of independence, land redistribution would be based on the 'willing buyer, willing seller' principle and for this period, this clause was protected from amendment. One scholar quotes the view of the Patriotic Front as saying in 1979 that:

> The Lancaster House conference produced a constitution which secured for the whites unhindered citizenship rights, a Bill of Rights which precluded the expropriation of private property …[32]

The legal architecture and limited financial resources limited the pace of land reforms in the 1980s. This view is echoed by Linnington who wrote:

> For the first ten years of independence the government was precluded from embarking on a meaningful process of land redistribution because section 16 of the Constitution was effectively insulated from amendment during that time.[33]

The government was restricted to buying land for resettlement but only on a 'willing buyer, willing seller' basis in respect of utilised land. It could compulsorily purchase under-utilised land but again this was subject to stringent conditions and in any event the criteria for determining whether land constituted 'underutilised land' eligible for compulsory purchase was fraught with complexities impeding its determination.

A free-market 'willing buyer, willing seller' basis was not entirely adequate for purposes of resolving the problem given that it depended on the will of the seller and the financial capability of the buyer to take up any offer. According to Moyo, land reform progress during the first decade and a half of independence was unsatisfactory as the 'land supply side of the redistribution effort [was, at the time] the least transparent and most contentious issue around which future conflicts will revolve'.[34]

In view of the historical contests over land, it is not surprising that section 16 of the Constitution became bitterly contested over the coming years. These contests culminated in the FTLRP post-2000 whose legitimacy has been the subject of litigation both in the Zimbabwean courts and the regional courts such as the SADC Tribunal. It is the Zimbabwean judiciary's reaction to the challenges to the FTLRP that are of concern in this chapter but as already argued the above context is important in analysing the approach they have taken.

Therefore, overall, the Lancaster House Constitution did not adequately address the contest between those who held land from the colonial era and those who had lost land during the same period the fact that this was a key issue notwithstanding. The Constitution recognised the existence of land rights under the umbrella of 'property rights' under section 16 of the Bill of Rights. It therefore protected the rights of those who had acquired land notwithstanding the contested nature of the manner of acquisition during the colonial period. It acknowledged, legalised and attempted to legitimise white hegemony over land whose moral legitimacy remained intensely contested. There were no specific measures in place for transitional justice to ensure that the wrongs of the past were dealt with adequately. The new Constitution paid little, if any, attention to the plight of the victims of the colonial system and this left a huge reservoir of protest which would later be exploited by politicians when political power appeared to be under severe challenge. Land grievances and claims were therefore unresolved, left instead to the operation of market forces through the 'willing buyer, willing seller' principle.[35]

The land inequalities which the Lancaster House Constitution perpetuated eventually gave the ZANU-PF government a platform to rally support based on claims of advancing social justice in which reclaiming lost lands from the white farmers and distributing it to the indigenous black Zimbabweans was a key part. In carrying out the FTLRP, ZANU-PF presented itself as a pan-Africanist party determined to continue and fulfil the expectations of the two 'Chimurenga' wars (wars of liberation) that had been waged in the 1890s and the 1970s. That is why the post-2000 land reforms are referred to as the Third Chimurenga.

9.4.2 Legal manoeuvres in the 1990s

It is important, however, prior to analysing the role of the post-independence judiciary in the reclamation of land rights by the new government, to set out the general framework in which the general process was set out. The role of the judiciary is best seen within the general context of the manoeuvres by the post-independence government to claim back land from the landed classes. In this case it is useful to divide the period into three segments. First there was the 1980 to 1990, during which the 'willing buyer, willing seller' principle was supposed to be the dominant mechanism for redistributing land from the white minority landowners to the black majority through the state. The second period is between 1990 and 2000 when the entrenchment of the right to private property expired and the government made further legal changes to facilitate land redistribution; and third, the period after 2000, when the government instigated and supported the FTLRP which was characterised by force and violence on the white commercial farms. In all three periods the role of the judiciary is pertinent.

> After the expiration of the decade-long entrenchment of the right to private property and acquisition based on the 'willing buyer, willing seller' principle there were legislative attempts to redress land imbalances. Initial attempts were largely moderate and focused on the constitution and new legislation. However later legal amendments took a radical thrust, effectively transferring responsibility for land compensation from the Zimbabwean state to the United Kingdom as the former colonial power. After 2000, the legal manoeuvres were accompanied by force and violence. The use of law and force to dispossess white landowners along racial lines after 2000 echoed the events of the colonial period. As in the colonial era, the courts have played a significant role.

9.5 Constitutional changes

The first step was the amendment of section 16 of the Lancaster House Constitution. The amendment came into effect in 1991 repealing elements of the provision relating to government compensation for acquired land.[36] Prior to the amendment, where the state, as an acquiring authority had acquired land, it was required to 'pay promptly adequate compensation' to the landowner. The new amendment required only 'fair compensation' be paid 'before or within a reasonable time' after the acquisition of the property, interest or right in it. This was an important change which demonstrated government's intention to remove what it considered to be impediments to easier and more rapid land reforms. Essentially by substituting the requirement for 'prompt' payment with 'payment within a reasonable time' and the compensatory change from 'adequate' to 'fair' compensation, it watered down the state's obligations, widening its discretion to acquire land. Later, section 16 was amended to bar judicial challenges questioning the fairness of compensation as determined by the Compensation Committee set up under the Land Acquisition Act 1992.[37]

The purpose here is not to assess the merits or drawbacks of these provisions, but rather to highlight the motivations of the key actors, in particular the government, which saw itself as legitimately pursuing a course of social justice. These were attempts at 'recovery' of land rights through executive and legislative action but also give an indication of the forces shaping judicial opinion in later years when they were called upon to adjudicate land disputes.

9.5.1 Land Acquisition Act 1992

The new law, namely the Land Acquisition Act 1992 sought to provide a new framework for land acquisitions. According to Moyo, the Act sought, 'an administratively swift process for acquiring selected lands by minimising legal contestations over land designated for acquisition'.[38] The Act was only passed after intense and often hostile debate. According to Tshuma, the Land Acquisition Bill 'polarised Zimbabwean society along racial lines' with passions running high on both sides of the racial divide.[39] Tshuma states that the 'white agrarian bourgeoisie' campaigned against the Bill on the basis that it would destroy agriculture and the economy. However, according to the same scholar, 'for blacks the Bill was seen as an opportunity for redressing historical injustices, an opportunity denied by the Lancaster House Constitution during the first decade of independence'.[40]

The Land Acquisition Act gave powers to the President to acquire land on a compulsory basis. Part IV of the Act allowed the relevant minister in charge of land affairs to designate rural land (essentially commercial farmland) for acquisition. The designation could be challenged and the minister was required to apply to court to confirm the acquisition.[41]

These changes were resisted by the farmers who sought recourse in the courts of law. In one high profile case, the constitutionality of land designation under the Act was challenged: *Davies and Others v Minister of Lands, Agriculture and Water Development.*[42] However, both the High Court and the Supreme Court dismissed the challenges.[43] Despite the success for the government in this case, it appeared the legal route was not yielding the desired results. While attempting to reverse colonial injustices through legislative change, it viewed the farmers' legal challenges as resistance to what it considered a historically just process of land reform. Legal challenges through the courts were interpreted as forms of resistance to land reform.

9.5.2 Compensation and souring of relations between Britain and Zimbabwe

The situation was exacerbated by the deterioration in relations between Zimbabwe and Britain, its former colonial power in the late 1990s, in particular after New Labour assumed power under the leadership of Tony Blair. The question of compensation for or generally funding the land reform process has always been a critical and controversial factor in the land reform. The government of Zimbabwe believes that the obligation for compensating the white farmers lies on the British government; a position that Britain resists.

The Mugabe-led government believed the New Labour government was approaching the land question with a different and wrong mentality compared to their Conservative counterparts, with whom they had always dealt with since the 1979 Lancaster House Agreement. The Mugabe-led government felt New Labour was downplaying Britain's responsibility for the colonial wrongs acknowledged at Lancaster House. Oft cited is a letter written in November 1997 by the then Secretary for International Development Clare Short. In the letter, Clare Short stated that the New Labour government would not accept the obligations of previous British governments. Part of the letter reads:

> We do not accept that Britain has a special responsibility to meet the costs of land purchase in Zimbabwe. We are a new Government from diverse backgrounds without links in former colonial interests. My own origins are Irish and as you know we were colonised not colonisers.[44]

This ill-judged letter was the start of a decade-long relationship of bitter acrimony between the two governments over the land question.

Meanwhile, towards the end of the 1990s, President Mugabe and his ruling ZANU-PF party were facing serious pressures domestically. In particular, there were pressures regarding land from the peasantry. The land occupations of the Svosve people in Svosve communal lands near Marondera displayed the vigorous discontent of many indigenous groups at what they felt was state collaboration with white farmers. This often understated event demonstrates the real manifestation of grievances over land by local groups that felt the government had not done enough to fulfil their promises of redressing the colonial wrongs of land expropriation.[45]

9.5.3 Legal changes in 2000: Constitutional Amendment No. 16

The government lost a referendum on a new constitution in February 2000. This represented a real threat to the ruling party's political power. The new Constitution itself had contained clauses seeking to empower the government to intensify the land acquisition process and reduce legal challenges through the courts of law. After the referendum defeat, war veterans supported by the government led farm occupations, forcefully and violently evicting white farmers.

The land occupations drew international criticism over the demise of the rule of law and violation of property rights. Just before parliamentary elections in June 2000, the government introduced Constitutional Amendment (No. 16) Act which sought to legalise and legitimise extra-legal land occupations already taking place and to expedite the land reform process. One clause placed responsibility for compensating evicted farmers on Britain, as the former colonial power, absolving the Zimbabwe government of that obligation. The amendment also stated that there would be no requirement for fair or adequate compensation – further watering down the government's obligations already undermined by the 1990 amendment. Here one can see the progressive erosion of the right to compensation, from the robust protections of the 1980 Constitution inherited from Lancaster

House to the weak provisions of the 2000 version guaranteeing neither fair nor adequate compensation.

ZANU-PF won the parliamentary election by a narrow margin and having amended the Constitution earlier the new government hastily changed the Land Acquisition Act 1992, stating that in the absence of a fund set up by Britain, the government of Zimbabwe would pay only for improvements on the land but not for the land itself. As under the previous provisions, no challenge would be allowed as to the 'fairness' of the compensation as determined by the Compensation Committee. The amendments also removed the process of designation, which according to Coldham, effectively removed what were considered land reform process bottlenecks. Coldham notes, 'controversial though they may be, these amendments to the law undoubtedly make it much easier for the government to acquire land for resettlement purposes'.[46]

9.5.4 Further legal changes in 2005: Constitutional Amendment No. 17

The government introduced a further amendment to the Constitution in 2005, namely Constitutional Amendment (No. 17) Act. Essentially, the amendments ousted judicial jurisdiction from determining land acquisition disputes. In Zimbabwe, the Constitution has traditionally provided for the right to the protection of the law under section 18 of the constitution. This clause effectively took away that right from those aggrieved by the government's land policy. Hitherto, an aggrieved person could challenge the acquisition, although challenging the fairness of compensation had since been eroded. This provision barred aggrieved persons from approaching the courts when their land had been acquired.

Two other clauses legitimised prior and current land acquisition without compensation. These *ex post facto* provisions were to apply retrospectively, giving legality to farms already occupied illegally. The changes were designed to legitimise the activities during the FTLRP, which were then illegal under law.

The constitutional amendments barring access to judicial jurisdiction were challenged before the regional court, the Southern African Development Community Tribunal (SADC Tribunal). The SADC Tribunal ruled in the case of *Mike Campbell (Pvt) Ltd et al v. Republic of Zimbabwe* [2008] SADCT 2, that white farmers had been racially discriminated against in the execution of the land reform programme and that this conduct by the Government of Zimbabwe violated SADC principles. It also ruled that the farmers were entitled to compensation for the loss of their land. However, the Zimbabwe government refused to pay compensation for the land, arguing that the obligation to pay compensation to the farmers rested on the British government, in its capacity as the former colonial power.[47] As Britain has refused to accept that it has such a responsibility,[48] the former commercial farmers have been left without effective recourse.

The attitude of the Zimbabwean government to the SADC Tribunal has been negative, casting doubt on its legality and legitimacy. In one instance during the hearing of the case, counsel for the Zimbabwean government walked out of the

Tribunal prompting the judges to hand down judgment in their absence. The matter was referred to the SADC Heads of State Summit as is required by the SADC Treaty and Protocol establishing the Tribunal. It is worth noting here that the Tribunal does not have effective enforcement mechanisms and so it relies on the good will and support of the States Parties. The legality of the Tribunal was brought into question by the Zimbabwe government resulting in the suspension of the Tribunal by the Summit. Therefore, at this point, for the white farmers, the situation is that after failing to find recourse through the Zimbabwean courts and despite finding some respite in the SADC Tribunal, that route has now been suspended.

9.6 Evolution of the Supreme Court and approach to the land question

It is important to note here that as part of the Lancaster House Constitutional Agreement, continuity in the judiciary among other things were seen as important mechanisms to also protect minority rights. The white minority received a package of protections including an exclusive White Roll under which they could elect their own Members of Parliament. In a parliament of 100 MPs, less than 5 per cent of the population was allocated 20 seats on the White Roll. As already indicated, the protection of private property was also seen as guaranteeing the land rights of the white minority who were the holders of the bulk of arable land.

These legislative and constitutional protections would however have been less effective without a strong judiciary that was independent of the executive arm of government that was dominated by the nationalists whose interest was to reform the economic order that privileged white landowners. Therefore a counter-force to the strong and potentially brash and forceful executive was an equally strong and autonomous judiciary. The Constitution provided guarantees for an independent judiciary. However, this would have been meaningless had the new government been able to remove the judges that had served during the colonial era and replaced them with their own appointees. Part of the negotiations at Lancaster House had produced a compromise that would see the retention of the colonial judiciary and the gradual injection of new appointees. These provisions were never written into the new Constitution and unlike the South African Constitution fourteen years later, no provision for redressing colonial imbalances in judicial appointments that produced disadvantaged groups was ever made.

Since they could not dismiss judges, and because they had to await the retirement of the members on the Bench, the government was stuck with a set of judges whose interests they had long suspected to be aligned to white landowners. For its part, the Supreme Court of Zimbabwe developed a liberal and pro-human rights jurisprudence. As the former Chief Justice of the Supreme Court Anthony Gubbay said:

> … Almost invariably since the inception of the Constitution, which came into force with Zimbabwe's independence on 18 April 1980, the Supreme

> Court has utilized the technique of a liberal interpretation with an eye to the spirit as well as the letter of constitutional provisions. We have endeavoured to move away from formalism and to use judicial activism as a tool for making human rights a practical reality for the people.[49]

Whilst this was in keeping with the spirit of freedom in the wake of independence, it also meant, ironically that as far as the land question was concerned, the same levels of protections were accorded to white landowners. Although the new nationalist government was keen to be seen as a protector of human rights, the protection of land rights posed a serious challenge to their own desire to acquire land with minimum hurdles. The legal machinations of the 1990s ought therefore to be seen against the background of a government that was keen to acquire land but also concerned to keep a façade of legality and adherence to the rule of law. They realised also that whilst they could change the laws, including the Constitution, the courts of law always stood as a big hurdle especially were the courts to rule against their legal manoeuvres. The government found the Supreme Court's liberal approach to human rights uncomfortable.

This discomfort is exemplified by the instances in which the government reversed through constitutional amendments several Supreme Court decisions that had expanded the application of human rights. A few cases in point here are relevant to illustrate this tussle between the executive and judicial arms of government.

9.6.1 Whipping of juveniles: section 15

In the case of *S v A Juvenile*[50] the Supreme Court outlawed whipping as a form of punishment, declaring it as a form of inhuman and degrading punishment contrary to section 15(1) of the Constitution.[51] Nevertheless, the executive moved to amend the Constitution to make it clear that whipping of juveniles as criminal punishment was permissible.[52]

9.6.2 Delays in executing the death sentence: section 15

When the Supreme Court ruled in the case of *Catholic Commission for Justice and Peace in Zimbabwe v Attorney-General and Others*[53] that the delay to carry out sentences of death was unconstitutional, the executive moved to amend the Constitution, thereby overruling the court.[54] The government condemned the judgment but it is notable that whilst it was being condemned at home, the judgment was receiving approval in other jurisdictions, notably by the Privy Council in the case of *Pratt v Attorney General for Jamaica*.[55]

9.6.3 Land case: section 16

Another instance is in respect of the more recent FTLRP which is the subject of concern in this chapter. The original application in the case of *Commercial Farmers*

Union v Minister of Lands, Agriculture and Rural Resettlement and Others[56] had been brought to the Supreme Court in 2000 by the Commercial Farmers Union, representing white farmers affected by land occupations led by the war veterans and supported by government.

It is important to note that the same case came before two different sets of the Supreme Court and was decided differently, therefore illustrating the different approaches and roles taken by the 'two' forms of the Court on the land question. The 'first' Supreme Court comprised of judges who had mainly served on the judiciary since the 1980s, going back even to the colonial era. Some of these judges were forced through intimidation and threats to leave office before their retirement. The Zimbabwe government elevated new appointees to the Supreme Court and the High Court, thereby creating a more pliable and sympathetic Bench. Therefore this case was heard and decided by these two different forms of the Supreme Court.

The decision of the first Supreme Court was that the prevailing land reform exercise was unconstitutional in that it violated section 16(1) of the Constitution which protected property rights. However, this judgment was not enforced by the executive. It is important to add also that at the time of hearing the matter, the Supreme Court building was invaded by war veterans who sloganeered and threatened judges with violence and death. The government, including President Mugabe, made serious adverse comments about the Supreme Court judges, accusing them of racism and agents of the old colonial order. The Minister of Justice, Patrick Chinamasa, told the judges that the government no longer had confidence in them and that their security could not be guaranteed. The ZANU PF-dominated parliament also passed a vote of no confidence in the Supreme Court and by March 2001, Chief Justice Gubbay had tendered his resignation before the expiry of his term of office. Although the vote of no confidence had no legal effect, it was a demonstration of political power against the Supreme Court judges.

The fact that the Chief Justice and some of the judges of the Supreme Court and the High Court were white and had roots in the colonial judicial system supported the perception promoted by government that the judiciary was there to serve white farmers' interests. To overcome the judicial impediment it was necessary to remove the judges and since they could not do it under the constitution, they resorted to extra-legal measures of intimidation and public criticism leading to forced resignations. In this process, ground was being prepared for the new Supreme Court to act as an instrument of 'recovery' of land rights as evidenced by the new Supreme Court's approach in the second but similar case which was brought before it.

A new application was brought by the Minister of Lands in 2001 before the new Supreme Court.[57] In an unprecedented move, the new Supreme Court granted the Minister's application to set aside the earlier judgment of the former Supreme Court. Notably, the basis upon which the relief was granted was a law that did not exist at the time that the matter was argued and no opportunity was given to counsel to make submissions and challenge the validity of that new law.

It is arguable that reliance by the court on matters that were not placed before them in evidence or submissions by counsel was wrong. The Court should have invited counsel to make submissions on the point of interest, especially one on which it would base its decisions.

Nevertheless, the case demonstrated the new approach of the Supreme Court in relation to the interpretation and protection of fundamental rights as guaranteed in the Constitution and more specifically the new role of the judiciary in reversing what was seen as the perpetuation of a colonial order in respect of the land question. The changes in the judiciary were also apparent in the reaction of the new Supreme Court to legal challenges advanced by counsel (who is white and prominent in the litigation on land issues) in the case of *Minister of Lands, Agriculture and Rural Resettlement and Others v Commercial Farmers Union*.[58] Here an application was made for the Chief Justice, Godfrey Chidyausiku (who had controversially succeeded former Chief Justice Gubbay in 2001) to recuse himself since he was an interested party as it was alleged that he was a beneficiary of the land reform exercise. The application was rejected and the Chief Justice made some stinging and threatening remarks against counsel and the litigants. He said:

> The unbridled arrogance and insolence with which the application for the reconstitution of this Court was made in this case is simply astounding and, to say the least, unacceptable. This is the first and last time when such contempt of this Court will go unpunished … The only reason why stern action was not taken *in casu* is that this case is of extreme national importance and distraction from the main issue was to be avoided at all costs.[59]

This indicates the extent to which the Court has itself morphed from being a liberal protector of human rights and defenders to potentially a threat to those who sought to bring applications for the security of their rights. The problems faced by lawyers in the justice system have been well documented and a rich and useful account of the trials and tribulations faced by lawyers and human rights defenders by law enforcement agents was given by Arnold Tsunga, then the head of the Zimbabwe Lawyers for Human Rights in an article written in 2003.[60]

The key change in judicial approach is that the judiciary became more defensive of the government land reform exercise and less inclined to protect private property rights. As the above discussion has shown, the liberal interpretation of the Bill of Rights since 1980 had become a hindrance to the government's land reform policy which was premised on compulsory acquisition with limited compensation for improvements and not for the land itself. The government's view was that compensation for land held by white farmers was the responsibility of the British government as the former colonial power. The judiciary could either be an ally or an opponent in achieving this goal. The Supreme Court's liberal approach to human rights protection meant that it would almost always be seen as a hindrance. The government made public pronouncements to the effect that they did not trust the judges to support what it regarded as a legitimate cause of empowering the previously disadvantaged black majority. Hence a change in the judiciary was necessary in order to more effectively legitimise the government programmes. A key factor in the transformation of the court was the forced removal of the judges and their replacement with judges steeped in the liberation tradition that the government claimed to represent and advance.

9.7 The 'human factor' and the judiciary in Zimbabwe

The idea of the 'human factor' is simply that when considering risks and failures in a particular system, it is important not only to consider the structural aspects but also the influence of the human agents operating or within that system.

It is a concept that is often applied in risk management but it is adapted here for purposes of assessing the influence of human agents operating within the constitutional system on the protection of human rights. At the risk of over-simplification, it simply means that the success or failure of a system, whether organisational or technological, is affected not only by its internal components but also by the behaviour of human agents responsible for its operation. In other words, organisations or technology might fail simply because of the risks posed by the people behind it.

As former Chief Justice Gubbay wrote:

> ... The mere fact that a given state has a justiciable declaration of rights in its constitution, no matter how well drafted, does not of itself guarantee the enjoyment of, or respect for, human rights. It is quite possible for two countries with identical declarations to have totally different experiences with the level of human rights that are actually enforced ... A justiciable declaration of rights can protect and enforce fundamental human rights only if the highest court in the land is *powerful enough*, and *independent enough*, to proscribe all attempted infringements thereof ... Judges need to be both independent and impervious to *extraneous influences*. Members of the court must also be able to bring to bear on the problems before them a *professional objectivity* which transcends *personal predilections*. [Emphasis added]

With these words, Gubbay CJ captures the essence of the 'human factor' and its influence on judicial decision making. The question whether the judge prioritises his 'professional objectivity' over 'personal predilections' and also whether he can resist the extraneous influences is dependent not on the nature of the rules alone, but on his own personality and the factors that influence it.

Applying this to the judicial context, whilst it makes sense to consider the strength and weaknesses of constitutional rules that define judicial independence it is also important to assess the identity, behaviour and attitudes of the human agents, i.e. the judges and other extraneous factors that influence their conduct. The sum total of the 'human factor' is the judicial culture which itself does not lend itself to easy measurement. However, we can see it for example in the context of human rights, in the way that different courts interpret the constitution that contains the same substantive rights.

For purposes of this chapter, the approach of the two Supreme Courts referred to above one can observe that the first Supreme Court was more liberal and its interpretations of the Constitution tended to favour the expansion of human rights and restricted state interference. Indeed, it ruled that the FTLRP was unlawful as it violated the Constitution.

However, the new Supreme Court in substantially the same case took the opposite approach, reversing in an unprecedented move the decision of the first Supreme Court. The new Supreme Court took a more conservative approach to Constitutional interpretation, restricting the scope of human rights and in particular the right to private property. Therefore in the space of a few years the new Supreme Court has undone almost everything that had been constructed on the basis of private property rights since the decision of the Privy Council in *In re Southern Rhodesia*. The whole structure of land ownership based on the right to private property has been dismantled by the state with the tacit support of the judiciary. However, nothing has changed as far as the constitutional protections of judicial independence are concerned.[61] What therefore accounts for the change in approach? It is that the argument regarding the human factor, represented the human agents responsible for interpretation of the constitution (the judges) has relevance.

Notwithstanding clear provisions regarding the protection of judicial office,[62] the treatment of judges post-2000 has been to effectively force their removal from office. As indicated before, after the contentious land-related cases, in which the executive accused judges of racism, the Minister of Justice also stated that the security of the Chief Justice and fellow judges could no longer be guaranteed by the government. As a result Chief Justice Gubbay tendered his resignation in circumstances that cannot be described as voluntary. Other judges followed, including Judge Michael Gillespie, Judge Ishmael Chatikobo, Judge Sandra Mugwira, Judge Ahmed Ibrahim, Judge James Devittie and Judge Nicholas McNally, mainly due to political interference and threats.

The removal of judges and replacement with another set of judges brought with it changes to the judicial approach to human rights, especially the protection of private property. Judges that were seen to be more sympathetic to the land reform agenda were appointed but other factors also played a role in the transformation. A report by Human Rights Watch states that 'since 2000 the government has appointed to the bench judges with previous connections and known sympathies to ZANU-PF'.[63] Perhaps the most dramatic appointment was the promotion of Judge Godfrey Chidyausiku to the office of Chief Justice ahead of more senior and experienced judges who had served in the Supreme Court, including Judge Sandura, Judge McNally, Judge Ziyambi, etc. Judge Chidyausiku had previously served in government and is widely perceived to be sympathetic to the government.

The remuneration of judges is one of the most important features that determine judicial independence. Judges ought to be adequately remunerated, from a source that is non-partisan and insulated from reduction or withdrawal of their privileges by the executive. The Constitution recognises the importance of a fair system of remuneration and to this end provides under section 88 that the salaries of judges are drawn from the Consolidated Revenue Fund as set by an Act of Parliament.[64] It also states in paragraph (2) that the salary and allowances payable to judges shall not be reduced during their tenure of office.

A key factor that is directly linked to the land question is that several judges of the Supreme and High Court are reported to have been beneficiaries of the FTLRP.[65] A Human Rights Watch report quotes sources who aver that most judges were beneficiaries of the land reform programme. Given that this was a contentious matter that was litigated before the courts many times, questions did indeed arise over the impartiality of the courts.[66] The allocation of land in a process in which they are supposed to be impartial adjudicators made them interested parties. As already indicated in this chapter, when a senior counsel asked the Chief Justice to recuse himself from a case involving determination of the constitutionality of land seizures from white farmers on the basis that he was an interested party, his reaction was hostile.

9.8 The judiciary as an instrument of 'recovery'

The above discussion has demonstrated the transformation of the judiciary in Zimbabwe from a liberal protector of human rights to one that is distinctly pro-government in so far as the land reform exercise is concerned. The first Supreme Court was seen by government as presenting impediments to the FTLRP. The changes in the judiciary have meant that the new Supreme Court has endorsed and backed the government FTLRP. It is in this context that the judiciary has been characterised in this chapter as an instrument of recovery – in terms of recovering the land rights that were lost during the colonial period. It is important to note also that the first Supreme Court, which had its roots in the colonial judiciary was accused of helping maintain the old order where land rights gained during the colonial period were ring-fenced and harder for the government to overcome in the land reform programmes. Thus the transformation of the judiciary through a change of the human agents played a critical part in changing the judicial attitude and approach to land reform in favour of the government. The judiciary was therefore to simply endorse and give a veil of legitimacy to an essentially political process.

In attempting to understand the events of the last 30 years and the judiciary's role in the FTLRP it is useful to note that the Declaration of Rights in the Constitution derives from agreements at the Lancaster House Constitutional Conference in 1979. At the time, the Declaration of Rights was created as an entrenched part of the Constitution placing it beyond amendment for a decade. This chapter has already noted that this deal was part of the measures put in place to assuage the fears of those who had historically enjoyed a privileged position in race-based politics and economic distribution but were about to lose political power. In respect of land, the Lancaster House Agreement did not deal decisively and adequately with this contentious issue. By entrenching the rights for ten years, it simply postponed the resolution of the problem between the claimants and the rights-holders of land. The 'willing buyer, willing seller' approach did not work as anticipated.

The new government accepted the Declaration of Rights but noted that whilst it recognised and protected existing rights, it did so on the erroneous assumption that every individual possessed such rights whereas in fact those rights were still the subject of bitter contest. The Constitution did a lot to safeguard property rights but did not provide a comprehensive solution to the problem of claims to land. It left it to the market to do so, on the assumption that there would not only be willing sellers and buyers but also the resources to fund this process.

When therefore the early courts were interpreting fundamental rights provided for in the Constitution, with the predilection towards the most liberal interpretation in favour of rights-holders, this approach appeared to solidify the approach taken at Lancaster House of safeguarding the *status quo*. This is particularly important in relation to property rights, which remained a politically contentious issue. Although attempts were made in the 1990s to change the legislative structure for land reform, this was met with legal challenges by the landowners. The judiciary therefore held a key position in so far as determining the legality and justification of the land reform programme. The early courts after independence were perceived to be more sympathetic to the white landowners.

The changes that took place post-2000 are therefore to be seen in this context, where the government was trying to create a more compliant judiciary that would act essentially as an instrument for the 'recovery' of land rights. It is not surprising, given this context, that when the government instigated extra-legal measures to acquire land post-2000, not only did it openly defy the courts it went further to purge the courts of judges who were considered to be part of the old order. It then replaced all those judges with new judges considered to be more sympathetic to its cause, leading in one case mentioned before in this chapter to an unprecedented reversal of the Supreme Court decision in the same matter.

9.9 Conclusion

By way of conclusion, this chapter attempted to trace the trajectory of judicial decision-making in respect of human rights by the Zimbabwean judiciary and looked specifically at the judiciary's role in relation to the hotly contested land issue. What is apparent are the continuities in the politicisation of the judiciary mainly in relation to the right to private property. The problems and challenges faced by the present judiciary are not new. Neither is the approach and role the judiciary has played particularly in respect of property rights. The executive saw after independence that the judiciary was a threat to its designs. It is not surprising that the judiciary has faced stern tests and reprisals in the post-independence era as it faced in the colonial period.

It is also notable that the forced changes in the composition of the judiciary in the post-2000 era is a culmination of the struggles and tensions during the 1980s and 1990s when the Supreme Court took a liberal pro-human rights approach to constitutional interpretation. The executive routinely reversed judgments of the Supreme Court and this was helped by the fact that ZANU-PF dominated political space and was able to amend the Constitution whenever it wished. Therefore the threat to democracy is also a threat to the judiciary as dominance by one party makes the judiciary's constitutional interpretations vulnerable to the whims of that single party.

We have also seen however that a closer look at the role of the judiciary from a historical viewpoint helps to better appreciate the current role of the Supreme Court under the ZANU-PF government. Without delving into the merits or demerits of that project, it appears that the Supreme Court is playing a role that is not dissimilar to the role of the colonial courts, as exemplified by the major decision in the case of *In re Southern Rhodesia*, in justifying the expropriation of land and property rights. In this regard, the judiciary has become part of the 'recovery' project in respect of claims to land under the so-called Third Chimurenga. These are perhaps continuities, albeit in different directions, of the role of the judiciary.

It is submitted that part of the problem was a failure of the independence Constitution, drafted and agreed at Lancaster House in 1979, to deal adequately and conclusively with the issue of property rights. It rightly recognised rights but provided little platform for the satisfaction of claims to such rights as property. This role is now been taken by the Supreme Court, in spite of the Constitution and in the process created confusion in respect of human rights. As stated earlier in the chapter, the judiciary has been used as an instrument of 'recovery' of property rights as much as it was an instrument of 'capture' of property rights in the colonial period.

Notes

* Senior Lecturer in Law, Kent Law School, UK.

1 79 *Judicial authority*

(1) The judicial authority of Zimbabwe shall vest in –
(*a*) the Supreme Court; and
(*b*) the High Court; and
(*c*) such other courts subordinate to the Supreme Court and the High Court as may be established by or under an Act of Parliament.

2 79A *Judiciary*
The judiciary of Zimbabwe shall consist of –

(*a*) the Chief Justice, who shall be the head of the judiciary; and
(*b*) the Deputy Chief Justice and the other judges of the Supreme Court; and

[Paragraph as amended by section 17 of Act 11 of 2007 – Amendment No. 18 with effect from 30 October 2007.]

The judiciary of Zimbabwe shall consist of –

(*c*) the Judge President and the other judges of the High Court; and
(*d*) persons presiding over other courts subordinate to the Supreme Court and the High Court that are established by or under an Act of Parliament.

3 79B *Independence of judiciary*
In the exercise of his judicial authority, a member of the judiciary shall not be subject to the direction or control of any person or authority, except to the extent that a

written law may place him under the direction or control of another member of the judiciary.
[Section as inserted by section 10 of Act 30 of 1990 – Amendment No. 11]

4 *Adopted* 10 December 1948, GA Res 217A (III), 3 UN GAOR (Resolutions, part 1) at 71, UN Doc A/810 (1948).

5 *Opened for signature* 4 November 1950, EurTS No. 5, 213 UNTS 221 (entered into force 3 September 1953).

6 *Adopted* in Banjul 27 June 1981, OAU Doc CAB/LEG/67/3/Rev.5.

7 *Adopted* 16 December 1966, 999 UNTS 171 (entered into force 23 March 1976), GA Res 2200 (XXI), 21 UN GAOR Supp (No. 16) at 52, UN Doc A/6316 (1966).

8 The rights covered under the Declaration of Rights include the following:

1 The right to life, personal liberty, protection of the law, and freedom from arbitrary search and arrest.
2 The right to freedom from slavery, from forced labour, and from inhuman or degrading punishment or treatment.
3 The right to freedom of conscience, expression, assembly, association, and movement.
4 The right to freedom from discrimination.
5 The right to protection against deprivation of property.
6 The right to be afforded a fair hearing within a reasonable time by an independent and impartial court or other adjudicating authority.
7 The right, if charged with a criminal offence, to legal representation of one's own choice and protection against self incrimination.

9 Also note that derogations are likely to be higher where a public emergency has been declared.

10 24 *Enforcement of protective provisions*

(1) If any person alleges that the Declaration of Rights has been, is being or is likely to be contravened in relation to him (or, in the case of a person who is detained, if any other person alleges such a contravention in relation to the detained person), then, without prejudice to any other action with respect to the same matter which is lawfully available, that person (or that other person) may, subject to the provisions of subsection (3), apply to the Supreme Court for redress.

11 *Section 24(3)* Where in any proceedings such as are mentioned in subsection (2) any such question as is therein mentioned is not referred to the Supreme Court, then, without prejudice to the right to raise that question on any appeal from the determination of the court in those proceedings, no application for the determination of that question shall lie to the Supreme Court under subsection (1).

12 *(2)* If in any proceedings in the High Court or in any court subordinate to the High Court any question arises as to the contravention of the Declaration of Rights, the person presiding in that court may, and if so requested by any party to the proceedings shall, refer the question to the Supreme Court unless, in his opinion, the raising of the question is merely frivolous or vexatious.
[Subsection as amended by section 9 of Act 15 of 1990 – Amendment No. 10]

13 1991 (2) ZLR 339 (SC). The court said, 'It is very difficult to imagine language which would give this court a wider and less fettered discretion.'

14 In the case of *Catholic Commission for Justice and Peace in Zimbabwe v Attorney-General and Others* 1993 (4) SA 239 (ZS) the court substituted a life imprisonment for the death sentence where persons who had remained on Death Row for a period that was held to be inhuman and degrading treatment contrary to section 15(1) of the Declaration of Rights.

In the case of *Retrofit (Pvt) Ltd v Minister of Information, Posts and Telecommunications* 1995 (2) ZLR 1 99 (S) the court invalidated telecommunications laws that it held to be contrary to the freedom of expression provided for under section 20(1) of the Declaration of Rights.

In most cases the Supreme Court issues a *declaratur* – a declaration – and leaves it to the executive to enforce and implement the decision although in some cases it has also directed the executive on how to deal with certain matters as in the case of *Conjwayo v Minister of Justice, Legal and Parliamentary Affairs and Another* 1992 (2) SA 56 (ZSC), a matter that involved the treatment of prisoners by the prison authorities and the court asserted that even prisoners enjoyed constitutional rights which the court would protect. In that case the court reaffirmed the right of a prisoner to have physical exercise.

15 Ramphal was the Secretary-General of the Commonwealth from 1975 to 1990. He made this comment in an interview with Gugulethu Moyo and Mark Ashhurst (2007: 160)

16 The decisive agreement was the Rudd Concession signed between Lobengula, King of the Ndebele, and Rhodes's emissaries, led by Mr Rudd. By that agreement, Lobengula was construed to have given away control of the land over which his powerful Ndebele kingdom ruled.

17 A British Colonial Office minute of 1888 quoted in the International Commission of Jurists Report on Racial Discrimination and Repression in Southern Rhodesia (1976), hereafter 'ICJ Report (1976)'.

18 Upon realisation of the consequences of white settlement on their land, the local African population instigated and participated in military uprisings in 1893 (Matebele Uprising) and 1896–97 (First Chimurenga) against the new order. They were defeated by the military might of the new settlers.

19 ICJ Report (1976), pp.11–12.

20 (1919) AC 210.

21 The core dispute was in fact between the new settler community and the BSAC over who owned the land. The settlers disputed the BSAC's assertion that it owned the land whilst the settlers believed that it could only own land that was in its administrative capacity and any new Government should be declared the rightful owner of unalienated land.

22 *In re Southern Rhodesia* (1919) AC 210, p. 233.

23 Palmer (1977) at p 134.

24 Ibid, p 134.

25 Ibid, p 178. On p 153 Palmer also quotes a Colonial Office official as having observed, 'I fear that a good deal of natives' grievances is the inevitable result of the white population ... The Ndebele in central Matabeleland were bitterly opposed to the forced relocation to distant and inhospitable reserves by aggressive white farmers ... '

26 Linnington (2001). See also Gauntlett J., Ninth Mofokeng Lecture entitled 'The Lie of the Land: Law and Land Seizure in Zimbabwe 1890–2010', 15 October 2010, also available at <http://www.cfuzim.org/index.php?option=com_content&view=article&id=1016:law-and-land-seizure-in-zimbabwe-1890-2010&catid=49:land-facts&Itemid=89> (last accessed 8 January 2011).

27 [1969] 1 AC 645.

28 Judges Fieldsend and Young are the two judges who resigned. Judge Fieldsend went on to become the first Chief Justice of the new Zimbabwe Supreme Court at independence.

29 Linnington (2001), p 37.

30 The Patriotic Front, consisting primarily of ZANU and ZAPU, was led by Robert Mugabe and Joshua Nkomo at the constitutional talks at Lancaster House. Mugabe and Nkomo were later to become President and Vice-President of Zimbabwe, respectively.

31 Africa All Party Parliamentary Group on Land in Zimbabwe (2009) Report on 'Land in Zimbabwe: Past Mistakes, Future Prospects', hereafter referred to as 'AAPPG Report (2009)', p. 26.

32 Moyo (1995).

33 Linnington (2001), p 427.

34 Moyo (1995), p 3. He was writing in 1994 and events of post-2000 in respect of the eventual conflict post-2000 goes some way to prove the accuracy of his prediction, which at the time went unheeded.

35 This view is also acknowledged by the Africa All Party Parliamentary Group of the UK parliament, AAPPG Report (2009). It states, 'The feeling that justice on land was denied at Lancaster House is felt strongly today, both in Zimbabwe and throughout southern Africa', p. 18.
36 Section 6, Constitution of Zimbabwe Amendment (No. 11) Act 1990 (Act 30/1990).
37 Section 16(2) stated, 'No such law [authorising acquisition of land] shall be called into question by any court on the ground that the compensation provided is not fair'.
38 Moyo (1995), p. 3.
39 Tshuma (1997), p. 129.
40 Tshuma (1997).
41 Moyo (1995) states that in 1993–94 40 per cent of farms that had been designated under the 1993 regulations were undesignated after challenges – which seemed to indicate that where valid contestations were made they were accepted.
42 1994(2) ZLR 294 (H).
43 1997 (1) SA 228 (ZSC).
44 The letter is published by *New African* magazine at <http://www.swans.com/library/art9/ankomah5.html> (last accessed 11 May 2010).
45 The Svosve invasions were not the first as stated by one author: 'Between 1983 and 1997, villagers from Mutasa, Chihwiti, Mhondoro and Nyamatsitu, communal lands that the state had leased to white commercial farmers were repeatedly invaded by those seeking to exert historical claims. In each instance, the government evicted these landless villagers by force. In June 1998, the Svosve people of the Marondera and Wedza districts undertook a series of illegal farm occupations. Earlier in October 1996, the land issue came to a head when a group of 200 land hungry peasants invaded an idle state farm adjacent to the Matobo Research Station in Matabeleland in defiance of the government. The unilateral action by otherwise law abiding citizens was an illustration of the growing impatience among thousands of landless Zimbabweans over the implementation of the nation-wide land redistribution programme to correct pre-independence imbalances.' Chikuhwa (2010).
46 Coldham (2001), p 229.
47 This is evident in section 16A of the Constitution of Zimbabwe, which states that:

(i) the former colonial power has an obligation to pay compensation for agricultural land compulsorily acquired for resettlement, through an adequate fund established for the purpose; and
(ii) if the former colonial power fails to pay compensation through such a fund, the Government of Zimbabwe has no obligation to pay compensation for agricultural land compulsorily acquired for resettlement.

48 AAPPG Report (2009).
49 Gubbay (1997). This was reaffirmed in the case of *Smyth v Ushewokunze* 1997 2 ZLR 544 (SC) 49 that it would accord, a generous and purposive interpretation and to expand the meaning of a fundamental right rather than to limit its scope. The idea, the court said, is to keep pace with changing conditions, social values and norms in order to meet the emerging challenges. Similarly, one of Zimbabwe's leading human rights' defenders Adrian De Bourbon (SC) has written, ' … litigating human rights during the 16 years between 1985 and 2001 was a great pleasure and privilege … In that time, huge advances were made in the field of human rights in Zimbabwe … (De Bourbon 2003).
50 1989 2 ZLR 61 (SC).
51 Adult whipping had already been declared unconstitutional in the case of *S v Ncube and Others* 1987 2 ZLR 246 (SC).
52 Constitution of Zimbabwe Amendment (No. 11) Act 1990.
53 [1993] 1 ZLR 242 (S).

54 Constitution of Zimbabwe Amendment (No. 13) Act 1993. Section 15(6), which was added, states that courts cannot issue a stay, alter a sentence or give any remission of sentence on the basis that since the sentence was imposed there has been a contravention of section 15(1) of the Constitution.
55 4 All ER 769 at 770–71 (PC 1993).
56 2000 2 ZLR 469 (SC).
57 *Minister of Lands, Agriculture and Rural Resettlement and Others v Commercial Farmers' Union* SC 111/2001.
58 Ibid.
59 At pp 6–7 of the original judgment.
60 Tsunga, A. 'The Legal Profession and the Judiciary as Human Rights Defenders in Zimbabwe in 2003: Separation or Consolidation of Powers in the part of the State?' Zimbabwe Lawyers for Human Rights, available at <http://www.kubatana.net/docs/hr/zlhr_legal_judic_hrdef_031224.pdf> (last accessed on 16 November 2010).
61 For example, section 86 of the Constitution provides that once appointed a judge can hold office up to the age of 65 years but he can elect before reaching that age to serve until he is 70 years old. When a judge elects to remain in office beyond 65 years old, a medical report confirming his mental and physical fitness to continue in office must be submitted to and accepted by the President after consultation with the Judicial Services Commission. A further provision safeguarding judicial tenure is section 86(3) which protects judicial office from abolishment save with the consent of the judge.
62 The question of removal of judges from office is addressed by section 87 of the Constitution which provides that a judge can only be removed from office in certain specified circumstances, i.e. where the judge is unable to discharge judicial due to infirmity of the body or mind or other cause or for misbehaviour. In all cases, the judge must be removed only in accordance with the provisions of section 87. These provisions require that the President appoint a tribunal to carry out an official inquiry into the matter. The tribunal reports to the President, recommending whether or not to refer the matter to the Judicial Services Commission. It also provides for the suspension of the judge from exercising his functions during the period of the inquiry. The judge will be removed from office if the Judicial Service Commission advises the President to remove him following consideration of the tribunal's inquiry.
63 Human Rights Watch (2008).
64 88 *Remuneration of judges*

(1) There shall be charged upon and paid out of the Consolidated Revenue Fund to a person who holds the office of or is acting as Chief Justice, Deputy Chief Justice, a judge of the Supreme Court, Judge President of the High Court or a judge of the High Court such salary and allowances as may from time to time be prescribed by or under an Act of Parliament.

[Subsection as amended by section 13 of Act No. 25 of 1981 – Amendment No. 2, and section 22 of Act No. 11 of 2007 – Amendment No. 18 – with effect from 30 October 2007.]

(2) The salary and allowances payable to a person under subsection (1) shall not be reduced during the period he holds the office concerned or acts as holder thereof.

65 A report by a team of eminent jurists into the state of justice in Zimbabwe stated that judges had received land under the government's programme and that this circumstance had caused problems with regard to the impartiality of the justice system.
66 See De Bourbon (2003), who recounts the problems faced by counsel in a land case where counsel applied for the Chief Justice to excuse himself from the case.

Bibliography

Books and articles

Chikuhwa, J. (2010) 'The Haphazard Land Reform' at <http://chikuhwa.net/zimbabwe-landreform.htm> (last accessed 14 May 2010).

Coldham, S. (2001) Statute Note, 'Land Acquisition Amendment Act, 2000 (Zimbabwe)', *Journal of African Law*, 45(2).

De Bourbon, A. (2003) 'Litigation – Human Rights in Zimbabwe: the Past, Present and Future', *African Human Rights Law Journal*, 3(2): 195–221.

Gauntlett, J. (2010) Ninth Mofokeng Lecture, 'The Lie of the Land: Law and Land Seizure in Zimbabwe 1890–2010', 15 October, also available at <http://www.cfuzim.org/index.php?option=com_content&view=article&id=1016:law-and-land-seizure-in-zimbabwe-1890-2010&catid=49:land-facts&Itemid=89 (last accessed 8 January 2011).

Gubbay, A. (1997) 'The Protection and Enforcement of Fundamental Human Rights: the Zimbabwean Experience', *Human Rights Quarterly*, 19(2): 227–54.

Gubbay, A. (2009) 'The Progressive Erosion of the Rule of Law in Zimbabwe', lecture at the Bar Council of England and Wales, 9 December. Full speech available at <http://www.newzimbabwe.com/opinion-1806-Gubbay+lecture+on+rule+of+law/opinion.aspx> (last accessed 10 January 2011).

Hatchard, J. (1993) *Individual Freedoms and State Security in the African Context: The Case of Zimbabwe* (Athens, OH: Ohio University Press).

Human Rights Watch (2008) *Our Hands are Tied: Erosion of the Rule of Law in Zimbabwe* (New York: Human Rights Watch).

Linnington, G. (2001) *Constitutional Law of Zimbabwe* (Harare: Legal Resources Foundation).

Moyo, S. (1995) *The Land Question in Zimbabwe* (Harare: SAPES Books).

Moyo, G. and Ashhurst, M. (eds) (2007) 'Sleight of Hand at Lancaster House', in Moyo and Ashhurst (eds) *The Day after Mugabe: Prospects for Change in Zimbabwe* (London: Africa Research Institute).

Palmer, R. (1977) *Land and Racial Domination in Rhodesia* (London: Heinemann).

Saller, K. (2004) The Judicial Institution in Zimbabwe (Cape Town: Siber Ink).

Short, C. (2010) Letter published at <http://www.swans.com/library/art9/ankomah5.html> (last accessed 11 May 2010).

Tshuma, L. (1997) *A Matter of Injustice: Law, State and the Agrarian Question in Zimbabwe* (Harare: SAPES Books).

Tsunga, A. (2010) 'The Legal Profession and the Judiciary as Human Rights Defenders in Zimbabwe in 2003: Separation or Consolidation of Powers in the part of the State?' (Causeway: Zimbabwe Lawyers for Human Rights), available at <http://www.kubatana.net/docs/hr/zlhr_legal_judic_hrdef_031224.pdf> (last accessed 16 November 2010).

Van Der Vijver, L. (2006) *The Judicial Institution in Southern Africa* (Cape Town: Siber Ink).

National legislation and international legal instruments

Universal Declaration of Human Rights. *Adopted* 10 December 1948, GA Res 217A (III), 3 UN GAOR (Resolutions, part 1) at 71, UN Doc A/810 (1948).

European Convention for the Protection of Human Rights and Fundamental Freedoms. *Opened for signature* 4 November 1950, EurTS No. 5, 213 UNTS 221 (*entered into force* 3 September 1953).

International Covenant on Civil and Political Rights. *Adopted* 16 December 1966, 999 UNTS 171 (*entered into force* 23 March 1976), GA Res 2200 (XXI), 21 UN GAOR Supp (No. 16) at 52, UN Doc A/6316 (1966).

African Charter on Human and Peoples' Rights. *Adopted* in Banjul 27 June 1981, OAU Doc CAB/LEG/67/3/Rev.5.

Constitution of Zimbabwe Amendment (No. 10) 1990.

Constitution of Zimbabwe Amendment (No. 11) Act 1990.

Reports

International Commission of Jurists (1976) 'Racial Discrimination and Repression in Southern Rhodesia' (London: Catholic Institute of International Relations; Geneva: ICJ).

Africa All Party Parliamentary Group (2009) 'Land in Zimbabwe: Past Mistakes, Future Prospects' (London: Royal African Society).

Browne *et al* (2004) 'The State of Justice in Zimbabwe', prepared by a team led by Desmond Browne QC, Chairman of the Bar Council of England and Wales (Brisbane: International Council of Advocates and Barristers), available at <http://www.barhumanrights.org.uk/docs/2010/7351_BHRC_Zimbabwe_Report.pdf> (last accessed 8 January 2011).

10 Property rights and land reform in Namibia

Sam K. Amoo and Sidney L. Harring†*

10.1 Introduction: the land problem in southern Africa

At the turn of the twenty-first century "land reform" has become a dominant political issue in southern Africa. The post-apartheid legacy of racism and inequality of Namibia has many manifestations, but the vast expanses of white-owned farms are among the most visible reminders. Violent land seizures in Zimbabwe highlighted a political problem with parallels in both Namibia and South Africa, with a message in the subtext: if deliberate legal measures are not taken to achieve land reform, the people will inevitably use force to "take back" the lands that were stolen from them during the colonial era.[1] As a legal issue, land reform is among the most challenging possibilities of the law: it requires a major transformation of property rights in impoverished and racist agrarian societies through peaceful, legal means.[2] As a historical issue, the justification for land reform is rooted in past injustices – colonial era land loss.

Land reform has many meanings, in different contexts, but in each of these southern African contexts it means "the redistribution of property rights or rights in land for the benefit of the landless, tenants, or farm laborers."[3] There is no need to include race in this definition, but all involved know from the racist and colonial history of the region that white farms are to be somehow acquired and redistributed to blacks: the "race issue" dominates all other issues in the post-apartheid era as a distinct "racial geography" divided southern Africa into "white" and "black" areas.[4] By definition, the land reform process transforms existing political and economic relations by creating wealth for people with nothing and politically empowering classes of people who have been poor and landless.[5] White farmers, who have held disproportionate political and economic power, lose much, most, or even all of their power to blacks, including their former farm laborers.[6] And, beyond lofty images of power and economics, land reform will enable black peasant farmers to have the chance to grow enough food to feed their families: a simple strategy of poverty alleviation in societies where children go hungry.[7]

This is especially important in southern Africa because of the recent legacy of colonialism, apartheid, poverty and war, continuing through the early years of the 1990s in South Africa, but only ending in 1990 in Namibia, and 1980 in

Zimbabwe.[8] The histories of these nations are clearly interrelated. South Africa governed Namibia from 1915 to 1990, nearly incorporating it into the apartheid era state.[9] Zimbabwe was founded by Cecil Rhodes, who had been Governor of Cape Colony and was South Africa's richest businessman, and, as Rhodesia, operated as one of Britain's most "colonial" of colonial societies, with its own system of apartheid.[10] Because of a moderate climate, and great economic opportunity, all three countries drew white settlers, and this permanent white settler population, heavily invested in agriculture, distinguishes these countries from other countries in sub-Saharan Africa.[11]

Namibia is a vast country occupied by only about 1.8 million people.[12] Eight hundred thousand of these people are concentrated in northern Namibia in Ovamboland, a former homeland that occupies less than 3 per cent of the land area.[13] Over 300,000, perhaps up to 400,000, crowd into greater Windhoek, leaving only about a half million people occupying the rest of the country.[14] The country has one of the most unequal economic structures in the world.[15] Whites, about 7 per cent of the population, may control 70 per cent of the economy. Nearly half of Namibia's blacks live at the subsistence level in rural poverty on an income of $US200 per capita a year or less.[16] But the most poverty stricken people in Namibia live on their traditional communal lands that, as overcrowded as these lands are, are still home.

One of the government's land reform strategies is the resettlement of previously disadvantaged Namibians and since 1990, the government has redistributed some 4 million ha of freehold or commercial land to these Namibians. The two principal acquisition methods are state acquisition through the Ministry of Lands and Resettlement and the Affirmative Action Loan Scheme through which formerly disadvantaged black Namibians are assisted by the state to buy freehold farms.[17] But, as stated in the same report,[18] it is felt by many that land reform is progressing too slowly. In a recent debate on land reform in Parliament, both Government and Opposition members of parliament bemoaned the slow progress of land reform. In his contribution to the debate, Prime Minister Nahas Angula is quoted to have said, "It is a travesty of justice that one family can own vast tracts of land in Namibia while many rural people are squeezed into small patches of land." He added that many white farmers declare themselves bankrupt so that their farms could be auctioned off, and farms are also auctioned off when their owners die, thereby driving prices up.[19]

10.2 The genesis of the skewed land policies in Namibia[20]

10.2.1 The colonial expropriation of indigenous lands

Land rights in modern societies are a juridical construct: land rights are defined in law. The "land title" is the legal document that serves as a representation of that land for all legal purposes: it can be sold, mortgaged, left to one's heirs, or given away. Under apartheid, as under the German regime, only whites could hold "land titles," thus only whites had a "legal" right to their land. Blacks held land, but under customary law, not under legal title. This regime is called "legal dualism" but it is not "dual," because black land rights were/are not backed by land titles.

The "stolen lands" issue, although world wide refers to the process of colonial occupation of indigenous lands, in Namibia derives more narrowly from the Herero/Nama War, one of the most violent of colonial wars. The colonial history of Namibia is complex and still, from the standpoint of the black people who live there, largely unwritten.[21] The Herero War has been the subject of a number of books, with scholars drawn to the unique character of German colonial violence.[22] While a number of meanings can be drawn from the war, the central outcome in terms of land law is clear: Germany terminated by conquest all Herero land rights in South West Africa, leaving the Herero with no land at all. Herero lands were then "sold" by colonial authorities to settlers – 90 per cent of them German – on favorable terms, with long-term loans subsidized by the colonial government.[23] These farms are now the heart of Namibian agriculture, occupying a wide swath from Omaruru to Gobabis and the Botswana border, the entire country to the west, north, and east of Windhoek. Further south, most Nama lands were also taken, although the Nama were left with reserves.

This violent dispossession followed a short colonial history. The ovaHerero were occupants of the high plains of central Namibia. A Bantu tribe, they had moved south into this region from Angola, arriving about 1750. A series of wars with the Nama, who live to the south, occurred in the mid nineteenth century, destabilizing the entire region.[24] Germany first arrived in South West Africa in 1884, using the dubious private land claims of a businessman, Adolf Luderitz, as the legal basis for establishing a protectorate over a vast desert hinterland, the first German colony in Africa.[25]

The Herero were not involved in these coastal land treaties, but on December 29, 1884 Chief Kamaherero, at Omaruru, entered into a treaty of protection with Great Britain, then engaged in a diplomatic dispute with Germany over what is now Namibia. Great Britain soon abandoned the contest, withdrawing to the Cape Colony and leaving the native people of South West Africa, with or without treaties of protection, to the Germans.[26] Different chiefs may well have had different strategies to deal with colonial authority and the Germans were beginning to implement a "divide and rule" strategy. It is also unclear what the Herero believed these "treaties of protection" meant. Such agreements did not, on their face, cede land or sovereignty.[27] Rather, the Germans agreed to "protect" Herero interests from rival tribes.

In 1895 colonial troops intervened in Okahandja on behalf of Chief Samuel Maharero in a Herero succession dispute. This military action cemented an alliance between the Germans and Maharero that lasted for nine years. During this time, Maharero "sold" vast tracts of Herero lands under various kinds of arrangements, some more "legal" than others. For example, traders took vast quantities of land in exchange for trade goods, including liquor. They, in turn, sold the land to farmers at huge profits.[28] Other Herero land was deserted as a rinderpest epidemic killed most of their cattle. Many lands were simply taken with no regard for legality – we have no idea how it was alienated from black ownership. Much closer attention needs to be paid by historians to the colonial land records.

In a 1922 *Memorandum on Treaties between the Late Government and Various Native Tribes in South West Africa* a colonial official bluntly (but confidentially) stated:

> I would like to mention here that in law there was no confiscation of the Khauash [*sic*] Hottentots property, and their Treaties with the late Government of the 9th March, 1894 and 4th February, 1885, are still valid. In fact the late Government confiscated their property, and omitted however to give this confiscation the force of law as prescribed in the Imperial Ordinance of the 26th December 1905. The German government in 1913 and 1914 was well aware of this mistake; as, however, nobody had yet found it out, it kept silence. Should the Khauas Hottentots come forward to-day and ask for the return of their former territory, of which a lot has been sold and is still advertised for sale, it would mean the return of one-quarter of the District of Gobabis. ... [29]

If this treaty is still in force, it may invalidate numerous land titles in this district.

Some black lands were lost through the actions, even duplicity, of their own chiefs, "sold" to whites, although it is unclear what the parties understood those transactions to mean. There was no history or law of land sales in Herero or Nama society at that time, and it is unclear how these legal transactions were translated into German. By 1902 the Herero only retained about 46,000 cattle of an estimated 100,000 head held 10 years before. In contrast, 1,051 German farmers and traders held 44,500 head. The number of settlers increased from 1,774 in 1895 to 4,640 in 1903. Of 83.5 million ha of land in the colony, 31.4 million ha remained in African hands[30] – although these figures include much land that belonged to Nama and other tribes. In an infamous proclamation, issued on 2 October 1904, the German General, von Trotha, ordered all Herero men killed, and all their lands and cattle seized.[31] After reading the proclamation to a group of Herero prisoners, he proceeded to hang 30 men then, after handing out printed copies of the document in the Herero language, drove the women and children out into the Kalahari Desert.

The details of the Herero War are well known and are not in serious dispute.[32] Historian Jan-Bart Gewald constructs a convincing account that the war was used as a pretext by the Germans to annihilate the Herero. But, accepting any account, it was a war over land. At least some Herero, offended by increasing German movement on to Herero lands, and subjected to demeaning and inhuman treatment by colonists and traders, rose in revolt. Once the revolt was under way, the Germans refused all attempts for a negotiated resolution.[33] This was not the only colonial war in Namibia: there was a series of such wars. The Nama, in fact, took advantage of the Herero War, attacking the Germans from the south, and carrying on a guerrilla war for several years after the Herero were defeated.[34]

But tribes in the north did not directly experience this war, nor this violent dispossession of their lands. This reality structures the land reform process in

Namibia: most blacks have lost no land to colonization, therefore the demand for "land reform" is not equally felt in all segments of the black population.[35] The government has rejected any model of "restitution of ancestral lands" in the land reform process.[36] Thus, unlike South Africa, where the land reform process includes a form of restitution for blacks dispossessed since 1913,[37] land reform in Namibia is not based on restitution of particular lands to aggrieved parties. The purpose is to promote national unity, but a model of restitution of ancestral lands would advantage the people of central Namibia who were dispossessed of their lands over the Ovambo and Kavango to the north, who were not, so there is a political advantage to this position.[38]

10.2.2 Classification of land in Namibia

In the early era of colonial expansion, as indicated above, protection treaties and rights of conquest were the most prominent tools of land expropriation and alienation. After 1915, however, land alienation by Europeans and the introduction of new property rights were implemented in a more systematic manner by legislation,[39] resulting in the classification of land which can legitimately be regarded as the genesis of the imbalances in land distribution and ownership in present-day Namibia.

The legal mechanism that was used by the colonial powers in South West Africa was legislation that was primarily geared at dividing the land on the basis of the settler–native dichotomy. This was done by the initial declaration of the territory as Crown land, followed by the declaration of tribal and trust land or communal land over land originally belonging to the natives. Ownership of land in the area demarcated as Crown land vested in the colonial power, whilst part of the land was reserved for the occupation and use of the natives. Within the area of Crown land the received law of the settlers was applied. Customary law applied to areas reserved for the natives. In most cases, the reservation of land for the occupation and use of the natives did not imply the complete ownership of that land by that particular tribal group. Rather, the tribal group had rights of occupation and use, or rights of usufruct.[40] The reversionary rights were vested in the colonial administration.

10.2.2.1 Creation of Crown land

The formal declaration of land inhabited or owned by the tribal groups as Crown land was effected by a series of laws. The Transvaal Crown Land Disposal Ordinance of 1903 was the initial piece of legislation used for this purpose. This ordinance was made applicable to South West Africa by virtue of the Crown Land Disposal Proclamation 13 of 1920. Firstly, the ordinance proclaimed the territory as Crown land and, secondly, in terms of section 12, certain areas of Crown land could be reserved "for the use and benefit of aboriginal natives." (The extension of Transvaal ordinances was made lawful and possible by virtue of section 4(1) of the Treaty of Peace and South West Africa Mandate Act No. 49 of 1919.[41])

The general effect of this ordinance was to vest ownership of tribal land in the state or, to be more precise, the mandatory power, South Africa. In 1967, another piece of legislation, the Reservation of State Land for Natives Ordinance 35 of 1967, was passed with similar provisions reserving state land for the use and occupation of the natives.

> The declaration of the territory as Crown land meant by necessary implication that the received law was to be used to determine property relations, but this did not rule out completely the application of the relevant customary law in areas where the land was substantially occupied by tribal groups. In this regard, mention should be made of section 4(3) of the Treaty of Peace and South West Africa Mandate, which authorized the Governor-General "in respect of land contained in any such reserve to grant individual titles to any person lawfully occupying and entitled to such land." The novelty of this provision was the introduction of the concept of private ownership to a community whose land tenure system was community-based. Property relations were to be determined by the received law, which allowed individual rights as opposed to the community-oriented land rights practiced by the indigenous people.

10.2.2.2 Reserves and trusts

The classification of land in South West Africa after the declaration of Crown land was determined according to identifiable tribes grouped under native reserves and tribal trust areas. The Native Administration Proclamation 11 of 1922, issued by the Governor-General, the official representative of the King of Great Britain on whose behalf South Africa administered the mandate, empowered the administration to establish native reserves. In 1928, the Native Administration Proclamation 15 of 1928, *inter alia*, gave the administrator the power to define tribal areas. Government Notice 122 under the Native Administration Proclamation 15 of 1928 indicates that as early as the end of 1923 about 14 native reserves had been established. The creation of the native reserves, therefore, cut the ties that natives had to their ancestral land, adding another dimension to the classification of land in South West Africa.[42]

Land allocation and utilization in the reserves were regulated by the Native Reserve Regulation 68 of 1924. The Regulations vested ownership of the land in the Administration and further provided that, after the land had been set aside as a reserve, "it [could] not be alienated or used for any other purpose except with the consent of both Houses of the Union Parliament."[43] As pointed out by Adams and Werner, traditional leaders in the Police Zone had no powers of their own with regard to the allocation of land in reserves. The regulations did make provision for a communal land tenure system, but the allocation of land for residential and agricultural purposes could only be made by Reserve Superintendents.[44]

The next step in the process of depriving the indigenous people of their rights to their ancestral lands was the "conversion" of the reserves into trusts. By virtue of the Development Trust and Land Act No. 18 of 1936, the native reserves were to be placed under a trust, known as the Development Trust, and the administration of native affairs was transferred from the Administrator of South West Africa to the responsible South African Minister. Under section 5(2) of this Act, all land placed under the Development Trust was declared the property of the state, to be administered by the State President of South Africa as trustee. In 1978, by virtue of section 2 of the Administration of the South African Bantu Trust in South West Africa Proclamation AG 19 of that year, the trusteeship was transferred from the South African State President to the Administrator-General of South West Africa.

10.2.2.3 Creation of areas for native nations

The next development in the land policy of the colonial administration was the creation of "areas for native nations." This was effected by the Development of Self-government for Native Nations in South West Africa Act No. 54 of 1968. This Act gave the various pieces of land assembled in the Development Trust special status by transforming them into areas for "native nations." Section 2 of the Act listed Damaraland, Hereroland, Kaokoland, Okavangoland, Eastern Caprivi, and Ovamboland as such areas. Section 2(g) empowered the State President of South Africa to "reserve and set apart such other land or area for the exclusive use and occupation by any native nation by proclamation." This was, for example, done for Bushmanland in terms of the Bushman Nation Advisory Board Proclamation R208 of 1976. Section 2 of the Proclamation recognizad Bushmanland, as defined in GN 1196 of 1970, as an area "for members of the Bushman Nation."[45]

10.2.2.4 Creation of communal land

By virtue of various pieces of legislation, the areas that had been designated for native nations were declared communal land. Examples of such pieces of legislation were: the Representative Authority of the Caprivians Proclamation AG 29 of 1980; the Representative Authority of the Kavangos Proclamation AG 26 of 1980; and the Representative Authority of the Ovambos Proclamation AG 23 of 1980. The Development of Self-government for Native Nations in South West Africa Act was repealed by section 52 of the Representative Authorities Proclamation.

In 1981, by virtue of the provisions of the Representative Authorities Amendment Proclamation AG 4 of 1981, the Administrator-General was made trustee of the communal lands. More importantly section 48(3) of this proclamation gave the executive authority of the representative authority – to the extent that it was authorized by an ordinance of the legislative authority or any other law – the power to confer ownership, or any other right into or over, any portion of such communal land, thereby maintaining the alien concept of private individual ownership among the tribal communities.[46] The Representative Authorities Proclamation, and those proclamations establishing representative authorities, were amended by the Representative Authority Powers Transfer Proclamation AG 8 of 1989, which dissolved the representative authorities and transferred the powers back to the Administrator-General. Article 147,[47] read with Schedule 8 to the Namibian Constitution,[48] repealed the remaining parts to the various representative authorities proclamations. However, as argued by Hinz:

> All those amendments and repeals, including the repeal by the Constitution … did not alter the status of the land, being communal land … This follows from the Interpretation of Laws Proclamation, 38 of 1920, which provides in section 11(2)(c) for the continuous legal validity of acts performed under the Act repealed. This appreciation for legal certainty also must apply to acts directly instituted by the repealed law itself.[49]

10.3 Land tenure after Independence

10.3.1 State land

Article 100[50] and Schedule 5(1)[51] of the Constitution maintain the status of state (Crown) land; Article 16(1) affirms the fundamental right to acquire, own and dispose of all forms of immovable and movable property (i.e. it maintains the status of private property); and by virtue of section 11(2)(c) of the Interpretation of Laws Proclamation 38 of 1920, Article 102(5) of the Constitution and the generality of the provisions of the Communal Land Reform Act No. 5 of 2002, the status of communal land has also been maintained.[52]

10.3.2 The communal lands

The government's proposals on communal land reform in the White paper on Land Policy are the subject matter of the Communal Land Reform Act No. 5 of 2002.[53] The primary purpose of this Act is to make the process of land allocation and land administration fair and transparent, and to enhance security of tenure in the communal areas by giving statutory recognition to existing land rights and by creating new rights. The Act also seeks to introduce a certain degree of uniformity in land policy throughout the country by laying down new procedures regarding land allocation, utilization and transfer or inheritance. It addresses, *inter alia*, the issues of administration of communal land, titles to communal land, security of tenure and reiterates the position in the White Paper that the ownership of rural land is vested in the state. With regard to rights over communal land, whilst recognizing the underlining principle that the ownership of communal lands is vested in the state, the Act creates two rights that may be allocated in respect of communal land: customary land rights and rights of leasehold.[54] The Act thus reaffirms customary rights of usufruct[55] granted to occupiers of communal land and seeks to confer on this tenure system statutory recognition. The Act does not go beyond the right of usufruct. It does, however, specify the duration of customary land rights[56] and makes provision for their registration[57] and upgrading to the status of leaseholds in order to encourage and promote the development of the communal lands. Registration only constitutes publicity or proof of title. It does not confer on the holder any additional security, for example, to use the title as collateral. The Act[58] also seeks to have one common position relating to the allocation of land to a surviving spouse in the event of the death of the holder of the right.[59]

The other right created by the Act is the right of leasehold, or statutory leasehold.[60] This right is meant to replace the existing PTO, which, as noted earlier, is granted by the Ministry of Lands for the use of land for any specific purpose, especially for commercial undertakings. In terms of the Act, the power to grant leasehold rights is vested in the Communal Land Board,[61] rather than the Ministry of Lands. The right is granted for a statutory period of 99 years. If the right is granted for a period not exceeding 10 years it is invalid unless approved by the Minister.[62] The grant of leasehold rights is subject to registration.[63] If the land in respect of which the right of leasehold is granted is surveyed land (i.e. land which is shown on a diagram as defined in section 1 of the Land Survey Act No. 33 of 1993), and the lease is for a period of 10 years or more, the leasehold must be registered in accordance with the Deeds Registries Act No. 47 of 1937.[64] These provisions therefore guarantee security of tenure, and could serve as a catalyst for the development of commercial activities in the communal areas.

The Act recognizes the role of traditional authorities in communal land administration by vesting in the Chiefs and the traditional authorities the power to allocate communal land, subject to supervision by the Communal Land Boards.[65] This provision should not be interpreted as a potential threat to the rights of traditional leaders under Article 102(5) of the Constitution, which provides for the establishment of a Council of Traditional Leaders by Act of Parliament "to advise the President on the control and utilization of communal land." Rather, the role of the Communal Land Boards must be seen as administrative and advisory.

10.3.3 The commercial farming sector

Land set aside for private ownership or freehold in the commercial sector is for the most part owned by whites. At the time of independence this constituted most of the commercially viable farming land, while the remainder of such land was held by the indigenous people in the communal areas.

The commercial farms, mostly in fact, ranches – about 6,000 in number, owned by about 4,200 whites (and now up to 700 blacks)[66] – occupy the high plateau that extends in all directions from Windhoek, the center of the country.[67] This area is not tropical, which meant that German farmers could settle there without worrying about dying of tropical diseases. This temperate country was "white man's country." The hotter and wetter land in the north, although better for agriculture, was left to blacks. In the German era blacks were substantially left alone there outside of the "police zone," a policed boundary line that still runs across the country, now remaining as the "red line," a veterinary fence that keeps "African" cattle in the north away from "European" cattle, segregating even the cows.[68] The "police zone" kept Germans inside its boundary, under the protection of the colonial government. The vast relocations of black people that characterized both South Africa and Zimbabwe, and make land reform there so difficult, happened in central Namibia but the majority of blacks in the north still occupy their traditional lands.

As mentioned earlier, the German farms were first settled beginning in the 1890s, with a great increase in settlement after the Herero/Nama War of 1904–07, and then again after World War I, but extending into the 1950s and even, in a few cases into the 1960s. White land ownership in Namibia does not always go back for "generations": only 458 farms date back to before 1904, four or five generations. In 1938 there were 3,305 farms, thus half of the farms in Namibia were taken up less than 70 years ago.[69] Up to 20 per cent of Namibia's farms have changed hands since independence.[70] Today these commercial farms constitute about 44 per cent of the land in Namibia, 36.2 million ha: an amount slightly larger than the "communal lands," about 43 per cent – 33.5 million ha – held by over a million blacks. The government owns the rest of the land, about 13 per cent held as national parks, the diamond district, and for other purposes.[71]

As stated by the Prime Minister, Hage Geingob, in his opening address to the Land Conference on Land Reform in 1991:

> There are about 6,292 farms. Out of these, 6,123 farms are white-owned, and cover 95 per cent of the surface area of the commercial districts (34.4 million ha). Within this ownership category the overwhelming majority of farms belong to individual white farmers, including non-Namibians. To be more specific, a total area of 2.7 million ha (382 farms) belong to foreign absentee farmers, that is to say 0.9 million ha belonging to citizens from Austria, France, Italy and Switzerland, while the bulk of 1.7 million ha is owned by South African residents. Similarly, there are individual Namibian farmers with more than two large farms, as against thousands of their landless fellow countrymen who live in squalid poverty.[72]

It was then clear that the imbalances in the distribution of land could not be redressed without government intervention, a process to which the SWAPO government has committed itself, as will be explained later, through its land reform strategies.

10.3.4 Land tenure in urban centers

10.3.4.1 Freehold titles

The historical classification of land in South West Africa along racial lines led to the development of urban centers in the southern and central parts of the country in the areas designated as non-communal areas reserved principally for white settlement. These urban centers maintained the dominance of white settlement through the pass law system, and through the reservation of property ownership to whites. Black settlement was only allowed as a source of labor. The black workforce lived in separate locations, which comprised less developed formal settlements and undeveloped informal settlements.[73] Black residents in the less developed formal settlements who were able to satisfy the requirements for registration in terms of surveying and adequate planning were granted freehold titles to the properties. This form of tenure, however, constituted the exception rather than the rule. Occupants of settlements without adequate surveying and planning could not get their properties registered and therefore did not qualify for titles. Informal settlement did not attract any grant of security of tenure.

Article 16 of the Namibian Independence Constitution guarantees everyone the right to private ownership of land. This provision means that black Namibians are now constitutionally entitled to own properties with freehold titles.[74] Freehold title over land in urban centers may be acquired either through alienation of land hitherto vested in local authorities under the Local Authorities Act No. 23 of 1992,[75] or through private treaties between individuals.

10.3.4.2 The permission to occupy

Apart from the freehold title, the other form of title granted to residents in the urban centers was the Permission to Occupy (PTO). Before independence, this constituted the only form of title to land, other than rights under customary law, that was available to the indigenous population of Namibia, considering the prevailing political, social and economic constraints on the capacity of blacks to obtain freehold title.

The PTO was formally introduced into the territory by the Development Trust and Land Act No. 18 of 1936. It is a license granted by the Act, which allows the licensee to occupy state land under conditions attached to the PTO certificate. There are two types of PTO: rural and urban. The former is issued by the Ministry of Lands and Resettlement, and the latter by the Ministry of Regional and Local Government and Housing and Rural Development. The urban PTOs are issued in respect of land that falls within the "old settlement areas."[76] All other PTOs are designated rural.

Despite the existence of the PTO since 1936, it was the establishment of the Bantustans (or homelands) after the Odendaal Commission's Report in 1964[77] that resulted in the proliferation of this form of tenure. The 1960s saw the growth of the capitals of the Bantustans or the communal areas of the northern regions of the territory as a response to the administrative and military needs of the colonial administration. Since these urban centers were situated in the Bantustans, it was a contradiction in terms for the colonial administration to grant freehold titles. To suit the apartheid design, the most appropriate title in the circumstances was the PTO. PTOs were granted mainly to residents who occupied government houses in the formal areas and to private persons who developed plots in the formal areas. They were designed to provide the residents thereof with some security of tenure for the development of a surface structure, which could be in the form of a house or a shop. In accordance with the overall objective of apartheid, therefore, the PTOs satisfied the colonial administration's need for a limited form of title for the indigenous population. As such, it is a leasehold *sui generis*. A PTO conveys no rights of ownership, but it does contain an option for the holder to obtain secured title to the land if, at any time during the currency of the PTO, such title becomes available. As indicated by Christensen and Hojgaard,[78] a PTO provides a limited right to occupy an identified site for a limited period. In theory, it cannot be transferred or mortgaged. In practice, however, because PTOs are the only form of legally recognized titles in unproclaimed towns, they are "transferable" (by cancellation and reissue to the purchaser). In certain instances, PTOs have also been used as collateral. The inherent limitations of the PTOs have, however, created a lack of confidence in the system among the holders and also the general public.[79] Current government policy[80] is thus to phase out PTOs in the urban areas as the full range of existing and projected tenure forms become available.[81]

10.3.5 Land tenure in resettlement areas

As mentioned earlier, the Namibian government's land reform program has land resettlement as an essential component. Resettlement involves both redefining and reconstructing of land rights that need to be vested in the settlers. The determination of appropriate land rights in these resettlement areas has been premised by the government's objectives of resettlement. The National Resettlement Policy (2001) states two objectives of resettlement as firstly, to enhance the welfare of the people through improvement of productivity and secondly to develop the destination areas where people are supposed to earn a living.

In view of the fact that with the acquisition of these holdings by the state, it is not only the freehold title but logically the allodial title that are vested in the state, the position of the government in the reconstruction of adequate titles for the resettlement areas is the retention of the freehold and allodial titles and the granting of lesser titles to the settlers. Consequently, the tenure system in the resettlement areas is based on non-freehold where the government provides long-term leases of 99 years to current holders and future generations. The leasehold tenure system allows settlers to use a lease as collateral to secure a loan from lending institutions for agricultural production purposes. However, the reality of the actual situation on the ground is that resettlement areas cannot be used for collateral purposes due to the following reasons:

1. The state is the registered owner of the property.
2. The ownership structure makes it difficult for the banks to repossess this land in the event of default in payment of loans.
3. The leasehold of 99 years granted by the government is not transferable, or "non-tradable."

The land rights may be granted as individual, group or cooperative holdings.

10.4 Land reform in Namibia

The concern for land reform in Namibia is raised in the opening paragraph of the White Paper in the following terms:

> Access to and tenure of land were among the most important concerns of the Namibian people in their struggle for independence. Since 1990, and following the 1991 National Conference on Land Reform, and the Consultative Conference on Communal Land Administration 1996 Namibia's democratically elected government has maintained and developed its commitments to redressing the injustices of the past in a spirit of national reconciliation and to promoting sustainable economic development. The wise and fair allocation, administration and use of the nation's urban and rural land resources are essential if these goals are to be met.[82]

Pursuant to various national conferences on the land question,[83] and consistent with its avowed policy of land reform, the government got the Agricultural (Commercial) Land Reform Act promulgated in 1995 (Act No. 6 of 1995). This Act is meant to provide the Namibian government with the necessary legal tools to acquire commercial farms for the resettlement of displaced persons, and for the purposes of land reform. To date the implementation of the policy has been facilitated by the state and by market-assisted acquisition schemes based on the "willing seller, willing buyer" principle. The state acquisition scheme known as the National Resettlement Program (NRP) acquires land for resettlement purposes in the market under the auspices of the Ministry of Lands and Resettlement (MLR). The Affirmative Action Loan Scheme (AALS) is a program implemented by the Agricultural Bank of Namibia on behalf of the Ministry of Agriculture, Water and Forestry. This program was introduced by the Agricultural Bank Amendment Act No. 27 of 1991 and the Agricultural Bank Matters Amendment Act No. 15 of 1992 with the aim, *inter alia*, of resettling well established and strong communal farmers on commercial farmland so as to minimize the pressure on grazing in communal areas. It assists formerly disadvantaged persons to acquire land themselves on the open market with subsidized interest rates. Between 1990 and October 2004, the two programs together redistributed 4.31 million ha, or 12 per cent of the total area of freehold land in Namibia, benefiting some 2,151 families. Since 1992, the AALS has distributed nearly four times the amount of land the NRP has distributed since 1990, namely 3.47 million ha compared with some 874,000 ha. In addition, the MAWF transferred 398,859 ha to the MLR in 1992.[84] In his address to the National Assembly in May 2010, the Minister, Alpheus !Naruseb, indicated that the Ministry of Lands and Resettlement had earmarked 15 million ha of freehold land to be redistributed by the year 2020.[85] The Minister added that in the 2009/10 Financial Year, the Ministry acquired eight farms with a total area of 26,000 ha at a cost of N$21.2 million and that the figure fell short of the set annual target of 534,000 ha. He explained that the slow pace at which land is being acquired had negatively impacted the rate at which Government can resettle people.

The implementation of the Act has, however, not been free from problems. As pointed out by the then Minister of Lands, Resettlement and Rehabilitation, Pendukeni Ithana, the government's policy of "willing seller, willing buyer" has imposed constraints on its ability to acquire fertile and more productive commercial farms.[86] This constraint was also alluded to by Minister Alpheus !Naruseb in his address mentioned earlier. However, an option that is open to the government as a possible solution to this constraint may be found under the provisions of Chapter IV of the Act. Section 20, read together with s 14(1), empowers the Minister to expropriate any commercial land for purposes of land reform in case of failure to negotiate the sale of property by mutual agreement.

Under Article 16 of the Constitution the government of Namibia has the sovereign power to expropriate private property.[87] Consistent with the norms of international law,[88] the Namibian Constitution provides for the justification of such expropriation on grounds of public interest and the payment of compensation. The power to expropriate, therefore, is a legal matter, while the decision to expropriate and determine the public interest is a political one. It is worth mentioning also that this clause is not entrenched and therefore can be derogated should a state of emergency be declared under Articles 24(3) and 26 of the Constitution.[89] The Namibian government has to date expropriated about nine farms. This may be attributed both to political reasons and budgetary constraints relating to the payment of compensation.

10.4.1 White agriculture in modern-day Namibia

Just as land dispossession has its history, so does the white agricultural order which followed. Namibian agriculture, under colonialism and apartheid, took on particular forms. In a land where farm ownership is politically and racially charged, it is not easy to determine exactly who owns the land because some ownership is concealed through various legal devices.[90] It is generally thought that about 4,200 families own about 6,000 commercial farms, with up to 700 of these farms held by blacks. Since independence, black businessmen and politicians have purchased farms and about up to 700 black farmers have been loaned money through various state affirmative action programs to buy commercial farms.[91] But the commercial agricultural sector is still overwhelmingly white, and is so perceived by Namibian blacks.

These 4,200 families represent much of the wealth in Namibia, with many urban residents owning farms that they use on weekends and holidays. At the same time, little of this wealth is actually generated by these farms, a situation much different from Zimbabwe where white-owned commercial farms were major sources of income, particularly foreign exchange. Many Namibian farms are held as "hobby farms," one asset of people wealthy from other areas of enterprise. Again, this data is difficult to get access to, but it is clear that the average Namibian farm does not produce a profit and the average farm is far in debt. At least 60 per cent, and up to as many as 70 per cent of all Namibian farms are unprofitable. Debt loads are large, with debt repayment amounting to about $N300 million a year; about one-third of Namibia's estimated agricultural income.[92] Debt loads are also rapidly increasing: in 1991 the average commercial farmer had to sell 31 per cent of his livestock to pay his debts; in 1998 this had increased to 64 per cent, effectively doubling debt in seven years.[93]

Debt per farmer has doubled since 1990, increasing from $N112,000 to $N227,000. Given that some farmers – perhaps as many as 30 per cent – carry no debt, the remaining farmers are even further in debt than these "average" data would indicate.[94] These farms, averaging about 8,000 ha each – 20,000 in the south – are losing money from year to year. This means that the present generation of white farmers with an average age of 55 is content with a rural life style that produces little cash income and are willing to borrow against their capital investment in order to maintain their agrarian life style.[95]

Ironically, it now seems that this was always the case with Namibian farms: they were never profitable and always heavily subsidized by the state. First, the German government, using the model of the yeoman German farmer that worked so well in Canada and the United States, subsidized small farmers in order to populate its colony with Germans, a necessary requirement to create a colonial settler society on the model of North America or South Africa. Later, the South African government moved thousands of poor Afrikaners to Namibia, setting them up in a rural welfare scheme, a bulwark of agrarian Afrikaner values.[96] Even the choice of cattle or small stock as the major "crop" was determined by South African officials: they loaned money only for particular types of agricultural enterprises. A vast road system was built; still among the best in Africa.[97] Wells were sunk all over the country in order to insure a constant supply of water in a semi-desert environment.[98] Dam building and canal projects were built, with plans developed to divert water from the Kunene and Kavango Rivers into central Namibia.[99]

Even with elaborate state efforts to develop water sources, drought is a periodic occurrence in Namibian agriculture. What rainfall that exists occurs during a few months between November and March.[100] But rainfall, even in the "rainy" season, is often irregular. Therefore, it is difficult to plan for herd development.[101] Periodic drought has also resulted in high levels of environmental degradation, that, ironically both lower the value of the farms making it easier for the government to purchase them, but also making it harder to successfully resettle black farmers on the land. Namibian grazing lands are stressed even under good conditions. Drought forces overgrazing, which has led to the permanent depletion of grasslands, desertification,[102] and bush encroachment, as worthless species of brush take hold where grass is gone, converting grasslands to shrubby wastelands.[103]

Since the 1950s, Namibian agriculture has become increasingly monocultural: cattle are the main cash source, and most farms are now "ranches," raising nothing but cattle.[104] Cattle herds in the commercial areas have declined by 27 per cent since 1990, now numbering under 1 million head.[105] Because Namibia has little grain, its cattle are grass fed, further stressing the environment. This means that it takes longer to raise them to market weight and that they produce an inferior grade of meat in the world market.[106] In the south, where there is too little grass for cattle, farmers raise over 2 million sheep.[107] Namibia, a vast agricultural land, is self-supporting only in beef and mutton. Most of its food products must be imported, almost always from South Africa.[108] Although cattle and small stock production dominates Namibian agriculture, there are several regions that support commercial crop production. A "maize triangle" in the north, where there is more rainfall, grows about half of Namibia's corn and wheat requirements.[109]

What is now left of Namibian agriculture is the remnants of a wasteful, politically determined, and subsidized system that never originally belonged in Namibia, but rather, was state subsidized for underlying purposes related to colonial policy that no longer exists.[110] The irony here is striking: even if those farms were vacated tomorrow, it is not clear that they should – or even could – be reoccupied as farms. To do so would simply continue a wasteful form of colonial era agriculture. If white farmers have required vast subsidies to operate in Namibia, it is also likely that black farmers will as well. Thus, the major expense of land reform is probably not the cost of the land itself, but the cost of generations of future government subsidies.

These commercial farms are at the core of an agrarian social structure that may provide jobs for about 15 per cent of the population. In 1997, 42,277 farm workers were employed in the commercial agricultural sector. An additional 38,125 were "unpaid family workers." With an average household size of 5.1, about 211,000 blacks are employed or supported by commercial agriculture.[111] Many black Namibians have worked on these farms their whole lives, and often have known no other home. While farm wages are generally low, farm workers may also draw benefits in terms of food, housing, and medical care that are much better than the average Namibian. Thus, any change in the ownership of these commercial farming operations will displace large numbers of poor blacks with no other homes, low educational levels, and few other job skills.[112] Thus, an irony of "land reform" is that most of the people displaced are poor blacks: most of the whites who own farms already live in cities.

10.4.2 Security of tenure in the Informal Areas

In terms of land holding rights and security of tenure, the other category that needs to be considered are residents of the informal areas. Most of these people obtain their rights of occupation from traditional leaders. Such rights approximate to rights of usufruct. This category of residence has, however, never been granted official land rights by the authorities. It is this group of residents, together with those in the spontaneous settlements on the fringes of proclaimed urban areas, at which the newly proposed form of tenure, the starter title,[113] is aimed.

With the advent of independence, more Africans were absorbed into the public service and, to a lesser extent, into the private and commercial sectors. This has resulted in the influx of more affluent Africans into the urban centers. The character of black settlement in the urban centers has consequently become more heterogeneous and, with the right of private ownership guaranteed by Article 16 of the

Constitution, more black urban dwellers are able to acquire property in the form of freehold title. Although this phenomenon may have corrected to a certain degree the effects of past racial discrimination, urbanization has its own inherent problems. It is thus estimated that urban areas in Namibia are growing at a rate of 3.75 per cent per annum on average. The fastest growing towns, Walvis Bay, Katima Mulilo and Rundu are estimated to be growing at a rate of approximately 6.5 per cent. Windhoek, with 34.5 per cent of Namibia's total urban population, has seen an annual growth rate from 1991 to 1995 of 5.45 per cent. This growth means that there is not only need for more land for urban settlement, but also for security of tenure for people whose rights are not recognized by the existing system. It is estimated that about 30,000 families presently live in informal settlements in urban areas without security of tenure.[114] Most of these residents are squatters on land belonging to individuals or local authorities.

One reason for the non-existence of a more secure tenure system for urban settlements in the former Bantustan areas was that it was the deliberate policy of the colonial administration to deny these urban centers official recognition as municipalities. This would have led to the establishment of local authorities with the jurisdiction to grant freehold title after the satisfaction of infrastructural and surveying requirements.[115]

The first democratic Government of Namibia reacted to this situation by establishing local authorities in these areas under the Local Authorities Act, 1992. The formalization of urban centers in terms of this statute involves, firstly, the proclamation of the area as an urban area under the jurisdiction of the relevant local authority. This step is then followed by the registration of the town in the name of the state or relevant local authority. The proclamation and subsequent registration enable the local authority to subdivide the area and create plots or erven of urban land. The occupants of such plots receive freehold title. In the formal areas, the intention is to sell existing erven to the relevant local authority, "subject to the holders of Permissions to Occupy being given the first option on the plots they occupy at the sale date."[116]

10.4.3 Reform of customary land tenure

10.4.3.1 Nature of customary land tenure

Apart from the maldistribution of land along racial lines, the Namibian land program has to be analyzed from the perspective of customary land tenure systems that operated in the communal areas within the general context of customary law. Some of the issues of customary land tenure discussed in this chapter center on the recognition and status of customary law and the nature of customary land tenure.

One of the legacies of colonization in Africa is the juxtaposition of the received law emanating from the legal systems of the metropolitan countries alongside the customary law of the indigenous African communities. This juxtaposition subjected the application of customary law to various tests of recognition. As Max Gluckman[117] and other students of the jurisprudence and legal systems of traditional African societies have acknowledged, before the advent of colonialism African communities had their own laws and legal systems regulating the behavior of individuals in society. These laws covered areas like civil and criminal liability, marriage, inheritance and succession and land tenure systems. Faced with the problem of accommodation, the colonial administration accorded limited recognition to customary law by subsuming it under the received law and by subjecting it to the all too familiar repugnancy clause test for equity, good conscience, and morality. This precondition for the recognition of customary law still exists in the constitutions and statute books of many African countries.

Customary law principles relating to criminal law generally did not withstand scrutiny under the repugnancy clause test. In the area of land law, however, the recognition and survival of indigenous legal principles depended upon different factors and considerations, including the ultimate colonial intent and design, economic factors, public domain concerns, and environmental and land use preoccupations. The general pattern was that in territories where the colonial administration did not intend to settle immigrants from the metropolitan country or from elsewhere in Europe, customary law relating to land tenure was given a fair amount of recognition.[118] In territories where the settlement of immigrants from Europe was the ultimate goal of the colonial powers, indigenous land tenure systems and property rights were given marginal recognition only, and the indigenous communities dispossessed of their property rights in favor of the immigrants and their property rights regimes. By legislation, land was classified into Crown or state land, native reserves or communal lands so that, as pointed out by TW Bennett,[119] "the authority of customary law recognized in the administration of communal lands was a creation of colonial authorities." In other words, native land was not communal land until the colonial authorities defined away all other forms of native land tenure. The latter pattern was more prominent in southern Africa, so that in these areas the characteristic feature of the customary law of land tenure is either the adulteration or lack of development of the indigenous systems. The Namibian pattern of classification, as described earlier, fits into this general southern African pattern.

With the promulgation of the Namibia Independence Constitution, customary law was recognized as one of the sources of law in Namibia. In its recognition of customary law as a source of law,[120] the Constitution removes the repugnancy clause and equates customary law with the common law. However, the Constitution left open the question of whether the new constitutional status of customary law in Namibia means that ownership of the communal lands is vested in the indigenous people as the holders of allodial titles to their ancestral lands. Article 100 of the Constitution vests ownership of all land in Namibia, except for the land otherwise lawfully owned, in the state. The application of customary law in the communal areas, coupled with the fact that communal lands were the creation of legislation, has left many uncertainties regarding the exact rights of the indigenous people who occupy the communal lands and the administrative authority of the chiefs.

The position adopted in the White Paper on National Land Policy is that in terms of Schedule 5(1) of the Constitution, communal land is vested in the state to be administered in trust for the benefit of traditional communities and for the purpose of promoting the economic and social development of the Namibian people. This position constitutes one of the underlying principles of the Communal Land Reform Act No. 5 of 2002, as discussed earlier.

10.5 Property rights of women in Namibia and HIV/AIDS

The colonial policy of apartheid, and more especially that of "bantustanization," that generally deprived a certain sector of the South West Africa/Namibian community of their basic fundamental rights was legitimized not only by the imposed political and social systems but also the legal system including legislation and some principles of Roman-Dutch common law. In terms of property rights the general black population was denied the rights to certain property rights, like for example, freehold titles, as a result of the Bantustan policy. The policies of the financial institutions requiring collaterals as a prerequisite for the granting of loans totally disqualified the generality of the black population from qualifying for the wherewithal and the empowerment necessary for the acquisition of property more especially immovable property. The situation was even more pathetic in the case of women who were not only subjected to the application of some of the discriminatory principles of the Roman-Dutch common law relating to matrimonial property rights (in the case of women who were subjected to the general law), but more especially the black women whose property rights were governed by the customary law of their tribal communities as a result of the Bantustan policy. In terms of property rights therefore, it is not only the black women who did not have the full legal rights to property and the means to acquire property, but also the white women whose property rights were governed by the general law that recognized the better titles of men to property.

These institutionalized and legally enforceable discriminatory policies constituted the genesis of gender inequality in Namibia. However, there is ample evidence that cultural and customary practices reinforced the state-sanctioned gender inequality. In Namibia there are eleven different ethnic groups all of whom are characterized by the norms and practices of patriarchy with ingrained gendered stereotypes that lead women to believe that men are biologically superior to women and thus lead to the male superiority and dependency syndrome.[121] In the context of the HIV/AIDS pandemic, as scholars and policy experts indicate,[122] gender inequality is a social factor that has significantly contributed to the spread of the virus since unequal power relations between men and women put women at a greater risk of HIV/AIDS infection.

At the time of independence the government of the day was confronted with the problem of adopting policies that will address the general policies of discrimination that affect not only the black population but the disadvantaged groups, and in the case of property rights, the generality of women in Namibia. The Government of the Republic of Namibia has committed itself to the policy of non-discrimination as enshrined under Article 10[123] of the Namibian Constitution and this underlies its National Policy on Land, including property rights.[124]

The government's position postulated in this policy is not only a political commitment but also a moral and legal/constitutional obligation.[125] Article 95 of the Constitution that deals with the principles of State Policy and the Promotion of the Welfare of the People states as follows:

> The State shall actively promote and maintain the welfare of the people by adopting, *inter alia*, policies aimed at the following;
>
> (a) enactment of legislation to ensure equality of opportunity for women, to enable them to participate fully in all spheres of Namibian society; in particular, the Government shall ensure the implementation of the principle of non-discrimination in remuneration of men and women; further, the Government shall seek, through appropriate legislation, to provide maternity and related benefits for women;
> (e) ensurance that every citizen has a right to fair and reasonable access to public facilities and services in accordance with the law.

These principles have been held in the case of *Government of the Republic, the Director of Legal Aid and the Prosecutor General v Geoffrey Kupuzo Mwilima and Others*[126] as "an expression by the State of its willingness" to provide those services and that "they are not enforceable in any court of law." In terms of access to property and the provision of the necessary framework, legal or otherwise, for the attainment of these rights by the erstwhile disadvantaged members of the community, especially women, this may not be a justiciable right, but the provision does impose a standing obligation on the government to be seen to be measuring up to its commitment. Furthermore, under the Constitutional Provisions on Apartheid and Affirmative Action[127] the government is enjoined to pass legislation to empower women, needless to say, to have access to property.

With regard to the rights to property, and more especially the rights of women, the Namibian legislature, since independence, has promulgated pieces of legislation aimed at redressing the injustices of the colonial legacy, including the discriminatory laws and practices relating to property rights, especially the rights of women. Apart from probably the Constitutions of the former Soviet Union and the other communist states in the Eastern Bloc, which made the provision of housing a constitutional obligation of Government, there are virtually no constitutions in the world that make the provision of housing to its citizens the constitutional obligation of the state and therefore justiciable rights of the individual. The Namibian government may therefore not be under such obligation but it has the duty to provide *within available means* adequate and affordable housing for members of the society in the lower income group brackets. It is recognized that since Government's resources are limited and Namibia has a mixed economy the private sector must of necessity play an important role in the provision of the wherewithal, credit facilities, for the acquisition of property. It is however, the function of Government to ensure that the policies of the private sector are not discriminatory, especially against women and that credit facilities are reasonably accessible to them. In addressing the general issue of the property rights of women attention will be focused on these specific areas:

(i) whether the legislation promulgated by Parliament has adequately redressed the injustices of the past with respect to the rights of women to property;
(ii) related to (i) above, whether the general rule inhibits women from enjoying the same rights as women in terms of rights to property;
(iii) whether the facilities provided by both the public and private sectors are equally accessible to both men and women in their own rights;
(iv) whether the promulgation of the Communal Land Act No. 5 of 2002 redresses the inherent inequities of the communal land tenure systems with respect to the rights of women, given the inarticulate premise, patriarchal biases and predispositions of the male-dominated traditional leaders;
(v) whether Proclamation 15 of 1928 should be amended, especially in s 18(2) for cognizance to be taken of the type of marital regime for the purposes of determining rights of widows in cases of succession to immovable property; and
(vi) possible national and international solutions.

10.5.1 Rights of women to property during marriage

In terms of the general law all single or unmarried women in Namibia have the right to own any property including the commercial land, subject to the laws relating to capacity. This is in terms of the law, but the questions of accessibility to credit facilities and other wherewithal of empowerment provided by both the public and private sectors will have to be addressed separately. The position with respect to married women, however, is more complex.

There are two types of marriages in Namibia, civil law and customary law and to a great extent marriage as an institution in Namibia is one of the factors that govern the proprietary rights of women and have contributed to some of the discriminatory laws and practices that prevent women from getting access to property.

Until 1996, the proprietary consequences of marriage in Namibia were governed by the Roman-Dutch common law which provided that all marriages were automatically in community of property unless, at the time of the marriage, the parties entered into an ante-nuptial contract, creating a property regime that was out of community of property. Under the Roman-Dutch common law principles relating to marriages in community of property, the property of the spouses, wherever situated, present and future, movable and immovable, including debts, is merged into a joint estate in which the spouses hold equal and indivisible shares regardless of their contributions.[128] The joint estate automatically falls under the administration of the husband by virtue of his marital power. As administrator of the estate, the husband has power to alienate, encumber, or otherwise deal with the property as he sees fit. More importantly, in terms of proprietary rights, the wife cannot contract or register property in her name without the consent of the husband.[129]

These two types of marital property regimes are still recognized in Namibia but the common law principles relating to the marital power of the husband substantially modified by the Married Persons Equality Act No. 1 of 1996. Section 2 of the Act abolishes the marital power of the husband acquired under the common law and removes the restrictions which the marital power places on the legal capacity of a wife to contract and litigate, including, but not limited to the restrictions on her capacity to register immovable property in her name.[130] It follows therefore that during marriage a married woman has the capacity to register any immovable property in her name. However, if the property forms part of a joint estate, she will need the consent of the husband if she wants to alienate, mortgage or burden with a servitude or confer any other real right in any immovable property forming part of the joint estate.[131] With regard to marital proprietary rights of black Namibians, the applicability of the Roman-Dutch common law rules relating to marriages in and out of community of property depended on the geographical location of the place that the marriage was contracted. The Native Administration Proclamation 15 of 1928, part of which to date is still in force in Namibia, makes a different rule for all civil marriages between natives north of the old "Police Zone" which took or take place on or after 1 August 1950. These marriages are automatically out of community of property, unless a declaration establishing another property regime was made to the marriage officer one month before the marriage took place. This position is not only discriminatory in terms of the equality provision of the Namibian Constitution but it also deprives the married women under this marital regime the right to the access of the matrimonial property accumulated during the marriage that ordinarily accrues to both spouses in marriages in community of property.

Marriages contracted under customary law are regulated by the customary law of a particular tribal community. The proprietary rights of women married under customary law to movable property are governed by a particular customary law. As mentioned earlier, since the promulgation of the Communal Land Reform Act No. 5 of 2002 the rights of women to the communal land are now given statutory force and in terms of allocation of communal land, the Act has eliminated most of the discriminatory customary practices. But the problem of widows being stripped of land and household goods by the husband's extended family members after his death are reported in some communities and in the context of HIV/AIDS this leads to women's dependence on men syndrome and the vulnerability of women to HIV/AIDS.[132]

10.5.2 Property rights of women after divorce

The property rights of spouses at divorce will be determined by the marital regime the marriage was contracted under, i.e., whether the parties were married in or out of community of property, in which case the Roman-Dutch common law principles will apply. If they were married in community of property, they share their property equally and if they were married out of community of property, each takes the share that belongs to him or her. This is however subject to the facts of each case with regard to the conduct of the parties because under current Namibian law, the property rights of spouses after dissolution of marriage by divorce is governed by the fault principle. It is worthwhile mentioning that in the case of a marriage contracted by African persons, the proprietary rights of the spouses will be governed by the relevant provisions of Proclamation 15 of 1928, which *inter alia* states that such marriage shall not produce the legal consequences of marriage in community of property between the spouses. There is a proviso to the extent that in the case of a marriage contracted otherwise than during the subsistence of a customary union between the husband and any woman other than the wife it shall be competent for the intending spouses at any time within one month previous to the celebration of such marriage to declare jointly before any magistrate or marriage officer that it is their intention and desire that community of property and of profit and loss result from their marriage, and thereupon, such community shall result from their marriage.[133] In the case of *Teofilus Mofaka*,[134] the respondent sued the appellant for a divorce and alleged in her Particulars of Claim that the parties had been married on 1 September 1995, at Onawa, Ovamboland, and that the marriage was in community of property. The Supreme Court, in its judgment *inter alia* affirmed the finding of the Judge *a quo* that s 17(6) applied to the marriage of the parties and that it was out of community of property unless declared or agreed otherwise.

The common law principles which govern maintenance, the distribution of the matrimonial estate and custody of children of the marriage have very scant parallels in customary law. The husband in most cases obtains the majority of the marital assets and because of the application of the consequences of *lobola*, he has custody of the children.

10.5.3 Rights of women to property upon death of spouse

The proprietary rights of a surviving spouse, or the widow, will be determined by the testate status of the deceased spouse, whether he died testate or intestate.

If the spouse died testate then the provisions of Wills Act No. 7 of 1953 will apply. In the case of intestate succession there is no uniform legislation applying to both whites and Africans. The Intestate Succession Ordinance 12 of 1946 as amended by the Intestate Succession Amendment Act No. 15 of 1982 applies to whites and, the provisions of Proclamation 15 of 1928 apply to Africans.[135]

In terms of the Intestate Succession Ordinance No. 12 of 1946, the surviving spouse of every person who dies either wholly or partly intestate is declared to be an intestate heir of the deceased spouse according to the following rules:

(a) if the spouses were married in community of property and if the deceased spouse leaves any descendant who is entitled to succeed *ab intestato*, the surviving spouse shall succeed to the extent of a child's share or to so much as together with the surviving spouse's share in the joint estate, does not exceed fifty thousand rand in value (whichever is the greater);

(b) if the spouses were married out of community of property and if the deceased spouse leaves any descendant who is entitled to succeed *ab intestato*, the surviving spouse shall succeed to the extent of a child's share or to so much as does not exceed fifty thousand rand in value (whichever is the greater); and
(c) if the spouses were married either in or out of community of property, and the deceased spouse leaves no descendant who is entitled to succeed *ab intestato*, but leaves a parent or a brother or a sister (whether of the full or half blood) who is entitled to succeed, the surviving spouse shall succeed to the extent of a half share or to so much as does not exceed fifty thousand rand in value (whichever is the greater);
(d) in any case not covered by paragraph (a), (b), or (c) the surviving spouse shall be the sole intestate heir.

With regard to marriages contracted between two Africans, the proprietary rights of the surviving spouse are governed by sections 18(1) and 18(2) which provide as follows:

18(1) All movable property belonging to a Native and allotted by him or accruing under native law or custom to any woman with whom he lived in a customary union, or to any house, shall upon his death devolve and be administered under native law and custom.
(2) All other property of whatsoever kind belonging to a Native shall be capable of being devised by will. Any such property not so devised shall devolve and be administered according to native law and custom.

The customary rules on intestate inheritance vary with different communities and inheritance is determined by whether the tribal community follows matrilineal or patrilineal system of inheritance.

It follows therefore that with regard to immovable property, the rights of a widow of such marriage will be determined by the relevant customary law. The provisions of this Proclamation have been challenged as unconstitutional and discriminatory. It must also be mentioned that the provisions of the Communal Land Reform Act No. 5 of 2002 which govern the allocation of customary land rights protect the rights of the widow who stands to be re-allocated the customary land right hitherto held by the deceased husband.[136]

10.5.4 Rights of women to private land freehold titles

As pointed out earlier, before independence, land set aside for private ownership was for the most part owned by white settlers. At the time of independence it was recorded that this constituted about 75 per cent of the commercially viable farming land, while a paltry 25 per cent of such land was held by the indigenous people in the communal areas.[137] Since independence, some indigenous people, comprising mainly civil servants and members of the private sector, have moved to the urban centers but the majority of the indigenous African Namibians continue to reside in the communal areas. In the context of the ownership of commercial farms the position of inequitable distribution of land and imbalances in land distribution remains and most Africans and particularly women, remain disadvantaged. This is compounded by the fact that most commercial farmers are men. Women do not have direct access and control over the commercial farms. Most women who interact with the dynamics of commercial farming are either housewives or workers.

The Namibian government in its attempt to correct these imbalances and empower the previously disadvantaged Africans, including women, promulgated the Agricultural (Commercial) Land Reform Act No. 6 of 1995. Under the authority of this Act the government has used the policy of willing buyer, willing seller to purchase some commercial farms for resettlement and farming purposes. To date the government has settled about 3,727 families at an average of six people per family giving a grand total of 22,362 people on commercial farms and 9,933 people at an average of six people per family giving a grand total of 59,598 people settled on the communal farms/land. Out of these 48 per cent of the beneficiaries are women.

As mentioned earlier, Article 16 of the Constitution guarantees everyone the right to private ownership of land. This provision means that black Namibians including women are constitutionally entitled to own properties with freehold titles. Freehold titles over land in urban centers may be acquired through alienation of land hitherto vested in local authorities under the Local Authorities Act No. 23,[138] or through private treaties between individuals.

10.5.4.1 Accessibility of commercial farms to Namibian women

The Namibian courts have upheld the principles of Article 10 of the Constitution[139] as one of the binding principles in the judicial and legislative processes of the country, especially in view of the injustices of the colonial past of the country and therefore as a matter of principle, and in the spirit of the strict application and implementation of the law and government policies relating to property rights of, especially, the previously disadvantaged members of the community these rights must be accessible to all members of the society, including women. It is imperative, therefore, to ascertain the myths and realities of this desired position.

10.5.4.2 The property rights of women under customary law

10.5.4.2.1 COMMUNAL LANDS AND CUSTOMARY LAND TENURE

As mentioned earlier, in the current property rights regime in Namibia, the rights to Article 66 of the Constitution recognizes the general application of customary law as source of law in Namibia subject to the proviso that it shall remain valid to the extent to which such customary law does not conflict with the Constitution or any other statutory law. The proprietary rights of women governed by customary law will be discussed within the general context of customary land tenure systems that operate within the communal areas. The relevant legal regime consists of the particular customary law of a tribal community and the provisions of the Communal Land Reform Act No. 5 of 2002.[140] As a matter of application of general principles, in the event of a conflict between the rules of these two regimes, the provisions of the legislation take precedence.

In terms of the provisions of the Act,[141] the proprietary rights of a woman to a communal land under the various statutory titles are guaranteed by legislation. But the Act fails to recognize the realities of the patriarchal nature of the traditional society and how this will influence the allocation of land by the traditional authorities and the Land Boards. It also fails to recognize the leadership role that a boy/man plays in the family and therefore the preferential/legitimate choice that is accorded him rather than the girl in family relations including land allocation.

In Namibia almost three-fourths of the population live rural agrarian lifestyles (CSO 2001). Therefore, the majority of people practice subsistence agriculture based on crop cultivation and livestock production of cattle, goats, sheep, chickens and donkeys. These rural people can only survive if they have access to land on which to grow crops and graze livestock. However, as indicated earlier, there is a great deal of insecurity regarding women's rights to land during divorce, when these relationships end, as women often lose their access to land, and thereby losing their ability to support themselves and their families.[142] Furthermore, in most communal areas in Namibia, traditional leaders such as headmen, chiefs, *indunas* and kings, control land although communal land is owned by the state. With the possible exception of the Nama, the majority of these traditional leaders are men and therefore patriarchal biases in the allocation of land in the communal areas cannot be completely ignored.

10.5.4.2.2 ACCESS TO CREDIT

As indicated earlier, a mere provision of legal rights to property is not enough. For one to fully realize the right to property one must be empowered or must have access to the wherewithal that will make the realization of the legal rights possible. In other words, the individual or in this context women must have access to credit. NDP1 (National Development Plan 1 (Namibia)) describes Namibia's financial sector as small and dualistic. It states that, "as is the case in many developing countries, there is on the one hand, a well developed financial system, mainly serving the urban centers, while on the other hand large portions of rural areas are left with little or no access to financial services." It has been observed that due to women's concentration in the rural areas, the distribution of credit institutions is a major barrier to rural women's access to credit.

Formal sources of credit in Namibia include five commercial banks, seven parasatals including the Namibian Development Cooperation (NDC), National Housing Enterprise (NHE), and the Agricultural Bank of Namibia (ABN). There are also the Build Together Program (BTP) administered by the Ministry of Regional and Local Government and Housing, as well as NGOs and a number of credit unions and rural saving schemes. Women's Action for Development (WAD), although not a source of credit, does provide financial support to a few female owned and operated income-generating projects.

Although there is, in theory, no discrimination against women by commercial banks and all customers are supposed to be treated equally, women tend to have more difficulty acquiring loans due to a lack of collateral and credit record. There are no statistics on loans by these institutions which distinguish between customers on the grounds of gender, so loan prevalence rates cannot be determined. However, in the past women married in community of property were required to have the consent of their husbands to enter into contracts and obtain loans due to the husband's "marital power" over his wife. This situation has changed as from 21 May 1996 when the Married Persons Equality Act was passed which abolished marital power.

Commercial institutions such as banks do not have any programs directed specifically at women and they do not have any significant programs or activities in the field of micro-economic enterprise development. Interviews with bank officials reveal they do not feel that they discriminate against women when extending credit. However, Standard Bank officials say that women can get loans if they have repaid previous loans on time. The Commercial Bank only gives loans to invest in the formal sector. All of these various criteria, although not specifically directed at women, form an effective barrier to women's access to credit, although women tend to have better repayment records on home mortgage loans than men.[143] For example, the figures released by the Agribank to The Parliamentary Standing Committee on Economics, Natural Resources and Public Administration indicate that during the 2003/04 financial sector, a total number of 553 farmers were granted loans.

10.5.4.3 The impact of HIV/AIDS on access to credit and insurance benefits

The historical imbalance that Namibia inherited from several forms of social and economic structural inequalities had a gender dimension which impacted negatively on the rights of women to property, as indicated above, unemployment and related social problems. The HIV/AIDS pandemic has added its toll to the impact of discrimination that women in Namibia face with regard to especially property rights, access to credit facilities, unemployment, and certain customary practices. This is particularly ominous given the fact that, out of the estimated 200,000 people living with HIV in Namibia, 60 per cent of these are women.[144]

As a matter of general legal principles, the respect for human dignity and equality and freedom from discrimination clauses in the Constitution of Namibia extend to all persons including both persons living with AIDS and those who are HIV positive. However, there are still some legal and cultural norms and practices that do not accord with the letter and spirit of the noble ideals of the articles mentioned.

In the area of property rights, it has been mentioned earlier that the mere provision of the right to the acquisition to property without the requisite workable and enforceable empowerment strategies and policies by government and the private sector will reduce the ideals of the constitution to a mere charade or façade. It will be therefore, worthwhile to look at the practices of the financial sector in relation to HIV/AIDS.

The financial sector comprises mainly the insurance banking and non banking financial institutions. In the context of property rights of women living with AIDS and those who are HIV/AIDS positive, the policies and practice of the financial sector play a very crucial role in determining the realization of the rights of women to property.

Insurance provides financial security against unforeseen and unpredictable events such as death and disability. Therefore, it is regarded as the key long-term investment made by working individuals. More importantly, it is also used as collateral in obtaining mortgage bonds for the purpose of property.

There are essentially four types of insurance cover that present difficulties for people living with HIV/AIDS. These are life insurance, assistance insurance, disability insurance and health insurance. A common factor with all these types of insurance is that the life/health is the basis for cover and to be more specific in the context of access to obtaining home loans by women living with HIV/AIDS, the current policies and practice of the insurance are closely interrelated. The policies and practice in terms of profit making may make good business sense and be justifiable but in terms of protecting the interests of people or women infected and affected by HIV/AIDS, there is much to be desired. The current practice will require legislative intervention or review by the insurance industry itself.

To obtain a home loan from a bank, one needs to provide the bank with some sort of security or a collateral. Usually this is done by ceding a life insurance policy to the bank. For people living with HIV/AIDS this is not an option as they are denied life insurance cover because of their HIV/AIDS status.

Notwithstanding the above, the insurance contracts contain exemption or exclusion clauses which exclude the liability if the insured was infected with HIV at the time of death or where in the opinion of the company, the claim is occasioned by infection with HIV. The inherent and apparent injustices of these policies are evident in the subjectivity of the absolute discretion given to the insurance industry in determining the cause of death as related to HIV/AIDS, irrespective of the direct cause of death. Women living with HIV/AIDS are disadvantaged by this practice. In the first place it is common knowledge that Namibia is a patriarchal society and most households in Namibia are headed by men. The Census Indicators for 2001 and 1991 are that 55 per cent of households are headed by males and 45 per cent by females. Depending on the credit history of a widow, a widow cannot claim under the policy of a deceased husband in such instances and furthermore the property which is not covered by a life policy is subject to foreclosure irrespective of the widow's wish to continue with payment of installments under the bond entered into between the husband and the insurance company. In the case of a single mother living with HIV/AIDS she is denied access to obtaining credit facilities or has to pay a higher premium.

Some insurance companies have, on account of pressure from activists revised their policies to include coverage for people living with HIV/AIDS. However, there is no indication that there has been any policy changes with respect to access to mortgages or house loans.

Lack of accessibility to property, either as a result of acceptable commercial practice not directly prohibited by the law or a customary practice and documented evidence from research from various sources indicate that these impact on lowering the social status of women *vis-à-vis* men. Hence women find themselves at risk of being exploited by men. As Le Beau puts it, "consequences of gender inequality and patriarchy, such as gender-based violence, women in poverty and women's lack of access to social and economic resources, place them at particular risk of HIV infection. Barcelona is not the only forum on HIV/AIDS where gender inequality and patriarchy have been linked to women's risk of HIV infection. At the 2000 Durban National Treatment Conference on HIV/AIDS, the Congress of South Africa Trade Unions (COSATU) General Secretary, Zwelinzima Vai, stated quite clearly that as long as we still have a patriarchal society that undermines gender equality we are far from defeating HIV/AIDS. Statistics bear testimony to this unequal relationship between men and women. Indeed the Namibia UNDP report (2001: 35) concludes that in Namibia, the major area where differences between women and men come to the fore is that of access to resources and decision-making."[145]

10.6 Observations and conclusion

1. Namibia's land reform is premised on correcting the imbalance created by the apartheid-skewed land policy. It is driven by the policy of reconciliation and is geared towards poverty alleviation, social and economic equity. In this sense, it is aimed at redistribution and restitution and it is necessary to ensure the long-term stability of the country. Poverty alleviation in the context of land reform can be realized through effective and productive utilization of the distributed land, which in turn contributes to increased agricultural productivity and improvement in gross national income. The land distribution policy based on the willing buyer, willing seller option embarked upon by the Namibian government is a strategy aimed at distributive justice and, in the context of the national policy of reconciliation, is regarded as the appropriate strategy, as it is seen as not generating conflict and racial tensions.

2. The operational mechanisms of land reform in Latin America after the Mexican revolution and elsewhere in Africa have taken two forms: expropriation and the willing seller, willing buyer principle promoted by the World Bank. The willing seller, willing buyer option is market-oriented and as indicated by Kay, the achievement of agrarian land reform through this mechanism involves "progressive land tax, land settlement and financing mechanisms, land markets, registration, titling and secure property rights."[146]

As pointed out earlier, the Government of the Republic of Namibia has not been able to realize the objectives and targets of the lands reform program through the willing seller, willing buyer option for a variety of reasons. But this has largely been attributed to the unwillingness of the proprietors of the commercial farms to sell to government the agro-ecologically viable farms and not to fiscal constraints. For example, $US50 million are allocated from Treasury to the Land Acquisition and Development Fund established under the provisions of the Agricultural (Commercial) Land Reform Act No. 6 of 1995 through the capital budget for land acquisition and development. Furthermore, the Fund is allowed to invest and earn interest on investment and benefit from donations as well. The introduction of the Fund has therefore enhanced the capacity of the land reform process to acquire and improve land in a sustainable manner without heavy reliance on the budgetary allocation from Treasury. One strategy that has been employed by the state is the imposition of land tax under the provisions of the Agricultural (Commercial) Land Reform Act No. 6 of 1995. The land tax serves as an important source of revenue to enable the government not only to fund the acquisition of land but also to help the resettled farmers start farming by supplying them with equipment and knowledge on modern methods of farming. It contributes $N30 million to the Land Acquisition and Development Fund and this is able to substantially boost the capacity of the Fund to finance, *inter alia* infrastructural developments on acquired lands.

In terms of poverty alleviation currently there is no statistical data to determine the extent to which land reform process has contributed to raising the income of those resettled and eventually to the gross domestic product. But one positive statement in this regard is that access to land and land redistribution constitute empowerment and besides land itself constitutes an economic asset and a factor of production. Land ownership represents wealth and power.

3. Expropriation is another operational mechanism open to the government. But the Zimbabwean experience and, as pointed out by Borras in the case of Brazil, expropriation without adequate preparation and careful planning can be politically contentious and counter-productive.[147] According to Sachikonye,[148] in the case of Zimbabwe following the implementation of radical fast-track land reform program, the amount of land acquired for distribution increased between 2000 and 2002 from 5 million ha to 11 million ha. He adds that the increase in land acquired did not translate into increased production. Agricultural output declined substantially during 2001–02, with tobacco production dropping from 236 million kg in 2000 to 165 million kg in 2002, due largely to, *inter alia*, lack of commitment on the part of black farmers who benefited from the land reform to production.[149] This coupled with the physical dislocation, economic distortions and conflict generated in the course of the fast track has discredited this approach. In Namibia, the Commercial Farmers Union has used the Zimbabwean experience to caution accelerated expropriation. But as stated earlier given the frustrations of the market-based willing seller, willing buyer approach, expropriation appears to be the ultimate option open to the government. Here, one is advocating a carefully planned process of expropriation, including capacity building and adequate support services. As Cloete puts it, for a successful land reform, beneficiaries should be provided with extensive basic training in personal value system

changes, personal and community development skills and agricultural, financial, technical, marketing and management support services.[150] The High Court of Namibia in the case of *Gunther Kessl v Ministry of Lands and Resettlement and Others*[151] has held that the state's power to expropriate is subject to the principle of reciprocity as demanded by the provisions of Article 18 of the Constitution, which deals with administrative justice. This means that the right of the state to expropriate must be exercised judiciously in compliance with the rule of law.

4. Finally, one may add as a matter of concern the growing rate of informal settlements in the urban centers, especially in the capital, Windhoek, in view of the recent "invasion" of vacant land belonging to the Windhoek Municipality. The government's White Paper on Land Reform addresses the issue of informal settlements and consequently a Bill proposing the creation of a range of rights over the informal settlements is in the legislative process. Land reform in Namibia will not be complete without a long-term solution to the issue of informal settlement.

Notes

* Faculty of Law, University of Namibia.

† City University of New York Law School.

1 The violence and land occupations in Zimbabwe in the spring of 2000 were the subject of extensive commentary and discussion throughout southern Africa. On the land situation in Zimbabwe see Moyo (1995) and Human Rights Watch (2002). On South Africa see van Zyl, Kirsten and Binswanger (1996). The occupation of farms in Zimbabwe was directly presented as pointing to the urgency of land reform in Namibia. See, for example, Owen-Smith (2000a); Ngava (2000: 2); Cousins (2000: 28).

2 Klug (1996).

3 Warriner (1969); van Zyl, Kirsten and Binswanger (1996); Christiansen (1996), pp 367–89.

4 Christopher (1994).

5 Adams and Howell (2001).

6 Wiley (2000).

7 Werner (2001).

8 Adams and Howell (2001).

9 United Nations Institute for Namibia (1986), pp 34–53.

10 Kay (1970), pp 37–58.

11 Almost all white farmers fled Angola and Mozambique at independence. Only Kenya was settled by whites to the extent that Zimbabwe and Namibia were – and most white farmers also fled Kenya at independence. Soja (1968), pp 48–54.

12 Namibia is 823,144 km^2 in size. Van der Merwe (1983), p 1. It is not clear what Namibia's population is: the first official census, in 1991, put the population at 1,409,920. Malan (1980), p 2. The results of the 2001 census are not yet published. Some preliminary estimates run as high as 2 million. The Namibian government's web site estimates the population at 1.8 million, <http://www.gov.na>.

13 Mendelsohn *et al* (2000), p 36.

14 Peyroux (2001). In 1991, one year after independence, Windhoek had a population of about 200,000. The end of apartheid coincided with much black movement to Windhoek, the only major city in Namibia, and by 2001 it is estimated to have doubled in size, to about 400,000, with most of the population living in newly established black housing developments but many in squatter camps. There is considerable

movement between Windhoek and the communal areas, especially among children and young people, as children are sent away to schools and young people search for work.
15 Schade (2000), pp 111–24.
16 Ingolf, Diener and Grafe, Olivier (2001), p 25.
17 Namibia, Ministry of Lands and Resettlement (2005), p 18.
18 Ibid, p. ix.
19 *Namibian*, 11 March 2009.
20 See also Amoo (2000), p 87.
21 There is a growing body of literature in this "new" Namibian history: Bley (1981); Hayes, Silvester, Wallace and Hartmann (1998); Hartmann, Silvester and Hayes (1998).
22 Gewald (1999); Drechsler (1980); Bridgeman (1981).
23 Werner (1998), p 48; Schmoekel (1985); Moorsom (1982), pp 21–24.
24 Malan (1995), pp 68–69; Hahn, Vedder and Fourie (1928), pp 153–208.
25 Esterhuyse (1968), pp 46–65.
26 Ibid, pp 66–83.
27 Shaw (1984), pp 46–48; Lindley (1926), pp 181–206.
28 Gewald (1999), pp 129–36; Werner (1998), p 43.
29 Anon. (1922), p 457.
30 Werner (1998), pp 43–44. These data represent cataclysmic social change: there were virtually no German farmers before the early 1890s. It took scarcely the decade of the 1890s for German herds to grow larger than Herero herds.
31 Quoted in Gewald (1999), pp 172–73. Gewald has dismissed the view that Von Trotha's proclamation has been interpreted "out of context," concluding that the proclamation meant what it threatened, a policy of genocide. The fact that it was printed in the Herero language and distributed to women and children about to be driven out into the desert (so they could widely distribute it) demonstrates that it was well planned.
32 Like much of German history, there is a right-wing "revisionist" interpretation of the Herero War that denies that genocide occurred: *Windhoek Observer*, 21 July 2001, p 2 (summarizing an uncited University of Hamburg (Germany) master's thesis claiming that (1) fewer Herero were killed in the Herero War than modern scholars claim and (2) that these deaths were not due to actions of the German army but to starvation). A point-by-point rebuttal was published a few weeks later: Silvester, Hillebrecht and Erichsen (2001), p 4. The major accounts of the Herero War (see n 22) agree on the essential details of the deaths of over 60,000 Herero people.
33 Gewald (1999), pp. 141–91, is the best account of the war. The two previous standard accounts are Drechsler (1980) and Bridgeman (1983), pp 132–63. Neither account disputes that the immediate cause of the Herero uprising was the loss of their lands, but Gewald challenges the idea that it was a widely planned general revolt of the Herero people.
34 Bridgeman (1981), pp 132–63.
35 Werner (2001), p 1.
36 Harring (2002).
37 Klug (1996b).
38 Harring (2002), p 3.
39 Amoo (2000), p 91.
40 See also Hinz (1998), pp 183–88.
41 During the conquest of Namibia by South African troops in 1915, the Union government was precluded from alienating or allocating any land on a permanent basis. However, the granting of the mandate over Namibia to South Africa in 1919 enabled South Africa to intervene more decisively on land issues. In terms of the mandate all land held by the previous German government was transferred to South Africa. Henceforth, only the Governor-General of the Union had the power to legislate in regard to the allocation of Crown land.

42 The creation of the reserves along racial lines was meant, *inter alia*, to accommodate white settlers on the prime land and to push the indigenous people on to more marginal land. By 1946, surveyed farms in the Police Zone comprised 32 million ha, representing just over 60 per cent of its area or 39 per cent of the country. By contrast, the area reserved for black Namibians in the Police Zone amounted to 4.1 million ha. By shifting the Police Zone further north and opening up land in the desert another 880 farmers were allotted farms between 1945 and 1954, bringing the total number of farms to 5,214. See also Adams and Werner (1990), pp 9–20.
43 Ibid, p 31.
44 Ibid.
45 See also Hinz (1998), pp 184–88.
46 Note that the executive authority of the representative authorities was established under the various Representative Authorities Proclamations.
47 Article 147 deals with repeal of laws, and repeals all laws set out in Schedule 8.
48 Schedule 8 is a list of repealed laws, mostly Representative Authority Proclamations.
49 Hinz (1998), p 185.
50 Article 100 provides that "[l]and, water and natural resources below and above the surface of the land and in the continental shelf and within the territorial waters and the exclusive economic zone of Namibia shall belong to the state if they are not otherwise lawfully owned."
51 Schedule 5(1) provides that "[a]ll property of which the ownership or control immediately prior to the date of independence vested in the Government of the Territory of South West Africa, or in any Representative Authority constituted in terms of the Representative Authorities Proclamation, 1980 (Proclamation AG 8 OF 1980), or in the Government of Rehoboth, or in Government or Authority immediately prior to the date of Independence, or which was held in trust for or on behalf of the Government of an independent Namibia, shall vest in or be under the control of the Government of Namibia."
52 For further discussion on the recognition of titles over communal lands see (10.4.3.1 and 10.5.2) below.
53 The Communal Land Reform Act contains the proposed provisions on the question of ownership, types of titles, security of tenure, and administration of communal land. In addition to this, the Traditional Authorities Act 17 of 1995 and the Council of Traditional Leaders Act No. 19 of 1997 give certain jurisdiction over the allocation and administration of communal lands to the traditional authorities.
54 See section 19 of the Act.
55 Under section 21 the customary rights that may be allocated comprise a right to a farming unit and a right to a residential unit. Section 20 vests the power to allocate or cancel any customary land right in the communal area of a traditional community in the Chiefs and Traditional Authorities.
56 See section 26.
57 See section 25(1)(b).
58 Section 26 provides, *inter alia*, that upon the death of the holder of a customary land right, such right reverts to the Chief or Traditional Authority for reallocation either to the surviving spouse of the deceased person, if such spouse consents to the allocation or in the absence of a surviving spouse to such child of the deceased person as the Chief or Traditional Authority determines to be entitled to the allocation of the right in accordance with customary law.
59 The traditional laws of the various tribal communities in Namibia relating to the rights of the surviving spouse to a communal land erstwhile occupied by a deceased spouse vary. The common position is contained in section 26.
60 See sections 19(b) and 30(1).
61 The Communal Land Boards are created under section 2(1) of the Act.
62 See section 34.

63 See section 33(1).
64 See section 33(2).
65 See sections 2 and 3. The establishment of the Communal Land Boards will be a completely new development in the law relating to communal land in Namibia, though Botswana and other countries have similar boards.
66 Throughout this study, the "commercial farms," predominantly white-owned, are contrasted with "communal farms," black-occupied agricultural lands. While this juxtaposition is essentially accurate, since 1990 some of the "commercial farms" have become black-owned. While exact data is unknowable because of secret ownership devices, it seems that as many as 700 of 6,000 farms are black-owned, or about 11 per cent, but many of these may be leased back to their white owners. All "communal" farmers are black, but some are grazing white-owned cattle, also through various (and concealed) ownership agreements.
67 Moorsom (1982), p 30. It is not clear exactly how many farm units there are because of inconsistencies in data collection, as well as the merger of some farms into others.
68 Adams and Devitt (1992), pp 5–6, 3–5.
69 Moorsom (1982) reports 458 farms in 1904; 1,331 in 1913; 3,305 in 1938; 5,216 in 1960; and 4,842 in 1970/71 (at p 30).
70 According to government data, 759 farms were offered for sale to the government, as required by Namibian law, up to 2001, about 13 per cent of the farms in Namibia. Odendaal and Harring (2002), p 76. Additional farms doubtless changed hands before the Agricultural Commercial Land Reform Act (1995) went into effect, and others have changed hands since 2001. Other farms have changed hands in private transactions that have not been reported.
71 Adams and Devitt (1992).
72 See Republic of Namibia National Conference on Land Reform and the Land Question (1991).
73 Tvedten and Mupotola (1995). See also Christensen and Hojgaard (1997), p 6. In the proposal for the introduction and development of a flexible land tenure system for Namibia, references are made to "formal" and "informal" areas of settlement. The former is used to denote areas that are planned and surveyed. These areas are most often serviced with water, sewage removal, roads and electricity. The latter are areas where people have not settled according to prior planning.
74 See 10.4.2 below.
75 See section 3(3)(a), 3(5)(b) and 30(1)(t) of the Local Authorities Act No. 23 of 1992.
76 The old settlement areas are the urban or urbanising areas where the colonial administration before independence carried out the surveying of some plots and in some cases provided water and electricity. These are also referred to as formal areas. If the PTO falls within such an area it is an urban one and will usually be located on one of the numbered surveyed plots.
77 In 1962, the South African government appointed a Commission of Inquiry to make "recommendations on a comprehensive five-year plan for the accelerated development of the various non-white groups of South-West Africa." This Commission was commonly known as the Odendaal Commission. The recommendations made by the Commission in its 1964 report had little to do with promoting the welfare of black Namibians. One infamous recommendation in the report was that Namibia should be fragmented into a series of economically unviable self-governing homelands or Bantustans for Africans, which would, of necessity, remain perpetually dependent on the "white" areas, and, through them, on South Africa. The Odendaal Plan was implemented by two pieces of legislation: the Development of Self-government for Native Nations in South West Africa Act No. 54 of 1968, and the South West Africa Affairs Act No. 25 of 1969. The effect of the implementation of the plan was to entrench both territorial apartheid in Namibia and the distribution of land along racial lines. See Duggal (1986), pp 37–41.

78 Gluckman (1954/1967), pp 59–92.
79 In a report prepared for the Social Sciences Division, University of Namibia, Howard (1995) states that the public's perception of the PTO is that of a second-rate form of title given to the black population by the previous regime whilst retaining the best title, freehold, for whites. He argues that if a revised form of PTO is to be accepted then it must be marketable, trusted by the target group until it gains popular acceptance.
80 *White Paper on National Land Policy* (Government of the Republic of Namibia 1997).
81 These projected forms of tenure are the starter title and landhold title. But it is now possible for holders of PTOs to acquire freehold title over such properties through alienation and transfer of rights of ownership.
82 Government of the Republic of Namibia (1997).
83 The Namibian government has held a number of consultative conferences on the land question since the National Conference in 1991. These have led to the enactment of legislation on land and related matters and to the drafting of the *White Paper on National Land Policy*. References to appropriate legislation and the White Paper are made elsewhere in this chapter.
84 Government of the Republic of Namibia (2005).
85 *Namibian Sun*, 20 May 2010.
86 See Nandjaa (1997), pp 1–4 and n 89.
87 See Article 16(2) of the Namibian Constitution and section 14(1) and 20 of the Agricultural (Commercial) Land Reform Act No. 6 of 1995.
88 See the Resolution on Permanent Sovereignty over Natural Resources 1962, adopted in the case of *Texaco v. Libya* (1977) 53 ILR 389.
89 This clearly means that the government, under such a state of emergency, can expropriate private property *without* compensation.
90 Because these various legal arrangements are secret it is not possible to say precisely how common these forms are, or even exactly what they are. Some "foreign" ownership, for example, is concealed by putting farms in the name of Namibian citizens. Other farms are held in the name of relatives, or corporations. Corporately held farms may legally appear in individual ownership. Still other farms may still be legally registered to their former owners, although ownership has been secretly transferred by an unregistered legal arrangement. Some Affirmative Action scheme farmers have apparently bought land from whites at inflated prices, then leased these farms back to the original owners. There are rumors that politicians do not want farms in their own names because it would reveal wealth that cannot be accounted for, thus the number of politicians (mostly black) who own farms is not known.
91 There is no firm data on the number of blacks who own commercial farms. While 500 loans have been taken out under an affirmative action farm loan scheme, it is not clear that 500 farms have been purchased with this money.
92 Werner (2000), p 33.
93 Ibid.
94 Ibid.
95 Adams and Howell (2001), pp 4–5. This is a logical conclusion, drawn from the above data. The farming sector is distrustful of the Namibian government and may want to appear stronger and more important to the nation's economy than it is, therefore accurate economic data is not easily gained. It should also be noted that the threat of expropriation has encouraged farmers to use various devices to raise the value of their farms, both to discourage expropriation, but also to increase the payment in the event of expropriation.
96 Schmoekel (1985).
97 Ibid; see also Moorsom (1982), pp 9–36.
98 Stern and Lau (1990).
99 Stengel (1963).

100 Moorsom (1982), pp 11–14; van der Merwe (1983), plates 10–14; Mendelsohn *et al.* (2000), pp 9–11.
101 Sweet (1998).
102 Seely and Jacobson (1996), pp 170–74; Seely (2001), pp 35–52; Timberlake (1994), pp 105–32.
103 Bester (1996), pp 175–77. Bush infestation is estimated to cover between 8 million ha and 14.4 million ha, the latter figure about 50 per cent of the commercial farming area. Sweet (1998), p 13.
104 Lau and Reiner (1993), pp 20–22, 43.
105 Werner (2000), pp 30–31; Sweet (1998: 4) puts the number of cattle on commercial farms as 790,699 in 1997. The same year blacks held 1.3 million cattle in the communal areas.
106 Cattle fed on poor grass take longer to mature and yield tougher, poorer-quality meat.
107 Sweet (1998), p 4.
108 Lau and Reiner (1993), pp 11–14; Elkan *et al.* (1992).
109 Sweet (1998), p 3.
110 Moorsom (1982), pp 30–36.
111 Werner (2002), p 4.
112 Ibid, pp 6–9.
113 These titles are the subject matter of the Flexible Land Tenure Bill which is currently in Parliament.
114 Christensen and Hojgaard (1997).
115 The *White Paper on Urban Land and the Proclamation of Local Authorities* states that prior to Independence many urban areas developed which, because of the discriminatory policies of the colonial regime, were never proclaimed as municipalities or townships and in which no local authority administration developed. The *White Paper on National Land Policy* requires the establishment and proclamation of urban and urbanizing areas as townships and municipalities where appropriate, to promote decentralization of government and the close involvement of communities in their own administration.
116 Ibid.
117 Gluckman (1954/1967).
118 Da Rocha and Lodoh (1995) state that in Ghana, for example, neither in theory nor in practice can it be said that all land is held from the state. Land in Ghana is held from various stools (skins) or families or clans, which are the allodial owners. The state holds lands only by acquisition from these traditional allodial owners. This right was recognized by Rayner CJ in a report on land tenure in West Africa, cited in the judgment of the Privy Council in the case of *Amodu Tijani v. Secretary, Government of Southern Nigeria* (1921) AC 399.
119 *Source Book of African Customary Law for Southern Africa* (1991), pp 384–96.
120 Article 66(1) of the Constitution states that both the customary law and the common law of Namibia in force on the date of Independence shall remain valid to the extent to which such customary and common law does not conflict with this Constitution or any other statutory law.
121 LeBeau, Iipinge and Conteh (2004), pp 2–10.
122 Kashkooli (2006).
123 Article 10 of the Namibian Constitution reads as follows: "Equality and Freedom from Discrimination: (1) All persons shall be equal before the law; (2) No person may be discriminated against on the grounds of sex, race, colour, ethnic origin, religion, creed, or social or economic status."
124 See n 82.
125 Article 95 of the Constitution has been declared to be obligatory on the Government.
126 Supreme Court of Namibia, Case No. SA 29/2001.
127 See Article 23 of the Namibian Constitution.
128 Voet 32.2.85.
129 See generally Hosten (1977, 1983, 1995).

130 Married Persons Equality Act No. 1 of 1996, section 3(a)(i).
131 Section 7(1)(a).
132 LeBeau *et al.* (2004), p 22.
133 Ibid, p 19.
134 Supreme Court of Namibia, Case No. SA 2/2002.
135 See also *Teofilus Mofoka v Josefina Nangula Mofuka*, Supreme Court of Namibia, Case No. SA 2/2002.
136 Section 26(2)(a) and para 3.2, above, n 139.
137 See Amoo (2000), p 96.
138 See sections 3(3)(a), 3(5)(b) and 30(1)(t) of the Local Authorities Act No. 23 of 1992.
139 Article 10 of the Constitution states that (1) All persons shall be equal before the law; (2) No person shall be discriminated against on the grounds of sex, race, color, ethnic origin, religion, creed or social or economic status.
140 See generally Amoo (2000), pp 103–08.
141 See para 3.2, above, n 139.
142 LeBeau *et al.* (2004), p xi.
143 Iipinge and Le Beau (1997).
144 Ministry of Health and Social Services (2008).
145 Le Beau (2004), p 9.
146 Kay (1998/2), <http://www.fao.org/sd/ltdirect/landrf.htm>.
147 Borras (2002).
148 Sachikonye (2003), pp 33–41.
149 Nampa/AFP (2005).
150 Cloete (1992), p 256.
151 2008(1)NR 167(HC)

Bibliography

A Source Book of African Customary Law for Southern Africa (Cape Town: Juta, 1991).

Adams, F. and Werner, W. (1990) *The Land Issue in Namibia: An Inquiry* (Windhoek: NISER, University of Namibia).

Adams, M. and Devitt, P. (1992) *Grappling with Land Reform in Pastoral Namibia* (Pastoral Development Network, No. 32a, London: ODI).

Adams, M. and Howell, J. (2001) *Redistributive Land Reform in Southern Africa* (Natural Resource Perspectives No. 64, London: ODI).

Amoo, S. K. (2000) "Towards Comprehensive Land Tenure Systems and Land Reform in Namibia," *South African Journal on Human Rights*, 17: 87.

Anon. (author's name illegible) (1922) "Memorandum on Treaties between the Law Government and Various Native Tribes in South West Africa," 4 September, National Archives of Namibia, p 457, S.W.A.R.

Bester, B. (1996) "Bush Encroachment: A Thorny Problem," *Namibia Environment*, 1: 175–77.

Bley, H. (1981) *South West Africa under German Rule, 1894–1915* (Evanston, IL: Northwestern University Press).

Borras, S. M., Jr (2002) "Towards a Better Understanding of the Market-led Agrarian Reform in Theory and Practice: Focusing on the Brazilian Case," *Land Reform, Land Settlement and Cooperatives*, 1: 32–51, <www.fao.org/sd/ltdirect/landrf.htm>.

Bridgeman, J. (1981) *The Revolt of the Hereros* (Berkeley, CA: University of California Press).

Bridgeman, J. (1983) "The Revolt of the Hereros," *Canadian Journal of African Studies*, 17: 132–63.

Central Statistic Office (CSO). 2001 Population and Housing Census: Preliminary Report, NPC: Windhoek.

Christensen, S. F. and Hojgaard, P. D. (1997) *Report on Flexible Land Tenure System for Namibia* (Windhoek: Ministry of Lands, Resettlement and Rehabilitation).

Christiansen, R. (1996) "Overview of Land Reform Issues," in J. van Zyl *et al* (eds) *Agricultural Reform in South Africa: Policies, Markets and Mechanisms* (Cape Town: Oxford University Press).

Christopher, A. J. (1994) *The Atlas of Apartheid* (London: Routledge).

Cloete, F. (1992) "Comparative Lessons for Land Reform in South Africa," *Africa Insight*, 22: 256.

Cousins, B. (2000) "Zim Crisis: Our Wake up Call," *Mail and Guardian*, 28: 11.

Da Rocha, B. J. and Lodoh, C. H. K. (1995) *Ghana Land Law and Conveyancing* (Ghana: Anansesem Publications).

Drechsler, H. (1980) *Let Us Die Fighting: The Struggle of the Herero and Nama against German Imperialism, 1885–1915* (London: Zed Press).

Duggal, N. K. (1986) *Namibia: Perspectives for National Reconstruction and Development* (Lusaka: United Nations Institute for Namibia).

Elkan, W. *et al* (1992) *Namibian Agriculture: Policies and Prospects* (NEPRU Research Report No. 5, Windhoek: National Economic Policy Research Unit).

Esterhuyse, J. H. (1968) *South West Africa, 1880–94: The Establishment of German Authority in South West Africa* (Cape Town: Struik).

Gewald, J. Bart (1999) *Herero Heroes: A Socio-political History of the Herero of Namibia, 1890–1923* (Athens, OH: Ohio University Press; Oxford: James Currey).

Gluckman, M. (1954) *The Judicial Process among the Barotse*, in P. Bohannan (ed) *Law and Warfare: Studies in the Anthropology of Conflict* (New York: Natural History Press, 1967).

Government of the Republic of Namibia (2005) *Strategic Options and Action Plan for Land Reform in Namibia* (Windhoek: Permanent Technical Team on Land Reform).

Government of the Republic of Namibia (1997) *White Paper on National Land Policy* (Windhoek: Ministry of Lands, Resettlement and Rehabilitation).

Hahn, C. H. L., Vedder, H. and Fourie, L. (1928) *The Native Tribes of South West Africa* (repr. London: Frank Cass).

Harring, S. (2002) "German Reparations to the Herero Nation: An Assertion of Herero Nationhood in the Path of Namibian Development?" *West Virginia Law Review*, 104: 1.

Hartmann, W., Silvester, J. and Hayes, P. (1998) *The Colonizing Camera: Photographs in the Making of Namibian History* (Athens, OH: Ohio University Press).

Hayes, P., Silvester, J., Wallace, M. and Hartmann, W. (1998) *Namibia under South African Rule: Mobility and Containment, 1915–46* (Athens, OH: Ohio University Press).

Hinz, M. O. (1998) "Communal Land, Natural Resources and Traditional Authority," in M. D'Engelbronner, M. O. Hinz and J. Sindana (eds) *Traditional Authority and Democracy in Southern Africa* (Tsumeb: Nation Press).

Hosten, W. (1977) *Introduction to South African Law and Legal Theory* (Durban: Butterworth).

Howard, J. W. (1995) *A Summary Review of Urban Land Policy Issues and Options* (Windhoek: Social Sciences Division, University of Namibia).

Human Rights Watch (2002) *Zimbabwe: Fast Track Land Reform in Zimbabwe* (New York: Human Rights Watch).

Iipinge, E. M. and Le Beau, D. (1997) *Beyond Equalities: Women in Namibia* (Windhoek: UNAM/SARDC).

Ingolf, Diener and Grafe, Olivier (eds) (2001) *Contemporary Namibia: The First Landmarks of a Post-apartheid Society* (Windhoek: Gamsberg Macmillan).

Kashkooli, K. (2006) "Gender Inequality and HIV/AIDS in Sub-Saharan Africa," paper presented at the annual meeting of the American Sociological Association, Montreal, Quebec, 10 August.

Kay, C. (1998/2) "Latin America's Agrarian Reform: Lights and Shadows," FAO, *Land Reform*, <www.fao.org/sd/ltdirect/landrf.htm>.

Kay, G. (1970) *Rhodesia: A Human Geography* (London: University of London Press).

Klug, H. (1996a) "Bedevilling Agrarian Reform: The Impact of Past, Present, and Future Legal Frameworks," in J. van Zyl *et al* (eds) *Agricultural Reform in South Africa: Policies, Markets and Mechanisms* (Cape Town: Oxford University Press).

Klug, H. (1996b) "Historical Claims and the Right to Restitution," in van Zyl *et al* (eds) *Agricultural Land Reform in South Africa* (Cape Town: Oxford University Press).

Lau, B. and Reiner, P. (1993) *100 Years of Agricultural Development in Colonial Namibia* (Windhoek: National Archives of Namibia).

Le Beau, D. (2004) *Structural Conditions for the Progression of the HIV/AIDS Pandemic in Namibia* (Windhoek: Pollination Publishers).

LeBeau, D., Iipinge, E. and Conteh, M. (2004) *Women's Property and Inheritance Rights in Namibia* (Windhoek: University of Namibia and Pollination Publishers).

Lindley, M. F. (1926) *The Acquisition and Government of Backward Territory in International Law* (London: Longman).

Malan, J. S. (1980) *Peoples of Namibia* (Pretoria: HAUM).

Malan, J. S. (1995) *Peoples of Namibia* (Wingate Park: Rhino Publishers).

Mendelsohn, J. *et al* (2000) *A Profile of North Central Namibia* (Windhoek: Ministry of Environment and Tourism).

Ministry of Health and Social Services (2008) "Report on the Estimation and Projection of the Impact of HIV/AIDS in Namibia and the Response Needed," unpublished document.

Ministry of Lands and Resettlement (2005) *Strategic Options and Action Plan for Land Reform in Namibia* (Windhoek: Ministry of Lands and Resettlement).

Moorsom, R. (1982) *Transforming a Wasted Land* (London: Catholic Institute for International Relations).

Moyo, S. (1995) *The Land Question in Zimbabwe* (Harare: SAPES Books).

Nampa/AFP (2005) "Zimbabwe blames new Farmers for Food Shortage," *New Era*, 2 November.

Nandjaa, T. (1997) "The Land Question: Namibians Demand Urgent Answers," *Namibia Review*, 6(2): 1–5.

Ngava, U. (2000) "The Vexed Question of Willing Buyer, Willing Seller: Zimbabwe Land Crisis a Pointer for Namibia," *New Era*, 5–7 May, p 2.

Odendaal, W. and Harring, S. (2002) *One day we will all be equal: A Socio-legal Perspective on Namibian Land Reform and Resettlement Process* (Windhoek: Legal Assistance Center).

Owen-Smith, K. (2000a) "A Clear Warning to Namibians," *New Era*, 2–May, p 7.

Owen-Smith, K. (2000b) "Zimbabwe Situation: Wake up Call for Farmers Here," *New Era*, 2–4 May, p 7.

Peyroux, E. (2001) "Urban Growth and Housing Policies in Windhoek: the Gradual Change of a Post-apartheid Town," in Diener Ingolf and Olivier Grafe (eds) *Contemporary Namibia: The First Landmarks of a Post-apartheid Society* (Windhoek: Gamsberg Macmillan).

Republic of Namibia (1991) National Conference on Land Reform and the Land Question, Windhoek, *Consensus Document* (Windhoek: Office of the Prime Minister).

Resolution on Permanent Sovereignty over Natural Resources, 1962.

Sachikonye, L. M. (2003) *The Scope and Process of Fast-track Land Reform: The Situation of Commercial Farm Workers after Land Reform in Zimbabwe* (Harare: Community Trust of Zimbabwe).

Schade, K. (2000) "Poverty," in Henning Melber (ed) *Namibia: A Decade of Independence, 1990–2000* (Windhoek: National Economic Policy Research Unit).

Schmoekel, W. (1985) "The Myth of the White Farmer: Commercial Agriculture in Namibia, 1900–83," *International Journal of African Historical Studies*, 18: 1–11.

Seely, M. (2001) "Environment: Harsh Constraints, Political Flexibility," in I. Diener and O. Grafe (eds) *Contemporary Namibia: The First Landmarks of a post-Apartheid Society* (Windhoek: Gamsberg Macmillan).

Seely, M. and Jacobson, K. (1996) "Desertification in Namibia," *Environmental Review* 1(1): 94–100.

Shaw, M. (1984) *Title to Territory in Africa: International Legal Issues* (Oxford: Clarendon Press).

Silvester, J., Hillebrecht, W. and Erichsen, C. (2001) "Waterberg Tragedy of 1904 Triggers Hot Debate," *Windhoek Observer*, 4 August, p 4.

Soja, E. W. (1968) *The Geography of Modernization in Kenya* (Syracuse, NY: Syracuse University Press).

Stengel, H. W. (1963) *Water Affairs in South West Africa* (Windhoek: Afrika-Verlag der Kreis).

Stern, C. and Lau, B. (1990) *Namibian Water Resources and their Management: A Preliminary History* (Windhoek: National Archives of Namibia).

Sweet, J. (1998) "Livestock – Coping with Drought: Namibia – A Case Study," paper prepared for United Nations Food and Agricultural Organization electronic conference "Livestock: Coping with Drought," December.

Timberlake, J. (1994) "Soils and Land Use," in World Conservation Union (ed) *State of the Environment in Southern Africa* (Harare: Southern Africa Office, World Conservation Union).

Tvedten, I. and Mupotola, M. (1995) "Urbanisation and Urban Policies in Namibia" (Discussion Paper No. 10, Windhoek: Social Sciences Division, University of Namibia).

United Nations Development Programme (UNDP) (2007) "Namibian Human Development Report", (Windhoek: UNDP).

United Nations Institute for Namibia (1986) *Namibia: Perspectives for National Reconstruction and Development* (Lusaka: United Nations Institute for Namibia).

Van der Merwe, J. H. (1983) *National Atlas of South West Africa* (Goodwood: Cape National Book Printers).

Van Zyl, J., Kirsten, J. and Binswanger, H. (1996) "Introduction," in van Zyl *et al* (eds) *Agricultural Land Reform in South Africa: Policies, Markets, and Mechanisms* (Cape Town: Oxford University Press).

Warriner, D. (1969) *Land Reform in Principle and in Practice* (Oxford: Clarendon Press), quoted in M. Adams, *Land Reform: New Seeds on Old Ground* (ODI Natural Resource Perspectives No. 6, London: ODI, 1995).

Werner, W. (1998) *No one will become rich: Economy and Society in the Herero Reserves in Namibia, 1915–46* (Basel: Schlettwein).

Werner, W. (2000) "Agriculture and Land," in H. Melber (ed) *Namibia: A Decade of Independence* (Windhoek: National Economic Policy Research Unit).

Werner, W. (2001) *Land Reform and Poverty Alleviation: Experiences from Namibia* (NEPRU Working Paper No. 78, Windhoek: National Economic Policy Research Unit).

Werner, W. (2002) *Promoting Development among Farm Workers: Some Options for Namibia* (NEPRU Research Report No. 24, Windhoek: National Economic Policy Research Unit).

Willy, L. (2000) *Land Tenure Reform and the Balance of Power in Eastern and Southern Africa* (ODI Natural Resource Perspectives No. 58, London: ODI).

Windhoek Observer (2001) "Researcher into the Waterberg Tragedy of 1904 Presents a New Radical Version," *Windhoek Observer*, 21 July, p 2 (summarizing an uncited University of Hamburg, Germany, thesis for a master's degree).

Statutes

Agricultural (Commercial) Land Reform Act No. 6 of 1995.
Agricultural Bank Amendment Act No. 27 of 1991.
Agricultural Bank Matters Amendment Act No. 15 of 1992.
Communal Land Reform Act No. 5 of 2002.
Council of Traditional Leaders Act No. 19 of 1997.
Intestate Succession Amendment Act No. 15 of 1982.
Local Authorities Act No. 23 of 1992.
Married Persons Equality Act No. 1 of 1996.
Namibian Constitution.
Native Administration Proclamation 15 of 1928.
Native Nations in South West Africa Act No. 54 of 1968.
Native Reserve Regulation 68 of 1924.
Representative Authorities Proclamation, 1980 (Proclamation AG 8 of 1980)
Intestate Succession Ordinance 12 of 1946.
Traditional Authorities Act No. 17 of 1995.
Treaty of Peace and South West Africa Mandate Act No. 49 of 1919.
Wills Act No. No. 7 of 1953.

Index

For Product Safety Concerns and Information please contact our EU representative GPSR@taylorandfrancis.com
Taylor & Francis Verlag GmbH, Kaufingerstraße 24, 80331 München, Germany

www.ingramcontent.com/pod-product-compliance
Ingram Content Group UK Ltd.
Pitfield, Milton Keynes, MK11 3LW, UK
UKHW020144200926
475702UK00005B/898
9780415587044